The Nigerian Revolution and The Biafran War

Major- General Alexander A. Madiebo, Ret'd
Commander Biafran Army

Fourth Dimension Publishing Co., Ltd.

First Published 1980 by
FOURTH DIMENSION PUBLISHING CO., LTD
16 Fifth Avenue, City Layout. PMB. 01164, Enugu, Nigeria.
Tel+234-42-459969. Fax+234-42-456904.
email: fdpbooks@aol.com, fdpbooks@yahoo.com
Web site: http://www.fdpbooks.com.

Reprinted 2002

ISBN 978-156-117-3

CONDITIONS OF SALE

Photoset and printed in Nigeria by
Fourth Dimension Publishers, Enugu.

*To my comrades-in-arms and to all those who lost
their lives in the civil war*

CONTENTS

Preface

PART I: The Revolution

1	Introduction	3
2	The Revolution — 15 January, 1966	15
3	The Overthrow of General Ironsi's Regime	29
4	The Counter-Revolution	61
5	The Gathering Storm	81
6	The Biafran Armed Forces	97

PART II: The War

7	Nigeria's Initial Attacks and Biafra's Effective Counter-Offensives	123
8	The Birth of "Sabotage" Politics and Consequent Disasters	145
9	Civilian Intervention or How Not to Fight a War	189
10	The Overrunning of the South in the Face of Biafra's Desperate Resistance	239
11	Biafra's First Collapse — September, 1968	267
12	Biafra's Attempt to Regain the Initiative	291
13	Biafra's Rainy Season Offensives — 1969	327
14	The Final Collapse	349

PART III: Epilogue

15	Why We Lost the War	377

ABOUT THE AUTHOR

Major General Madiebo (Ret'd) joined the Nigeria Army in May, 1954 as an Officer Cadet. His military training was undertaken at the Regular Officers' Special Training School (ROSTS) in Teshie, Ghana; Eaton Hall Officer Cadet School in Chester, England, and Royal Military Academy Sandhurst in Camberly, England. He was commissioned into the Nigeria Army Artillery with the rank of a Second Lieutenant in December, 1956. He took part as Troop Commander of the Reconnaissance Squadron in the Cameroun uprising and in Kinshasa. Before returning to the Congo (now Zaire) in late 1962 he served in Ibadan as the Adjutant of the Third Nigeria Battalion during the political crisis of that year.

He returned to England and the U.S. for further training in 1963-64 and became the first Regimental Commander of the Nigeria Army Artillery Regiment in July, 1964.

During the Nigeria/Biafra War, he first commanded Biafra's 51 Brigade for two months before assuming full command of the Biafran Army with the rank of Major General from September, 1967 to the end of the war.

MAP OF EASTERN NIGERIA
DECLARED BIAFRA 30th MAY 1967

1 : 1750 000

Legend
—— Main roads
—··—··— Provincial boundaries
·········· Divisional boundaries
▨▨▨ Effective control by
Biafra as on 8th Jan
1970

Source: N. U. Akpan, *The Struggle for Secession 1966 - 1970: A Personal Account of the Nigerian Civil War* (London: Frank Cass, 1971), p. 20.

PREFACE

This book is not intended to serve as political propaganda material for the benefit of any section or group of individuals. It is rather a genuine attempt on my part to render a dispassionate account of the Nigerian revolution and the civil war which took place from January 1966 to January 1970. I believe I owe it as a duty to Nigerians particularly, and indeed to the rest of the world, to initiate a post-mortem on those events in which I was deeply involved, first, as the Head of the Nigeria Army Artillery and later as the General Officer that commanded the Biafran Army throughout the war.

I believe the world would like to know why it was necessary for some army officers in Nigeria to topple their civil government in January, 1966 in order, as they claimed, to ensure that Nigeria remained united and stable. I am sure many people would like to know why the tremendous joy and happiness, expressed by all Nigerians in support of that coup, appeared to have been short-lived. Some people may also want to know why a section of Nigeria later reacted very violently against that coup by first carrying out massive civil riots in May, 1966 which cost the country over 3000 lives, quickly followed by a military counter coup and pogroms also directed against the same people at an estimated cost of over 50,000 lives, all in an attempt to secede from the rest of the Federation of Nigeria. Serious doubts may still exist in many minds as to why Lt. Colonel Gowon (later General) suddenly did a complete turn-about and rather than secede as he had originally planned and said, preferred to plunge Nigeria into a civil war, which took a toll of an estimated three million lives, in an attempt to re-unite the same Nigeria he had set out initially to break up.

Most important of all is that those who made up Biafra and the rest of mankind may like to read authentic eye-witness accounts and inside stories of how Biafra fought a war with virtually nothing and yet survived for almost three years, under a total blockade and complete isolation from the rest of the world. For Biafrans, such an account becomes vital if they are to appreciate fully their extraordinary courage and achievements, as well as their sad mistakes during that war which they had to fight. On the other hand, armed with some important facts about the revolution and the war, the world, particularly the powers that be, will be in a position to judge more realistically, the role Biafrans played. It is also hoped that if this book can clear the existing doubts by presenting the facts, sufficient lessons may be learnt by those presently in a position of power to discourage a re-occurrence of a catastrophe of that magnitude anywhere in Black Africa. The confusion that exists has been provoked and encouraged by a spate of books containing inaccuracies and misinformation which have been written and published in New York, London and Paris during and since the war.

Finally, I seize this opportunity — an opportunity I never had before — to express my gratitude and thanks to the members of the Army and the civil population of Biafra, for the support they gave me during the war, as the General Officer Commanding the Biafran Army.

I

THE REVOLUTION

Chapter 1

INTRODUCTION

POLITICAL BACKGROUND

The Federation of Nigeria, as it exists today, has never really been one homogeneous country, for its widely differing peoples and tribes are yet to find any basis for true unity. This unfortunate yet obvious fact notwithstanding, the former colonial master had to keep the country one, in order to effectively control his vital economic interests concentrated mainly in the more advanced and "politically unreliable" South. Thus for administration convenience Northern and Southern Nigeria became amalgamated in 1914. Thereafter the only thing these peoples had in common became the name of their country. That alone was an insufficient basis for true unity.

Under normal circumstances the amalgamation ought to have brought the various peoples closer together, and provided a firm basis for the arduous task of establishing closer cultural, social, religious, and linguistic ties among the people — ties which are vital for true unity. The prevailing circumstances were far from normal. For the colonial master, such a union, if allowed to develop, would have amounted to a major threat to the very economic interests he was striving to protect. It was to remove this unwelcome threat that Britain introduced the Divide and Rule system of government for the country.

The important aspect of this system is that it laid emphasis on the differences among the peoples, while encouraging social apartheid. As a result, there was division, hatred, unhealthy rivalry,

3

and pronounced disparity in development among the various peoples of the country. The ultimate result of this situation was that the possibilities of a co-ordinated national resistance against foreign domination were reduced, if not completely removed.

All the same, social integration among the various Nigerian peoples was taking place to a commendable extent all over the country. However this integration proceeded faster in the South than in the North which always saw an uncontrolled integration of tribes as a threat to its religion, culture and customs. Thus, we find that in all Northern Nigerian cities and towns, the Northern indigenes lived in the "cities" while the Southern strangers occupied the "Sabon gari" or ‹strangers' quarter. This system made the problem of identification of strangers easy whenever there was a need to locate them.

Indeed some expatriates, who were often more "Nigerian" than the Nigerians, did their utmost to encourage this separation both in civilian life and in the Army. Soon, top political leaders in parts of the country began to speak on television and radio to condemn and vilify Nigerian "strangers" in their midst in an attempt to emphasize the need for separate existence and their determination to ensure its realisation. The colonial master, determined to ensure a continued uninterrupted economic exploitation of the country even after independence, recognised that this could only be done not by keeping the country one but by ensuring that the effective political and military powers were left in the hands of that part of the country they could trust, the military power being necessary to ensure a stable government of such a big country as Nigeria, made up as it is of diverse and heterogenous elements.

At independence therefore, Nigeria became a Federation and thus remained one country. Soon afterwards the battle to consolidate this legacy of political and military dominance of a section of Nigeria over the rest of the Federation began with increased intensity. It is this struggle that eventually degenerated into *coups d'état* and a bloody civil war.

The growth of nationalism and the subsequent emergence of political parties were based on tribal rather than national interests, and therefore, had no unifying effect on the peoples against the colonial master. Rather, it was the people themselves who were the main victims of the political power struggles which were supposed to be aimed at removing foreign domination.

The Islamic and aristocratic Hausa-Fulani tribes of Northern Nigeria formed the Northern Peoples Congress (NPC) as their political party. In Western Nigeria, the predominantly Christian Yorubas formed the Action Group (AG), until their ranks were infiltrated with promises of power and money, and that succeeded in splitting them into many opposing political groups. In Eastern Nigeria, where the Ibos were in the majority, the main political party was the National Convention for Nigerian Citizens (NCNC). Other numerous tribes, some of them, more populous than many independent world nations, were conveniently grouped into "minorities." These minorities were used by major political parties at home and by other interested outside powers for power-juggling exercises during the frequent political crises in the country.

Thus, the political struggle and the consequent drifting apart of the various peoples of Nigeria went on over the years unchecked, to an extent that the Federal Parliament was reduced to an intertribal battlefield. Sporadic physical violence erupted from time to time between the various peoples of Nigeria to mark the end of each phase of the rapid drift towards total disintegration of the country.

The last phase of that drift appeared to have started with the 1959 Federal elections, for it was then that the political rift in the country between the leader of the Northern Peoples Congress, the Sardauna of Sokoto, and the leader of the Action Group, Chief Awolowo, dominated the political life of the country. By 1962, the controversy had become virtually uncontrollable and thus a major threat to the very existence of Nigeria as a nation, despite genuine attempts made by Dr. Azikiwe, the then Governor General of the Federation, to reconcile them. Chief Akintola, the Premier of Western Nigeria, had earlier in the year been expelled from the Action Group for his alleged anti-party activities beneficial to Northern Peoples Congress and the Sardauna. He was replaced by Chief Adegbenro. The confused situation that followed disorganised the Action Group and appeared to have neutralized Chief Awolowo on a permanent basis.

When therefore the new Western Nigeria House of Assembly met on 29 May, 1962 and was about to begin the business of the day, supporters of the new opposition, NNDP, rose from their seats and began a weird dance on the floor of the House. One of the dancers seized the Mace, danced towards the Speaker, Prince Adedoyin, took aim at him and, missing, broke the Mace on his table. Federal police quickly moved in and dispersed the members with tear gas. Following this incident, a state of emergency was declared in the West by the Federal Prime Minister, Sir Abubakar who appointed Dr. Majekodunmi, a Federal Minister of Health, the Sole Administrator of the Region. Later, the 3rd Battalion of the Nigeria Army, whose adjutant I was at the time, went down to Ibadan, the capital of Western Nigeria, to enforce the emergency.

The obvious unpopularity of the NNDP in Western Nigeria notwithstanding, Chief Akintola was restored to power by the Federal Government at the end of the emergency period. At the same time, the emergency administration had restricted Chief Awolowo and a good number of his top supporters, including Chief Anthony Enahoro. They were later charged with treasonable felony and some of them were sentenced to long terms of imprisonment.

The tension created by the disturbances in Western Nigeria and the trials that followed, were still fresh in many minds when the Federal elections became due in 1964. Again the nation was disappointed but not exactly surprised at the brazen manner in which the elections were manipulated in some parts of the country in such a way as to make a mere mockery of democratic parliamentary election practices. Some political parties were prevented from campaigning in parts of the country only to make it possible for candidates of the ruling party to be returned unopposed. In such areas of the country, more candidates were returned unopposed than those said to have been elected, even though all parliamentary seats had many contestants. The dust raised by the census fiasco of 1963 had not completely settled and that, coupled with allegations of gross election malpractices, forced the Eastern Nigeria Regional

Government to, rather unwisely, boycott the elections in exaspiration. To control the Federal Parliament, the Sardauna's NPC merged with Akintola's NNDP to form the Nigeria National Alliance (NNA). In desperation, the NCNC and the AG, apparently with no other alternative, consummated a marriage of convenience which gave birth to a party alliance called United Progressive Grand Alliance (UPGA).

The people of Western Nigeria found some consolation for the unfortunate political situation in their Region in the fact that they would have full opportunity to rectify the situation during the Regional parliamentary elections which were due to be held soon. Chief Akintola, who had hitherto ruled without an opportunity of having his popularity and that of his party tested in an election, had the chance of doing so in October, 1965. However, when the elections finally came, they were conducted in a way that can only be described as the height of political folly, an expensive political exercise which ended in a complete fiasco. Even before the elections, the ruling party was alleged to have boasted publicly that they would win the elections whether or not the people voted for them. True to his words, Akintola did "win." Again, massive fraud was alleged, and details of how election malpractices were carried out by government supporters were being discussed publicly. It was alleged that all the government appointed returning officers went into hiding after accepting election papers from government sponsored candidates, thereby making it impossible for AG candidates to register their candidacy. Those who registered had to discover their Returning Officers in their hiding places and forcibly bring them back to their constituencies to do their duties. On election day, the government began to release election results over the radio even for constituencies where voting was still going on.

The Federal Government accepted the results of this election which were entirely rejected by the opposition UPGA. The people of Western Nigeria now realised that they had lost their only opportunity under the constitution of getting a government of their choice in the Region They also knew that the Federal Government was most unlikely to shift its stand on this issue. The ultimate result was a

7

serious outbreak of rioting and violence throughout the Region which spread gradually towards Lagos. As the situation in the Region deteriorated, it became more necessary than in 1962 to proclaim a State of Emergency. If in May, 1962 a broken Mace in the Regional House of Assembly provided sufficient justification for the proclamation of a State of Emergency, one should have thought, in 1965, that the loss of lives through bloody riots that had shown no sign of stopping, was more than an adequate justification for the Federal Government to take emergency action. However, Sir Abubakar appeared to be quite satisfied with the situation, which, by his own assessment, did not require Federal Government's intervention.

To give an impression of normalcy in Nigeria 'to the world at large, the Nigerian Government called a Commonwealth Prime Ministers Conference in Lagos in January, 1966, not to discuss the crisis in Western Region of Nigeria, but the Rhodesian problem! This action ignited a time fuse which was to set off the Nigeria powder-keg before long. For the Prime Minister, Sir Abubakar this conference was to be his last public engagement before the coup of January 15, 1966 in which he died.

MILITARY BACKGROUND

When I joined what is now the Nigeria Army as an officer cadet in 1954, it was merely a part of an all-embracing British Western African Army called the Royal West Africa Frontier Force (RWAFF). This force included the armies of Nigeria, Gold Coast (now Ghana), Sierra Leone and Gambia. Then there were eight indigenous Nigerian officers in the entire Army, the rest being British officers. Even at that stage, it was already clear to a few Nigerians and, of course, to the British authorities that the future stability of a nation such as Nigeria depended to a large extent on the existence of a reliable army. It was also obvious that only the group that controlled the Army could aspire to run a stable Nigerian Government.

Unlike politics where the people thought they knew their rights and quite often fought for them successfully, the average Southern Nigerian had little interest in the Army. It was therefore easy for a few interested persons to do whatever they wanted with the Army without being challenged, and the British Government, being among the interested, took full advantage of the situation. For a start, they saw to it that almost all military installations were concentrated in one area of the country. To illustrate this fact, below is a list of major military installations in Nigeria and their locations, before the January 1966 coup:

Northern Nigeria

3rd Battalion	Kaduna
5th Battalion	Kano
1 Field Battery (Artillery)	Kaduna
1 Field Squadron (Engineers)	Kaduna
88 Transport Regiment	Kaduna
Nigeria Military Academy	Kaduna
Ordnance Depot	Kaduna
44 Military Hospital	Kaduna
Nigeria Military Training College	Kaduna
Reconnaissance Squadron and Regimental Headquarters	Kaduna
Nigeria Air Force	Kaduna
6th Battalion (while under formation)	Kaduna
Ammunition Factory	Kaduna
Recruit Training Depot	Zaria
Nigeria Military School (NMS)	Zaria

Western Nigeria

4th Battalion	Ibadan
2 Field Battery (Artillery)	Abeokuta
2 Reconnaissance Squadron	Abeokuta

Eastern Nigeria

1st Battalion	Enugu

There were no military units in Midwestern Nigeria and those in Lagos were either administrative or ceremonial. Both the 2 Field Battery and the 2 Reconnaissance Squadron at Abeokuta in Western Nigeria were moved there from Kaduna in 1965, after the political coming into being of the Sardauna-Akintola alliance.

To some senior military officers of Southern Nigeria origin this concentration of military establishments in one part of Nigeria did not appear as a mere coincidence, and so they sounded a note of warning to some Southern Nigerian politicians and leaders who were invariably uninterested. Thus, in 1964, the late Lt. Colonel Arthur Unegbe, then the Quartermaster-General fought a one-man futile battle to prevent the establishment of the 6th Battalion in Kaduna, and almost lost his job in the process.

With all major military installations safely in Northern hands, the next phase of the operation to gain control of the Army was to secure absolute majority within the rank and file of the Army itself. Here the problems were formidable for the British Government because with the unlimited opportunities awaiting them in the fields of politics and administration, the Northerners showed little or no interest in the Army. The ethnic quota system of recruitment into the Army, which was introduced shortly before Independence, provided the solution to the problem. Under this system, whenever new recruits were needed for the Army, Northern Nigeria would provide 60 percent, Eastern and Western Nigeria, 15 percent each, and Midwestern Nigeria, 10 percent. The North could hardly fill their quota and some Southerners took advantage of the situation by passing for Northerners and thus getting recruited into the Army. In the name of "ethnic balance" military hospitals were staffed with doctors trained in Kano for about three years in preference to doctors of Southern Nigeria origin with internationally recognised diplomas.

The result of this system was that standards fell within the Army and soldiers became politically conscious. In order to ensure the loyalty of the military majority thus established, the criterion for promotion and advancement in the Army was based more on political considerations than on efficiency or competence. Thus, a course mate of mine, just for coming from the privileged part of the country, was able to attain the rank of Lieutenant Colonel and to attend all available courses in military training colleges in Britain without even bothering to take the compulsory local "Captain to Major" promotion examination in Nigeria. At the same time his colleagues who trained with him in the Royal Military Academy Sandhurst were still Captains.

This situation forced some Southern officers who were politically conscious to identify themselves openly with political parties and politicians, in order to gain military promotions and appointments without any hinderance. Junior officers joined in the bitter struggle for military success through politics — a massive exercise which reduced the Army and its promotions to a ridiculous farce. It could best be described as a football pool in which rich dividends were paid out to successful stakers.

For soldiers of Northern Nigeria origin, the question of political alignment posed no problems for they were by birth aligned to the privileged political establishment. Indeed, it was risky for a Southern Nigeria commanding officer to punish a Northern soldier for fear of being accused of victimisation. For instance in 1964, I sentenced a Northern soldier to 14 days imprisonment for being drunk on duty. This soldier wrote a petition to the Minister of State for Army — a Northern Nigerian — accusing me of victimisation. It took me well over six weeks to clear myself by justifying the punishment. Ironically, three years later, in 1967, during the Biafra-Nigeria war, I was astonished to meet this same soldier in Biafra. He confessed he had been a fake Northern Nigerian all the time he was in the Nigeria Army.

The height of political manoeuvring among the military came when the commander of the First Brigade, Brigadier Samuel Ademulegun, a Yoruba, closely identified himself with the Northern Peoples Congress, in 1964, hoping by this move to achieve his ambition of becoming the first indigenous General Officer to command the Nigeria Army on the departure of the last British General. In his eagerness to demonstrate his loyalty to the party, he consented to the request of the Northern Nigeria Premier, the

11

Sardauna of Sokoto, for troops to be sent to the Tiv Division to quell political riots without clearance from the Army Headquarters in Lagos. The Commanding Officer of the 5th Battalion, Lt. Colonel Unegbe, whose troops were to be sent, opposed the move, insisting on the need for proper procedure. He not only failed to stop the move, but was immediately relieved of his command and posted to Lagos on the orders of the Sardauna. Major Michael Okwechime and I also made our views on the matter known publicly, and this made life uncomfortable in the Army for both of us until the death of Brigadier Ademulegun during the coup of January, 1966.

As the division within the Army widened, intensified by the unofficial move of troops to the Tiv Division, Major Nzeogwu once met Colonel Unegbe and myself in the former's office in Kaduna, and while speaking on the subject advised that we "go easy with the Brigadier, for when a strong wind blows, all the grass bends low to allow it to pass." This proverb was not sufficiently clear enough to enable us to have an idea of what the Major was referring to. How closely Brigadier Ademulegun and the Sardauna were working at this time can be illustrated by this story told by Lt. Colonel David Ejoor shortly before the January 1966 coup.

Colonel Ejoor, a Midwestern Nigerian, who was the senior General Staff Officer (GSO) at Army Headquarters, while on an official tour of the First Brigade, paid a courtesy call on Brigadier Ademulegun in his house one Sunday morning. The Brigadier was upstairs when he arrived but a big, and rather richly dressed Northerner was sitting on the carpet in the living room. Colonel Ejoor completely ignored this man and sat on a chair cross-legged reading a magazine while he waited for the Brigadier to come downstairs. When the Brigadier came down, he introduced the man on the carpet to Ejoor as Sir Ahmadu Bello, the Sardauna of Sokoto and Premier of Northern Nigeria. The Colonel was frightened out of his wits, and after a trembling handshake, he staggered out of the back door and disappeared in utter confusion.

Ademulegun's close political association with the Sardauna made him rather too confident about his chances of superceding Brigadier Ironsi as the next General Officer Commanding (GOC) and, in an army where competence and seniority were of no real value, his confidence seemed quite reasonable. However, he probably talked and boasted too much to the embarrassment of his political supporters and benefactors. When the time for the appointment eventually came, Ademulegun did quite a lot of open campaigning to strengthen his position. Thus, Ademulegun, with the help of the Sardauna, fought and succeeded in having Ironsi, who had just returned from the Congo as a General, revert to the rank of Brigadier. Then using the Northern Government press and radio, he widely publicised his curriculum vitae and that of Ironsi, making sure that his was the more impressive. The bulk of the Southern army split into two opposing sides to campaign for Ademulegun and Ironsi, the latter of whom showed little interest in the exercise.

Ironsi was eventually appointed the GOC on the advice of Brigadier Maimalari but the struggle had created a permanent division in the Army. Some officers, however, preferred to be neutral for, apparently, they considered a *coup d'etat* the only way of restoring the country's political and military situation to normalcy. These neutral officers, acting as umpires, saw no possibility of a return to normalcy through the democratic means unless there was a change of the Federal Government. In Nigeria, like most parts of Africa, where the policy is "once in power, always in power," only force could remove a government. It was not enough for the North to gain full control of the Army, it also went a step further to use that Army with abandon for the benefit of the Region exclusively. For instance, the Reconnaissance Squadron under Major Robert Scott, between 1958 and 1960 when I served in that unit, did nothing but carry out the wishes of the Northern Government. Major Scott who, as Lieutenant Colonel, served in the British Embassy in Lagos as the Military Attaché during the Civil War, was at that time a personal friend of the Sardauna, and therefore very influencial among the Northern civil servants and politicians. In 1958, a part of this unit, under my command, conducted an operation throughout the Northern Region designed to exterminate the Quitia birds that destroyed grain. In 1959, I again took a part of this unit to the Northern Camerouns (now Sardauna Province) to destroy lions alleged to be killing cattle in the Mambila Plateau. Apart from those specific tasks, the Army carried out "flag matches" all the year round in the Northern Region to reassure their leaders — privileges which were not extended to the South.

The involvement of the army in politics took a turn for the worse during the Western Nigeria Parliamentary elections in October, 1965. The Commanding Officer of the 4th Battalion at Ibadan was alleged to have arranged for a training cadre on how to use military automatic weapons for Chief Samuel Akintola, the Premier of Western Nigeria, and his Ministers. The Premier was later killed in the January 1966 coup. The malpractices that were alleged during the Western Regional elections were possible only because the Army was said to have encouraged the dumping of ballot papers into the boxes in the polling booths by supporters of Akintola while they intimidated supporters of the opposing AG. I paid a one-day visit to Abeokuta during the elections and discovered that the Army was far from being impartial in its role of ensuring fair play. It had become clear that Nigeria was overdue for a change.

By October, 1965, rumours of an impending coup were already circulating within the country. A circular letter was passed around all army units to alert commanders to the possibility of a coup. Major C. K. Nzeogwu, the Chief Instructor at the Nigeria Military Training College (NMTC) had been preparing for a demonstration exercise since October, 1965. For this exercise, he sought and had the authority of First Brigade Headquarters to have elements of all army units in Kaduna represented in the demonstration team. For this reason, Nzeogwu had for this exercise, in addition to troops of the NMTC, a Company of 3rd Battalion, a troop of guns, one engineer troop, one reconnaissance troop and representatives of other support arms and services.

Chapter 2

THE REVOLUTION — 15 JANUARY, 1966

Major Hassan Katsina, Inspector of the Reconnaissance Regiment and I travelled together to Lagos from Kaduna on 10th January, 1966 to attend a conference on the purchase of new equipments for our respective units. At the airport also was Major Chukwuma Nzeogwu who had come to see off a colleague of his, Major Wole Ademoyega, who was also travelling to Lagos after a short visit to see Nzeogwu in Kaduna. I can well remember Major Nzeogwu in a conversation with Mrs. Katsina at the airport asking her some searching but apparently irrelevant questions such as — when her baby was due, how many children she had and their ages, how many more children she would like to have, and so on. Mrs. Katsina answered these questions very patiently and it is possible that her answers may have saved her husband's life during the coup that followed five days later.

When the plane touched down at Ikeja airport, a big American car belonging to the Minister for Lagos Affairs, Alhaji Yar'Adua, whisked Katsina away to the plush residential area of Lagos called Ikoyi. Major Ademoyega, cuddling a big briefcase, disappeared into the crowd while Major Eze took me in his car to the Officers' Mess at Apapa, the principal port of Nigeria in Lagos. For various reasons, the Brigade Commanders, Battalion Commanders and most of the other senior military officers were either already in Lagos or were being expected. Most of these senior officers were booked in Ikoyi Hotel but twice, in my first two days in Lagos, Major Christian Anuforo, the Staff Officer in Army Headquarters responsible for arranging accommodation for these officers, attempted to oust me from the Mess VIP chalet where I was staying in order to put

15

Brigadier Ademulegun who was being expected from Ghana. When the Brigadier came in, he chose to stay in a private accommodation. Judging from subsequent events, it would appear Anuforo was merely trying to put the Brigadier where he could be easily held. His decision to stay in an undisclosed private lodging, on the 12th of January, 1966, may have contributed to the postponement of the date of the coup.

While in Lagos, a few officers through their conversations with me, gave clear indications that they were, as individuals dissatisfied to the extent of resorting to violence if need be, to rectify their personal and national grievances. No one however made it known to me that a definite decision had been taken by some of them to carry out a coup. Major Emmanuel Ifeajuna, for instance, invited me for lunch, during which he expressed a view that an immediate coup was the only solution to the nation's numerous political problems. In agreeing with him, I expressed my doubts on the chances of success of such an exercise in a country where tribal loyalties were much stronger than the national and ideological ones. He immediately changed the topic of the conversation and never mentioned it again. Also Major Donatus Okafor, later buried alive for his involvement in the January 1966 coup, as the commander of the Federal Guards, had the occasion to speak to me angrily over his problems with the commander of 2 Brigade, Brigadier Zakari Maimalari. Major Okafor said it was his immediate intention to deal with Maimalari before Maimalari succeeded in dismissing him from the Army for punishing a Northern soldier who went absent without leave.

In another conversation, Major Anuforo condemned Colonel Yakubu Pam, the Adjutant-General and a Northerner from Jos for being brutal to Tiv rioters of Northern Nigeria while he was in charge of operations there as commander of Third Battalion. Talking of Pam, Anuforo commented that an officer who had caused the death of so many people should be punished. The comments and opinions of these officers meant very little to me then, but became very significant when those same officers turned out to be the leaders of the January coup in Lagos.

I left Lagos for Kaduna on the morning of the 13th of January with Hassan Katsina. Major Alphonsus Keshi, the Brigade Major First Brigade, telephoned my house at 0545 hours on the 15th of January, 1966 to inform me that a coup had started at midnight and was still going on. According to him, the coup was being led by Major Nzeogwu and appeared to be going on successfully. It had already resulted in the death of some senior military and civilian leaders including Brigadier Ademulegun, Colonel Ralph Shodeinde, the Commandant of NMTC; the Sardauna; the Premier, and a few others. Major Keshi condemned the whole exercise but requested that I come down to the Brigade Headquarters to assist him in handling the very explosive situation. I considered a hasty move through the town to the Brigade Headquarters unwise at that stage, for I was yet ignorant of Major Keshi's real role and my relationship with those executing the coup. My first reaction was to walk across to the near-by Artillery Officers' Mess and alert my officers. There I found only a young Northern Nigerian, Second Lieutenant Nasko, who told me that all other unit officers had gone on a night exercise and were not yet back. I briefed him on the situation without going into the details of casualties and instructed him to go immediately to the unit and alert the men and await my arrival.

I got to my office soon afterwards, and discovered that those unit officers on the "exercise" took with them almost all the guns and a good quantity of ammunition, as well as most of the serviceable motor vehicles. As these were not authorised for this exercise, it became clear they were a part of the coup, even though there was no shelling going on. I spoke to what was left of the unit on the situation a·.d asked them to prepare to repel any attack from any quarter. In addition, the remaining vehicles were fuelled ready to move troops to anywhere on orders from competent authority.

At about 0900 hours of 16 January, 1966 the young officers under me who took part in the coup — Lt. Bob Egbikor and Olafemiyan came back to the unit and reported in my office. They talked glibly of how they had gone on an authorised exercise, during which they suddenly realised it was a coup, and they were forced to take part against their will. I could not possibly believe them because

17

of the amount of equipment and ammunition they took away without my permission. As a matter of fact, I thought they were sounding my opinion in order to report back to Nzeogwu. Therefore, when they wanted to know from me whether to continue to back Nzeogwu or revert to the normal channel of command, I humourously told them to "render to Nzeogwu what was his and to the old establishment what was theirs." I, however, advised them to return the guns to barracks as they were unnecessary for the exercise they were doing.

Needless to say, they failed to carry out this instruction. There was no doubt they may even have shot me if I had given them the slightest indication of disapproval of the revolution, judging from the ferocity of their looks and how well armed they were even in my office. Probably they were acting under instructions. Shortly after their departure, Major Israel Okoro, the second-in-command of the Third Battalion came into my office, looking quite ruffled and nervous. His commanding officer, Lt. Colonel George Kurubo, had suddenly left Kaduna the previous afternoon by air to Lagos, without explanation. There was a chance that he had been tipped off. Okoro therefore found himself commanding the battalion on this turbulent day.

Major Okoro advised that I disarm and stand down my troops to avoid a misunderstanding and perhaps a confrontation with Nzeogwu who he said was already in full control of all military units in Kaduna. He knew much more of what was happening than I did for he had already gone to see Nzeogwu who was now occupying the Brigade Commander's seat and issuing instructions to the entire Brigade. He also confirmed the death of those already mentioned earlier by Major Keshi. Major Okoro told me of how he was awakened at midnight by a group of soldiers led by Captain Timothy Onwuatuegwu, after they had gained forced entry into the house. Onwuatuegwu had told Okoro what was happening and demanded to know his opinion. Naturally, he declared his full and unqualified support, with all those rifles pointing menacingly at him.

While Okoro was still there, I telephoned the 5th Battalion Kano and spoke to the Commanding Officer, Lt. Colonel Ojukwu.

When I had told him what was happening in Kaduna, his only comment was a series of "good," "good," "good." I rang off and promised to telephone him again, which I never did. It was difficult from this telephone conversation to guess what his real views and stand were, and, I'm sure, he also did not know what I was thinking. However, it seemed that Ojukwu already knew all that I told him.

On the advice of Okoro, the two of us drove down to the Brigade Headquarters to see Nzeogwu. When we arrived, Nzeogwu was sitting in the Brigade Commander's Office with a heavily bandaged neck, surrounded by soldiers of Northern Nigeria origin. There was no doubt he was in pain but appeared calm and very serious. He expressed delight in seeing me and from then on, not only did he confide completely in me, he accepted the advice I gave him right to the end of his "regime." He explained that the aim of his revolution was to get rid of the corrupt and incorrigible politicians and have them replaced with true nationalists. He regretted that it had become necessary to use force to do this when it could have been done through a democratic election — a system which was no longer possible in Nigeria.

Nzeogwu then gave me a quick briefing on what he had done so far and expressed satisfaction with the progress of the revolution in Northern Nigeria. He disclosed that it had been his intention to carry out the revolution in December, 1965, at Enugu, during the annual Army inter-unit shooting competition, which was to have been attended by all senior army officers including Ironsi, the General Officer Commanding. According to Nzeogwu, he had arranged to round up all senior officers and put them under sedation until he had peacefully taken over the government. The plan was shelved and the date postponed because Brigadier Sam Ademulegun and a few others failed to attend. He added that he had given instructions that I should not be disturbed the previous night because he expected that I would join the revolution when I learned of it.

I thanked him for reposing so much confidence in me and congratulated him for his efforts and achievements. I however advised him to go to hospital and get good treatment for his neck which he injured as a result of a grenade explosion during his

19

encounter with the Sardauna in his house during the night of the coup. He rejected this, and preferred to have all treatment he needed in the office.

The Governor of Northern Nigeria, Sir Kashim Ibrahim was being held prisoner in the Brigade Major's Office while many Northern Nigeria soldiers surrounded the building demanding that he be killed for his important role in a regime of corruption, oppression and dishonesty. I clearly overheard Captain Onwuatuegwu trying very hard to convince the soldiers to spare the life of the Governor, and later threatening that the Governor could only be killed over his dead body. In the end, Onwuatuegwu, with the timely intervention of Nzeogwu, saved the Governor's life. Explaining later his reasons for protecting the Governor's life, Onwuatuegwu said he was personally responsible for arresting the Governor during the night of the revolution. What had impressed him was that the Governor, unlike many others, had behaved toward him very well, and had given him full cooperation during his arrest.

Judging from the soldiers in the Brigade Headquarters, it was very striking that Nzeogwu was conducting his coup almost entirely with soldiers of Northern Nigeria origin. His medical attendants, driver, escorts and guards were all Northern soldiers and he only ate meals prepared by his Northern batman. Nzeogwu was a Southern Nigerian.

Because of Nzeogwu's intention to replace the old politicians with what he called "honest progressives" who would work under military supervision, he prepared a proforma to be signed by all politicians pledging their loyalty to the new regime and promising not to engage in any political or other activities likely to obstruct or retard the progress of the revolution. All the politicians who were in Kaduna at the time of the coup signed this form before they left for their villages. Top civil servants were called into Nzeogwu's headquarters and after pledging their loyalty were briefed on their new duties under the new regime.

As I observed these civil servants coming in and out of the headquarters, their faces portrayed nothing but joy and excitement. The only visible exception was perhaps Alhaji Ali Akilu, the

Secretary to the late Premier, whom Nzeogwu however intended to arrest as a likely obstacle to the course of the revolution. I personally thought his arrest would do more harm than good because it could not be justified at the time and could be misunderstood to be victimisation. Other officers held the same view and the idea was dropped by Nzeogwu. Alhaji Yesufu, the Commissioner of Police for Northern Nigeria, also showed open resentment over the conduct of the revolution and, in fact, refused to go and see Nzeogwu when he sent for him. But for my timely intervention he could have lost his life, for soldiers had been detailed to go and gun him down. I promised Nzeogwu I was going to speak to the Commissioner and if I failed to get him realigned, action could be taken against him. I later visited Yesufu in his office at the Police Headquarters and, after a chat with him, he realised the foolishness of his obstinacy. He later came down to the headquarters to make up with Nzeogwu and pledge his loyalty. From then on, he carried out all instructions issued to him by the leaders of the revolution.

I had been in the Brigade Headquarters for over three hours and had not seen Major Katsina, or even heard his name mentioned. I developed a suspicion that he may have been killed during the night as well, for inside Nzeogwu's headquarters, no one talked about the dead. I telephoned the Reconnaissance Unit from the Brigade Major's Office and was told that Katsina was in the house. I drove to his house to ensure this was true and there I found a nervous, absolutely shaken Katsina holding fast to a glass of whisky he was carrying. His wife and children were with him and every minute his wife stood up and peeped out of the window to reassure herself all was still well.

According to Katsina, he knew about the coup at about 0430 hours on the 15th and then went straight to his unit to alert his troops. He was still addressing them and getting them prepared for action when Major Nzeogwu himself came in with a few soldiers. Nzeogwu, Katsina said, asked him on which side he was — on the side of the revolution or on the side of the "old establishment." Katsina said he had no choice but to declare his support for Nzeogwu, but on further reflection, he was more convinced that

21

Nzeogwu's exercise was "justifiable." Having got his assurance, Katsina went on, Nzeogwu shook hands with him, ordered that the remaining armoured vehicles in the unit should be dispatched to the Brigade Headquarters and left amidst cheers from all the men on parade. I later had lunch with Katsina and left him much more relaxed.

News about the conduct and progress of the coup in Lagos began to trickle in by mid-day and it appeared things were not moving well for the revolutionaries. At best, they could be said to be partially successful with a task well planned but badly executed. Sir Abubakar, the Prime Minister; Chief Festus Okotie-Eboh, Federal Minister of Finance; Chief Akintola, Premier, Western Nigeria; Brigadier Maimalari, Commander Second Brigade; Colonel Largema, Commanding Officer, Fourth Battalion; Lt. Colonel Pam, Adjutant General Army Headquarters and Lt. Colonel Unegbe, Quartermaster General were all reported killed or missing. It also appeared as if General Ironsi was successfully foiling the coup in Southern Nigeria, thereby forcing the young officers who started it to flee into hiding in panic and fear. Soon after this, what was left of the civilian regime quickly handed over full responsibility for the government of Nigeria to Ironsi.

Nzeogwu was utterly disappointed with this development and began to plan a deliberate attack on the South to crush Ironsi's men. He blamed his failure on certain officers who had failed to implement their part of the coup even though they had given their full support during the planning stages. Nzeogwu's opinion was that this sudden betrayal deserved punishment because it was due more to consideration for personal reward by Ironsi than to cowardice.

The following day, 16th of January, 1966, Major Nzeogwu called a conference of all officers in Kaduna to brief them on what had been achieved and to issue instructions for future operations. Addressing the conference, Nzeogwu stressed his determination to deal ruthlessly with those who showed signs of "sitting on the fence" and the "opportunists." In this connection, he announced that Ojukwu and Katsina were enemies of the revolution and would be disposed of as soon as possible. He accused Katsina of showing insufficient interest in the revolution by never showing up at the Brigade Headquarters and failing to attend the conference without excuses. He accused Ojukwu of being a "let down" for reasons best known only to Nzeogwu himself. On my advice, in the conference hall, Nzeogwu agreed to give Ojukwu one more chance of joining the revolution and immediately appointed me to go to Kano and find out from him what his real stand was.

While in Kano, Nzeogwu also wanted me to collect £ 500,000 sterling from the Central Bank for the payment of soldiers in Northern Nigeria under his command. Speaking about future operations, Nzeogwu announced he had grouped all forces under his control into three Task Forces. The first Task Force was given the task of moving further north to Zaria and Kano to consolidate his control on those areas and to remove all opposition where it still existed. The second Task Force had the assignment of moving through Jebba to take Ibadan, the capital of Western Nigeria and subsequently Lagos. The third Task Force was to move on the eastern axis through Makurdi to take Enugu, the capital of Eastern Nigeria and later Benin, the capital of Midwestern Nigeria. The task of the Air Force (NAF) was to fit machine guns to their training aircrafts (Piagsos and Doniers) in preparation for strafing and bombing Lagos when orders were given after the fall of Ibadan. The Air Force bombs were to be hand grenades and the pilots were already practising at the outskirts of Kaduna how to strafe with machine guns and release grenades from their planes. Most, if not all the officers attending this conference, listened to Nzeogwu's orders with absolute joy and excitement. When Nzeogwu in conclusion said "Nigeria has a population of 50 million. We can afford, and we are prepared to sacrifice a million to achieve our aims and objectives," the conference hall was virtually brought down by the applause of the young officers. The D-day was to be the 18th of January, 1966 and each Task Force had artillery and armoured vehicles in support. Before the end of the conference, Major Ukpo Isong, a Calabar officer under Katsina's command, was appointed by Nzeogwu to take a small force and go and arrest Katsina, with orders to shoot him if he resisted.

Alone with Nzeogwu in his office after the conference, I very carefully and cautiously disagreed with his plans and future intentions. I argued that I was the wrong person to go to Kano to meet Ojukwu as well as collect soldiers' pay, because my presence was necessary in Kaduna at all times. For this task I thought a junior officer would do. Nzeogwu accepted this suggestion. Also I advised that Katsina should be persuaded to come down to the Headquarters as opposed to his being arrested. I thought no harm ought to come to him until it was positively proved beyond all doubt that he was against the revolution. Finally, I advised Nzeogwu again, rightly or wrongly, to give up the idea of launching an attack on the South. My points of argument were that the civil regime had been overthrown and the Army was in control of the Federal Government, thus fulfilling his overall aim. If he therefore attacked Southern Nigeria, it would be seen as a military struggle for power between him and Ironsi — a struggle which could degenerate into a civil war, and blood bath. Moreover, I thought Nzeogwu would very easily and quickly lose his military advantage over Ironsi who was in a position to call for outside military assistance. A point Nzeogwu tended to overlook was the fact that the bulk of his soldiers were from the tribes of Northern Nigeria who could easily switch their loyalty if the confrontation lasted too long. With these points, Nzeogwu decided to cancel the offensive against Ironsi and the South.

When later Katsina was brought to the Brigade Headquarters and it appeared as if he would get into trouble, Captain Isong pleaded for Katsina's life and was prepared to die for him, as he was his commanding officer. Yet during the subsequent July 1966 counter coup, Captain Isong was allowed to be killed by people who were in a position to save his life.

Soon afterwards, on the evening of the 16th of January, news came from Kano that Captain Ude, who had gone there with a message from Nzeogwu for Ojukwu, was under arrest and was being held in the 5th Battalion Guardroom. The following day, when I got to the Brigade Headquarters in the morning, there was tension and feverish activity. Outside the Headquarters, a strong Company group, supported by two ferrets and a saladine armoured car, formed up under Captain Onwuatuegwu, an instructor under Nzeogwu at the Military College. This force, as I soon found out, was about to leave for Kano to ensure that 5th Battalion joined the Revolution. Their instruction was to avoid the use of force and the consequent loss of lives, unless it became necessary. Realising that the special task force was formed to do battle in Kano, I convinced Nzeogwu to cancel the operation, and he did so. He then asked me to devise a more peaceful means of ensuring the full cooperation of the 5th Battalion in Kano, and the release of Captain Ude from arrest.

I had by now discouraged all future operations, and in my attempt to get a quick and tidy end to Nzeogwu's revolution I had created a stalemate. Ironsi was sitting in Lagos ruling the South and Nzeogwu was ruling the North from Kaduna, and there was no real link or dialogue between the two of them. I thought Nzeogwu should submit to Ironsi, and for this reason I began to speak to him about the need for a unified military leadership of the nation under Ironsi. I also pointed out that unless the wandering troops were disarmed and sent back to the barracks at once, they could eventually get out of hand. Already, numerous illegal road blocks had been set up all over the towns where the Army was stationed in Northern Nigeria by soldiers of all military units, and civilians were being dispossessed and molested. On my initiative, I had ordered the gunners deployed in Kaduna town to go back to barracks with their guns, but they refused to do so unless the instructions came from Nzeogwu.

Later that day, both Ironsi and Gowon spoke to me over the telephone. Ironsi said my new task was to bring Nzeogwu down to Lagos dead or alive and then handed me over to Gowon to work out the details of how that was to be done with him. Over the telephone Gowon passionately described how he had come back from Britain on the night of 14th January, 1966, a day before the coup started. Gowon narrated the story of his narrow escapes from death in the hands of the revolutionaries who, he said, were after him the whole night and throughout the following day. He suggested that I find sufficient troops to attack and destroy Nzeogwu. I refused to do this because as I told him, all troops were already under Nzeogwu's

25

control in the North. In addition, I pointed out that even if troops were available, it would be unwise on my part to fight against what appeared to be a popular revolution. Gowon then suggested that I should arrange with a doctor to sedate Nzeogwu while appearing to be treating his injured neck. Nzeogwu could then be brought down to Lagos in that state. I once again had many reasons why this could not be done; foremost among them was the fact that only one doctor — a Northern Nigerian at that — treated Nzeogwu and this doctor would definitely not have consented to such a suggestion. I explained to Gowon that the coup was completely over in the North and Nzeogwu was prepared to settle with Lagos under two main conditions. One was a guarantee of safety for himself and others who took part in the coup and the other was an assurance that the aims of the revolution would be upheld at all times by the Lagos regime.

Later, I telephoned Ironsi again and gave him those conditions as demanded by Nzeogwu and promised to convince Nzeogwu to hand over power completely to him if these assurances were honestly given. Ironsi accepted the conditions and invited Nzeogwu to Lagos. Nzeogwu formally handed over power to Ironsi and agreed to go to Lagos in a telephone conversation during the evening of the 18th January, 1966. This enabled Ironsi to announce the appointment of Military Governors, one for each of the four Regions: the North, West, East and the Midwest. Major Katsina was appointed Governor of the North, Lt. Colonel Francis Fajuyi for the West, Ejoor for the Midwest and Ojukwu for the East.

Immediately after the announcement of the new Governors, Major Keshi, the Brigade Major First Brigade, telephoned my house to say that, in his view, the appointment of one of the Military Governors was a grievous mistake. Major Keshi also expressed the same view to Nzeogwu who said he would take up the matter with Ironsi when he arrived in Lagos. He thought that by that appointment cowardice had been rewarded in a revolution designed to bring to the forefront only the best the nation could muster. Nzeogwu also felt that Ironsi ought to move the new Governors to Regions other than their Regions of origin.

By the time Colonel Conrad Nwawo, Military Attaché,

Nigerian High Commission, London, travelled from Lagos to Kaduna to escort Nzeogwu to Lagos, all was already set for his departure. On 20th January, 1966, in a short ceremony outside the Brigade Headquarters, Nzeogwu handed over the affairs of Northern Nigeria to the newly appointed Governor, Katsina. Katsina made a short speech in praise and support of Nzeogwu and all he stood and fought for. In the presence of the world press and radio, including the British Broadcasting Corporation, he expressed his determination to ensure that Nzeogwu's efforts would not be in vain. In a show of great emotion, Katsina embraced Nzeogwu before his final departure.

The January coup was widely acclaimed all over the country including the Northern Region, where top civil servants celebrated its success, and apparently happy ending by holding parties both in their homes and in public places. Acting against my advice that it was improper from the protocol point of view, Katsina visited my house immediately after his appointment. He brought with him his entire entourage of police outriders and patrol cars and a carload of drinks. We all drank to the health of Ironsi. We drank to the health of the new Governors. We drank to the survival of a new Nigeria. Katsina would probably say now, I did all that to deceive old Alex into believing all was well. I sincerely believed that he was acting in good faith that night we drank the toasts.

Western Nigeria probably benefitted most from this revolutionary turn of events. The Military takeover brought to an end a long nightmare of bloody riots which were triggered off by the rigged Western Nigeria Parliamentary elections. In the East, Midwest and Lagos, the entire people and press hailed the change with absolute joy and optimism for the emergence of a new Nigeria free from corruption, tribalism and nepotism. Therefore, when people argue nowadays that Eastern Nigerians were massacred in retaliation for their role in the January coup, it sounds ridiculous. The January revolution was not a total failure for it achieved its primary objective — the removal of the discredited civilian regime. What went wrong was the inability of the coup to exploit its success.

When, therefore, the inevitable counter-coup came, the Ironsi regime wobbled and collapsed.

It may be relevant to mention that the coup only attained limited success in Lagos because Nzeogwu, in his determination to ensure success, selected Majors Ifeajuna, Anuforo, Okafor and Ademoyega — officers who had personal grievances against various senior military commanders — to lead it in the Federal Capital. The personal grievances clouded their thoughts and unfortunately adversely affected their judgements and therefore the entire Lagos operations.

Without doubt, it could now be argued that if Nzeogwu had been given a free hand to kill Ojukwu, Katsina, Yesufu, and Ali Akilu and then attack the South, as he intended to do, things might have developed differently in one way or the other, in Nigeria. Against this argument, one can only bear in mind that it could have been worse. But then, the disaster that followed the coup was entirely due to weakness and lack of clear realistic political objectives and discipline on the part of the military regime which inherited power. The January coup was sufficiently successful for that regime to have rectified whatever was done badly and still retain power, discipline and respect. What happened was that Nigeria, which was being treated for an overdose of compromise by those who carried out the coup, was being administered with more doses of compromise by Ironsi's regime, which inherited power after the revolution.

28

Chapter 3

THE OVERTHROW OF GENERAL IRONSI'S REGIME

The Initial Plot

The plot to overthrow General Ironsi's Government was slow, deliberate and systematic. Said to have been conceived in Ahmadu Bello University, Zaria, it was worked out in detail by Northern Nigerian civil servants and politicians and executed by the entire Northern civilians and their military counter-parts. This regime, formed in the first instance on basis of compromise between Ironsi and Nzeogwu on the one hand, and Ironsi and the politicians on the other, aspired to rule successfully by compromise. For this reason it tried to placate those who sought to destroy it and took no action on various substantiated reports available to it concerning plans to overthrow it.

The first sign of trouble for the Ironsi regime came from Ahmadu Bello University where it was alleged that a group of expatriate and Nigerian lecturers were inciting Northern students against Southerners shortly after the coup. These lecturers were said to be openly advising the Northern students on the need for an immediate counter-coup to restore Nigerian political power to the North; the alternative, they claimed, was for the North to be enslaved by the South for an indefinite period. One of the ex-patriates involved had a good personal reason for wanting to dethrone General Ironsi. He had applied to serve with U.N. forces in the Congo in 1962 at the end of his military contract with the Nigeria Army. This application was turned down by General Ironsi who was then commanding the U.N. forces in the Congo. In taking his decision, General Ironsi probably took into consideration this

General Ironsi watching a mortar concentration at Kachia near Kaduna in 1966, shortly before his overthrow. Some of the officers shown are (from left to right): Lt. Col. Imo, Major Obioha, Lt. Col. Okoro (with umbrella), Lt. Col. A. Madiebo, Major Ogbemudia (with map), Col. Bassey, Major General A. Ironsi, Lt. Col. O. Kalu, Lt. Col. M. Shuwa, Lt. Col. J. Akagha, etc.

gentleman's political activities while he was in the Nigeria Army — activities which Ironsi was most reluctant to promote in an already troubled Congo.

When therefore the expatriate eventually gained employment in the Ahmadu Bello University, he saw in the crisis which was taking place, a good opportunity to have his own back on General Ironsi. Right from the start, his activities were fully reported to the General through the First Brigade Headquarters in Kaduna, as a steady flow of information came to it from students of Southern Nigeria origin in Ahmadu Bello University. For unknown reasons, these reports were never acted upon.

In Lagos, the General surrounded himself with more Northerners than the late Premier Balewa ever did in the height of his political power and glory. Alhaji Kam Salem was his Inspector General of Police following the suspension of Mr. Lewis Edet, the former Police boss. Alhaji Yesufu who had moved down to Lagos from Kaduna immediately after the revolution, was appointed the head of the Police Special Branch. Lt. Colonel Gowon emerged out of nowhere to become the Army Chief of Staff and for all practical purposes, the commander of the Nigeria Army. Brigadier Babafemi Ogundipe preferred a quiet job of "advising" Ironsi and re-allocating living quarters vacated by former Federal ministers. The other very senior officer left was Colonel Robert Adebayo who was away in Britain at the time of the revolution. He had rushed back home immediately after the coup in the hope of becoming the Military Governor of Western Nigeria. Ironsi sent him back to Britain and he left a very disgruntled man.

Thus, while the Northerners were carefully getting themselves into strategically important political positions, Southerners were as usual chasing after the most comfortable ones. With the situation as it was, only few reports got to Ironsi and on these, he got the wrong advice or none at all. Gowon was instructed to investigate and report to the Supreme Military Council on the January 1966 coup and the degrees of involvement of various persons to enable disciplinary action to be taken. Some special junior afficers were appointed by Gowon to do this investigation but it is still doubtful if Ironsi and

31

some members of his Supreme Military Council got copies of this report.

Northern officers were becoming increasingly aware that Ironsi was prepared to do anything to please them and, for this reason, they were becoming more daring in their open criticism and even mockery of him and his entire government. A young Major under my command in the Artillery, when writing to me from America where he was at the time of the coup, bitterly condemned and criticised Ironsi and his team; and threatened that on his return, he would ensure that another coup was organised to overthrow Ironsi's government.

Katsina, who worked very closely with me immediately after the coup, began to avoid my company and advice after a month in office as Military Governor. In Kaduna, Lt. Colonel Duke Bassey was sitting in as the Brigade Commander after his return from Lagos where he had fled in disguise as a Cow Fulani during the coup. Bassey later came back a very frightened man and was only too pleased to hand over the command of his Brigade to Governor Katsina contrary to regulations stipulating the powers and functions of the Military Governors. Having ensured his own personal safety by deploying two armoured vehicles in front of his house, "papa" Bassey delegated the power to employ and deploy the rest of his Brigade to the Governor. This practice did not go without protests from me as the most senior officer in Northern Nigeria, but my protests and reports to Lagos on that development fell on deaf ears.

The real turning point came at the beginning of March when one morning the Governor of the North called a conference of all army officers in Northern Nigeria. Addressing the conference in an angry voice, the Governor charged that certain military officers of Southern Nigeria origin, according to his information, were unhappy and jealous of him for being the Governor of the North. He went on to accuse certain Southern officers of trying to displace top civil servants in the North from their jobs, and assured his audience that such officers would fail. Speaking about the January coup he described it as a well organised "murder operation" for which the participants ought to have been punished if the Lagos authorities were fair and sincere to all. He warned that when the Northerners were ready for their own coup, it would be conducted in broad daylight and would be very "bloody indeed," unlike the January coup when cowards went around by night murdering people in their sleep.

On that note, the Governor left the conference hall followed closely by his chief aid, Ali Akilu, who stood grim-faced and tense beside the Governor during his speech. What Katsina said did not come as a surprise to anyone. What was a mystery was the reason and the need for him to make his intentions public. My view was that Katsina and the people of the North were still very frightened over what happened in January and felt that the Southerners were planning a repetition. For this reason, he wanted to intimidate these Southerners to discourage them from doing anything before the North was ready. Details of Katsina's address were forwarded to Supreme Headquarters, Lagos both by the Brigade Headquarters and by various individual senior officers. It would appear no action was again taken.

To give an impression of working with Ironsi, a Central Administrative Committee was established in Kaduna to deal with serious civil and military problems and advise the Governor accordingly. The Committee which had three Northern Permanent Secretaries and myself as members, had also a top British official as virtually its chairman. This Committee met three times before it wound up. Even the few times it met, the committee did no formal work except that members expressed their dissatisfaction with Ironsi's handling of the officers who carried out the January coup. The argument was that those officers ought to have been brought to trial as opposed to their present detention. The discussion appeared to have been meant for my consumption, being the only Southerner in the Committee. I absorbed all that was said and promptly reported to the right quarters in Lagos. I submitted a memorandum to the chairman of the Committee in February, 1966 for discussion, but no more meetings were held, nor did I get an acknowledgement. The next time I heard about this memorandum was in September, 1966, after the second coup and the pogroms. It might be of interest to mention that while I was a refugee at Enugu, I got a letter from the Committee chairman, saying that a committee meeting was to be held in Kaduna at the end of September, 1966 to discuss my memorandum! I was requested to attend. I still had enough humour and spirit left in me to enjoy the joke, which it was intended to be.

As time went on, the clandestine campaign against Ironsi's government, which was initially localised around Ahmadu Bello University, grew into an open and nationally organised exercise, and appeared to have the official blessing and recognition of Northern Nigeria Government authorities. By April, 1966, top civil servants, ex-politicians and senior police officers were known to be holding frequent meetings which could no longer be said to be secret. Many politicians who had earlier fled from Kaduna immediately after the coup were back again in town, this time buying up all available shotguns and cartridges in the local shops, indeed, in the same way these guns were being bought up in all other major cities in Northern Nigeria. I called Katsina's attention to the new development. He thought that probably the ex-politicians, as displaced persons, had taken a fancy to hunting as a means of livelihood!

To reassure me that he still thought of peace from time to time, the Governor created what he called a Peace Committee, made up of two Ibos and four Northerners. They were given the task of trying to restore confidence and mutual understanding between Northerners and Southerners in Kaduna. They were to report their difficulties and any other information they had to the First Brigade Headquarters which would take action or refer the matter to Katsina. This committee looked like a mockery of attempts being made by Ironsi to bring the North and the South together once again. Otherwise, how could four semi-illiterate Northerners assisted by two semi-illiterate Ibo traders bring peace to Kaduna if the Governor himself could not do so. Even if the committee had succeeded in bringing peace to Kaduna, what arrangements had been made to bring peace to other Northern towns which were in as tense a state as was Kaduna? The Committee soon died a natural death after the senior Ibo representative failed to get a hearing at the Brigade Headquarters after several attempts.

By the end of April, 1966, the press and radio of the North had joined in the hostile campaign against the South. These mass information media were then fully employed in preparing the people's minds for the coming counter-coup. Starting from the beginning of May, 1966, Radio Kaduna played every day for three weeks, recorded speeches of late Sir Abubakar and Sir Ahmadu. These political campaign speeches were carefully selected to arouse tribal feelings, passion and hatred against the people of the South. While the Radio networks blared the speeches, the official Government daily newspaper, the *New Nigerian*, carried daily for some time serialised articles on the Islamic war of Conquest or Jihad, both in English language and local vernaculars.

I saw the handwriting on the wall. Indeed no one could have failed to recognise the signs of the impending disaster. But to reassure myself, I personally forwarded a report to Army Headquarters in Lagos attaching texts of some of the speeches and publications. I did not expect any reaction from Lagos and there was none. I also protested to Katsina against the Radio broadcasts and the newspaper publications and implored him to intervene and save what was left of the country by ordering an immediate stop to these inciting declarations. He refused to intervene on the ground that "what was left of Nigeria" was still supposed to be a democracy where people were free to express their views and feelings freely. When I suggested, as an alternative, that military personnel be deployed in key ministries as a check against anti-government acts, I received no answer.

"ARABA" TEST RIOTS — 29 MAY, 1966

I was not exactly surprised when I got an unofficial report in my house at 1500 hours on the 29th of May, 1966, to the effect that serious riots against Southern Nigerians were going on inside Kaduna city. According to this report, Southerners were being beaten up and their cars smashed by Northern mobs. What surprised me though, was the fact that policemen were said to be actively participating in some areas. The Duty Officer at Brigade Headquarters confirmed the report over the telephone and pointed out that reports of more bloody and widespread riots had been received from such big Northern cities as Kano, Zaria and Jos. He said he had contacted both the Brigade Commander, Bassey and Governor Katsina. According to the Duty Officer, Katsina had told him that it was only he, as the Governor who had the authority to order an intervention by the Army. If what the Duty Officer said was right, that amounted to usurption of the responsibilities of the Brigade Commander and the Army Headquarters by the Governor. When I telephoned him later to find out the true facts, Katsina said he was acting under the provisions of special emergency powers just conferred on him by General Ironsi over the telephone. I advised him to turn out the Army immediately before the situation got out of hand but he refused on the grounds that the police were capable of handling the situation.

I telephoned Lagos, and told the Duty Officer at Army Headquarters what the true situation was and also recommended that the Headquarters should order an immediate military intervention. For unknown reasons, there was no reaction from Lagos.

Many other senior officers in the North, including officers of Northern origin, appealed to the Military Governor for immediate action but failed to convince him. The riots therefore went on all over the North unchecked for more than 24 hours. From reports already received, a good number of Southerners — men, women and children — had been killed and were still being killed all over the cities and towns in Northern Nigeria.

Around noon of 31 May, 1966, Governor Katsina telephoned me to request that I go by air to Kano and Katsina and bring back for him an on-the-spot situation report to enable him to advise Ironsi. Initially, for many reasons, I refused to do that. I had a suspicion that the trip could be a trick to get me out of Kaduna and lead me into a trap which might well cost me my life. I also felt that the trip would achieve nothing as the riots in Kano were already dying down and there were no riots at all in Katsina town at the time. A trip to Zaria and Jos would have made more sense. I also had at the back of my mind the fact that Katsina, being a much junior officer to me, was in no position to give me orders. If I accepted and acted on those instructions without comments, I would be creating a precedent which would be difficult to erase in the future. I was equally angry that the Governor, who had for 48 hours of rioting turned down all my advice and suggestions to him, should now consider me the most appropriate person to scout round for situation reports on his behalf. It was most unlikely that my report would be accepted under the circumstances and that my trip was merely being used to reassure Ironsi.

To ensure that I went on this trip, the Governor got Ironsi to issue the instructions again, this time as orders. While passing Ironsi's orders to me, Katsina assured me of my safety. He explained that he had already turned out the troops in Kano and the situation there was back to normal. To avoid taking any risks over my life, he said he had detailed a special protection party to travel with me. This party as far as I was concerned could be a firing squad but I had no alternative but to go with them. The Sergeant in charge of my protection party was always so close behind me breathing hot air down my neck that I feared he might drive a knife through my back without anyone taking any notice. I was forced, at Kaduna airport, to tell him to get off my back, and give me a chance to swing my arms while I walked.

Two hours of relatively rough flight in our special plane brought my reconnaissance party to Kano airport, shortly before 1700 hours. I also had with me the new Police Commissioner for Northern Nigeria, Alhaji Hamman Maiduguri and Mallam Capinta of Katsina's Office. Capinta insisted that we call up Colonel Muhammed Shuwa, the Commanding Officer of the 5th Battalion, to the airport to brief us there, so as to save time. I had no objection and he telephoned Shuwa who came up immediately to the airport to meet us. Colonel Shuwa gave a detailed and frank briefing on the Kano riots which had just ended. According to him, he had a pre-warning early on the 29th of May, 1966 about the intentions and preparations of Northerners to attack Southerners in Kano later in the day. For this reason, he later drove round the town and

37

discovered that already a large crowd of Northerners were assembled outside the city gates. In the Sabon Gari (Strangers' Quarters) he also noticed small groups of anxious Southerners huddled together in street corners. Some of them were already shutting up their houses. According to Shuwa, he then drove to the Police Station to acquaint the police with the explosive situation. The police confirmed they were fully aware of what was happening but had instructions not to do anything until they were given instructions by Katsina and by no one else.

Shuwa said he then went back to his barracks and immediately dispatched a Company of soldiers with instructions that they be deployed in the area of Kano Stadium midway between the "City" and Sabon Gari. The Company, which also had instructions to prevent a confrontation between the Northerners and Southerners, took up position just in good time to do this, for the Northern mob was already advancing towards Sabon Gari when the Company arrived at the Stadium. Shuwa said he was happy and proud of his action particularly when he noticed that the Northern mob appeared to lack determination and were in fact drifting slowly backwards towards the city gates.

The presence of the troops created a lull during which Shuwa said he telephoned Katsina to report these commendable achievements. Shuwa claimed that when it was learnt in Kaduna that he had deployed troops, instead of being praised for using his initiative to an advantage, he was ordered to withdraw the troops back to barracks without being given reasons for such a line of action.

According to Shuwa, as soon as the troops left, the Northern mob again advanced, this time unchallenged, into the town. Thus began the very bloody riots and massacres. These he said went on unchecked neither by the police nor by the army for over 24 hours. During the riots, he said he had telephoned Katsina several times to appraise him of the true situation and to try to convince him to order military intervention but failed. As he went around the town unable to do anything, Shuwa said he saw private homes, churches, shops. schools and market stalls belonging to Southern Nigerians, in flames. He saw crying children, the young and the old, both men and women being chased about and being beaten to death while their homes were looted.

On the 30th of May, 1966, the riots began again rather early. The rioting was much fiercer than the previous day, and the Commanding Officer himself with the assistance of his escorts, had to go round the town trying to disperse the mobs by firing in the air. In places where he rescued people who were still alive, he arranged to send them to the military medical centre for treatment.

A story was told of a whole family that was locked up inside their house and the house set ablaze. I also listened to the story of an incident at the Kano Railway Station where a large crowd of Southerners had gathered, waiting to escape by train. They were attacked by a mob which killed or maimed most of them, and their property was looted. By mid-day the Commanding Officer felt that he had seen enough atrocities and murders to decide to turn out his troops on his own initiative and face the consequences. By 1400 hours he had deployed two Companies of armed soldiers all over the town with instructions to deal ruthlessly with the rioters. His troops did a good job as they met little or no opposition from the mobs, who appeared to be surprised that troops were being used against them after all.

It was then that a belated message came from the Governor's office at 1700 hours authorising him to employ troops to quell the riots, knowing fully well that he was already doing so. Apart from burning houses and corpses all over the town, the whole area was now quiet and the situation could be said to have returned to normal. Shuwa finally added that he had information that similar riots were due to be held in Katsina. In order to prevent a repetition of what took place in Kano, he said he had already, on his own initiative, dispatched a Company of armed soldiers to that town.

My investigations showed that Shuwa's efforts to control the riots made him unpopular with the local leaders and politicians. These people had, between February and May, 1966, sent many unsuccessful delegations to him urging him to organise a counter-coup in retaliation for the January coup. I was personally very impressed with Colonel Shuwa, whose role and actions I greatly admired. He had done much of his military service before the January, coup among the Ibos at Enugu and had grown to understand them as human beings, in spite of all their faults and foibles. I am sure that, in spite of all that has happened since then, including the atrocities of the pogroms and the war, he is still the same fair-minded and humane person whose courage I admired so much that day. My plane party took off for Katsina, shortly afterwards.

When we touched down at Katsina airstrip we were met by a local government official from the Emir's palace. Katsina town is the home of Governor Katsina and I therefore expected that we were going to get the best briefing of our trip there. Rather, the official who met us also decided to speak to us at the airport. He assured me that all was well and normal inside the town. He announced that the Emir had offered protection to all Southern Nigerians and most of them were already living happily inside the palace grounds, as a precautionary measure. The Emir's emissary was very anxious that we did not go into the town because, in his opinion, that would irritate an already angry and tense people if they knew someone had come to spy on them. I sent a message of thanks to the Emir through his emissary and congratulated him also for his successful attempts to preserve the peace in his Emirate.

When we returned to Kaduna, I drove straight to the Governor's house and reported to Katsina. I gave him as many details as he cared to listen to and made it quite clear that in my opinion, the Kano disaster could have been avoided if Colonel Shuwa had been given a free hand to handle the situation properly, before it got out of hand. I then praised Shuwa for his initiative in sending troops to Katsina to prevent any riots breaking out there.

Contrary to my expectations, Katsina was of the opinion that Shuwa's action in sending troops to Katsina was unnecessary and provocative in view of the fact that his father, the Emir had already taken appropriate action. Soon afterwards, Shuwa was ordered to ensure the withdrawal of all troops in Katsina back to Kano within 24 hours. When this instruction was carried out, the stage was set for another bloodbath.

From Katsina's house, I called the Brigade Headquarters to get a briefing on the situation in other parts of Northern Nigeria. The Brigade Major, Major Sam Ogbemudia, said that the expatriate staff at Ahmadu Bello University were leading the rioters in Zaria. According to him, these gentlemen were even using their personal cars to move the rioters quickly from one part of the town to another. Their cars also had anti-Ironsi slogans pasted on them. As was the case in Kano, many houses were being burnt, while free-for-all looting was being carried out. People had been killed or injured and the Army, as in other places, had stood by and watched. Ogbemudia said that in Jos it was the same story if not worse, as there were no soldiers stationed there and even if the Governor wanted to use the army there, it would take some time to get them there. In Jos and Zaria, the riots lasted for three days and stopped only when the rioters were tired of rioting.

The news of an outbreak of riots in Katsina came as a climax to the whole exercise. The rioters were said to have attacked the Emir's palace, where many Southerners were seeking protection, and inflicted heavy casualties on them after the Emir had tried un-success-fully to stop the mob from entering the palace. Thereafter the riots moved from the palace into the town to hunt down those who had not sought refuge with the Emir. These tragedies may not have occurred if the troops sent to Katsina town by Shuwa had not been withdrawn prematurely.

I spoke to Katsina over the telephone during the riots in his hometown and expressed regret that his father had, despite all his efforts, failed in his attempt to give effective protection to the Southerners. He explained that an Ibo man had been found with a loaded shotgun in his house and that had angered his people. He, however, assured me that the police were trying to bring the situation back to normal.

The Sokoto operation was swift. There in Sokoto, while other towns rioted, the Southerners went into their Church to pray to their God for the return of peace. While they all gathered there and prayed the church was cordoned off. Having poured petrol over the church building, it was set ablaze, and the multitude died while praying for peace.

41

After seven terrifying days, serious rioting stopped in most major cities of the North, apart from a few remote villages. Strange enough, the peoples of Northern Nigeria could not agree on a common reason for the riots. There were those who said they fought against Ironsi's Federal Government Decree no. 34 (Unification Decree) which "endangered" the position of Northern Nigerians as free citizens of Nigeria. Others said they rioted simply to avenge the death of their leaders in January. But a great majority simply wanted secession. According to them they had no intention of being a part of a Federal Nigeria not ruled by Northerners. This explains why most of the placards carried by the rioters in all towns bore the word "ARABA" — the Hausa word for "secession." Various versions of these "Araba" placards were collected at Brigade Headquarters and sent down to Lagos, but even these gave Lagos no cause for concern or deep reflection on the matter.

Immediately the riots came to an end, certain questions came to my mind and perhaps to the minds of many others as well. Why did the Northern members of the Supreme Military Council not advise Ironsi against Decree no. 34, but instead approved it? Assuming they had not anticipated a hostile reaction from the North at the time of its promulgation, why did they not alert Ironsi when they found that to be the case subsequently? Could they truly say they were not aware of the resentment of their people against this Decree? Why were the riots directed against innocent civilians who had nothing to do with the January coup carried out by officers and men drawn from all Regions, or with the Supreme Military Council that passed the "notorious" Unification Decree, a Council which had more representatives from Northern Nigeria than from the East? If the competent authorities had cared to find out the answers to these questions, the situation may have been rectified permanently after the riots. But everybody appeared quite happy that the worst was over even if it had cost over 3000 lives.

During the first half of June, 1966, a massive exodus of Eastern Nigerians from the North was taking place amidst appeals and assurances from various quarters asking them to stay on. Katsina's immediate reaction was to try and revive his Kaduna Peace

Committee as a way of reassuring Southerners of their safety in the North. The Committee packed up after the first day's meeting. He then went on to reassure Ironsi that Easterners, or for that matter any other Nigerian, would never again be molested in Northern Nigeria. Ironsi accepted Katsina's assurances and sent up Lt. Colonel Patrick Anwunah, General Staff Officer at the Army Headquarters, to Kaduna to tour the affected parts of the North and deliver to him a first-hand report. Ironsi later appointed a board to inquire into the root causes of the riots, establish degrees of involvement and make recommendations. Finally he deported Major Boyle from Nigeria, which was a futile exercise, for soon after Gowon seized power this man came back as a hero.

Following Katsina's assurances of safety for the Ibos in the North, both Ironsi and Ojukwu, the Governor of Eastern Nigeria, encouraged those who had fled the North to go back there and resume their normal lives. Even then, tension in the North was on the increase but, that notwithstanding, many Southerners, particularly those from the Eastern Region, went back in large numbers. Rumours of another Ibo coup were rife during the month of June, 1966. The May, 1966 operations proved a failure because, even though the Ibos suffered heavy casualties, the objective of changing the government in Lagos was not achieved. Northern soldiers were now being pressured to strike back quickly in self-defence before the "Ibo second coup." After the "May Test Riots" Lagos Military Government even redoubled efforts to placate the North, instead of admonishing the authorities of that Region. This tended to confirm that something more drastic could be done against the regime in Lagos without meaningful opposition.

Meetings of Northern Nigerian leaders from all walks of life were on the increase and more regular, both in Kaduna and elsewhere in the Region. Governor Katsina was alleged to have attended many of these meetings, particularly those held in Kaduna. As a result of these meetings, a major conference of all Emirs and chiefs of the North was held in Kaduna during the month of June. At this meeting, the Emirs and chiefs forwarded to Ironsi certain

43

conditions which he had to meet if the North was to remain a part of Nigeria. Chief among them were:

1. That Decree no. 34 be immediately abrogated followed by a return to the pre-January coup status quo of the Regions.
2. That those who took part in the January 1966 coup be tried and severely punished.
3. That no investigations be conducted into the May, 1966 riots.

This meeting and the demands of the Emirs and Chiefs were very significant. The North had discovered that Ironsi's "military" regime could be pushed around without danger. Ironsi was considering their demands without realising that he had created an impossible situation for himself.

Northern military personnel all over the country were now very active. Governor Katsina had gradually gained complete control of the First Brigade in Northern Nigeria, while Brigade Commander Bassey, knowing what had happened and was likely to happen, was most reluctant to get involved.

An incident that took place about the 15th of June, 1966 left no doubt in any ones mind about Colonel Bassey's attitude to chaos and disorder in the country. On that day, at midday, sounds similar to rifle shots and machine gun bursts were heard at his Headquarters. Everyone thought the next coup had begun. Colonel Bassey without as much as saying "good-bye" to his staff, ran out of his office and downstairs. As he scampered into his car he was heard saying "they should have told me; they promised to give me sufficient warning." He never quite said who were "they," but he had said enough to alert everyone to the fact that certain people were going to do something dangerous. Later, the Brigade Major dispatched some armed soldiers in the direction of the "shooting" to find out exactly what was happening. They brought back a report that a goods train was off-loading planks in a nearby railway station.

Soon after this, Bassey was transferred to Lagos on "medical grounds." To be fair to Bassey, he was not the only one who fled the Brigade Headquarters for as soon as he disappeared from his Head quarters, most of his staff also fled — the Northern elements were running away together in one direction and the Southerners in another. As they fled the common question on everybody's lips was "Who is doing it this time?" This story, when it got to Lagos served more as a piece of entertainment than serious intelligence information of security value.

Northern army officers were now alleged to be holding frequent secret meetings in and around Kaduna as well as Zaria and Kano. All reports on such meetings were dismissed by the Governor as rumours no matter how well substantiated they were. Ironsi invariably agreed with him. By chance, I discovered also that many officers of Northern origin were sending their families away to Britain at that time. I received a report that Captain Abdul Wya, an artillery officer under my command, was applying for a loan of money direct from First Brigade Headquarters to enable him to send his family away to Britain. The procedure was irregular and the request itself most unusual. I spoke to Wya on the matter, and after admonishing him for dealing directly with the Brigate Headquarters, advised him to drop the idea which amounted to a luxury he could ill-afford, particularly as his wife had only been in Nigeria for nine months. He explained that his young Irish wife was very lonely following the departure to Britain of certain army officers' wives who were her close friends and associates. He cited Major George Otigba's wife as an example. His story was childish for an officer whose rank was really a Second Lieutenant, but who had been recommended for a specially accelerated promotion by me, to enable him to maintain his foreign wife.

Wya was desperate to see his wife go away from the country and was not prepared to listen to any advice to the contrary. I was due to attend a one-year artillery course in Britain in September, 1966 and I immediately offered it to Wya so that he could go with his wife and live there at Nigerian Government expense. I informed Lagos and necessary changes were made. Two days later Wya came back to say his wife was so miserable and lonely she could not wait till

45

September. She had to leave at once. I arranged for her to leave at once and her husband to join her later. I did not realise that I was an accessory to an impending coup. I was only concerned for his psychological well-being.

THE FINAL PLOT

On the 18th of June, 1966, Mr. Anueyiagu, a member of the Kaduna "Peace Committee" requested an interview with me in my house. He sounded excited and warned me against refusing to see him. I granted him the interview and he came to see me almost at once. He informed me that a certain friend of his, Alhaji Suya (the correct name is withheld), a cousin of the late Sardauna had an urgent and very important message to pass on to me. He however pointed out that Suya would like to meet me secretly that day at 1800 hours at the Railway Club, Kaduna. This, he explained, was to avoid his being seen in my house by the military guards who were mostly Northern Nigerians. I definitely ruled out the question of meeting him outside my house for security reasons. Rather I suggested he could come much later, say at 2100 hours when it would be dark. I promised to wait for him outside the house to take him in, thus preventing the guards from stopping and questioning him, and thereby establishing his identity.

Even before he arrived at my house, I took security precautions, for it was difficult for me to convince myself that a cousin of the Sardauna, whose death had already cost the Ibos so many lives, could pay me a genuinely friendly visit. I invited the Commanding Officer of the Third Battalion, Colonel Okoro, and Colonel Anwunah to my house at 2030 hours. Colonel Anwunah was still in Kaduna on the first leg of his fact-finding tour of the North in connection with the May riots. I had enough time to brief the two officers before Suya and Anueyiagu arrived. A light-machine gun was well concealed in my sitting room ready for use if the need arose.

Alhaji Suya, using his notes, narrated a long and depressing story of a plan by the Northern military government and other leaders of the North to launch an attack on the people of Southern Nigeria with a view to achieving independence for the North separate from Nigeria. He explained that many plans had already been worked out, but the main drawback was still the apparent reluctance or even unwillingness of their military counterparts. He expressed confidence that the Army would eventually take part but added that if they failed to do so, there was a special plan that would exclude the Army, initially. By this plan, Northern Nigeria civilians would be secretly trained as soldiers and given Nigeria Army uniforms which were made in the North. These men, on the completion of their training, would then be used to attack various Army barracks and kill a few Northern soldiers to give them the impression that the Ibos were again on the offensive. It was hoped this would sufficiently provoke the Northern soldiers into action against the South. Once that happened, they would be directed according to the plan. According to him, rumours were already being circulated among the Northern population of an impending Southern coup to give credence to this plan if it had to be used.

He revealed that already about 500 civilians were receiving training in the area of Lokoja, and military uniforms for them were being made in Kano and Zaria. On the day of the operation, Suya added, Governor Katsina would leave Kaduna on the pretext of touring parts of Northern Nigeria. This was to ensure that Ironsi did not get in touch with him to issue embarrassing instructions about intervention of the Army. He gave dates and places of the last three meetings and pointed out that Ali Akilu had a car accident near Zaria. A quick check later confirmed that Akilu indeed had this accident near Zaria.

Okoro asked Suya why he had decided to reveal such vital secrets to his "enemies." Suya explained that at the early stages, he fully supported the idea of eliminating a carefully selected group of Southerners followed by a possible succession only if an effective retaliation was imminent. He said he preferred that the operation should aim at restoring the power at the centre to Northern Nigeria

47

and no more. However, he went on, he changed his mind during the last meeting when it was decided to kill all Southerners in the North particularly the Ibos irrespective of age, sex or social status. He felt the new development was unnecessary as enough people had already been killed in May. He explained that the aim of his mission to me was to help us save as many people as possible by giving them timely warning. He warned that during the operation the intention was to blow up both Jebba and Makurdi bridges — the only links between Northern and Southern Nigeria. He said he was probably doing his last duty to the Ibos with whom he had had a long social and business association — a people who had contributed so much to his success as a businessman and the overall development of Northern Nigeria. He regretted he did not yet know the date of the operation but promised to let us know as soon as it was fixed.

As soon as Alhaji Suya left, we had a full discussion on the situation and arrived at a decision that I should fly down to Lagos the following morning and give General Ironsi the information. Colonel Mike Okwechime telephoned my house from Enugu shortly after. I gave him the summary of the information we had just received and asked him to make a booking for me to see Ironsi because the Kaduna-Lagos line was out of order. He later telephoned me back to confirm the booking. First Brigade Headquarters, which bought my air ticket did not know the true reason for my trip to Lagos, and Army Headquarters Lagos did not even know I was visiting.

Colonel Tony Eze, the Commanding Officer of Lagos Garrison, met me at Ikeja airport in his private car at 1500 hours on the 19th of June and drove me directly to the State House. I entered Ironsi's office after a very rigorous search at the door. Major Mobalaji Johnson, the Governor of Lagos was seated next to Ironsi as was the practice throughout that regime. It was said he always sat with Ironsi to prove to the Nation that Ironsi did not hold any secret meetings with the Ibos. Though disappointed that Johnson was present, I narrated my story to Ironsi very bluntly without mincing words. It was my first opportunity of meeting him since he became the Supreme Commander and I had no doubt in my mind it was most likely to be the last, unless he took some prompt action on this matter. While Ironsi remained speechless for over a minute following my narrative, Johnson fidgeted and dropped his pencil on the floor twice. The office was air-conditioned but young Johnson had begun to sweat. I had an awful feeling I was going to "lose my name" for rumour mongering.

As soon as he recovered. Ironsi took up the telephone and summoned to his office Kam Salem, Yesufu and Gowon, the three people who were said to represent the Northern Revolutionary Council in Lagos. Ironsi asked me to tell my story in their presence, which I did. Naturally the three gentlemen denied the story and advised Ironsi to treat it as a wicked and malicious rumour fabricated to discredit them and tarnish their good names. They expressed disappointment with me for being a party to rumour mongering. Ironsi telephoned Katsina to hear his views on the matter, and Katsina also promptly denied any knowledge of the existence of such a committee. Ironsi reprimanded me for rumour peddling and warned against the grave consequences. He however asked the Inspector General of Police, Kam Salem, and the head of the Special Branch, Yesufu, to investigate the information. With only Gowon, Johnson and I left, Ironsi sent for Njoku the commander of Second Brigade in Lagos and briefed him. He was then ordered to dispatch a Company of soldiers to Lokoja to locate the alleged training camp and destroy it.

Despite all the denials, I was convinced that the story I brought down to Lagos was true. In my view the handling of this matter was very unsatisfactory. Ironsi had lost his last opportunity to survive by asking the very people who were alleged to be plotting to overthrow him to investigate their plot and report to him. He was ordering the destruction of their private army in the presence of their military leader. If the allegation were true, the plotters now had enough warning to change their plan into something else which no Suya would know and tell. I was now more concerned about my personal safety and that of my family who were living in the North than with saving a reluctant Ironsi and his regime. I was now exposed to danger beyond rectification and my survival rested entirely with me and my chances were very slim if I got caught in Northern Nigeria by a counter-revolution such as was described by Suya.

Later I discussed with Colonel Eze the conduct of my interview with Ironsi and he agreed with me that I should get out of the North with my family very quickly. For this reason I decided to move my Artillery Headquarters to Lagos where it really ought to have been. Colonel Eze, the Commanding Officer of Lagos Garrison was already making arrangements to provide official accommodation for my family by the time I left for Kaduna on the 20th of June, 1966.

As soon as I got to Kaduna, I alerted Colonel Okoro and other senior Southern military officers to the dangerous situation and my intention to move down to Lagos. Within 48 hours I had packed up and despatched my baggages to Lagos in advance, even though Gowon, as the Chief of Staff did not approve the move. I had a few personal matters to sort out in Kaduna and I could not leave before the 1st of July, 1966.

On the day of my departure to Lagos, an Ibo artillery soldier visited my house in the morning with the information that the First Field Battery Commander, Wya, was making what appeared to be a secret arrangement to "line" the route to the railway station with artillery soldiers in my honour. I naturally suspected this exercise of "honour" being planned for me particularly as I was not told about it officially. As far as I was concerned, it could be one of those innocent military exercises that eventually end up as a coup. To avoid tempting anybody into such a coup, I decided to leave for the railway station two hours before the scheduled time, before the soldiers could take their positions along the route. I felt much safer among the crowd in the station. The artillery officers, realising later that I was already at the railway station, came down there to see me off but without their soldiers. Wya regretted that I did not know about the intention of the artillery to line the route for me but explained that he had wanted to give me a big "surprise." I apologized for the disappointment he and his men must have felt. We managed to have some beer at my expense before the train's departure for Lagos.

Tension was equally high in Lagos particularly within military circles. But one felt better and safer living with what appeared to be a friendly population. Gowon moved around Lagos with heavily armed escorts, the only officer who was given that privilege by Ironsi. With the exception of Gowon, or someone carrying a written authority from him, no military officer could enter the Federal Guards barracks which had been placed out of bounds to all Southern army officers by Northern officers and men serving with the unit. Major Linus Ohanehi, an Ibo officer, who had visited the barracks for routine liaison duties, had been immediately surrounded, stripped naked, and severely beaten with sticks, leather whips, and rifle butts until the soldiers thought he was dead. They had taken his "corpse" to Yaba Military Hospital, for burial. There the doctor discovered he was not dead and fought desperately but in great secrecy to save his life. As soon as he revived sufficiently to undertake the journey, he was smuggled away to Eastern Nigeria. When it was known in Army Headquarters that the Major was alive and had escaped to the East, he was dismissed from the Army for "cowardice." Throughout the Ohanehi incident, neither Ironsi nor Army Headquarters could or did interfere to save his life. This officer later commanded Biafra's 15 Division during the civil war that followed.

Northern army officers were very bitter against Ironsi and expressed this feeling freely inside Army Headquarters. Major Murtala Muhammed was particularly bitter, and on the few occasions when he visited me in my office, he made it clear that Northern Nigeria would deal with Ironsi and his regime ruthlessly. He went as far as to call Ironsi a "fool" for ever conceiving the ideas contained in Decree no. 34. He said the people of the North were prepared to fight with their bows and poisoned arrows on their horsebacks against Ironsi's army if he tried to implement his Decree. According to him neither Katsina nor any other Northern senior officials would be allowed to leave the North to other Regions in the name of unity of one Nigeria. In short, discipline in the Army, with regard to Northerners was virtually non-existent. General Ironsi's reaction to this state of affairs was to conduct a mass promotion exercise in which people he wanted to appease were promoted arbitrarily. Even then, the Northern officers promoted were far from satisfied with the situation.

After four days in Lagos, I managed to break through the formidable barrier of guards in front of Gowon's office and paid him an informal visit. Gowon laboured hard to crack some of the old jokes we used to share, but it was clear he was no longer the same "Jack" I had known and lived with since 1954 when we joined the Army together as officer cadets. He was pensive and avoided looking at me in the face all the time I was with him. It took us a lot of beating about the bush before we could start off a reasonably sensible conversation. When Gowon eventually spoke, he expressed his regrets for ever having joined the Army at all, in view of what was happening and likely to happen in the near future. He said he would have liked to leave the Army and settle for a quieter job. He thanked me for the role I had played in ensuring that the January coup did not get out of hand and expressed a desire to see me back in Northern Nigeria very soon. In this connection, he offered me the post of acting Brigade Commander in Kaduna, for, according to him, I was virtually the only senior officer of Southern origin who enjoyed the confidence of the people of the North. I thanked him for his nice sentiments and agreed that the best thing for us to do was probably to leave the Army. I however rejected the offer to go back to the North, because I knew for certain that it was unsafe for me. Later Colonel Philip Efiong was appointed the acting Brigade Commander in Kaduna.

My personal association with Gowon is a rather long one. I joined the Army with him in May, 1954. At the end of our six months initial training at the Regular Officers Special Training School (ROSTS) Accra, Ghana, we left together for Britain in January, 1955. We completed the courses at Officer Cadet School Eaten Hall, Chester, and Royal Military Academy Sandhurst together and were commissioned in December, 1956. While in Sandhurst, we even went on a skiing holiday to Austria together in the summer of 1955. During our training in Sandhurst, an extremely formidable drill Sergeant-Major "sought" and obtained Gowon's permission to call him "Jack" for ease of pronounciation. The following encounter

A physical training session in R.M.A. Sandhurst. The author is about to grab the rope while Gowon and Anwunah advance on his left and right respectively.

between the Sergeant-Major and Gowon on the drill square brought about the change of name.

Sergeant Major (CSM): "That West African gentleman, you, yes, the small one, what is your name, Sir."

Gowon: "Yakubu Gowon, Sir."

CSM: "Pacing stick! What language is that, Sir?"

Gowon: "Nigerian, Sir."

CSM: "You expect me to remember that name, Sir, do you, Sir."

Gowon: "Yes, Sir."

CSM: "You are idle, Sir. My God, you are."

Gowon: "Yes, Sir."

CSM: "Let me hear the name again, Sir, slowly."

Gowon: "Yakubu Gowon, Sir."

CSM: "That first one sounds like "Jack." Do you mind if I call you that, Sir?"

Gowon: "No, Sir."

CSM: "You better not, Sir. Christ, you better not. And if you want to be a "Jack" you must work hard. Do you understand, Sir?"

Gowon: "Yes, Sir."

From then on, Gowon became known as "Jack" throughout the Academy. He brought the name back to Nigeria and has kept it since then.

Gowon, for unknown reasons has always been very popular with the British authorities both during his training in Britain and throughout his military service in Nigeria. For this reason, his progress in the Army was so remarkable and extraordinary that even his fellow Northern officers were beginning to grumble. For instance, when he was chosen to attend the Camberley Staff College, England in January, 1962, Major Pam, a Jos officer senior to him called him a "sneaky sucker." While together in the Nigerian Army the two of us maintained as close an association and friendship as Nigerian politics would allow. As an individual, he was very helpful to his Southern colleagues by occasionally putting in a good word for them to the authorities. The last time he paid me a visit at home we discussed the problems and complications confronting him in his bid to marry an Ibo girl.

By the middle of July it was clear that the D-day was fast approaching. Northern officers in Western Nigeria and Lagos held conferences every Sunday afternoon in Colonel Muhammed's Ikoyi residence. In addition, there was a daily gathering of those residing in Lagos in Federal Guards barracks which, as I said, was out of bounds to Southerners. Young Muhammed was now very vocal and boastful.

Gowon then convened a commissioning board to select officer cadets. The board was to meet in Kaduna on the 30th of July and its members included most of the Southern Nigerian senior officers and a few Northern officers. All Southern Nigerian Lt. Colonels were included on the board except me. However, many of these officers were aware of the danger involved and tried to wriggle out of it without much success. The reason I was initially left out of the Board was that Gowon wanted me to attend a military course in England towards the end of July. He had telephoned me on the 20th of July to tell me he had secured a place for me at the Joint Services Staff College, England. He added that there had been a great deal of competition for the only one vacancy allocated to Nigeria, and he had used his good offices to ensure that I was nominated for it. He advised that I leave immediately to get used to the weather again, before the course started middle of August, 1966. He also expressed a fear that any unnecessary delay on my part could result in Ironsi changing my nomination as a result of overwhelming pressure from other senior interested officers.

For a start, I did not want to attend the course because of the explosive situation in the country and the fear that my family was unsafe in Lagos in my absence. Gowon worked very hard to convince me to attend the course, so I accepted to attend but insisted on leaving during the first week of August. Gowon even asked me to go with my family.

However, on the 25th of July, Gowon again telephoned me to say he would like me to attend the Selection Board in Kaduna. According to him, Colonel Okoro, who was to chairman the Board had suddenly left for India on a course, and he wanted me to replace him, as the chairman. He pleaded with me to regard this assignment as a personal favour and the last one he would ask of me before my departure to Britain. He suggested that I should get to Kaduna on the 29th, 24 hours before the first meeting of the Board so as to have sufficient time to sort out some minor details. I reluctantly accepted this job, knowing fully well that the Northern Region was not a place a Southern officer, particularly me, should visit at the time.

Later on that afternoon, Colonel Adebayo suddenly came into my office. It was indeed a big surpirse for me and many others who saw him for he was supposed to be in England attending the Imperial Staff College. He was, as usual, in high spirits and laughed heartily. He explained that he was on his way to Australia with a section of the College, but thought he should drop in and see Ironsi to find out what the Nigerian policy towards Australia was. I understand the Colonel went round and saw all other senior officers with the same story. On my part I could not quite understand why a military officer should abandon his course of study to chase around for his country's policy towards various other countries. As mentioned briefly before, three days after the January coup, Adebayo had abandoned his course in Britain and returned to Nigeria allegedly to demand that he be appointed the Governor of Western Nigeria. General Ironsi, who had already appointed Colonel Francis Fajuyi, rejected his demand and ordered him back to England. He left disgruntled and bitter. He was now back. There was no coup, nor a vacant post for a Governor, but with the situation as it was, the prospects for a vacancy were good.

Even at that late and very dark hour, while the North was putting finishing touches to their plan, Ironsi was still confident he would reverse the ugly situation. He hoped to do this by touring all Regions of Nigeria to explain to their leaders the merits and good intentions of Decree no. 34 and to reassure them generally. All Southern leaders — army and police officers, politicians, intellectuals and others — who could reach Ironsi advised him against undertaking such a tour but he was determined to go ahead with it.

Ironsi first visited the North, and there it was an arduous effort to restrain young Northern Nigerian officers from seizing advantage of his visit to commence their coup. What actually happened was that the more mature Northerners and their advisers did not want Ironsi killed in the North. Neither did they want to risk a confrontation with him in Lagos where all major units were being commanded by Ibos, with whose help he could easily foil the coup before it gained momentum. Midwestern Nigeria was most unsuitable for such an operation because no troops were stationed there and a sudden movement of troops towards that Region would have alerted him. It was clear that Western Nigeria was going to be the battleground for it satisfied all the necessary requirements. The only battalion in Western Nigeria was under the command of a Northerner, Colonel Joe Akahan, and the men on the exercise would be dealing with an indifferent population.

That Ironsi himself realised the dangers he faced was doubtful, but he was advised by all who knew the true situation to halt his tour and remain in Lagos for awhile. However, he was determined to continue his tour. When he came back from Northern Nigeria, he left for Midwestern Nigeria on the 27th of July and, as expected, never returned.

I was playing lawn tennis with Colonels Eze and Nwajei and other officers at Yaba Military Hospital Court in the evening of 28th July, 1966. At about 1800 hours, a military Landrover pulled up near the court and a Sergeant Major who came out of the vehicle, began to discharge some sten machine guns. Nobody appeared to be surprised or to have taken any notice of this unusual practice. I called Eze's attention to the Landrover which bore his unit sign, but he said he knew about it. Shortly afterwards, the game was temporarily suspended, and the officers trooped along to the Landrover and began to sign for weapons. It was then that Eze explained to me that the guns were necessary because he had very reliable information that the Northern Nigerian coup was due to start at any moment. I could hardly believe my ears. It was absolutely absurd if not silly for us to be playing tennis in the full knowledge that a coup aimed against us was due to start at any moment.

I signed for a machine gun and left for my house after advising against the continuation of the game. It was getting late, and the setting sun also symbolised a possible end of Ironsi's regime. It was very painful to think that we had all watched the conception of this monster, and its development to the final stage, without causing an effective abortion. The normal tendency to underrate the Northerners was evident. The hard fact always overlooked is that in Nigeria, the North always works with a powerful "friend," and therefore can never walk alone.

Assuming Eze's story was correct, the situation was almost too late to be redeemed; yet I was only too anxious to try if only I could find enough senior Southern Nigeria officers sufficiently interested. I was also very anxious to get an official confirmation of these facts to enable me to decide whether I should go to Kaduna the following morning or not. For this reason, still dressed in my tennis clothes, with my gun in the car, I drove to Colonel Anwunah's house. Colonel Anwunah was General Staff Officer at Army Headquarters at the time, and I thought he ought to be able to give me the official version of the situation report. On my way, I saw Colonel Nwajei near the "An" barracks gates, dressed and on his way into town. I told him my intention and advised him to come with me so that between us, we could work out a quick counter-attack plan. He remarked, rather sarcastically that rumours of coups were a part of the life in Lagos for the past four months. He added that he was sure I would get used to the rumours and learn to ignore them when I had stayed long enough in Lagos. On that note, he gave me a short nod and a wave and drove off. I should have turned back if I were not within 400 yards of Anwunah's house already. My wife who was in the car thought we might as well get there and if nothing else, say hello to him.

Lt. Colonel Anwunah, stripped to the waist, was sitting in his living room, starring into the ceiling and completely ignoring his numerous guests made up of both civil and military persons who were in the room with him. The only army officer I can still remember who was present was Captain Ben Ejiofor of Army Base

Workshops, Lagos. Before I had a chance to speak to Anwunah he went upstairs to receive a telephone call.

When he came downstairs again, he was very agitated and nervous. He walked straight out of his house and asked me to follow him. He said he had just received a call from his very reliable contact man serving with the Federal Guards confirming that the coup was due to start during the night. According to this contact man, Northern troops in Lagos were already moving into position. I then suggested that we go down to Army Headquarters and open an emergency operations room to instruct and control units all over the country. Anwunah considered this premature. He explained that earlier on that evening of 28th July, 1966, Muhammed had visited his house and the two of them had had an open and violent confrontation. The quarrel started when Anwunah accused him of planning a coup and reminding him that everybody was waiting for him, well prepared. Anwunah was of the view that the confrontation would force Muhammed to change or abandon his plans. For this reason, according to Anwunah, we should not rush into any counter measures. I then suggested that we assemble all senior army officers in Anwunah's house for the night and from there, we could issue co-ordinated instructions to various units as well as defend ourselves more effectively. Anwunah preferred that I went back to my house and waited for further and more definite developments. He advised that I should travel to Kaduna as scheduled the following morning, unless I heard anything to the contrary from him over the telephone during the night. I got back to my house at about 10 p.m. and very soon Captain Ejiofor, who is my cousin came in to find out what was happening. When I briefed him, he advised that I should move away with my family from the house for the night. He said he was going to park his car in a garage and sleep in it. I slept in my house with my mind absolutely made up to do nothing more about the coup if I was not to make myself a laughing stock.

Chapter 4

THE COUNTER-REVOLUTION

29 July, 1966

When I woke up at 0530 hours on the morning of 29th July, 1966 it was apparently very peaceful, regardless of a night of nightmares. There had been no telephone call from Anwunah, or anybody else during the night, and with difficulty I resisted the urge to telephone and find out the situation. Outside the house the staff car which was to take me to the airport was already there. I reminded my wife about the need to be cautious in the next few days and gave her sufficient funds to keep as her emergency reserve, should anything happen in my absence. I left the house for the airport at about 0615 hours.

Life was perfectly normal on the road to the Ikeja airport. The airport itself was calm and peaceful and my plane took off at 0705 hours, five minutes later than the scheduled time. When the plane touched down at Kaduna airport, life was also perfectly normal with a crowd of people waiting to meet various passengers. An old friend from the Governor's office was the first person to speak to me. Immediately I entered the lounge, he approached me with his mouth wide open in what appeared to be amazement. He expressed surprise that I was able to come up from Lagos with the plane. I asked for clarification and he went on to say that the Army had overthrown the Federal Government and seized power in Lagos and Western Nigeria. He added that all airports in those Regions were in the hands of the rebels. He said his information was that both Ironsi and Fajuyi had been kidnapped from the Government House at Ibadan and were still missing. He added that according to rumours currently circulating, similar mutiny was also taking place in Eastern Nigeria, even though no confirmed reports had been received yet. He said he was at the airport to despatch a special plane to collect "my friend" Governor Katsina from Kano, as he was "touring parts of the North." He was anxious that Katsina should return immediately and re-establish contact with Ironsi. I tried to explain, without making an impression, that all was well in Lagos. The confidence, excitement and happiness on his face showed clearly that he knew what he was talking about. Suya had warned that Katsina would be on "tour" before the D-day and now Katsina was indeed on "tour." This was the first indication I had of the commencement of the long expected coup. The long suspense had been nerve-shattering and, in a way, I felt slightly relieved at the thought that it had started at last.

Captain Dilibe, an Ibo Staff Officer at the First Brigade Headquarters who had come to meet me at the airport was miserably huddled in one corner of the airport lounge, lost in thought. He did not even appear to realise that the plane he was waiting for had landed for more than fifteen minutes. I woke him up with a mild reproach and got him to clear my baggage. Having cleared the baggage and apologized for his absent-mindedness, he advised that we get out of the airport as quickly as possible, for it could soon be dangerous. While we drove into town, I narrated to him what I had heard at the airport and he confirmed the whole story to be true, and gave further details. Dilibe said the Brigade Headquarters had received information that Northern soldiers at Ikeja barracks had seized Lagos after inflicting heavy casualties on their Southern counterparts, particularly the Ibos. He went on to say that Ikeja airport was taken over by the soldiers at 0715 hours (ten minutes after my departure) and he never really expected me to arrive in Kaduna. In Western Nigeria, he said, these Northern soldiers had seized Abeokuta barracks and killed the Garrison Commander, Lt. Colonel Gabriel Okunweze; the Commanding Officer of the Second Reconnaissance Squadron, Major Obienu, and several other junior officers, and men.

He revealed that Ironsi had telephoned the Brigade

Headquarters from Ibadan at 0730 hours to say that the Government House where he was staying was surrounded by soldiers. Ironsi also informed the Brigade that he had already made several attempts to get a helicopter sent to him from Lagos but had failed.

Dilibe went on to explain that the previous night an Ibo policeman had made a secret report to the Brigade Headquarters that soldiers were loitering around various key and vulnerable installations in Kaduna. These soldiers and their officers were rounded up immediately. The officers claimed to be on a night map reading exercise from the Third Battalion. Neither the commanding officer nor the adjutant of the Battalion knew about this exercise, so all those arrested were placed under close arrest. It was Dilibe's view that this was probably the reason why the coup had not started in Kaduna. He revealed that the coup started in Abeokuta at 2359 hours on the 28th July, 1966, at Ikeja at 0600 hours and Ibadan at 0630 hours July 29th. In other words, the coup was already going on in Lagos when I left the city.

Information I gathered later showed that Anwunah was informed about the coup at midnight, immediately it started at Abeokuta. He was probably too upset to remember to telephone me. Thus, I found myself trapped in the middle of Northern Nigeria which I had worked so hard to leave four weeks before. If I had taken Gowon's advice and left immediately for the U.K., I would not have found myself in my present predicament. Perhaps Gowon had tried to save an old friend.

The acting Brigade Commander, Colonel Efiong, was away attending a meeting with local leaders in an attempt to forestall a possible eruption in the North. Most of his senior staff officers were Southerners who appeared to be very happy with themselves for having prevented the coup in the North through their timely arrest of potential participants the previous night. At the time I got into the Headquarters, Major Ogbemudia, the Brigade Major, was questioning a young Hausa Second Lieutenant from the Training College. This officer was seen going from house to house the previous night, passing messages to various Northern Nigeria officers. The officer denied the charge and, with tears in his eyes.

charged Ogbemudia with maltreating him because he was a Northerner. Ogbemudia apologized and sent him away. Later this young officer led the Training College section of the coup, and with a group of men he very nearly succeeded in killing Major Ogbemudia who had a miraculous escape.

Telephone lines to Lagos and the South were now cut, and I was only able to get Army Headquarters on the Brigade wireless set. I spoke to Captain Martin Adamu, the Intelligence Officer at Army Headquarters, who appeared to be the only officer at the Headquarters. In briefing me, he assured me that nothing serious was happening in Lagos. He explained that a minor incident had taken place earlier when some drunken soldiers tried to molest civilians, thereby causing general panic. Those soldiers, he said, were quickly arrested and taken to the barracks. He denied any knowledge of a military mutiny in Abeokuta and Ibadan. He was sure such a serious incident would not have taken place without the knowledge of the Army Headquarters. He said Gowon wanted those who were already in Kaduna for the Board meeting to stay for 24 hours during which period a firm decision would be taken on whether or not the Board would still hold.

As Efiong was still absent from his Headquarters, I ordered Ogbemudia to instruct all units under command to disarm all ranks and lock up their weapons in unit armouries. These armouries, I suggested, should be guarded by an equal number of unarmed soldiers from the North and the South. As a follow-up to the above instructions I telephoned all unit commanders of Southern origin in Kaduna, to drive home the need for them to carry out these instructions to the letter and promptly too. They all agreed with me except Colonel Okoro, the Commanding officer of the Third Battalion, who hated the idea of disarming his men. He told me he had just held a muster parade in his battalion to brief the men on the situation, and on that parade, all ranks had promised to be absolutely loyal to him and Ironsi's government. Okoro added that his Regimental Sergeant Major, Mallam Ahmadu Bello (from Sokoto) had advised him against disarming the troops for security reasons and he had accepted this advice. He revealed that Bello had worked out a good alternative plan which was to disarm the entire battalion less a Platoon to be selected by Bello himself. When Efiong came back later, I briefed him on what I had done in his absence and he approved. Okoro was so sure of his battalion that later he telephoned to invite me for lunch in the battalion. I turned the invitation down without giving it a thought.

Throughout the morning, officers of Northern Nigeria origin were coming in and out of the Brigade Headquarters for no definite reason. Their countenance invariably betrayed the thoughts in their minds — they were definitely set for a showdown. When Major Kyari of the artillery came to the Headquarters at 1100 hours, he was deliberately calm and expressed no surprise at seeing me in Kaduna. He thanked me for successfully rectifying an error on his military seniority which had been long outstanding in the Army Headquarters. He thereafter broke a kola-nut and offered it to all officers around who were almost all Southerners. As he gave each officer he wished him "good luck."

In the course of a conversation which followed, the Brigade Deputy Assistant Adjutant and Quarter-Master General, Major Emelifonwu, condemned the coup going on in the South, and asked Kyari to do all he could to assist in preventing a similar occurrence in the North. Kyari disagreed with Emelifonwu in his condemnation of the coup in the South. As he stormed out of the office, he promised to pay me a courtesy visit at Hamdala Hotel late in the evening. As his Regimental Commander, it appeared perfectly normal for Kyari to pay me a courtesy visit. But with the prevailing situation, I was suspicious of everyone.

I telephoned Colonel Ogbugo Kalu, Commandant of NMTC and asked him to come to the Brigade Headquarters and discuss with me. When he arrived he was more confident and relaxed having disarmed his unit in accordance with Brigade instructions. I alerted him to the fact that the net was closing in on us and time was fast running out. Following a lengthy discussion, the two of us decided to recommend to Efiong that a conference of senior officers of Southern Nigeria origin be called to work out an immediate counter measure. The meeting was held at about 1330 hours at Colonel

Efiong's house and was attended by Kalu, Emelifonwu, Ogbemudia, Ogunro and myself. Okoro again had a "good" reason for being absent, and being the commander of the only infantry battalion in Kaduna, the meeting was thus rendered ineffective and fruitless by his absence. It was however decided that all officers should stay with their troops throughout the night and do their best to prevent any acts of violence within their respective units. At the end of the conference I told Kalu that I wished to stay in his house for the night and he gladly agreed. While Kalu left for the Officers Mess where he intended to make a brief stop, I went across to the Brigade armoury to sign for a revolver.

On my way to Kalu's house, I stopped to collect him at the Mess and there was a big party going on there. Inside the Mess there were many Northern officers drinking with notably Kalu and Captain Idika as the only Ibo officers present. There might have been a few others I did not see. I was told a "send off" party was being held by officers of the Training College in honour of Idika and others who had just completed a course of instruction at the School and were due to leave for Lagos the following day. I was convinced that we, as Southerners were doomed beyond redemption if we could still accept invitations to parties on the very day we had lost the Head of State and of the Army as well as several other officers in the South. In the first instance, why should a section of the Army be engaged in a coup to topple the government while another section of the same Army finds it appropriate to hold drinking parties? I politely turned down all offers of drinks and went out of the Mess immediately, requesting Idika and Kalu to come out with me. While outside, I warned them about the danger of their continued stay in the Mess. I expressed an opinion that the party was just the beginning of a coup that could start at any moment. The longer any Southerner stayed around the Mess, the more likely he was to get into trouble. Idika was quick in reciting the latest situation to me giving details of those who had already been killed. He sympathised with all senior officers from the South, who he thought were the obvious targets. He offered to render maximum assistance to any of us who might need his help. Kalu agreed to leave at once with me but Idika thought he ought to have "one for the road." Unfortunately what the young man had was "one for the grave," for he was killed when the coup eventually started. It was too late for him to learn that the coup plotters had no intention of discriminating between junior and senior officers in the selection of their victims.

When I got to Colonel Kalu's house with him by 1800 hours, I was still wearing the same lounge suit I had on when I arrived in Kaduna in the morning. My official military driver, a Northerner, had been with me since morning and did not even ask for a break for a meal. I was now suspecting everything and everybody including this driver who I thought might have been planted to report on my final destination for the day. Before the driver left, I gave him instructions to report back at the house at 0800 hours the following morning to take me to the office. I did this to reassure him I was spending the night at Kalu's house. As soon as he left, however, I told Kalu that I no longer thought it safe to sleep in his house and expressed my desire to go into the town and stay with a civilian friend. He gave me all assurances of safety in his house and revealed that he had a carefully selected guard of 15 Ibo soldiers to guard the house for the night. My mind was made up, for nothing could prevent Northern soldiers from attacking the house with a Company of 150 soldiers. To maintain absolute secrecy on my movements from his house I refused to be driven to town in his private car which was pretty well known. I prefered to walk using side streets and lanes.

I had bidden Kalu farewell and wished him luck when Major Simeon Uwakwe drove in accompanied by his wife he had married only four months before. This officer had gone to the Eastern Region on a compassionate leave to bury his father and was just reporting back to his commanding officer. He had left Enugu very early in the morning and had driven all day. He was therefore completely ignorant of what was happening in the country. Kalu gave him a quick briefing and asked him to report to the unit as soon as he had dropped off his wife at home.

Major Uwakwe left me at the Kaduna Recreation Club where I expected to find the friend I wanted to stay with. Having wished each other good luck the officer left for his unit. He was later shot at the back of the neck and the bullet made a clear exit through his mouth removing all his teeth. His assailants abandoned him as dead but when he was picked up by relatives he was found to be alive. An emergency crash treatment restored him sufficently to undertake a secret air journey to Enugu where he fully recovered eventually, and was able to play a commendable role in the civil war that followed.

From outside the club house, I tried in vain to attract Mr. Raphael Nweke's attention through the window without being seen by others. The billiard room was full and morale of all, irrespective of tribes, appeared high. Almost everybody else had seen me and was urging me to come in for a drink before Nweke looked in my direction. This was exactly the type of reception I anticipated in the club I had been a member of for nine years and only left four weeks before. I knew every member of the club very well and it was with a lot of difficulty that I convinced them that I could not stay immediately for drinks. I promised to be back at night.

My main difficulty was to convince Mr. Nweke to come outside and have a chat with me. He explained that he had waited for two hours for his turn to play a game of billiards and he had no intention of losing his chance. When eventually he agreed to come out for five minutes I gave him a quick summary of the situation and requested that he take me away to his house without delay. He needed no further convincing for within two minutes we were already racing towards his house in his car. Immediately the car stopped in front of his house, I dashed through the front door straight into the bedroom, making sure nobody saw me go into the house. During the night, a few visitors came to see Mr. Nweke but none of them knew of my presence in the house. At about 2200 hours, Nweke and I decided to inform another good friend of mine, Mr. Christopher Ozieh, of my presence. He lived less than a hundred metres away and was soon in the house to say hello and encourage me.

My main preoccupation was to work out a quick plan for getting out of the North immediately. I held a meeting with my friends Nweke and Ozieh on the situation at 0900 hours the next day and there Ozieh suggested that I lie low for a couple of days to allow the situation to improve a bit. I rejected this and explained to them that the situation was likely to worsen as time went on. For with time, the rebels would become better organised. Ozieh then offered to take me in his car to his in-laws in Kafanchan from where I could make my way to Eastern Nigeria. This suited me perfectly. When Nweke and Ozieh went back to their various departments, they had no difficulty at all in getting the weekend off from their jubilating Northern Nigerian bosses.

MY NARROW ESCAPE

When Nweke and Ozieh were ready for the journey, I almost made a fatal mistake by entering the car and consenting to an immediate departure. It dawned on me all of a sudden that the route ought to be checked first for road blocks before the journey even though my civilian friends considered this unnecessary and a waste of time. I insisted that they should first go along the route for a minimum of 20 miles and report back on locations and strengths of all military road blocks. They did the reconnaissance in Ozieh's Volkswagen car and reported two road blocks between milestone 4 and 6 from Kaduna. The last road block, they said, was manned by a strong contingent of artillery men, most of whom were likely to know me. These gentlemen now realised the gravity of the situation and the amount of danger facing me.

I was confident I should be able to leave Kaduna making maximum use of my thorough knowledge of the town and the surrounding villages. Before long I presented a simple plan to them which was carried out with success. The plan was to take me in Mr. Nweke's Peugeot 403 to Kaduna South. Before the first road block we would turn left into a lane which leads for two miles into a new housing estate mostly occupied by expatriates. At the end of this lane the major road block could be seen 400 yards to the right. I was to be dropped off there, from where I was to make my way on foot through the villages till I finally came out at milestone 12 along the road to Kafanchan. My instruction was that they should be at the rendezvous by 1500 hours to give me enough time to get there. I stressed the need to use the Peugeot car to avoid suspicion that would arise if the Volkswagen was used again, particularly as it had been thoroughly searched during the reconnaissance.

By 1300 hours I was ready to move, having changed into a big Hausa gown and cap donated by Mr. Ozieh. All I now had on me was my revolver and £50 cash which Gowon had given to me for the payment of my hotel bills at Hamdala. By 1320 hours I was already making my way through peaceful villages which were still completely unaware of what was happening in town. I spoke sufficient Hausa language to go through those villages without arousing curiosity or suspicion and this proved to be a very useful asset.

Before 1500 hours I was inside the bush opposite the rendezvous. A Peugeot car was packed there facing Kaduna rather than Kafanchan. I crawled close to the car which was similar to Nweke's, but I was not in a position to see the registration number. The most intriguing thing was the fact that there was no sign of life anywhere near the car. I thought of all sorts of possibilities. Could it be that my friends had been discovered, and, after a confession, the car had been brought up to drive me triumphantly back to Kaduna? After lying down there and watching the car for fifteen minutes, I decided to make a move towards the car in the hope that I could shoot my way out of trouble if I encountered any. With my revolver at the ready, I came out to the main road and looked around the car. It was indeed the right car, but there was nobody around. Soon, I heard some noise on top of a nearby tree. As I crawled into cover, I heard a burst of laughter. I looked up towards the tree and my two friends were climbing down. They swore their actions were more of a security measure than a joke. They explained that the car had to face Kaduna so as not to give an impression that someone was running away to passers-by who knew the situation. They also claimed that the idea of hiding on top of a tree was to give a false impression that the car had broken down and had been abandoned by the owner.

There was no time for argument and very soon the car was speeding towards Kafanchan at a very fast pace. We prayed that we should not run into another road block on our way. We had only one incident on the way and that was at Kachia 86 miles from Kaduna. There, outside the town a lorry was parked by the side of the road with many civilians and a few soldiers milling around it. The scene was what one would see in a typical road block, and I could have sworn it was one. We stopped the car about 300 yards before the crowd, I got out and slipped into the bush. Nweke and Ozieh drove on to find out what exactly was going on. Before my friends came back to report to me, the crowd had all entered the lorry which was now moving towards me, on its way to Kaduna. Apparently it was a public transport lorry which only made a routine stop to allow the passengers to ease themselves. The soldiers we saw were mainly Ibo soldiers returning to Kaduna from leave, ignorant of the situation. I was not in a position to advise them to turn back, otherwise I should have done so.

The nearer we were to Kafanchan the more relaxed we became, and soon we were sufficiently relaxed to crack jokes. There was a lot of argument between Nweke and Ozieh on the question of who should be given credit for what, in the planning and execution of the escape operation. At a village 20 miles from Kafanchan, Ozieh wanted us to call at the house of a Northern friend of his, called Audu, who had been at school with him. I agreed to this when he insisted. After all, his request could be considered to be a modest one after the personal risks he had taken to bring me out of Kaduna. My view, though, was that we were beginning to dramatize this escape and thus were running a risk of leaving trails behind us. I was introduced as Mr. Mensah Brown from Ghana to Mallam Audu who might not have heard about the coup in Kaduna, and therefore could not have suspected anything. But a Mensah Brown in Fulani robes would cause doubts in anybody's mind.

As I suspected, this unwise visit almost brought total disaster on me, for five days after my departure from my hiding place near Kafanchan, two plain clothes men called on my host and wanted to see Mr. Mensah. It was only Audu who knew our destination and must have alerted the police as soon as he knew I was being looked for and that Ozieh was suspected of having removed me from Kaduna.

Mr. Iloanya, Ozieh's brother-in-law who was to harbour me, lived on a Government plantation which he managed in a small village of Sabon Gida, 25 miles from Kafanchan. His family, however, lived inside Kafanchan itself. The village was easily the better and more secure place for me to go and by 1930 hours we were there. It was a good thing we did that because Iloanya's family at Kafanchan was down at the village for the weekend. Ozieh told our story and Mr. Iloanya gave an assurance of his willingness to ensure that I got through safely to Eastern Nigeria. The following day, Sunday the 31st of July, 1966, my friends Nweke and Ozieh returned to Kaduna. The same day I travelled with Iloanya to Kafanchan in the hope of catching a train for Enugu.

All trains were overcrowded, but Kafanchan was perfectly normal. All around, one could easily identify fleeing officers and men of Southern Nigeria origin, despite their attempts at disguise. Inquiries at the railway station revealed that the River Benue bridge at Makurdi had been sealed off by Northern troops. All trains were thoroughly searched for Eastern Nigeria officers, and those identified were said to be shot on the spot and thrown into the river. Troops stationed at Makurdi at the time were from 5th Battalion Kano, under the command of Captain Daramola, and I had no doubts that Daramola and most of his troops would recognize me even if I wore a mask. Having come so far I did not want to take a single risk and, though disappointed, I decided to go back to my hide-out at Sabon Gida and try again a few days later when things would have improved. Lt. Akpuaka and a few others I met in town that day decided to make the journey to Makurdi and cross the river by canoe. They did this successfully.

Life in Sabon Gida was dull and tense and there was no news coming in on the grave situation. The radio stations carried little or nothing about the situation in Nigeria. It is true that Gowon announced he had taken over power and also said something about the basis for unity in Nigeria not being there. It is also true Ojukwu said something about not recognizing Gowon. But these statements added to the confusion in my mind rather than clarify it. As days passed by, reports on the situation at Makurdi bridge showed gradual deterioration. By now train passengers all got down on the Bridge while searching and interrogation took up to eight hours for a passenger train.

After ten days at Sabon Gida I thought I had had enough and just had to make a move. The situation was worsening gradually to the stage where friendly Southern civilians were also beginning to pack and move away towards Enugu. I was not even sure Mr. Iloanya and his family would not suddenly wish to move, thereby forcing me into an unplanned and ill co-ordinated journey. Moreover, Northern civilian labourers in the plantation were beginning to be curious about my presence, and could have told anybody who wanted to know that a stranger was around.

On the 9th of August, 1966, I suggested and Iloanya completely agreed with me that I ought to get moving. Later that day, we travelled together to Kafanchan to catch a train to another town yet to be decided, but at least nearer to Makurdi. When Mr. Iloanya made contact with the Station Master, Mr. Ojeh, an Ibo man from Midwestern Nigeria, he was pleased to help and revealed that he had successfully passed many officers including Colonel Kalu and Major Okon. He added that a few more military persons of various ranks were in his house waiting to be passed that day or the next. For reasons of security and also for lack of accommodation, Ojeh advised that I find other accommodation in town rather than his house until he was ready to send me off. He pointed out that he was packing up from Kafanchan as soon as he had finished with the batch of military refugees he had because the situation was becoming very dangerous even for civilians.

Iloanya put me into his house in town which was recently abandoned by his family. Besides a bed and mattress, the house was empty. Ojeh later brought word that we would travel the following day and Iloanya decided to go back to Sabon Gida village immediately to be with his family. Before he left he bought for me enough cooked food to last at least 24 hours, and assured me that Mr. Ojeh would pick me up from the house at the right time the following day. His advice was that I must not be seen by any of the neighbours who were now mostly Northerners, the Southern elements having fled. When he left, I locked up all the doors and windows, and there was no question of trying to sleep throughout the night. Only once I slipped out to ease myself, and ran head long into a female neighbour doing the same. I was almost sure she would take me for a thief and raise an alarm. Rather she accepted my greetings kindly and took no more action when she saw me going into the house confidently and locking the door behind me. All the same, I had a window half open for the rest of the night, in case of any emergency requiring a quick get-away.

Mr. Ojeh picked me up from the house at 1030 hours the following morning. He regretted that the special train he had hoped for would not run. He was still sure I would be able to make my destination in safety. His plan was to move all of us to Ayalagu, 20 miles from Makurdi. There he said, another Ibo Station Master with whom he was in touch, would arrange to pass us through the bridge safely. To kill time, we drove round the town in his old Consul car and also visited a few of his Southern friends, most of whom were packing up.

When the train pulled into Kafanchan, it was so full that people sat on top of coaches. There were others strapped unto parts of the train by relatives and friends who wanted them out of Northern Nigeria dead or alive. A good many of these people never made it for some died en route, while others fell off the train. I put in a spirited 30 minutes' effort before I gained a foot-hold on the steps of a coach entrance. Once there, I soon consolidated on two feet and was holding tight to a metal rod, ready for the journey. No civilians had been attacked yet anywhere in the North. Some of those leaving did so because they were warned or threatened by their Northern neighbours. Others were simply afraid or panic-stricken. A sizeable crowd of curious Northern civilians were at the railway station. The majority of them expressed alarm and shock at what they saw, but there were very few who thought it was all a big joke. The journey to Ayalagu was extremely slow and tedious and by the time we got there, four of the children and a woman in my coach were dead. It would have been useful to find out how many people had died in each of the ten coaches at Ayalagu and how many more died by the time the train got to Enugu more than 200 miles south of Ayalagu.

Only a few people got down at Ayalabu when the train made a stop there at midnight and, before long, the majority of those that stopped had left the station for the town. Inside the office, I approached a railway official who appeared to be in charge and expressed my desire to see the Station Master. Without looking up, he asked me to wait outside if I had a message from Mr. Ojeh. I assumed he was the Station Master himself. Outside the office, a few other men in tatters whispered their conversation in Ibo language. I was sure they were soldiers on the run.

The Station Master, who introduced himself as Mr. Akukwe, came out to join me at 0100 hours and soon the other gentlemen in tatters joined the two of us. As I suspected, we were all soldiers with a similar problem. Akukwe was very frightened by our presence and wished we had not involved him by stopping at his station. He loathed the very idea of our continued stay within the railway compound and decided to take us to the nearby house of an Ibo merchant for the rest of the night. We walked the distance of about half a mile under a drizzling rain and experienced considerable difficulty getting the merchant out of the house at that time of the morning. This very prosperous Ibo merchant, after hearing our story, bluntly refused to have anything to do with us because the local chief was his close friend and he was not prepared to strain the relationship for fugitives he did not know.

Back at the railway station Mr. Akukwe asked us to move into the bushes just outside the station until daybreak. At this stage, an Ibo railway worker who had listened to Akukwe offered us his "Doki house" near the platform. By about 0300 hours on the 11th we were settled inside the hut and I got to know my three companions better. One was a Sergeant Major Chief Clerk and the other an Education Instructor Sergeant both from the Third Battalion Kaduna. The third man was a private soldier from the Military Hospital, Kaduna. I did not have to introduce myself to any of them for they all knew me. The Sergeant Major had very badly bruised hands. He narrated how his commanding officer, Lt. Colonel Okoro was shot at midnight on the 29th, in front of the Battalion guardroom. He had been lured out there by his Regimental Sergeant Major who told him there was a very urgent matter requiring his presence. Having shot the commanding officer, an alarm for a battalion muster parade was sounded, with the battalion yet unaware of the death. On the parade ground, Eastern Nigerians were extracted and loaded into waiting trucks. The trucks then drove to mile 18 on the Kaduna-Jos road where the passengers were lined up to face firing squads in their turns. According to the Sergeant Major, after the execution of each group or truck load, the soldiers inspected the corpses using vehicle head lamps. When they were all certified dead, all valuables on the victims particularly watches and rings were removed. The Sergeant Major said he was not hit by a bullet but fell down with the dead and lay perfectly still during the inspection. He was covered in blood of others, and only lost his wristwatch during the inspection. Immediately after the inspection and the lights went out, the Sergeant Major said he crawled away to safety and later made his way to Jos. The Ibos in Jos gave him a change of clothing and money, and arranged for him to continue his journey to Enugu.

The Sergeant Education Instructor confessed he was really absent without leave on the fateful night. He had spent the night at his girl friend's house in town and did not realise there was trouble during the night. On his way back to the barracks early the following morning, he got to know what was happening. He simply turned round and started making his way to Eastern Nigeria.

The private soldier said he was on night duty on 29th July, 1966 in the Kaduna Military Hospital. Just before 0100 hours on 30th July, 1966, a military Landrover stopped in front of the reception to the officers' ward. A few soldiers dismounted and ordered the duty sergeant to arrange to remove a "parcel" in the vehicle which they had brought for the hospital. When a member of the staff went to collect the "parcel" it turned out to be the corpse of Lt. Colonel Okoro. As the hospital staff, who were nearly all Eastern Nigerians stood there speechless, one of the soldiers who brought the corpse remarked in Hausa "Ana yi ku, kwo ba ku gani ba?" — there is a coup going on, or don't you understand? As soon as the Landrover left. the staff took fright and scattered in all directions.

The three soldiers were very worried about our outright rejection by the Ibo merchant and were convinced it was most unsafe for us to stay any longer in the town. By daybreak the following morning they had all decided to leave for Enugu by the next available train and hoped to pass through the bridge unidentified. My assurances to them that it was reasonably safe where we were failed to impress them. All efforts to get them to exercise patience were futile. They left at 0830 hours and by 1800 hours that day Mr. Akukwe informed me that both the Sergeant Major and the Sergeant were identified, shot and dumped into the Benue River. Only the private soldier passed unidentified to the South.

I stayed alone in the "Doki" hut for four days without seeing daylight. Food was passed in by Akukwe through a small opening at the rear, opened long enough to slip in new plates and collect old ones. Each day various unsuccessful arrangements were made to get me across the Benue River. There was Akukwe's plan to move me down by train to a village ten miles from Makurdi. From there I was to hire a bicycle for myself and a local Ibo guide who could take me to an obscure beach head from where I could cross by canoe. My view was that this plan was fragile and loose, and I rejected it. I was not sure I could find a suitable and reliable guide in a completely foreign village; neither was I sure I could find bicycles. In the event of my not finding a guide or bicycles or both, I would be unable to find a place to stay until those arrangements were made. Above all, it was now being said that soldiers at the bridge were already aware of these side-crossings and were taking counter-measures, including the use of search lights at night.

I put forward my own plan which was to enter the wagon of a goods train and have it sealed up. I hoped this would discourage the soldiers at the bridge from opening and searching it. Akukwe rejected the plan as being dangerous to my life we were trying to save. He explained that priority is always given to a passenger train along the line. If therefore one such train overtook my goods train before Makurdi bridge I would have to remain sealed up for up to six hours while the passenger train was being searched. He was sure I could not survive it. I agreed with him but then wè again reached a complete dead lock.

At midday of 14th August, 1966, Akukwe informed me that I had a good chance of crossing the bridge safely later at night. He said he had spoken to an Ibo driver of a goods train which went up North earlier on in the morning, but would be returning to Makurdi later at night. The train driver was only too willing to help and was very sure he would do that successfully without difficulty. Akukwe said this driver revealed to him that he had already crossed a few people in his water tank including Lt. Colonel Kalu.

As I waited for nightfall anxiously, my nerves were becoming over-strained. I had become very nervous. When a goods train stopped just outside the main platform at 2000 hours Mr. Akukwe came and collected me. All he told me was to go to the driver's compartment and join him. He wished me good luck and disappeared. I walked briskly through the platform, all the time looking backwards over my shoulders and restraining myself from breaking into a run. As soon as I got to the engine-end, the driver beckoned me in, and without saying a word, moved the train which was not meant to stop at that station. Later the driver introduced himself as Mr. Ifezue. He said he intended to stop briefly at a point five miles from the bridge and there, I would change into a spare fireman's suit to preserve the only clothing I had on. Then I would be lowered into the water tank in preparation for the crossing. He said it was possible the soldiers at the bridge could open the tank even though it had not been done before. If they did so, he said, I should remain absolutely quiet and well hidden to the side, for he was sure they would not come in to wet themselves unless they saw me. He advised against answering any call to come out from the outside. I was only to answer calls from him, but he would always give his name before such calls. It was a good briefing which gave me complete confidence and a feeling that the operation would succeed.

By the time the train made the stop I was already changed. The fireman dashed out and I went after him. As soon as the tank cover was lifted, I slid into the freezing water assisted by the fireman who immediately screwed back the cover. I was crouching in a corner in pitch darkness with water up to my chest. In less than ten minutes, the train was again slowing down and the rumbling echos were a clear enough indication that we were over the bridge — the notorious bridge which later became known as the Red Bridge of Makurdi. Soon after, when the train came to a complete stop, heavy footsteps of boots could be heard on both sides of the train and on top of it. A soldier patrolled even on top of the water tank and when he stepped on the lid, my heart missed a couple of beats. I was certain that the lid was about to be opened.

The stop had not lasted more than fifteen minutes when a rude jerk by the train clearly conveyed the good news to me, that the train had been cleared and I was on my way to safety and freedom. After a couple of short moves and stops, the train finally came to a standstill and the lid of the water tank was slowly removed. In accordance with previous arrangement, it required the train driver himself to get me out of the tank after he had clearly spelt out his name. When I came out, I found the train inside the locomotive shed with the coaches already detached at the station siding. It was 0200 hours in the morning, but without doubt, life appeared to be perfectly normal. Everybody on duty seemed to be of Southern Nigeria origin, and yet they went about their work happily and without fear. It was almost unbelievable that such a normal situation could exist in a railway station less than a mile from the Red Bridge where Southern soldiers were being killed every hour of the day. I put on my dry clothes and was taken into an office by a group of Ibos on night duty, who had gathered to see me and hear my story.

At daybreak on the 15th of August 1966, I went across to the platform to catch a train for Enugu. I felt much more relaxed, and mingled freely with what was left of the good people of Northern Nigeria. I came under heavy pressure from the Ibos who knew I was around to stay and rest in Makurdi until evening. They meant well, but I was in a position to know that such a rest could be eternal. I also knew that their confidence that Makurdi would continue to be normal indefinitely was misguided and I told them that. As a risky compromise, I stayed back for breakfast with the Ibo Station Master and there, I told the others my story and the general critical situation

79

in the country. I hoped that briefing would make them sit up and plan their immediate future realistically without delay.

I got into the open wagon of a locomotive train overflowing with a desperate crowd. This wagon was also carrying a car of a friend of mine from Kaduna, who allowed me a seat inside his car. The moment the train pulled out of the station, I became pretty sure I would make Enugu for no more military road blocks were expected. Less than two miles from Makurdi main station, I observed a military road block at a railroad junction, very close to the railway line. I thought I should relax a bit after a fortnight of gloom. So, as the train crawled through the junction, I came out of the car waving furiously to the Northern soldiers and shouting "power, power, power, to the North." The soldiers became very excited and waved back joyfully without realising that the person at whom they were waving was one of the individuals for whom they had set up that road block. While we relaxed in his car, my friend briefed me on the latest situation and the current rumours circulating throughout the country about me. According to him, some people believed I had hi-jacked the plane that took me to Kaduna on the 29th of July, 1966 to Ghana where I sought and was granted political asylum. Others said I had been killed in Kaduna and claimed to have seen my corpse in the public mortuary. He confirmed I was looked for in the village of Sabon Gida by the Northern authorities five days after my departure from there.

The train got into Enugu at 1800 hours and by a lucky coincidence a cousin of mine, Police Constable Nwachukwu, was on duty at the station. He shed a few tears, in uniform (which probably is against police regulations), when he recognized me in that very pathetic condition. He soon secured for me a clean shirt so that I could remove the Hausa gown I had been wearing for fifteen days. I passed that night at Dr. Anwunah's house and, for the first time, it dawned on me that my whole family, my wife and three children were still in Lagos. I telephoned my house in Lagos but there was no reply. The following day however I discovered them at Onitsha, still performing the last stages of my burial ceremony. This had cost them a considerable amount of money, and soon I had to find an equally large sum of money to go through my "waking ceremony."

Chapter 5

THE GATHERING STORM

THE RESUMED POGRAMS

By the end of August, 1966, civilians of Southern Nigeria origin became the main targets of the mass killings all over the country. This was perhaps because there were no more soldiers to be killed and yet the killings simply had to go on somehow. Very soon the majority of Easterners from all walks of life were back in Eastern Nigeria and many more were still returning daily. An announcement by Gowon about his intention to convene an Ad Hoc Constitutional Conference in Lagos on the 12th of September, 1966, came as a big relief for all Easterners. For them, it held the last glimmer of hope for an end to the pogroms and a return to peaceful life.

In his message to the conference, Gowon asked the delegates to completely rule out a unitary form of government in all their deliberations. This announcement brought general morale in Eastern Nigeria to its climax, and churchmen who had spent all their days in prayers and fasting thought that the Good Lord was at last listening. On 13th September, 1966, a high-powered Northern Nigeria delegation which represented Gowon himself, suggested a system of completely autonomous states with a Common Services Organisation, similar to the defunct East African Federation. Under this system, the North envisaged each Region or State having its own Army, Police, Civil Service and Judiciary, as well as a right to secede unilaterally from the union. The joy of the people of Eastern Nigeria turned out to be premature and short-lived, for on 20th September, 1966, when the conference reopened (after a break to enable various

81

delegations to hold consultations with their respective Regional Governments), the Northern delegation did a complete turnabout. All they wanted now, and were not even willing to discuss it, was a strong Central Government in Lagos and the creation of more States. Nigeria was before a Federation of four Regions or States, with a measure of Regional or State autonomy. The conference then took a break, to enable various delegations to again hold consultations with their Regional Governments, and resumed sittings during the last week of September. This time, while it sat, there began, on 29th September, 1966, an organised massacre of Eastern-ers, particularly the Ibos, by Northern soldiers and civilians all over Northern Nigeria on a scale yet unprecedented in the history of Black Africa. One began to wonder whether the Northern delegation actually went home to consult on issues pertaining to the conference or to give the green light for the new wave of killings.

Ojukwu, as the Governor of the Eastern Region, tried in vain to safeguard the lives and property of the people of the East by pressing that all soldiers should return to their Regions of origin in accord-ance with an agreement reached between Gowon and the Regional Governors in August, 1966. Gowon not only ignored this plea but went further to announce the "suspension, indefinitely of the Ad Hoc Committee," on the grounds that it could no longer serve any useful purpose. On this assertion, Gowon was dead right. For this committee really served as a deceptive measure designed to divert attention while preparations for a final show-down were being made.

With increasing confidence, Gowon announced that he was not prepared to consider the question of a temporary confederation. He revealed that he had already drafted some proposals himself, which he would discuss with other Military Governors in an attempt to find a peaceful solution to the country's problems. Indeed, soon after, he announced that he had appointed a special committee to draft a constitution which he would submit for discussion to a constituent assembly to be formed by him. In brief, what he was actually telling

Victims of the progroms in Northern Nigeria

83

the nation was that from then on, he was the judge and the jury. Indeed, Gowon issued a universal threat to use force to subdue any individuals or groups who stood in his way in his efforts to preserve Nigeria as one. It was astonishing and almost unbelievable that a man, in a short space of a few weeks, could shift his policy from secessation, to confederation of autonomous states, and then straight back to one and indivisible Nigeria with a unitary government — the very system against which he had earlier told the whole world he had taken up arms.

The resumed killings brought with it an influx of refugees into Eastern Nigeria from all over the Federation of Nigeria. They came back by air, land and sea, in pathetic and shocking conditions. Most of them had one or the other part of their bodies either broken or completely missing. Thousands of children arrived, some with severed limbs and many others emasculated. The adults bore the full brunt of the killings and very few arrived from the North unharmed. Those whose limbs were not severed, brought them back shattered and had to be amputated anyway. Many others had their eyes, nose, ears and tongues plucked out. The highlight of this horror was the arrival in Enugu of the headless corpse of an Ibo man! Women above the age of ten were raped and many of them came back in stretchers. The remaining Eastern Nigerian soldiers in Lagos came back by air. They arrived either naked or in underpants and the big gashes on their bodies showed they had been thoroughly beaten and tortured. There was hardly a single family in Eastern Nigeria which did not suffer a loss through these massacres.

As could be expected, tempers were extremely high, particularly when those who managed to come back told their stories of carnage and atrocities. From Kano came the story of how Easterners who had assembled at Kano international airport in an attempt to fly away to safety were rounded up by Northern troops and killed. In Jos the mobs were said to have combed out all Easterners. All of them, including men, old women and children, were either killed or maimed. Young women were raped until some of them collapsed and died. Some pregnant women they said had their wombs cut open and their unborn babies brought out and publicly executed. In Zaria, there was an attempt to imitate the system tried out in Sokoto in May, 1966. Most of the Ibos were hounded into a church, and there, rather than burn the church down, their assailants were sent in with matchets and other weapons to cut them down.

Officers from Lagos also told their own stories. Colonel Eze said he had telephoned Gowon on the 1st of August, 1966, after two days in hiding, to find out from him the true situation as well as seek his advice. Gowon assured him all was well and advised him to go back to work the following day. He took Gowon's advice and went to work. He was not in his office for more than 30 minutes when his orderly ran in to tell him that a section of Northern troops armed with automatic weapons were advancing towards his office in an extended line. Eze said he jumped out through the office window to the rear and as he ran towards the barbed wire fence he came under heavy fire from the soldiers. He tore through the barbed wire with his bare hands and escaped into town without being hit. His skin was badly torn and looked like that of someone rescued from the claws of a lion. He ran into a nearby house and was put up by a young girl he had never met before. She also arranged for medical attention and his transfer to a safer place from where he was smuggled out of Lagos by friends as soon as he was well enough to travel. The attacking soldiers, very angry for missing Eze, went back to his office and arrested his staff officer, Captain Iloputaife. They tied up the Captain hands and feet, and bounced him on the tarmac in front of the office until he was dead. Another officer from Abeokuta Garrison revealed that Major Okafor who was held in detention for his role in the January coup was brought out of jail and buried alive. He also said that both Colonel Okunweze and Major Obienu were shot in the Officers' Mess, Abeokuta during a conference to find ways of preventing the coup on the night of July 28th.

Ironsi's Air Force ADC, Captain Nwankwo, who was with Ironsi at the time of his death, later told us the story in Enugu of how the General died. According to Nwankwo, at 0630 hours on the 29th of July, 1966, Ironsi, Fajuyi, the Governor of Western Nigeria and himself were arrested at Government House, Ibadan by Northern troops under the command of Captain Danjuma. Colonel Hilary Njoku, who was also present, escaped with multiple bullet wounds. The troops used to affect the arrests were those detailed to protect the General during his tour. The captives were driven to an isolated jungle just outside Ibadan. By the time they got there, the three prisoners had been so thoroughly beaten that the older two — Ironsi and Fajuyi — could hardly stand up. Shortly after, Fajuyi was shot and then, Ironsi.

While Ironsi was being shot, Nwankwo said he ran into the bush and escaped. He emphasized that his escape was not due to his cleverness, but because his colleague, the Hausa ADC who was also present, wanted him to escape. Nwankwo explained that during the month of June, 1966, he and his Northern colleague had discussed the possibility of another coup. The Northern officer was emphatic the Ibos were going to do it again, but Nwankwo swore it was going to be done by Northerners. According to him, at the end of a long but heated argument, they came to an agreement that whichever side did it, the man on the winning side should save the other's life. Based on this agreement, the Northern ADC whispered to Nwankwo to escape while Ironsi was being shot, and also discouraged the soldiers from chasing after him. Nwankwo said he later made his way to Lagos and contacted this Northern officer again, who not only hid him for a couple of days, but eventually took him out of Lagos in the boot of a car.

THE CRISIS OF CONFIDENCE

The dangerous situation notwithstanding, there appeared to be very little that was being done in the Eastern Region in the way of preparing to resist any further attempt to carry the massacres into the Region. It appeared as if the Military Authorities there were much more concerned with the threat to their offices by the presence of many senior military officers in the Region than with that posed by the apparent determination of some sections of the country to exterminate a whole tribe. This unhappy situation was further worsened by the presence also of some young officers who took part in the January coup and were now released from jail by the Eastern Nigerian Government. They felt that they had the right to rule and not those who had attained high offices by betraying the January revolution at the last moment. No one knew for certain to whom the young majors were referring or whether their allegations were true or not. Nevertheless, this created a lack of mutual trust between the Army and the Government.

The unfortunate state of affairs resulted in the complete exclusion of all Armed Forces personnel from all national policy-making bodies throughout the period of the war, probably as a means of ensuring the security of the Military Governor. Surprising as it may sound, it is true that not a single military officer to my knowledge, received an official briefing on the explosive political battle which was going on between Gowon and Ojukwu. The military got news of what was going on either from the civilians, or through the wireless. Thus, the news of the Aburi Conference, the Ad Hoc Constitutional Conference and even the very declaration of independence came to the Army as a surprise over the national radio network. These actions, though seemingly the best thing to do at the time, may have been executed slightly better if Ojukwu had taken his military colleagues into confidence. Even if the Army had had no advice to offer on these matters, the sense of belonging which this show of confidence could have produced might have made the Army fight with more zest.

The crisis of confidence between the Army and the Military Governor assumed dramatic proportions in April, 1967. During that month, what was left of the Army in the Region was conducting a night exercise in preparation for a possible war. Shortly before H-hour, the exercise was cancelled and the entire police force was alerted with the information that the exercise was a camouflage for a coup to unseat Ojukwu as the Military Governor of the Eastern Region.

Thereafter the Governor went into hiding in the University Campus of Nsukka for four days. On his return to Enugu, he suspended Major Nzeogwu and a few other officers from performing military duties. All future military exercises and large troop movements were banned.

Colonel Njoku, the Army Commander at the time pressed very hard to be allowed to sit at Executive Council meetings, and also to be briefed regularly on the political situation. This was immediately seen as a threat to the office of the Governor. His requests were rejected and, soon afterwards, rumours of Njoku's doubtful loyalty to his people were deliberately spread throughout the Region.

In frustration Njoku convened a conference of all senior army officers and there he read out his letter of resignation which he intended to submit to Ojukwu. I immediately assured Njoku during the conference, and in the presence of all officers, that if his resignation was accepted, I would also resign my commission. A few other officers also gave him a similar assurance. Major Frank Obioha, the special military intelligence officer for State House warned Ojukwu against the acceptance of Njoku's letter of resignation. His resignation was rejected and later he was asked to go to Ireland for medical attention to remove three bullets still lodged in his thigh following an attack on him by Northern soldiers at Ibadan. Even though the problem of Njoku had been solved, albeit temporarily, the basic crisis of confidence still existed.

I was equally in the bad books of Ojukwu as a result of a strongly worded letter I wrote to him criticising the nepotic practices going on in the University Teaching Hospital, Enugu. In this letter I charged that the hospital was being staffed from the Chairman to the ward maids by either Nnewi people or their friends. Ojukwu is from Nnewi. I pointed out that our present struggle against the evil forces of oppression, nepotism, tribalism and corruption for which Nigeria was known, would be meaningless if we were going to settle for the same vices on a larger scale at the end of the struggle.

I was soon accused of disloyalty and planning to overthrow the government. Various groups of people and delegations were sent to preach to me in an attempt to discourage me from executing my "plan." I got away with this lightly because we were then still Eastern Region of Nigeria. After the declaration of Biafra, I had to be extremely careful not to get my name associated with anything that would give rise to rumours relating to disloyal acts. I am not therefore surprised that Colonel Ojukwu failed to tell me we were going to declare independence on the 30th May, 1967, even though I met and had a brief conversation with him the previous day in Army Headquarters, Enugu.

The Army in Eastern Nigeria, therefore, had more than enough reasons to be of very low morale indeed. Most of the soldiers came back in rags, having lost all they had, and there was no prospect of replacements. Wherever they went, it seemed they were unwanted because the civilian refugee problems were overwhelming and demanded immediate action. Those officers and men who remained in Enugu soon left for their villages in frustration when they felt they were not really required or wanted. Those who still remained in Enugu, including very senior officers, had to make their own arrangements in town for accommodation of their families. Lt. Colonel David Ogunewe, the Commanding Officer of the First Battalion Enugu, made it quite clear he did not want any senior officers, particularly the Colonels, to interfere in any way with the running of his Battalion which was the only military unit in the Region. He discouraged even visits to the Battalion by such officers. His fear was that unless he was careful he might be displaced from his command by someone else. All senior officers finding that they could neither go to the Governor, nor to Colonel Ogunewe, retired to a common house given to them at the Independence Layout, Enugu. There we played cards and checkers all day completely disinterested in what was happening around us.

It was in this state of mind that one morning in March, 1967, while we were playing cards, we got the information that Nigerian troops, advancing through Midwest Nigeria, had entered Onitsha town. According to the information, the invading troops were moving up to Enugu unchallenged. The news of the invasion, which came from police sources, appeared to be authentic and realistic in view of the fact that Northern troops had earlier moved into that Region, removed all Ibo detainees in the Benin prison and executed them. About ten officers were around when the news was received and they all jumped into their cars to move to the First Battalion barracks. When I got to the barracks, not a single officer had arrived there. What in fact these officers had done, was to drive into hiding or straight to the security of their respective towns and villages. The Military Governor had also taken off to an unknown destination, but my information was that he had chosen Udi where he had served as an Administrative Officer, as his hiding place.

Colonel Ogunewe, alone and dejected, was trying to marshall some troops the best he could. With my assistance we were soon able to despatch about a hundred armed men towards Onitsha. Shortly after the departure of the troops, another message from Onitsha revealed that the story of the invasion was false. Unfortunately, Colonels Eze and Ivenso had left Enugu earlier that morning to Abakaliki and Onitsha respectively — Eze to see his parents since his escape from Lagos, and Ivenso to collect from a friend the remnants of his belongings collected from Lagos. Later, when the runaway officers returned they expressed no regrets, neither were they ashamed of what they had done. Rather, they said they would do exactly the same thing again if the situation arose until such a time the Army was told what was happening and where the weapons of war were hidden.

That incident was the best indication that the Army was neither ready nor yet conditioned for a meaningful resistance against an invading force from Nigeria. To improve on our intelligence, Colonel Eze and I, acting on our own initiative, visited various parts of the Northern Nigeria border almost every night in an attempt to get information from friendly natives. For this dangerous task, we were unable to convince either Ogunewe or Colonel Ojukwu to issue military weapons to us, for fear that we might use them for other purposes.

This crisis of confidence between Ojukwu and the Army may well be the reason why he leaned entirely on the civilians for all military purchases including weapons. These weapons, when they arrived in Eastern Nigeria were hidden in villages around Nnewi, under arrangement outside military control. From there they were brought up to Enugu by night in trickles, and handed over to the

Army. The Army, ignorant of what was available to it at any given time, could not plan in advance. In addition, this system proved to be a colossal waste of money because a good percentage of these weapons were unserviceable. Lt. Colonel George Kurubo soon had an open and violent confrontation with Ojukwu against this practice, as a result of which he was given money to arrange for the purchase of weapons, abroad. For Kurubo it was too late because his mind was made up already against Ojukwu and his system of "military" government. The main cause of Kurubo's bitterness, however, was the displacement of his cousin, Dr. Graham Douglas, from his post as the Attorney-General of Eastern Nigeria by Mr. C. C. Mojekwu at the end of September, 1967. Mojekwu later became Biafra's Commissioner for Home Affairs while operating abroad as Ojukwu's special envoy in Lisbon. Kurubo explained to me in Dr. Douglas' house at Enugu shortly before his resignation that his cousin's powers and rights were already completely stripped and his resignation would only be a formality. It should not have come as a surprise to any senior army officer in the Eastern Region that Kurubo defected to Nigeria in the long run because in the presence of other senior officers, before the declaration of Biafra, he told Ojukwu that he was unwilling to serve under him because both of them, as members of the Supreme Military Council under Ironsi, had equal status.

The Military Governor, however, had a few military friends and perhaps confidants, but each one of them seemed to have a reason for being so close. In fact the only known confidant and friend was Major Chude-Sokei. He later performed top secret military and civil assignments both inside and outside the Region. There was Colonel Victor Banjo, a Yoruba, who was in detention in the Eastern Region for his role in the January coup. He was released and moved into State House to live with Ojukwu. Major Ifeajuna, also a released January 1966 coup detainee, was a close friend of Ojukwu with special privileges. He not only refused to accept any field appointment within the Army, but was also accommodated at government expense in the Progress Hotel, Enugu while much more senior officers lived in slums in the town.

91

There were rumours that the Governor was trying to appease those privileged officers for personal reasons not unconnected with the January 1966 coup. If these rumours were right, then these tactics failed woefully because the same privileged group, in September, 1967, made an unsuccessful attempt to overthrow the Governor.

THE FINAL PLUNGE

The news that Colonel Ojukwu was in Aburi, Ghana with other Military Governors on the 4th of January, 1967 to try to find a peaceful solution to the current disturbances in the country came as an encouraging surprise to me and many other senior military officers in the Eastern Region. At the end of the two-day conference some important decisions were reached, among which were:

1. The immediate resumption of the Ad Hoc Committee to work out a constitutional future for Nigeria.

2. The payment of salaries until the 31st of March, 1967 of all staff and employees of Government and Statutory Corporations and any others who were forced to leave their posts as a result of the disturbances.

3. The setting up, in the meantime, of a committee to look into the problem of rehabilitation of displaced persons and the recovery of their property.

4. The exclusion of the use of force as a means of settling any difference within the country.

5. The repealing of all decrees which tended to over-centralise power at the expense of Regional autonomy. This would be followed by the enactment of a decree before the 21st of January, to restore the Regions to their political position prior to January 15, 1966.

On the advice of some Federal senior civil servants, most of whom were acting on foreign advice, Gowon rejected most of these decisions, particularly those pertaining to the payment of displaced persons and the reconvening of the Ad Hoc Constitutional Conference. As a follow-up, Gowon enacted Decree no. 8 which gave him power to declare a state of emergency in any Region irrespective of the wishes of the Governor of that Region. Later Gowon published these as the official outcome of the Aburi conference. The above measures were a clear indication that Gowon was no longer giving much consideration to the possibility of a peaceful solution. Rather he was rapidly preparing the ground for the use of force.

The Eastern Nigerian Government, then absolutely helpless, passed a couple of Edicts to protect the interests of its people and avoid a total economic collapse of the Region. These Edicts were meant to serve as temporary relief while a more permanent solution was being sought. Foremost among these Edicts were the Registration of Companies Edict, the Revenue Collection Edict and the Court of Appeal Edict. As a punishment for these measures taken by the Eastern Nigeria Government, the Lagos Government imposed economic sanctions on the Eastern Region.

As a result of the deteriorating situation, Colonel Ojukwu convened a meeting of the Advisory Committee of Chiefs and Elders at Enugu, on the 26th of May, 1967 to acquaint them with the latest developments and seek their decision. He gave the committee three alternative solutions to the crisis:

1. To accept the terms of the North and Gowon and thereby submit to domination by the North; or
2. To continue the present stalemate and drift; or
3. Ensure the survival of the people by asserting their autonomy.

On the 27th of May, the Consultative Assembly mandated Colonel Ojukwu "to declare, at the earliest practicable date, Eastern Nigeria a free sovereign and independent state by the name and title of the Republic of Biafra." Lagos' reaction to this was swift and immediate for Gowon at once announced a new constitution for Nigeria based upon the division of the existing four Regions into twelve States. By this arrangement, the Eastern Region was unilaterally split into three States: Rivers, East Central and South Eastern States.

Completely engulfed in an apparently misguided optimism, we perhaps spent by far too much time and money on propaganda with little left for military preparations. When the Head of State of Biafra told the nation that no country in black Africa could defeat Biafra by land, air or sea, the nation went wild with joy and thought that any further delay on our part in launching an attack against Nigeria was senseless. Yet the Commanders of the Army, Navy and the Air Force had not been told where the forces referred to, were stationed. Even the announcement by the Head of State that if we were attacked the grass would fight for us, was taken literally by many, who were beginning to ask for nothing but war. In an attempt to demonstrate the strength of the Biafran Army, Colonel Ojukwu took some top civilians to the firing range of the First Battalion at Enugu. There, some newly acquired machine guns and automatic rifles were displayed and later fired. The noise produced was impressive and sufficiently indicative of strength. When Chief Awolowo visited Enugu, just before the outbreak of war, two helicopters painted in Army colours, put up a short demonstration for him to illustrate our air power. When the helicopters finally landed on the grounds of the State House, and the fierce-looking pilots jumped out smartly, it was clear that the chief from Yorubaland was highly impressed.

With the people's minds thus prepared for war, demonstrations were organised and held all over the country demanding immediate action against Nigeria. Everywhere the cry on everybody's lips was "Ojukwu Nyeanyi Egbe" (Ojukwu give us weapons). Finally, on the 30th May, 1967, the Head of State declared Eastern Nigeria an independent and sovereign state of Biafra. In doing this he was merely acting in accordance with the mandate given to him earlier by the people. The mandate had authorised him to do so "at the earliest practicable date." The question was whether the date chosen was "the earliest practicable date." Almost all senior army officers thought the answer to that question was an unqualified "No." The thought of being independent of Nigeria was simply glorious but to make this a reality was going to be a miracle; yet there was universal jubilation.

By June, expatriates began to leave Biafra because of mounting pressures to do so from both the Lagos Government and their respective embassies. I remember some American staff, at the University of Nigeria, paid me a visit at my Nsukka Headquarters, on 4th July, 1967 to seek advice on the question of leaving Biafra. They disclosed that they had been told by Lagos to leave Nsukka immediately for Gowon's Army would go through that town on 6th July, 1967. While admitting the fact that the situation was very critical, I explained to them that Gowon's march through Nsukka, if it took place, would be resisted, and certainly long enough to allow them time to pack up and leave the town or even the country. I however pointed out that the choice to remain in or leave Biafra rested entirely on them in the final analysis. I think they stayed on till the outbreak of the war when I also realised the significance of the date they had mentioned.

Later on that day, Dr. Nnamdi Azikiwe, also at Nsukka, called me in to seek advice. He pointed out that, if all stories he had heard were to be true, and if all outstanding threats from Lagos were to be executed, Nsukka would be unsafe for civilians pretty soon. He was therefore contemplating a move from Nsukka after he should have heard from me. My advice was that a more before the actual outbreak of hostilities would be premature as the direction of the initial invasion was not known.

Chapter 6

THE BIAFRAN ARMED FORCES

THE ARMY

An agreement arrived at in August, 1966 between Gowon and the other Military Governors stated that all soldiers be repatriated to their Regions of origin without their weapons. For this reason all soldiers who returned to the Eastern Region did so without arms. In a separate arrangement between Gowon and Ojukwu, Northern soldiers at Enugu were to go with their weapons for self-defence, but on the promise by Gowon that the weapons would be returned to Eastern Nigeria as soon as the soldiers were safely in Northern Nigeria. The Northern soldiers left Enugu in August, 1966 with their weapons and without any incident, under Major Benjamin Adekunle, who later became the Commander of Nigeria's Third Marine Commando Division.

What was left of the Nigeria Army at Enugu barracks after the departure of the Northerners amounted to about 240 soldiers, the majority of them technicians and tradesmen. As weapons taken away by the Northern soldiers' were never returned, not all the remaining soldiers had weapons. A decision to set up Regional Military Commands in the four Regions with Army Headquarters still in Lagos was taken at Aburi Conference, held in Ghana. When later, a conference of military representatives of all Regions was convened in Benin, the capital of Midwestern Nigeria, the North failed to send any representatives. The conference broke up before it could begin when Major Olutoye, who was an Education Officer in Lagos before the crisis, turned up in Benin flying the flag of the Commander of the Second Brigade, and posing as the Commander of that Brigade. Senior delegates from other Regions demanded that he stop flying the flag in Benin. He refused to do this, and immediately left for Lagos with members of his delegation. Thereafter the conference dispersed and from then on, there was no further contact between the Nigeria Army in the East, and Army Headquarters in Lagos. Intensive recruitment into the Army began throughout Nigeria except in the Eastern Region where Gowon warned seriously against such an exercise. When a report came in that Major Appolo was in Europe to buy weapons for the Lagos Army, the East had to do something about it.

The threat from Lagos was now real and Ojukwu could no longer keep the senior officers in cold storage. Colonel Njoku came out of hospital in January to preside over the first conference of senior army officers held in Enugu. The conference tried to find the best possible ways of establishing formally the Eastern Nigeria Command, as approved by Lagos, using resources available. The conference recommended the formation of two new infantry battalions to be called the 7th and the 8th Battalions, to be commanded by me and Colonel Kalu. These Battalions were to be based at Nsukka and Port Harcourt respectively. The task of the 7th Battalion was to defend the entire Northern border while the 8th defended the South, with the First Battalion acting as the army reserve force in addition to looking after the Niger riverline to the West. A training depot was to be established under the command of Lt. Colonel David Okafor, inside the Enugu Prisons. This was to ensure that Lagos did not know we were recruiting and training soldiers. An officer cadet school was to be established just outside Enugu and run in absolute secrecy.

There was no difficulty at all in finding recruits for the Army. Several hundreds of people turned out daily in front of the First Battalion barracks to be recruited. The majority of these were refugees, who were very bitter over the treatment they had received from their fellow Nigerians and were anxious for vengeance. The rate of intake of these recruits was unfortunately very slow due to inadequacy of existing training facilities as well as acute shortage of weapons and essential administrative support. By the middle of

April, 1967, the 7th and the 8th Battalions had received sufficient small arms to go round, as well as a few machine guns, and were deployed in the field.

With my 7th Battalion Headquarters based at Nsukka town, I deployed the rifle companies as follows: A Company at Okuta was responsible for the defence of the 80-mile stretch between Okuta and Onitsha to the south. B Company at Enugu-Ezike was responsible for the defence of 30 miles of frontier between Okuta and Obollo Afor main road (exclusive). C Company at Obollo Afor defended from there to Obollo-Eke, 40 miles to the East. To facilitate their task, a detachment of platoon strength, from C Company, was based at Eha-Amufu to look after the area of Eha-Amufu closely. Two Companies of the First Battalion were placed under command for the defence of the entire Ogoja Province almost 200 miles from my Headquarters at Nsukka.

Effective supervision of these two Companies was a near impossibility for me. When therefore a Northern fighting patrol crossed the border in that sector in May, 1967, and attacked one of our outposts, our soldiers reacted poorly. As a result we lost the only heavy machine gun available to an entire Company. The lesson learnt from this skirmish was that a more effective command arrangement was urgently needed for that sector. It also became abundantly clear that two Companies were most inadequate for the effective defence of 150 miles of frontier. The only force which I still had uncommitted was my reserve Company at Nsukka, which I was determined not to commit. First Battalion rear at Enugu could not render further assistance. They had two more Companies left, one of them permanently based at Onitsha for the defence of the River Niger bridge and the other remained as the Army reserve.

The 8th Battalion in the South was in exactly the same predicament as the 7th. With its Headquarters at Port Harcourt, a Company each were deployed at Ahoada, Calabar, Oron, and a Platoon at Bonny. The extreme southwestern coastline, covering a distance of more than 100 miles, remained undefended due to lack of troops.

When more weapons were received in May, 1967, a decision

was taken to form two new Battalions to be called the 9th and the 14th Battalions. The First, 7th and the 14th Battalions would then be grouped to form the 51 Brigade, under my command, for the defence of the Northern Sector. The 8th and the 9th Battalions would form the 52 Brigade under the command of Colonel Eze, with the responsibility of defending the Southern Sector. Colonel Eze was promised a third Battalion to bring his Brigade up to strength as soon as possible. This unfortunately was not possible before the outbreak of the war. Under this arrangement, the rest of First Battalion still at Enugu moved to Ogoja under the command of Major Pat Amadi. The 14th Battalion under Major Ohanehi, was forming at Abakaliki and the 9th under Major Ogbo Oji was doing the same at Calabar when shooting began.

The Biafran Army had nothing other than old bolt-action rifles made available by government civilian agents. A few machine guns were issued at the scale of about one or two per Company. In the way of support weapons, only the First Battalion had 6 x 81 mm and 6 x 3" mortar barrels, inherited from the Nigeria Army. For these, the bombs available were extremely limited. Other units had to rely entirely on local devices as substitutes for support weapons and then fortified their defences with ditches, mines and armoured vehicle traps.

THE AIR FORCE

Many pilots and technicians formerly of the Nigeria Air Force returned to Eastern Region where they had neither new planes to fly nor old ones to mend. In the course of time, two old planes, a B26 and a B25 were acquired together with three new helicopters. The two planes were fitted with machine guns and locally-made rockets and could deliver bombs also made locally. The helicopters became very effective for bombing when the Air Force perfected the art of throwing a bomb out of the door of a flying helicopter, and scoring a direct hit on objects about 300 metres below. The helicopters did an extremely marvellous job at the initial stages of the war. They not only inflicted heavy casualties on the enemy, but also served as the only available means of silencing enemy guns and mortars. For whenever they were in the air, the enemy stopped all shelling and mortaring, and our soldiers were able to rest and reorganise.

While the B26 wandered round the North wrecking military installations and equipment, the B25 was never able to take off for she was just too old to fly. For a short period, a Dove executive plane recovered from Shell BP Port Harcourt played a commendable role in tackling strategic targets. Like all good things, our luck and joy were short-lived for the entire Air Force was driven aground and into hiding by the appearance of Russian jets on the Nigerian side. When this happened it became much easier for the enemy to begin their successful push to Enugu.

However, our hopes for a dramatic recovery of the Air Force were kept kindled throughout the war by monthly assurances given to me by Colonel Ojukwu that we would get jet planes. Unless I am mistaken, these jet planes never quite made the journey to Biafra till the end of the war. The BAF, however, made a dramatic comeback in 1969 with their newly acquired "Minicons" aircrafts. These Minicons performed extremely well against carefully selected strategic targets and reduced considerably Nigerian shipping as well as their oil industry. Count Von Rosen played a commendable role in the operations of these small aircrafts which he nick-named "Biafran Babies."

THE NAVY

The Biafra Navy (BN) started off in Calabar with a small patrol boat, formerly used by the Nigeria Navy before the revolution, for anti-smugglers operations. At the time, the people of the East found naval consolation in a rumour that the Nigerian flagship, the "NNS Nigeria" had been destroyed through sabotage in a Lagos harbour by Eastern Nigerian guerrillas. Even if such damage was done to the ship it could not have been very serious because it played a dominant role in all naval battles with Nigeria throughout the war. In the course of the war, the BN found more boats locally; these were armour-plated, fitted with light guns and machine guns, and used most effectively to present formidable opposition against the Nigerian Navy, with all its modern equipment.

THE MILITIA

It is appropriate at this stage, to mention briefly the Biafra Militia which had been developed with the outbreak of the war and was already playing an important role in the war effort. Due to acute shortage of weapons and lack of money for personal emoluments, the majority of Biafrans could not find their way into the Army at the initial stage. Yet these people were determined to be actively identified with the struggle in one form or the other. For this reason, several organisations which later became known as Militia, sprang up in various provinces. In these organisations, local leaders and ex-servicemen trained young men and women in the use of whatever weapons the individuals had. These weapons were mainly imported and locally manufactured shotguns. When it became increasingly clear to the Government that the Army could hardly hold back the enemy, the need arose to reorganise all Militia units into an effective and disciplined force under one command. Efiong, who was then a Brigadier, was appointed to command this force with special emphasis on administration. At the time the tasks of the Militia were given as follows:

1. To provide a ready source of man-power reinforcement for the regular Army;
2. To assist with military administration immediately behind the frontlines;
3. To garrison all areas captured or regained from the enemy;
4. To help educate the population on the reasons why Biafra was fighting.

Initially many people detested serving with the Militia and preferred the Army. In the course of time, however, the Militia, for reasons to be shown later became so popular that it drew all available man-power, to the extent of threatening the very existence of the Army. At that stage it had to be disbanded.

When the 53 Brigade fell back from Nsukka, and left all routes and flanks undefended, the Militia from Enugu moved in with their shotguns, dane-guns and locally-made mines and explosive devices. Together with elements of the Biafra Police, they managed to hold the enemy back for several days. The men of the Militia did many brave deeds during their Nsukka battles. On one occasion, a militia officer crawled to a ferret, climbed up on it and dropped a grenade. This officer lost his life trying to escape but the ferret crew must have lost theirs too. It is noteworthy, that all militia officers in the field were entirely civilians with no formal military training. They included intellectuals, businessmen and professionals. As will be seen later, they got more involved in the fighting as time went on and finally became almost as committed as the regular Army.

No sooner was the Militia formed than it split into two powerful and often opposing factions called the National Militia and the Port Harcourt Militia. Reconciliation attempts which started under General Efiong when he was in charge of the Militia continued under Police Commissioner Chinwuba who took over command from Efiong. In the end, the Militia remained unreconciled. The Militia, which was completely independent of the Army, was highly political in many ways and the Army steered clear of its affairs for a long time, to avoid a political confrontation which would develop.

However, with the fall of Port Harcourt, I thought I had sufficient reasons to demand that the Militia be disbanded. I boldly put forward my views to Colonel Ojukwu in complete awareness of the personal risks I was taking in the event of a hostile public reaction. I was of the view that the Militia had outlived its usefulness because the aims for which it was established no longer applied. We had so far captured no territory for them to garrison since the collapse of Midwestern Nigeria and the likelihood of such an event taking place in the immediate future was remote. The Militia had expanded very rapidly to a point of being as strong as the regular Army at a time the Army was beginning to be short of man-power. As a result of this rapid and uncontrolled expansion almost everybody in Biafra who was not in the Army claimed to be in the Militia and was automatically entitled to all Militia benefits at the expense of the Army. The Army now shared her food, clothing, transport and fuel with the Militia. Arms and ammunition which were grossly insufficient for the Army had to be issued to some militiamen, who were yet to do their basic weapon training. For the above reasons and many more, my view was that all men of military age should either join the Army or keep off fighting completely.

Colonel Ojukwu accepted these proposals and the disbandment of the Militia began. As I expected, I came under public criticism but succeeded in disbanding this force and thus releasing talents trapped and misapplied within the organisation.

THE BIAFRAN ORGANISATION OF FREEDOM FIGHTERS (BOFF)

Shortly after the fall of Port Harcourt and the disbandment of the Militia, Colonel Ojukwu announced that Biafra would start guerrilla warfare against Nigeria in addition to the conventional warfare already being fought by the Regular Army. I did not hold any discussions on this issue with the Head of State before or after his announcement, so I assumed that he had his own secret plan for initiating the operation. When, after a fortnight, it became clear to me that there was no follow-up action being planned by anyone, I began to work on a plan in my Headquarters without knowing exactly at the time, who was going to implement that plan.

The indomitable Colonel Aghanya paid me a visit shortly afterwards and, in the course of a general discussion, we touched on guerrilla warfare and discussed it at length. In the end, he volunteered to form a guerrilla force and run it. We discussed the paper I had written on it and agreed on all points raised. In outline, the paper warned against setting up a force similar to the Militia we had just got rid of, for the nation could not afford it. What we wanted, I stressed, was a controllable group of dedicated Biafrans who were prepared to operate in enemy territory without being given pay, clothing, food, accommodation and even arms and ammunition by the government of Biafra. Those who insisted on having all or some of the above facilities, I maintained, should be encouraged to join the Army. These guerrillas who would only be given a small quantity of weapons and ammunition initially, must thereafter arm themselves with weapons they would have to capture from the enemy. In addition, they were to live off the soil, sleeping wherever they could find shelter in their areas of operation.

I was fully aware of the difficulties which the Biafran guerrilla would have to face in enemy-held territories. For instance, with very little civilian population in the occupied areas at the time as a result of the enemy's initial ruthlessness, a strange face in those areas could easily be identified. I was also conscious of the fact that a successful guerrilla action in any occupied area would bring about a ruthless and massive reprisal against the Biafran civilians still living in the area. For these reasons I was of the view that our guerrilla force should limit its operations to Nigeria, particularly the Midwest, the West and probably Lagos. If that was done effectively, the enemy would be forced to tie down a sizeable force in those areas. Inside Biafra, with few or no hide-outs due to close concentration of towns, I thought the best the guerrillas could do was to conduct raids on military locations and installations, as well as lay ambushes on known enemy routes. That, they could do from bases inside Biafran-held areas. I took into consideration a factor which was likely to reduce quite considerably the effectiveness of guerrilla warfare within Biafra. That problem is the multiplicity of languages and dialects spoken by the people of Biafra. In other words, for a successful guerrilla operation in any given area, one had to send only people who spoke the language and the dialects of that area perfectly well. To do that was, to say the least, not in the best interest of national security, at least in certain areas.

Colonel Aghanya later saw the Head of State with my proposals and was soon given the mandate to go ahead, and his efforts resulted in the formation of the Biafra Organisation of Freedom Fighters (BOFF). I am not in a position to write fully on BOFF operations and their achievements because it functioned independently of the Army and under the direct control of the Head of State. However, if their reports are anything to go by, then they did extremely well.

105

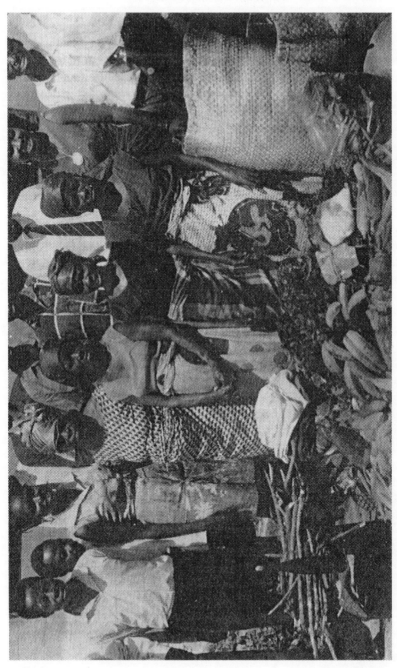

A Biafran Civil Organisation standing beside the food they had just donated to the Army during the initial stages of the war

Towards the end of the war, though, the BOFF was beginning to pose exactly the same problems to the regular Army as the Militia had done. It had grown so big and drained all available man-power that one would have been tempted to work towards its being drastically cut down in size, if not disbanded, had the war gone on much longer.

I do not want to be drawn into a lengthy discussion on guerrilla warfare. I therefore hope that what I have said contains enough points to convince those who say that we should have changed to total guerrilla warfare when we appeared to be failing in the conventional way, that was rather too late and no longer possible at that stage. We would have had to surrender formally first, before embarking on a meaningful guerrilla warface. If, when we were attacked by the Nigerians on the 6th of July, 1967, we had not offered any resistance but rather allowed the enemy to go anywhere he had wanted, normal life would have continued in Biafra and the setting would have been perfect for a very effective guerrilla warfare soon afterwards.

ADMINISTRATIVE SUPPORT FOR THE ARMY

In order to understand fully the overwhelming difficulties of the Biafran Army during the war, and to appreciate the efforts it made, the issue of the administrative support available to it should be discussed at this stage. A well-equipped army with poor administrative support cannot sustain its achievements and success. But, an ill-equiped army with poor administrative support should never take to the field if it can be avoided. Unfortunately for the Biafran Army, the field could not be avoided.

Before the war, the small Biafran Army under formation was almost completely administered and maintained by donations from the civil population. For an army of that size, particularly in peace time, that arrangement was tolerable on a temporary basis. All soldiers lived together in various camps and fed together, thus minimizing administrative complications that might have arisen. With the Army completely dependent on the goodwill of the people for its administrative support, it became imperative that the situation must continue to be normal enough to permit the people to render these services. In short, they must have enough food, transport, fuel, clothing and houses for themselves and to spare for the Army.

The whole idea was a magnificient gesture by a people fighting for survival, but that was as far as it went. As an Army officer with training and years of military experience, I considered it a rather unsuitable way of running an Army expected to engage in a shooting war at short notice. The truth, as already mentioned, was that no one expected a shooting war and whatever assistance the Army got was on compassionate grounds, and intended to be temporary. We appeared to lack nothing in Biafra (still Eastern Nigeria) and the need for formal administrative planning for the Army appeared frivolous to the civilians who handled military affairs. After all there were thousands of vehicles in the Region, the number of which had increased tremendously with the return of refugees from other parts of Nigeria. All large markets and shops were fully stocked throughout the Region and what they held appeared inexhaustible Many therefore got away with the wrong impression that we could go on indefinitely without outside administrative assistance or internal planning.

Immediately after the declaration of Biafra on 30th of May, 1967, General Efiong (then a Colonel), alarmed at the administrative chaos within the Army, submitted a paper to Ojukwu suggesting an administrative set-up for the Army and giving details of the Army administrative (support) requirements for six months, in the event of war. All items listed by Efiong were available in Biafra in large quantities except a few items like boots and web equipment. Even if sufficient quantities were not found in Biafra, they could have been purchased from Nigeria with which we still had common currency and unrestricted movements across the borders. Efiong's paper was discarded as being too expensive and completely out of tune with the requirements of the Biafran Army — an Army which, in the opinion of many, needed only determination and will-power to fight a just cause successfully. No further attempts were made at building up an administrative machinery to support the armed forces until the outbreak of the war. In the meantime, a few officers were appointed to purchase Army requirements from the local markets from time to time.

When war finally broke out, the government created civil administrative directorates to cater for both the military and the entire civil population of the country. Foremost among these were the Food, Fuel, Transport and Clothing Directorates. I became aware of the existence of these Directorates when I took over command of the Army in September, 1967, three months after the outbreak of hostilities. During my three months as a Brigade Commander, I had thought the food my soldiers ate was donated locally by villagers. Most of it actually came from the Food Directorate.

The Food Directorate

The Food Directorate was by far the largest of the lot, very controversial, and extremely difficult to run. It was responsible for the purchase and distribution of all food, drinks and cigarettes to the Army and the nation. These items were sent in bulk to civilian organisations established to support each major military field unit. From there they were prepared for consumption and sent up to the front-line troops. The first problem identified with this system was that military operations had to be timed to fit in with meal timings as determined by various civilian cookhouses, over which the Army had no authority. For this reason, the Army lost flexibility and surprise unless one was prepared to forego some meals.

Soon, another problem and a much more serious one came to light. Each time the Army lost ground, the cookhouses dispersed and took several days to reassemble and re-establish in another location. In their absence the troops went without food. By December, 1967 when such places as Nsukka, Ogoja, Calabar and Enugu had fallen to the enemy, the Food Directorate had many refugees added to its ration strength, and at the same time, less food was available to it. Even those who were not yet refugees were becoming increasingly unable to feed themselves as a result of the war and had to get themselves attached somehow to the Directorate. Consequently, the Army suffered tremendously. As a result, the Biafran Army Service Corps (BASC), was formed to assist the Food Directorate with the distribution of food to Army rear units. As the war progressed and Biafra territory shrank, the number of people fed by the Food Directorate increased, and the amount of food getting to the Army decreased. By early 1969, we had lost almost all food-producing areas, and the Food Directorate had little or no money to buy the little amount of food still being sold at cut-throat prices.

At this stage the food problem assumed new dimensions with everybody placing his personal survival and that of his dependants above every other consideration. Malpractices and cheating became the order of the day. Food Directorate officials, when they bought their food, made generous allowances for their dependants. BASC officials and unit representatives did exactly the same whenever they drew food from the Directorate. In addition, Army units, rather than draw food only from the Food Directorate depot allotted to them, went to other depots and obtained food from the civilian staff by deceit or intimidation. In order to get sufficient food, ration strengths forwarded by units to the Food Directorate were anything up to five times the actual figures. The Directorate, with no military staff or even a system of checking the figures, operated on these false strength returns.

By the middle of 1969 the Army was getting not more than 10 percent of all food available to the Directorate and this amounted to a meal in four days for each soldier. In desperation, the Army and the Food Directorate quarrelled but each had a good case to present. The Army charged the Directorate with negligence and paying more attention to the civilians. The Directorate accused the Army units of inflating their ration strengths and failing to deliver the little food they collected to the front lines.

In an attempt to solve this problem, I forwarded a memorandum to General Ojukwu listing the faults of the system and making recommendations. Among the anomalies I identified with the Directorate was the fact that they worked daily from 0800 hours to 1500 hours and did not work at all on Sundays. Their services or assistance were therefore not available to the Army over the weekends. The most frustrating aspect of the system was the fact that the Army had no authority whatsoever over the running of the Directorate. If the Directorate thought any particular unit was trying to impose itself on it, that unit could be punished by a cut in their rations.

My recommendation was that the Directorate be split into military and civil sections. The staff of the military section, I felt, should either continue to work as civilians but under complete control of the Army and subject to Army rules and regulations or be merged with the BASC. If this had happened, the Army would have had better control of the staff and exercised a bit of flexibility in the distribution of the little food available. It would have been almost impossible for soldiers who obtained food fraudulently from civilians to do the same successfully from military food depots.

Unfortunately, the Food Directorate saw in this proposed system an attempt by the Army to close it down and take over its duties. The Directorate put forward a counter proposal suggesting the complete dissolution of the Biafra Army Service Corps. The argument was that the unit was a luxury which the nation could ill afford at a time when all soldiers should be in the front lines. The Directorate was sure it would do the job much better without interference by soldiers. What they conveniently overlooked was that if the majority of them put on uniforms, they could have made good soldiers and also gone to the front line. I did not tell them that.

Soldiers continued to endure prolonged and intensive hunger but at the same time performed extremely well in the battlefield. The civil population did their best to help, but their best was not enough with a deteriorating food situation. Civilian communities supported only units operating in their areas and the problem was heightened when the Red Cross decided to stop its "mercy" flights in July, 1969 after one of its planes was shot down by a Nigeria Air Force Russian Jet Fighter. Many still believe that the Red Cross had other reasons for halting its relief operations in Biafra.

The Biafran civil population did not consider hunger as a good

111

reason for soldiers to lose ground. When, therefore, field commanders came under bitter criticism from the public, rather than go round explaining to everyone that soldiers were hungry, all formations created what was known as "Survival Companies." For each Division, there was a survival company made up of convalescing officers and men. These companies helped to relieve the food shortage. It did this by growing some food in rear areas and also harvesting crops abandoned close to the front lines, and at times, behind the lines. When any areas were cleared of the enemy, survival companies moved in quickly and removed whatever they could, in the way of food, before a counterattack by the enemy. This system soon became the most reliable source of food for field units. Those who did not benefit from this practice were the rear units because they were not allowed by Divisions to operate "Survival units" in their sectors.

Survival companies notwithstanding, the problem of hunger within the Army remained unsolved and cases of kwashiokor were on the increase among front-line troops. This, as should be expected, adversely affected morale and will-power. Soldiers admitted into hospital for battle injuries ended up as kwashiokor cases, thereby making recovery either very slow or impossible.

Soldiers in the rear were left with only one alternative — stealing from the local farms. This was an exstremely risky business because whenever they were caught by civilians they were killed on the spot. In August, 1969, four hungry and convalescing soldiers from Army Garrison at Isu, went to a nearby farm and dug up some yams to eat. They were caught but two of them managed to escape. The other two were killed on the spot by local farmers. It was with difficulty that Biafra Army Headquarters prevented a massive military retaliation by men of the Garrison. The sum total of the ugly food situation was that a good number of soldiers in the front lines either moved back in search of food or stayed on and fraternised with the enemy in the hope of getting presents of food and cigarettes from him.

Transport and the Transport Directorate

The operational procedure of the Transport Directorate was similar to that of the Food Directorate. As a result, the armed forces experienced similar difficulties. At the beginning of the war, Infantry battalions had as many as 200 lorries and as many cars as they cared to keep. As the Goverment could neither replace these vehicles with new ones nor even repair them due to lack of spares, the number of vehicles on the road decreased rapidly. At the same time, the Army expanded with equal rapidity and so did the demand for vehicles, from both the Army and the civil population.

Issue of vehicles or spares to individuals or formations was based almost entirely on "old boy's net" during the last six months of the war. By then it was easier for a popular junior rank to get things from this Directorate than the Army Commander. For instance, I could not get a replacement for the gasket of my staff car, which was burnt during the Umuahia battles in April, 1969, until the war ended. I was fully aware that many junior officers and civilians were replacing their gaskets at will and frequently, too. General Ojukwu's solution to this problem was that I should find a popular enough officer to go and get it for me. I did not find one.

When authority was given to units and formations to commandeer vehicles for their use, the privilege was abused and the situation worsened. Individuals set up illegal road blocks and converted the vehicles they commandeered into personal use. Army authorities could do nothing to check this malpractice for it was difficult to differentiate between such commandeered vehicles and legitimately acquired private-owned vehicles. Moreover those who indulged in this practice made sure they did not bring the vehicles into military establishments for fear of confiscation. By the middle of 1969, very few vehicles were available to the Army, and some units had none at all. Casualties were either abandoned or evacuated by use of porters whenever possible. The Army Electrical and Mechanical Engineers Unit was in existence but hardly functioned. The reason was that spare parts, when they were available, went direct to the Directorate and other allied transport organisations but

113

never to the Army. Army vehicles had to be sent to the Directorate for repairs, and there they took their turn with hundreds of other vehicles sent in by civilian organisations.

Army Headquarters, in a memorandum signed personally by me, put up a suggestion to the Head of State requesting that all vehicles intended for the Army be issued in bulk to Ordnance Depot for orderly distribution to Army units. It was further suggested that the Directorate should make available to Army Headquarters, details of all vehicles already issued to the Army, to enable it to recover and redistribute them properly on basis of need. These simple measures could have given Army Headquarters better control of vehicles available to it, but unfortunately the Head of State considered them unnecessary and rather provocative. His view was that the Army should set up road blocks and recover these vehicles — a system that had been tried several times without success. The majority of those stopped at the check points either claimed that they were driving their personal cars or that they were using unit vehicles for urgent military assignments. Any attempt to check every such story could have caused serious disruption within the Army. No further attempt was made by the Army towards solving this problem, the effects of which were seen very clearly later.

Fuel and the Fuel Directorate

The problem of fuel was closely interwoven with that of transport. As soon as Port Harcourt fell in May, 1968 and, with it, most of the oil fields and the refinery, a shortage of fuel was felt all over the country. A Petroleum Management Board (PMB) was established to control what was available as well as find ways of affecting replenishments. The Board designed and built a sizeable and efficient fuel refinery at Uzuakoli. What they produced was not sufficient for the needs of a nation at war, thereby making petrol rationing imperative. The Research and Production Board, which considered no problem impossible to solve, soon stepped in to assist. It designed and built several refineries and produced petrol and

114

diesel at a considerably fast rate. With its initial assistance also, all major armed forces units and formations, as well as civilian organisations, set up oil refineries. Products of these numerous refineries were generally fair and satisfied the urgent fuel needs of the nation even after the main refinery at Uzuakoli was lost to the enemy.

With the completion of their new refinery at Amandugba near Owerri, the PMB grew resentful of the practice of uncontrolled fuel refining within the country. Pressure was brought to bear on General Ojukwu by the middle of 1969 to ban all oil refining except by PMB. He did this through an appropriate Decree. The reasons given by PMB for wanting an absolute monopoly in the field of fuel refining were logical and good. The Board revealed that the quality of products from the mushroom refineries was so poor that they damaged the few vehicles available. They also pointed out that most of the fuel produced was diverted for sale on the black market for the benefit of individuals.

Unfortunately when all refineries closed down, the PMB developed so many problems that it was almost impossible for it to produce petrol on any meaningful scale. First was the problem of shortage of tankers for the collection of crude oil. To combat this the Army and all other bodies holding all tankers were ordered to hand them over to the Board. Yet, no petrol flowed, for the electricity supply had broken down. Army Headquarters responded by making available to the Board the generator that supplied light to the Headquarters. Still no petrol flowed because the road to Egbema oil field was so bad that vehicles got bogged down. When the road was repaired, enemy aircrafts destroyed a good number of tankers on their way to collect crude. When the tankers were repaired, the same aircrafts damaged the refinery itself. There was no end to the problems which were real, and could not be blamed on anybody. As a result, no petrol was delivered to the Army for a whole month. When the Board eventually started production, the average quantity of fuel made available per Brigade was 20 gallons per day. I was in full sympathy with the PMB which worked round the clock to overcome their insurmountable problems. All the same my heart ached for the Army whose fuel problems by October, 1969 were simply pathetic.

In a desperate effort to solve this problem, I forwarded a memorandum to the Head of State. In it, I put up a suggestion that Army and Division Headquarters should be allowed to revive their refineries if the war was to continue. To ensure that PMB efforts were not disrupted, I suggested that units devise their own methods for crude oil evacuation, other than by the use of tankers, which should all remain with PMB and the Directorate for Fuel Supply (DFS) which distributed refined products. I also suggested that the PMB should give the Army exact times of the day or night for collection of crude, to further ensure that PMB operations were not hampered. These suggestions were turned down by the Head of State for reasons I do not know. Military administrative support for the fighting forces ground to a halt. Towards the end of the war, reinforcements, supply of food, and ammunition and the evacuation of casualties were all done on foot, over very long distances. By December, 1969, the rules on refining were relaxed for Army Headquarters and 14 Division which defended the oil field itself. Within a fortnight, the two formations had produced a considerably large quantity of fuel and were helping other formations. The only difficulty came from Colonel Joe Achuzia, who, as the officer responsible for the prevention of illegal refining, ambushed and seized most of the crude on its way from Egbema to Army Headquarters. He may not have been told about the relaxation of the rules, but he continued this practice even after he had been reported to the Head of State several times.

Clothing and the Clothing Directorate

Several other Directorates such as Clothing, Housing, Propaganda, Requisition and Supply and Medical rendered invaluable assistance to the armed forces. Of these, the closest to the Army and the only one worth mentioning here in any measure of detail is the Clothing Directorate. Clothing was the first administrative difficulty experienced by the Biafran Army. By the end of October, 1967 the problem was already acute. In December that year, I ordered all staff officers in Army Headquarters, particularly those who came back to Biafra from the Nigeria Army, to give up all their army uniforms in excess of two suits. I also gave up mine and these were issued to soldiers within the Headquarters who still wore civilian dress. In most units a good percentage of soldiers wore civilian dress with the Biafra Sun sewn on to indicate they were soldiers. The Clothing Directorate evacuated baft from Aba and Onitsha textile mills, dyed them green, and sewed uniforms for the Army. Only a small percentage of the Army got these uniforms which were grossly insufficient and incapable of enduring more than a fortnight of battle.

When, however, Onitsha, Port Harcourt and Aba had fallen, and all big markets were lost, the problem of clothing assumed crisis proportions. From then on, anything with the Biafra Sun was acceptable as army uniform. When civil dress was no more available or too expensive for soldiers to buy, a lot of them went damned in rags. Divisions received, on the average, about fifty pairs of boots every six months for issue to the troops under command and in most cases, these did not go beyond the confines of the Divisional Headquarters. The luxury of steel helmets was never contemplated; neither were dialogues held in earnest which could lead to the acquisition of ammunition poaches and haversacks. Admittedly the last two items could well have been unnecessary for troops who hardly held more than a maximum of ten rounds of ammunition at any given time and had absolutely no other items of military kit to carry. Colds and pneumonia were frequent with the frontline troops. At a certain stage of the war there were more casualties inflicted on the Army by the weather than by the enemy.

The enemy, realising that we wore no boots, surrounded his defensive positions with broken bottles and sharp objects to discourage an infantry charge by our troops. This very simple device was effective. Biafran soldiers soon formed an opinion that the only way to get boots and clothes was to capture them in battle, and this belief ruined numerous operations which could have otherwise been very successful. As it was, as soon as our troops overran their first objective, they halted to defrock prisoners and enemy casualties, thereby losing the momentum of the attack. Before they realised what they were doing, the enemy would be staging a counterattack. As soon as the enemy realised this weakness on our part, he began to abandon items of clothing on his pre-arranged artillery and mortar targets, as bait. It was virtually impossible to stop this practice with soldiers who would always tell you they had no alternative but to do what they were doing.

The Biafran soldier therefore fought for almost three years naked, hungry and without ammunition. All he had was his will to survive and a genuine determination to realise this aim. It will be seen later how he did it. The first four lines of a popular frontline song within the Biafran Army illustrates the cynical attitude of the soldiers to the acute shortage of administrative items to support them:

> Take my boots off when I die
> Send my clothings to the camp
> Give my gun to someone else
> to fight for fatherland, etc.

RELATIVE STRENGTHS OF NIGERIAN AND BIAFRAN FORCES

With limited resources available to it, it was obvious that the Biafran Army could not win a war against Nigeria. One was not even sure whether the Army could put up a meaningful defence. Apart from any new additions it may have made since the crisis, the Nigeria Army was a formidable force in comparison with what Biafra had. Nigeria had an Army of six battalions, well equipped by modern standards. In support were two artillery units holding a total of 16 x 105 mm Pack Howtzers in addition to two Reconnaissance Squadrons equipped with ferret and saladine armoured vehicles, not to mention mortars of various calibres. It had a sizeable Navy and Air Force that could be made combat ready at short notice. Biafra had none of these and the prospects of getting them were rather remote.

In support of their belief that Nigeria would never attack Biafra, Biafrans argued that, having destroyed thousands of Biafran lives and property, the Nigerians were more likely to be sorry for what had happened, and would therefore avoid further bloodshed at all costs. Others argued that as Biafra had never accepted Gowon's rule, any attack from Lagos would amount to a continuation of the July 1966 coup. It was therefore thought that the whole world would either watch in absolute neutrality or perhaps come out in support of Biafra which represented the rump of a universally recognised Ironsi's Nigeria. Others, assuming that the initial Northern Nigeria coup objectives (to massacre the Southerners and secede from Nigeria) were still the same, argued that an attack on Biafra by Lagos would be pointless. They held the view that Southerners had been massacred and the North was then in a position to secede without a challenge from any quarter of Nigeria. To support their argument they never failed to point out that Gowon was already flying the flag of his new Republic at Ikeja barracks, having said that there was no basis for unity in Nigeria.

Logical as all this reasoning seemed, we were proved wrong and we realised this fact rather too late. For Gowon had new aims and objectives and as soon as he was ready, almost the entire world closed ranks and gave him all the assistance he wanted. But then, a new precedent had been created in Africa. Anybody who intends to overthrow his government only has to gain control of the capital. To complete his task, he stands entitled to assistance from the rest of the world. Another point we probably overlooked was the fact that Gowon had been winning all the time since July, 1966 and the natural tendency would be for him to continue to attack.

II

THE WAR

Chapter 7

NIGERIA'S INITIAL ATTACKS AND BIAFRA'S EFFECTIVE COUNTER-OFFENSIVES

Ogoja Battles

At the beginning of June, 1967, I handed over the command of the 7th Battalion to Major Adigio, and thereafter directed my efforts towards establishing a headquarters for the newly created 51 Brigade which I was to command. My continued stay at Nsukka was merely to enable me to carry out this assignment, using the material and human resources available in the 7th Battalion as no further issues were to be made to the new headquarters. Soon my Brigade Headquarters was functioning with a staff captain, Captain Nebo, a clerk and five other soldiers. The town of Udi was selected as the permanent Brigade Headquarters location and the target date for me to be fully "operational" there was 12th July, 1967. By the end of June, 1967 whatever I had been able to pinch from the 7th Battalion was loaded into a vehicle and despatched to Udi with an advance party of ten men.

In view of the massive Nigerian troop movements, and a reported concentration in Makurdi I planned to visit all battalions under my command between the 5th and 9th of July, 1967 before settling down at my new headquarters in Udi. My intention was therefore to inspect from the 5th to the 7th July the First Battalion at Ogoja, and the 14th Battalion at Abakaliki on the 7th and 8th of July and then return to Nsukka on the 9th. The aim of this tour was to alert the field commanders on the impending invasion and ensure they were making necessary preparations to counter it.

I arrived at Ogoja in good time on 5th July for lunch with Major

Amadi, the Commanding Officer. All appeared normal in Ogoja and from Amadi's briefing, his three Companies deployed, one each at Garkem, Obudu and Akpoha bridge, had not reported any unusual movements or occurrences in their sectors of operation. The 4th Company was still at Onitsha bridge head. I expressed my desire to visit all Company locations starting with Garkem, immediately after lunch, and continuing with Obudu and Akpoha the following day, 6th July.

At Garkem, about 30 miles from Ogoja town, the defensive position was pathetically inadequate. The entire Company, under two Second Lieutenants, sat together on the outskirts of the town, on both sides of the Garkem-Afikpo road, watching very keenly the long stretch of grassland in front of them which formed the Nigeria-Biafra territorial boundary. These young officers who appeared totally lost, explained that both the company commander, Captain Ude and his second-in-command, Captain Ojukwu, were ill and admitted in Ogoja General Hospital.

Ignoring the fact that they may not have had a chance of being trained I severely reprimanded them for apparent idleness. Together with Major Amadi, I selected trench positions and sighted the company machine guns. I then ordered the digging of trenches which must be completed for my inspection the following morning. In order to get the officers and men to understand the need for trenches, I explained that unless they had trenches, they would have to abandon their position and flee, or stay and be killed, should the enemy decide to shell them. I was merely trying to spur them into working harder, for I was almost convinced Nigeria would not use such weapons on us, even if she decided to use force.

The only complaint the company had was that Garkem natives appeared to be unwilling to assist the Army in any way. Trench digging was in full swing and to make the setting more military, I ordered a reconnaissance patrol to go out and obtain information from the enemy territory. With that on, I left the location for Ogoja at 1800 hours.

That night, a small party was arranged at the Progress Hotel in my honour by a few senior government officials. Among those present were the Provincial Secretary, Mr. Nwakoby; the Provincial Police boss. Mr. Aguliefo; the Provincial Magistrate, Mr. Onyechi and a few others. Major Amadi was the only military personnel in attendance besides me. It was a good party and lasted till 0200 hours on the 6th of July. As we went to bed I never dreamt that was going to be the first and almost the last party I was to attend in Biafra, for a major war, quite unknown to anyone, was only three hours away.

THE BATTLE OF GARKEM

Mr. Nwakoby woke up Major Amadi and I at 0600 hours on the morning of the 6th of July. He was wet with sweat and his shaky hand just about managed to hold on to the cigarette he was smoking. With a stutter, he said he had been hearing some heavy rumbling noise in two directions towards the North, since 0530 hours. He expressed his fear that it was some sort of military action. We all went outside to listen again, more carefully and it was indeed the sound of heavy artillery shelling we were hearing. In less than ten minutes Amadi and I were in his battalion headquarters three miles away from the house. There, the duty officer explained that he had received no reports from the forward troops, and he had assumed that what we had been hearing all morning was heavy thunder. He had not quite finished talking when the first set of casualties began to come in with the story that the war was indeed on. The Company had absolutely no wireless communication.

The enemy attacked in Garkem at 0530 hours with two battalions, advancing on two axes right and left of the main Garkem-Afikpo road. His preparatory bombardment using artillery and heavy mortars was extremely heavy and sustained. Our own troops, even though they had suffered some casualties, were still firmly in their newly dug trenches but with no over-head cover. By 0900 hours the first enemy assault of three ferret and one saladine armoured vehicles came in. A landrover mounted with a 106 RR anti-tank gun moved in with the attacking armoured vehicles which rained bullets in all directions and knocked down the mud huts of the village. As the vehicles approached the trenches, our troops were

125

ordered to withdraw to both flanks and advance to make contact with enemy infantry if they could be seen.

Thus, bypassing the armoured vehicles in the village, our troops soon made contact with the two assaulting enemy infantry battalions which were advancing half-heartedly some 400 yards away from the village. Fighting began with each enemy battalion poised against two platoons of Biafran Army. After two hours of intensive exchange of fire, the enemy turned round and broke into a run towards their start line. They were obviously surprised and for that reason suffered heavy casualties, and conceded a number of prisoners of war. One of them turned out to be a bore for he spent several hours muttering to himself "in other words, the Biafrans have arms and ammunition." No one could stop him!

The Biafran troops, anxious to exploit their success, continued to advance but soon ran into heavy enemy fire both from the front and from the armoured vehicles which were now speeding back to rejoin their troops. Our troops again moved to the flanks to allow these monsters to pass. From there, the troops returned to their trenches at Garkem to face a fiercer concentration of artillery and mortar fire, the intensity of which showed clearly that it was meant to be a punitive measure from an angry enemy. Thanks to the trenches dug the previous night our troops could withstand the bombardment.

Reorganisation in the midst of this bombardment was a near impossibility. One of the Second Lieutenants was already a casualty, and the Regimental Signals Officer, Captain Anah, was dispatched to command the Company. Before midday, the enemy put in another attack, this time with the infantry following closely behind the armour. While the enemy attack was coming from the right flank, Captain Anah was already advancing through the left to attack the enemy concentration at the rear. His operation was extremely successful. The concentration was completely disorganised and the soldiers there fled. Anah's force, too weak to attempt to hold any ground, destroyed as much enemy equipment as they could and brought with them those things they could carry together with a few prisoners for interrogation.

When our attacking troops returned from their mission, they discovered that the town of Garkem had virtually fallen into the hands of the enemy who were using completely fresh troops for their second attempt. Most of the enemy infantry men were still lagging behind on the outskirts of the town while the armoured vehicles and the 106 gun ravaged and destroyed the town. The two platoons left behind at Garkem had resisted enemy entry into the town for over two hours and had withdrawn to the outskirts. Captain Anah, dropping off all he had captured including the prisoners, launched another attack from the rear against enemy infantry. For one reason or the other, enemy guns and mortars opened up a short but an intensive bombardment on both our troops and enemy troops in the town. In the confusion that followed, all troops got mixed up and scattered in various directions — the Biafrans running down South, and the Northerners, up North. Only the armoured vehicles remained in the town of Garkem.

As the enemy resumed heavy shelling of Garkem and environs, our own troops reorganised the best they could south of Garkem. There was no question of counter bombardment to silence enemy guns for no guns or mortars were available to us. But the greatest menace remained the presence of the armoured vehicles in the absence of anti-tank weapons. The enemy had by now switched round troops more than three times and Biafran troops were extremely tired and depleted. Besides, the Battalion Headquarters defence platoon, sent up at 1000 hours as reinforcement, had been fighting all day without a single break for rest, food or water. As fresh enemy infantry entered Garkem by 1600 hours, Anah again put in a flanking attack with two platoons, which represented what was left of his Company. Even at this stage enemy infantry still ran but then the whole operation was proving obviously futile, particularly when the gallant Anah sustained an ugly shell wound on the right leg. We had learnt from this battle that we were not going to have much difficulty dealing with enemy infantry. What remained to be sorted out, and quickly too, was the problem posed by the guns, mortars and the armoured vehicles.

By 1600 hours, Biafran troops, completely exhausted, were

digging in and constructing obstacles against armoured vehicles, three miles south of Garkem. Though taken aback by the unexpected weight and nature of the attack, they had developed high spirits and morale with the realisation that the enemy soldiers were no better than they were. When before dark, the enemy again advanced towards their new defensive line, the soldiers fought very well to check further advance for the day.

The Battle of Obudu

While the battle of Garkem raged, a similar battle based almost on the same pattern and tactics had developed at Obudu. The "D" Company of the First Battalion, stationed at Obudu, was extremely strong and well led by experienced Captain Michael Olehi. More than half of his Company of 450 men were old Nigerian soldiers with the commander himself in a position to boast of 18 years of military service. At the end of two hours of bombardment which lasted from 0600 to 0800 hours, the enemy put in a straight forward infantry battalion attack. This was quickly halted and beaten back. We followed up with an immediate counterattack which was so successful that the enemy was completely routed and set on the run. Enemy casualties were very heavy and the amount of stores, equipment and weapons captured, considerable. During the almost uncontrollable chase which followed many enemy stragglers were taken prisoners. By midday we had captured enough weapons to form another armed platoon, the only limitation being the restricted quantity of ammunition captured with these weapons.

Later in the afternoon, the enemy again attacked with a fresh battalion. The shelling was heavy but the enemy infantry effort was poor. They were again beaten back and chased towards Ishangev, on the Adikpo road. From then on the enemy did nothing but shell our position. We could not shell them back, neither could we go into the offensive because of our obvious inadequacy in equipment, communications and administrative support. The day at Obudu ended in a stalemate.

INITIAL BATTLES AT NSUKKA

I got in touch with the 7th Battalion at Nsukka over the rear link to find out the situation there at 0700 hours on the 6th. I spoke to the second-in-command of the battalion, Major Ben Gbulie, who said his battalion commander Major Adigio had gone forward. According to him, besides the free use of para-illuminating bombs and flares, used for the first time the previous night by the enemy, everywhere was still calm. He expressed his fears and anxiety about the tense situation but was confident they would do their best.

One hour later, Major Gbulie was on the air telling me that the enemy had launched massive attacks on two fronts — Ankpa-Ogugu-Enugu Ezike and Ida-Adoru-Okutu. On both axes, he said, the enemy was shelling massively and advancing with armoured vehicles, despite all attempts by our troops to stop them. He wanted me to return to Nsukka soonest to assist them. I agreed with him because I knew the ground and troops over there pretty well.

In the evening, a Biafran Air Force helicopter came up to Ogoja to collect a sitrep for Army Headquarters and I decided to go down to Enugu with it on my way to Nsukka. At Army Headquarters Enugu, the Army Commander, Lt. Colonel Njoku ordered that I should go back and look after Ogoja sector while I established my Brigade Headquarters at Abakaliki. He revealed that he had already sent for Lt. Colonel Eze, Commander 52 Brigade, to come up from Uyo and take command of Nsukka sector. In the meantime, he explained, Lt. Colonel Efiong was already at Nsukka to hold on till the arrival of Eze.

I got more details of the fighting at Nsukka from Njoku. The enemy force, advancing on the Okutu axis, had pounded their way through Okutu town and were short of Okuje despite their heavy casualties. On the Enugu Ezike axis, the enemy had passed or bypassed most of the obstacles with armoured vehicles, and were already in control of Ete and beyond, to about two miles from Enugu Ezike town. Njoku was very unhappy and paced his office ceaselessly. He said that with all the fighting going on the whole day, he had failed to convince Ojukwu to show or tell him where the available arms and ammunition were hidden. As a result, he went on, it was impossible to plan and issue any sensible orders to the fighting troops, for he had very little ammunition left under his control. I could do nothing about this but console him before I left for Abakaliki that night. It was however distressing that even with a war on, mutual confidence had not been restored among top military leaders.

I moved into the 14th Battalion temporary location at Abakaliki, where I started all over again trying to form a brigade headquarters. All I had was Captain Nebo, my driver and a staff car. The first day of fighting had shown quite clearly we would get into serious trouble soon, unless the Nigerians stopped their attacks or a miracle happened in our favour. Right then, we simply had no answer to the military might of Nigeria as already displayed in one day. Major Ohanehi, the commanding officer of the 15th Battalion rendered all assistance he could, and in less than 24 hours I was operating a Brigade Headquarters with a skeleton staff of four men in a building of three rooms.

THE DESTRUCTION OF ENEMY AT OBOLLO AFOR

My newly established Headquarters became the 51 Brigade Headquarters with the First and the 15th Battalions under command, and Nsukka sector was detached as a separate and independent 53 Brigade. As time went on, the situation at Ogoja was deteriorating with mounting enemy pressure particularly on the Garkem front. No reinforcements were available and the Company that started the fight was hardly more than a platoon after three days of continuous fighting. Even though the Obudu front remained stable, there was increasing danger of its being cut off if any further advance was made by the enemy into Ogoja town. If that happened, the Company could only rejoin the Battalion by withdrawing southwards to Ikom and then to Iyahe on the Ogoja-Abakaliki main road. That distance of 100 miles of almost unmotorable road should have taken them almost a month to complete.

By the time a detachment of 150 men arrived at Ogoja from

Obudu, as reinforcement for Garkem, the town of Ogoja was badly threatened. 12th Battalion which was ordered to move from Ahoada to Ogoja by Army Headquarters, had not arrived and the withdrawal of the First Battalion from Ogoja was ordered by Army Headquarters. The enemy was already in full control of the town by the time 12th Battalion began to arrive. The first two companies that arrived were deployed on a defensive role, one at Okpoma bridge 12 miles from Ogoja, on the main axis, and the other at Ikom from where it would patrol to Ajasso bridge at the Cameroun-Biafra boundary.

On the 4th day also Nsukka town had fallen when I checked with Major Gbulie over the army wireless net. In fact, Gbulie had told me that the 7th Battalion was reorganising at Eke, with the Brigade Headquarters at Ukehe, 20 miles from Enugu. I had not realised then that the situation was all that bad, so when I opened a map and saw a town called Eke, 15 miles inside Northern Nigeria, I thought that was the one he meant. I was glad, but could not understand why the infantry should be moving forward while the Brigade Headquarters was moving back. I rechecked with him and found to my utter amazement that the Eke he meant was barely 12 miles to Enugu, capital of Biafra. At that particular time, the only force on the road between Nsukka and Enugu was the 53 Brigade Headquarters. If the enemy had made any attempt to advance on the 10th of July they would have had absolutely no difficulty driving straight into Enugu without opposition.

My view at the time was that if Enugu fell, the war was virtually over and lost, and, having started fighting, the people of Biafra did not want such an abrupt end. For this reason, I put forward some proposals to Army Headquarters, aimed at checking more effectively any further advance of the enemy from Nsukka. My view was that the whole of my Brigade less the 12th Battalion should move to Eha Amufu and from there conduct offensive operations against the enemy at Nsukka from the right flank. This would give 53 Brigade some breathing space for reorganisation and, subsequently, joining in a two brigade offensive to destroy the enemy at Nsukka. According to this plan, 12th Battalion would remain in their present

131

defensive locations around Ogoja, and if they were further pushed, they could always fall back behind River Aya, blow the bridge, and defend the riverline indefinitely.

I am glad the Army Commander completely agreed to this plan. While the necessary moves were going on, policemen and civilian volunteers called Militia had moved up to the front. Fighting with little or nothing, they were able to keep the enemy confined to Nsukka town. I moved my Brigade Headquarters to Eha Amufu town and the First Battalion to Obolo Eke, one and a half miles from the Northern Nigeria border. The 14th Battalion deployed two Companies at Agaya on the Ikem-Nsukka road. The battalion headquarters and the remainder of the battalion remained at Eha Amufu with me as the brigade reserve. Morale was pretty low in First Battalion because of the withdrawal from Ogoja. Even though they looked tired and battered, I still prefered to use them for the first offensive if it was going to be impressive as well as effective. 15th Battalion had not yet seen action but were fresh and green, and not nearly as well equipped as the First. I spoke to all ranks of the First Battalion at a muster parade in an attempt to improve on their morale. In a one hour's address I reminded the men of the reasons why we were fighting, praised them for the efforts they had already made, and explained the consequences of losing the struggle. I think I said almost all the nice and encouraging things one is supposed to tell a distressed soldier. Apparently this worked, for the parade ended up in song — songs and war songs, and everyone wanting to fight. With that, we began to plan the next offensive.

51 Brigade under my command managed to complete its reorganisation and rest without interruption by the enemy. I was also aware of the fact that the enemy was concentrating at Obollo Afor for a final massive thrust through 53 Brigade area to Enugu through Opi Junction and Ukehe. Such a move could never have been checked by 53 Brigade judging from the state of morale and battle worthiness of the Brigade. The need therefore for my brigade to act quickly was urgent. My outline plan for the operation, as approved by the Army Headquarters was as follows:

Four strong companies of the First Battalion, each of 250 men, were to be moved through the right flank of Obollo Eke to Obollo Afor, leaving behind two companies to guard the base and defend all flanks to the right of it. At Obollo Afor, A and B Companies would attack the market. Having cleared it, A company would reorganise in the market and thereafter assume the role of a reserve force for future attacks or exploitations. B Company would exploit to a maximum of one mile westwards towards Enugu Ezike. C Company was to be in a strong ambush position along the Obollo Afor-Orokam road. Their task was to prevent enemy soldiers or their equipment from escaping to Northern Nigeria as well as preventing reinforcements from that Region coming into Obollo Afor. On orders, the Company would exploit to the border three miles away and re-occupy the trenches we had there before the war. The task of D Company was to attack and clear the Rest House on the left of the market. From there they would wheel left and exploit southwards towards Opi with a view to making contact with 53 Brigade elements. They were, however, not to exploit beyond the town of Eha Alumona, so as to have an opportunity to withdraw through Ikem route if we suddenly lost Obollo Afor again.

In arriving at this plan, I got very little information from the 53 Brigade in whose area we were about to operate. I was not sure where the Brigade headquarters and its subordinate units were located, but I knew they were not in Obollo Afor. Neither Colonel Eze nor myself had the time for a liaison visit but I sent a note telling Eze what we were about to do in sufficient detail. In addition, I requested that his Brigade should put in diversionary attacks on various objectives around Nsukka town to prevent the enemy from concentrating all his resources at Nsukka into Obollo Afor, as reinforcement.

The support available to First Battalion was impressive by our standards at the time; after all they were the only unit within the Army that had any form of heavy support. There were 2 x 81 mm Tempella mortars with 68 rounds as well as 3 x 3" mortars with 100 rounds. These mortars and bombs were left behind at Enugu when the battalion was at Ogoja because nobody imagined that the war, if it came would assume such proportions. We were now going to

133

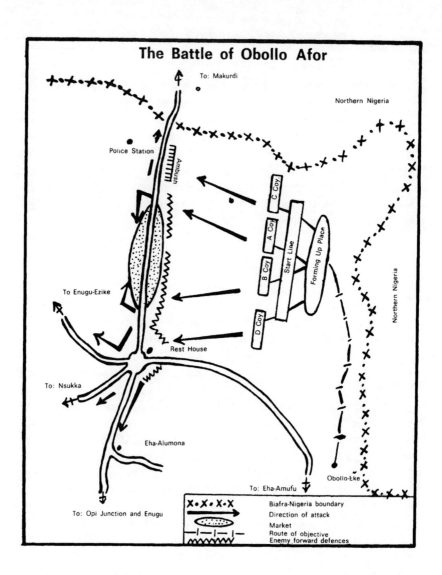

The Battle of Obollo Afor

To: Makurdi

Northern Nigeria

Police Station

Ambush

C. Coy

A. Coy

B. Coy

Start Line

Forming Up Place

To: Enugu-Ezike

D. Coy

Rest House

Northern Nigeria

To: Nsukka

Eha-Alumona

Obollo-Eke

To: Eha-Amufu

To: Opi Junction and Enugu

X•X•X•X	Biafra-Nigeria boundary
→	Direction of attack
⬭	Market
–I–I–I–	Route of objective
⌇⌇⌇	Enemy forward defences

134

launch our first deliberate offensive of the war and it was therefore imperative that we put in everything to impress and frighten the enemy. For this reason, I ordered that 90 rounds of 3″ mortar bombs and 50 rounds of 81 mm bombs should be used for the offensive leaving as a reserve only 10 and 18 rounds respectively. Natives of Obollo Afor and Obollo Eke were only too willing to help with detailed reconnaissance of routes and acted as guides and porters. At the last minute an additional plan to attack the gun positions at Orokam with a platoon, during the attack, was called off as being unlikely to succeed due to the long distance involved. All was ready and the D-day was fixed for 20th of July at 0530 hours.

On the 19th of July, 1967 at 2200 hours, the long column of soldiers, guides and porters, moved out in a single file from Obollo Eke on its way to Obollo Afor. Control and direction were maintained by guides posted at one mile intervals all along the 8-mile route to the objective. The need for guides was absolutely necessary to ensure companies did not stray into Northern Nigeria which was as near as 400 yards in some places along the route. The native porters and guides were so excited that we were always at alert to stop any of them bursting into a war song. By 0300 hours the following day, troops were already in their forming up places and making final preparations. Mortars were laid and their bombs prepared. Ammunition was distributed to individual soldiers. All was ready by 0430 hours and as the troops moved to their startlines, the civilian guides and porters were left at the forming up places. They however had instructions to move to the forward administration base, two miles further back, if their present location became untenable.

At exactly 0530 hours the mortars opened up on the market and the Rest House. Cheers could be heard from our soldiers in all locations. They simply could not restrain their joy because for the first time, we were shelling the enemy. In less than ten minutes the shells were exhausted and the mortars were silent, but there was no doubt we had made a terrifying impact on the enemy. Soon enemy counter bombardment began with two artillery guns and about 8 x 81mm mortars. As enemy showered bombs and shells in all

135

directions, our own troops were already advancing towards their objectives. Before long very heavy fighting had begun in C Company location where the sound of ferret cars and browning machine guns were evident. Also very heavy vehicle movements started in many directions — some appeared to be moving northwards out of the battle area, while others seemed to be moving south into it from the Northern Region. During the encounter C Company destroyed several vehicles and an armoured car. Even though some enemy vehicles and men managed to escape to the North, scarcely any reinforcement got into Obollo Afor.

A and B Companies fought in the market place until 0930 hours and inflicted extremely heavy casualties on the enemy but had to return to the startline to get more ammunition issued and to reform. The system of returning to the startline for ammunition was the only solution to the unavailability of ammunition pouches. While A and B Companies reformed and reorganised, C and D Companies remained in action.

At 1100 hours, both A and B Companies again advanced into their second assault while D Company halted to rest and reform. Thus the fighting went on wave after wave amid an ever increasing enemy heavy bombardment. The decrease in the volume of small arms fire by the enemy was very noticeable. By 1645 hours, B Company, which had almost achieved its objective noticed what appeared to be a strong enemy force advancing from the left towards the market. B Company wheeled left and engaged this new force inflicting very heavy casualties on it. It was rather odd that rather than return fire against B Company, the enemy force appeared to be engaging a completely different target on the extreme left flank of the market. As our troops closed in on this enemy force, it was soon identified as our own D Company. Apparently the Company had cleared the Rest House, and rather than wheel left towards Opi as instructed, wheeled right towards the market in pursuit of fleeing enemy soldiers. In doing this they had moved into the objective of B Company. This unhappy and demoralising incident created a lot of doubts as to who was exactly where.

The time was about 1715 hours and it was decided to call off the attack, after 12 hours of non-stop fighting. Our own troops were rather disappointed for not being able to clear Obollo Afor despite a spirited effort such as we put in. I was personally unhappy too at the thought that, if the strongest force in Biafra could not clear the town of Obollo Afor, we had very little chance of clearing any other town, let alone Nsukka. Even though the enemy must have used over 4000 rounds of shells for the battle, the shelling was inaccurate and resulted in low casualty, except for D Company where we inflicted the casualties on ourselves, in error. Throughout the fighting, there was no sign of any military activity in 53 Brigade area and this, of course, made the task much more difficult.

All troops that took part in the Obollo Afor operation were back to base at Obollo Eke before first light on the 21st of July. That day, in the morning, some native civilians from Obollo Afor reported to Major Amadi, the commanding officer of First Battalion, that the enemy was no more at Obollo Afor. Rather, they said, the town was littered with hundreds of dead enemy soldiers as well as wrecked vehicles and equipment. They said that already, many villagers were coming out of hiding and returning to their houses, while burial of the dead and general tidying up of the town had begun. A strong Company was immediately despatched to investigate the story but not to fight if the enemy was still occupying the town. The Company found the story to be absolutely correct. 53 Brigade had also got the information and sent soldiers to evacuate all abandoned stores and equipment, leaving behind only the dead.

I was angry with 53 Brigade for what they had done, for it was fully aware that the only way a unit could add to its resources and become stronger was to capture those things in battle. It was therefore unfair of them to have removed everything. I asked Amadi to despatch another Company to Obollo Afor to join the one already there so that they could garrison the town till such a time 53 Brigade took over their responsibility. Amadi, apparently also very infuriated with the action of 53 Brigade decided to walk the 8 miles to Obollo Afor and from there visit 53 Brigade Headquarters and lodge his protest. Taking a big and perhaps unnecessary personal risk, he went through Eha-Alumona, Opi and finally found the Brigade

Headquarters at Ukehe. He threatened in anger to launch a battalion attack against the whole of 53 Brigade unless they returned whatever they took away from Obollo Afor battlefields. Colonel Eze, the Brigade Commander, soon succeeded in appeasing him and offered him some drinks. In a more friendly atmosphere Amadi convinced the Brigade Headquarters to move up a bit towards Opi. This they did the following morning and thereafter consolidated their defences around Nsukka more solidly. The Obollo Afor battle was therefore a complete success. It not only destroyed the enemy concentration completely but also gave the 53 Brigade sufficient time to get itself ready for combat once again.

ENEMY'S DISASTER AT OBOLLO EKE

As his diversionary measure to assist Nsukka, the enemy began further moves in the Ogoja sector which had been quiet and neglected for some time. Employing all his usual support of artillery, mortars and armoured vehicles, the enemy attacked on the main axis from Okuku towards Utukpo and Iyahe bridge. The men of 12th Battalion of the Biafran Army put up magnificient resistance for six days. Finally on the 6th of August our own troops were compelled to withdraw behind the river and to blow the Iyahe bridge. On the enemy side, the armoured vehicles again stole the show. Still completely lacking in anti-tank weapons, we had not found an answer to the armoured car menace. Ditches, traps and obstacles we constructed simply delayed but did not prevent enemy advance.

Once deployed behind the Iyahe riverline it became necessary to redeploy the 12th Battalion whose main threat had shifted from the west to the north. One company was left to defend the riverline while the rest of the battalion, with its Headquarters at Ngbo, was deployed to cover all approaches from the north between Agala and Aloma to the west. By this deployment, I obtained the best concentration and control of my Brigade for the defence of over 80 miles of frontier. It was now possible to plan brigade operations involving up to two of the battalions at a time.

So far, all operations within my Brigade had been planned and executed within the formation. It was almost impossible for Army Headquarters to give tasks to field units because not only was the enemy many times stronger than we were, it was only a field commander who could correctly determine what task he could accomplish having given careful consideration to his resources as well as anticipated opposition. Enemy reaction to his great losses at Obollo Afor was to create a new Third sector of the Nigeria Army, independent of his troops at Nsukka. The task of the Third sector was primarily to destroy our forces at Obollo Eke. At the beginning of August, 1967, all intelligence information pointed to the fact that the enemy new command was forming up very quickly in the area of Orokam. The same very reliable intelligence source also revealed that the attack would come from the right flank with Obollo Eke as the objective, with a view to completely cutting off Obollo Afor and the two companies up there. With my present deployment, I had no doubts about my inability to withstand a strong enemy attack either at Obollo Afor or Obollo Eke. My Brigade had cleared and held Obollo Afor in trust for 53 Brigade for almost a week and there was yet no sign that 53 Brigade was ever going to be in a position to take over from us. I decided to concede Obollo Afor back to the enemy by withdrawing the troops there in preparation for the impending battle at Obollo Eke.

On the 30th of July, Obollo Eke came under very heavy artillery and mortar concentration from 0600 hours. The shelling was so heavy that movement within the battalion area was virtually impossible for the first 30 minutes. When the commanding officer, Major Amadi, recovered from his initial daze, he ordered the two Tampella mortars to lay on Ogobido, the only likely enemy concentration on the right flank, and then fire off their remaining ten rounds. When this happened, enemy shelling also stopped completely, and it seemed as if the infantry assault would come in at any time. When this did not happen, our force of two companies advanced to make contact, in two different directions. What we saw when the enemy was sighted was very amazing and initially very difficult to understand. The whole enemy force numbering several hundreds, was seen scampering away in all directions, in absolute confusion, without firing a shot in anger. Several of them who had completely lost their sense of direction ran right into the warm embrace of Biafran soldiers, among them were both the sector commander himself, and the commanding officer of the attacking battalion. We spent the rest of the day bringing in enemy stores, the most valuable of them being 81mm mortar bombs which we no longer had at all.

Later, in the Officers' Mess basher, the enemy battalion commander, over a glass of beer, explained what had happened. According to him, they had arrived at Orokam the previous day under Major Sotomi who left them there and returned to Lagos. Their task was to move immediately and destroy the Biafran force at Obollo Eke and affect a link-up with Obollo Afor immediately after. They were told to spend little or no time in preparation and reconnaissance because the Biafran troops there were Nzeogwu's guerrillas with no heavy support and unserviceable rifles. When the attack started, he said, his mortar team spent their 500 rounds in less than 30 minutes and then left for Orokam to collect more bombs. He explained that it was at this stage that the Biafran shells which they never expected, began to drop right in their midst in the forming up area. As soon as that happened, all ranks scattered in all directions and thereafter it became a question of everybody to himself. It was during this confusion that those who had gone for more mortar bombs arrived. In fact this enemy battalion commander expressed his thanks to us for our wisdom in not shelling heavily — otherwise, he said, it could have been a disaster. He did not realise we gave them all the shells we had at the time. The sector commander was wounded and had to go to Enugu Hospital at once. This very short encounter was very rewarding and represented the second consecutive major success of the 51 Brigade within a fortnight. Confidence among the ranks and file which was badly shaken if not destroyed at Ogoja, was now fully restored, and all ranks wanted nothing but action.

Greatly encouraged by our recent successes, I decided to carry the war into the Northern Region for a change. On my front, numerous tracks existed through which one could move deep into the Northern Region without opposition but such moves could have been fruitless and difficult to sustain. Administrative support for a move of that nature could have been very difficult because the roads were not motorable. In addition, in the absence of wireless communications, control of troops on deep penetration operations would have been absolutely impossible. As a compromise, I decided to launch the 12th Battalion on a limited task of capturing Igumale. This would give us a good chance of linking it up with Ihama and thus reducing the brigade frontage very considerably. A few days before the offensive, 12th Battalion was withdrawn to Onitsha by Army Headquarters, in preparation for the Midwestern Nigeria offensive and the Igumale operation was abandoned indefinitely.

THE EHA-AMUFU MIRACLE

The situation all over 51 Brigade front was quiet enough to tempt me into undertaking a tour of my administrative base at Nkalagu Cement Factory seven miles south of my Eha-Amufu Headquarters. It was to be my first administrative inspection since the outbreak of the war. This was a particularly important visit during which I was to work out with the civilian authorities a form of flexibility with regard to the very rigid feeding hours. I left my Headquarters at 1300 hours for this inspection.

At 1630 hours I received a telephone call from my Headquarters to return immediately because the enemy was launching a strong attack on the Headquarters itself from the right flank. On my way back to the Headquarters the roads were already flooded with civilian refugees and a few military administrative vehicles which were beginning to pull back. Eha-Amufu town itself was in utter confusion as the population began to evacuate. My Headquarters was half packed up and most of the stores were in vehicles.

Major Ohanehi, the commanding officer of the 14th Battalion, whose Headquarters was in the same hut as mine, was in the office. He said the enemy of an estimated battalion strength, was advancing from Agala on our right to attack Eha-Amufu town. Thick smoke from far away burning villages was a clear evidence that the enemy was indeed advancing even though there was neither small arms fire nor shelling. Civilian refugees and informants when asked to give a rough estimate of enemy strength simply said they were so many no one could ever attempt to count them. As far as I was concerned, it could well be a brigade advancing.

I turned out the only company available to me as a reserve force. Leading them myself, with Major Ohanehi assisting, we moved out through Eha-Amufu market towards the direction of enemy advance. When we approached the foot bridge 800 yards from the market and attempted to cross it, we came under heavy small arms fire and shortly after, heavy shelling of the town began. The situation was extremely dangerous. With only a big stream separating the enemy of unknown strength from my Headquarters 800 yards away, and with only a company available with which to stop them, I was inclined to believe that my Headquarters would be captured intact. Besides losing my Headquarters, the loss of Eha-Amufu from that flank would have meant the seizure, by the enemy, of the only line of communication to both the First and the 14th Battalions, and consequently the complete disorganisation of my Brigade.

While the company already in position fell back behind the river and returned fire, I contacted Army Headquarters for assistance but there was none available. As an alternative, I ordered the First Battalion to despatch a company reinforcement together with their two 81mm mortars. This company arrived under Major Olehi of Garkem at 2100 hours, with only ten rounds of mortar bombs. I thought it was too late to waste these bombs which undoubtedly would be required more early in the morning when a major attack was expected. However, even at that time, the enemy was still shelling indiscriminately and, this was rather irritating. The nearest village to the river on the enemy side was burning furiously, and in anger, I asked the mortars to lay roughly on the burning village and fire off their rounds. As soon as this was done, the enemy stopped shelling. Thereafter, there were occasional outbursts of small arms and machine gun fire till 0200 hours.

As we waited for a dawn attack, I returned to my Headquarters hut by 0300 hours. My wireless set was off the air because the aerial wire had been cut to bits by shells. The wireless operator who was the only person remaining in the building told me that the enemy commander at Nsukka had telephoned my Headquarters at 0100 hours to find out if their men had occupied Eha-Amufu. I could not understand how this could have been possible as one had to go through Enugu exchange to get Eha-Amufu from Nsukka. Enugu, fully aware that Nsukka was in enemy hands, could not have handled the call. Later on, I found out it was Colonel Ogunewe who had telephoned from Enugu to find out whether indeed my Headquarters had been overrun. He disguised his voice the best he could and spoke in Hausa, on the pretext that he was speaking from Nsukka.

We waited for the enemy attack until 0630 hours in the morning but it did not come, so we crossed the river and advanced. There was no enemy around anymore except the dead and the injured. Our advance quickened into a pursuit and after three miles, there was still no organised enemy resistance or presence. There, the Army halted its advance and asked the civilians to continue the chase to the border, which was still another seven miles away. Apparently the enemy had withdrawn in a very disorderly fashion during the night leaving behind their dead and wounded and abandoning a considerable amount of stores and light equipment.

This was the third major victory for the 51 Brigade but it was a lucky one. We won due to enemy mistakes. During his advance into Eha-Amufu from Agala, the enemy stopped to burn down all villages on their route in addition to killing off the livestock. By so doing, they lost speed and surprise. Markings on stores and equipment captured showed it was an enemy battalion which launched the attack. It was evident that there was a good number of policemen and convicts in the battalion — a fact that was later confirmed by prisoners of war. A major lesson learnt from this battle was that the flanks were much more vulnerable than many field commanders would care to imagine, therefore rendering a defensive position unsafe unless the flanks were well protected.

Apart from our defeat at Ogoja where we were caught completely on the hop, 51 Brigade was winning all its battles until now, and it was difficult to imagine that the enemy could ever again overpower the Brigade in any battle. This happy trend of events soon changed for two reasons — one was the formation of 101 Division and the other, the invasion of Midwestern Nigeria. Thereafter things began to be difficult for not only 51 Brigade but the whole of the Biafran Army.

Chapter 8

THE BIRTH OF "SABOTAGE" POLITICS AND CONSEQUENT DISASTERS

THE LOSS OF OBOLLO EKE

The ill fortunes of 53 Brigade were so frequent and stereotype that they no longer appeared to be coincidental. For a long time, each time they planned an operation against the enemy, they were attacked exactly 30 minutes before the H-hour on that particular front, thereby neutralising their proposed offensive. My fears of foul play were heightened by the fact that Colonel Banjo and Major Alele were already going round spreading a rumour that saboteurs existed in 53 Brigade and the Army Headquarters.

It was not difficult to see that the two men were actually accusing the Army Commander, Colonel Njoku, of sabotage. Major Alele in fact gained access to the radio station at Enugu and made a broadcast in which he alerted the nation to the fact that there were top-ranking saboteurs in Biafra. He did not mention names but the nation understood clearly to whom he was referring. Thus, that dirty word "sabotage" which completely tore the nation into tiny bits and contributed so much to the loss of the war was cleverly introduced. From then on, the Army lost the absolute confidence and admiration which it had hitherto enjoyed from the entire population. It was difficult for the Army to understand how Colonel Banjo, a Yoruba who found himself in Enugu by chance, and Alele, a civilian political commissaire wearing an honorary rank of a Major, could be the first Biafrans to detect acts of sabotage in the front lines from their offices in Enugu. Yet everyone believed them and gave them maximum assistance in their campaign against Njoku in particular, and the Army in general. It was much later that I learnt from Eze that Banjo insisted and did attend all his briefings preparatory to his futile offensives and near disasters.

Shortly after Eha-Amufu battle, Colonel Banjo visited my Headquarters for the first time since the outbreak of the war. He had no time to waste on congratulating the Brigade on their achievements so far. He went straight on to a lengthy speech about Colonel Njoku's sabotage and collaboration with the enemy, which had resulted in the enemy knowing in advance all plans made by 53 Brigade. According to Banjo, he had already held a series of discussions with Colonel Ojukwu on this problem and their solution was to form the 101 Division which would have 51 and 53 Brigades under command. He revealed that the Divisional Headquarters was already established in Enugu and was fully operational. According to him, it was the wish of the Head of State that, with effect from that date, the above-mentioned Brigades should deal directly with the new Divisional Headquarters and should on no account discuss operations with Army Headquarters or Njoku. I made it abundantly clear to him that his facts and assessments about Njoku were wrong for a person of such a strong character, with a couple of Nigerian bullets still buried in his right thigh. I also asked for formal official instructions to cover the points he raised. Later, I got these instructions in writing.

Now, acting as the commander of 101 Division, Colonel Banjo brought out his plan for my next offensive. In outline, it boiled down to the following:

The Brigade was to move from its present location to attack and recapture Obollo Afor, which we had abandoned because we had no troops to garrison it. From Obollo Afor the Brigade would then move to capture Enugu Ezike deep behind the enemy locations at Nsukka, after leaving behind sufficient troops to garrison Obollo Afor and all approaches to it. From Enugu Ezike, the Brigade would move on three axis — northwards to capture Ogugu and exploit beyond it; westwards to seize Nadu and Akpanya and southwards to take Nsukka from the rear. By so doing, Banjo explained, the 51 Brigade would completely surround the enemy at Nsukka for a final destruction by 53 Brigade. He explained that 53 Brigade had already been given detailed instructions on their move into Nsukka and a subsequent link-up with me.

In my view, all that Banjo said was absolute nonsense which showed a remarkable ignorance of basic military tactics. For a start, the 101 Divisional Headquarters was comprised of himself, Captain Christian Ogbu, and Major Alele, and it was impossible that such a team could handle two Brigades in battle without assistance from Army Headquarters. I reminded Banjo that the task he gave me could hardly be achieved by a well equipped division, let alone a Biafran brigade. I pointed out to him that, with my Brigade defending 80 miles of front, I could only conduct an offensive with a maximum of one battalion at a time, particularly at a time when the 12th Battalion was standing by to move to Onitsha. By my own assessment, I could not even carry out a meaningful offensive against Obollo Afor alone, unless I had at least a replacement battalion, for the following reasons:

1. After our previous successful offensive on the town, we were unable to hold it due to lack of troops. It would be pointless repeating the operation unless one had sufficient forces to hold the town, particularly now that the enemy had reinforced the town considerably.

2. We were unlikely to achieve surprise again because we could only attack the town from the right flank and had done that once. I was sure if we tried again, the enemy would be waiting for us.

3. My greatest fear was that, since our successful repulsion of enemy attack on Obollo Eke, his presence on that flank was being felt increasingly in the area of Orukpa, only three miles away. That menace did not exist when we conducted our first offensive against Obollo Afor. I warned Banjo that to move out the troops at Obollo Eke to go chasing eight miles away at Obollo Afor would with out doubt, result in the seizure of our base from the right flank in our absence. If that happened the Brigade would be cut into bits and destroyed permanently.

147

My suggestion to Banjo, based on the above reasons, was that the operation be postponed indefinitely till such a time as we could afford such an ambitious task. I thought the most sensible and urgent alternative in the meantime would have been a limited offensive to make our right flank more secure.

I am afraid I did not impress the new Division Commander who insisted that the operation must go on, exactly as he had outlined it. I sent for Amadi who was most likely to command the battalion for that operation to give him a chance of expressing his views before Banjo. His views were that the operation would be suicidal, and his alternative plan was to clear the right flank as I had previously suggested before his arrival. Banjo remained relentless. Before his departure to Enugu, he ordered that the operation be started within 72 hours and that it was my duty to forward to him the details of the D-day and H-hour as soon as they were fixed. I told Banjo clearly about my willingness to relinquish command of 51 Brigade or even resign my commission rather than carry out that suicidal and absolutely fruitless operation, but he paid no further attention to me.

Later on that night, Major Amadi paid me a visit during which he tried to persuade me to accept the operation. He reasoned that my action could easily be misinterpreted as disobedience with all its disasterous consequences particularly in a time of war. He also saw this as a chance for Banjo to brand me a saboteur and if this happened it would be almost impossible to convince the people of Biafra to believe otherwise. I later gave my approval and the operation was fixed for 0530 hours on the 3rd of August, 1967. This information was duly passed to Banjo and nobody else.

Only the 2nd of August was available for reconnaissance of enemy locations at Obollo Afor where the enemy was now in strength and appeared to be very well entrenched. At 2300 hours on the 2nd of August the entire battalion left through the usual routes to Obollo Afor. Only one company was left behind, this time to defend Obollo Eke and the right flank. At 0530 hours the following morning we put in an attack on Obollo Afor but to our greatest surprise, the enemy, that was there the previous day, was hardly there any more. As our own troops were going through the town, heavy artillery and mortar bombardment of Obollo Eke began at 0600 hours. This bombardment came from Orukpa on the right flank and was being done with 4 x 105 mm guns and several mortars, and was by far the heaviest concentration so far of the war.

Exactly what I told Banjo would happened was happening, but there was hardly time for apportioning blame. Obollo Eke with only a company defending it could hardly be said to be defended at all. I was therefore compelled to order the immediate withdrawal of the rest of the battalion from Obollo Afor back to Obollo Eke to defend it, and what was more, to secure our entire rear down to Enugu.

It took the troops considerable time to walk back the eight miles of bush tracks. In the meantime, after two hours of intensive pounding, the enemy put in the first wave of attack by 0800 hours. This was repelled by our company with casualties on both sides, after a twenty minutes encounter. Two hours later the enemy did the same thing again and withdrew, but at the end of each brief attack, the volume and rapidity of the shelling increased considerably. It appeared as if the enemy did not want to get hurt but to shell us out of the position.

As tired troops returned from Obollo Afor they joined in the fighting. It was almost impossible to supply food and other necessities to the fighting troops because the shelling had assumed such proportions as to denote angry impatience and frustration on the part of the enemy. Our attempts at advancing were halted by heavy and extremely lavish firepower. When shelling stopped at 2330 hours on that first day, all available assistance was rushed in, including a reinforcement of 400 militiamen, which was all that was available in the way of reinforcement. At that time of the night, it was quite difficult to locate all troops and feed them before daybreak; as a result a good number of them went without food or water, as no soldier had mess tins and collective feeding was the practice.

The following day, the 4th of August at 0600 hours, heavy shelling resumed, followed every two hours by half-hearted probing attacks by the enemy. By the end of that day, most of the soldiers were completely exhausted, most of them having gone without food or water for 48 hours. The Militia requested to be withdrawn because they thought they were taking unnecessary punishment without coming into contact with the enemy responsible for that. They were withdrawn back to Eha-Amufu that night from where most of them left for Enugu to reorganise. Unfortunately we had not a single round of mortar bombs because they had been fired off at Obollo Afor during the futile second attempt of the 3rd of August.

At the end of the third day, it had become clear that our own troops could no longer stay in Obollo Eke for the enemy was bent on completely reducing the town to ruins. As we had no reinforcement prospects nor any plans to silence the enemy guns, further stay in the town appeared to be unwise. I therefore ordered the withdrawal of the battalion during the night of the 5th, immediately shelling stopped. I warned 14th Battalion to prepare to move up to the area of Obollo Eke to allow the First Battalion sufficient time to reorganise at Nkalagu Cement Factory. It would, no doubt, take the 14th Battalion anything up to 24 hours to assemble from their various defensive locations and move forward but we could ill afford the time.

All the same, First Battalion had to be brought out at once to avoid disaster. For this reason, I moved up the 14th Battalion standby D Company stationed in my Headquarters as a reserve force under Captain Wilson Odo to act as a protective force for the withdrawal. Their instructions were to secure the bridge half a mile to Obollo Eke and defend it, as a possible startline for a future attempt by 14th Battalion to regain the town if the enemy entered it during the change over. This company moved up quickly while First Battalion moved out. At 0400 hours 6 August, Captain Odo came back to my Headquarters with the information that his company had found Obollo Eke extremely calm on getting there, and had therefore entered and physically occupied it. In his misguided optimism and uncontrolled excitement he swore he was able to hold the town and meant to do so to the last man. Fully aware that Obollo Eke was his home town, I understood the sentimental aspect of his thinking which was badly syncronised with the prevailing military situation. I was angry with him and would have had him arrested for disobedience but for the fact that he had troops in the frontlines to command. I still took time off to explain to him that his attempt to hold a location with a company — a location which a battalion could not hold, amounted to suicide. I warned him that unless he withdrew his company before daybreak, he might never be able to do so again as soon as the pounding started.

Captain Odo left my Headquarters at 0500 hours and had not gone for more than 20 minutes when the shelling began at Obollo Eke. By the time he got into the town, his company was already badly battered and he only met about half of the original strength in complete disarray and confusion. By 1000 hours, the company had completely disintegrated, and Odo himself ended up in hospital with severe shell shock which took him well over three months to recover from.

Thus, the enemy entered Obollo Eke on the 6th of August, 1967 after four days of non-stop shelling and practically no use of infantry. The Biafran troops had put in a most magnificient show and were not exactly demoralised by the outcome. I was, however, personally demoralised and so was Amadi because many things required some explanation with regard to both our offensive and that of the enemy. Why was it that the enemy moved exactly from the right flank as I had previously warned Banjo? Why did we not find the enemy at Obollo Afor when we attacked even though they were there in strength the previous day? Why was it that the only battle I had planned from outside the Brigade failed so woefully, in exactly the same pattern as most of those planned by 53 Brigade at Nsukka? Could it be a mere coincidence that in whichever sector Banjo operated, the out-come of all efforts was invariably disaster-ous? The real answers to these questions may never be known but thereafter the 51 Brigade never again knew real success in battle for a very long time, for the First Battalion was the real pride and strength of the 51 Brigade. 14th Battalion must have put in over six counter attacks against Obollo Eke without success.

THE LOSS OF EHA-AMUFU

For the first three weeks of the war, the south was very calm. On the 25th of July after the routing of the enemy at Obollo Afor and while the threat to Obollo Eke was fast developing from the right flank, I received by telephone through Christian Ude, then the Chief Operations Officer at Army Headquarters, Enugu, the news of the invasion of Bonny.

According to Ude, the Nigeria Navy had shelled the tiny town heavily for over six hours and then landed a battalion which swiftly swept away our force of one platoon stationed there. The sad aspect of this new development was that the Biafran Army at the time was almost unable to check the enemy advance from the north. If, therefore, such an advance was to develop simultaneously from the south, the situation could quite easily get out of control. There were no troops available for reinforcements anywhere and, in fact, existing formations were being thinned down in order to get sufficient troops for the Midwestern Nigeria offensive.

There was nothing the 51 Brigade or indeed 53 Brigade could do to assist in the south. The loss of Obollo Eke and the total neutralisation of the First Battalion had broken the 51 Brigade completely. The enemy seemed to realise it and was bent on exploiting the situation to the fullest. The enemy therefore, pushed on with all his apparently limitless resources from Obollo Eke towards Ikem and Eha-Amufu. The 14th Battalion battled relentlessly to halt them but bolt action rifles, ditches and mines proved grossly ineffective against enemy fire power, armour and tremendously heavy support. Whenever enemy infantry were contacted, heavy casualties were inflicted on them but they were not easily seen.

As a last resort and for the first time during the course of the war, I called for the support of the Air Force helicopters in the hope that they would help delay enemy advance. The helicopters did a good job by inflicting casualties on the enemy but failed to halt the advance. Very soon the enemy also learnt to lie low and completely freeze up whenever a helicopter was in the air over him, and to resume the offensive as soon as it was gone. This made it difficult, if not impossible, for the enemy to be identified anymore from the air, thus reducing the usefulness of the helicopters considerably. The enemy retaliated in the air by conducting an air raid with the Dunier 27 aircrafts over my Brigade Headquarters at Eha-Amufu. The planes flew very low and dropped buckets of explosives mixed with mortar bombs. As the pilot of one of the planes flew slowly over me outside my Headquarters, he dropped one of these buckets almost on my head before I realised it was an enemy plane. My orderly immediately engaged it with a sten machine gun, and the left door of the plane fell down on the ground. The plane got away all the same, but the pilot was no longer grinning as he was when he dropped the bucket. Of all buckets dropped, only the one that fell in the half empty town market exploded. This represented the first Nigerian air raid on Biafra.

When the enemy entered Ikem town, an armoured vehicle, manufactured in Port Harcourt, was sent up to me for a counter-attack. It was the first occasion my Brigade was going to employ armour in battle and despite the numerous limitations of that particular vehicle, its very presence was a source of hope and morale. It was an enormous mass of steel on wheels and capable of not much more than a maximum speed of ten miles per hour, in addition to overheating after every thirty minutes of operation. The driver who brought the vehicle from Enugu was a civilian who claimed that his task was to deliver the vehicle to the brigade and return immediately to Enugu. I could not let him go because nobody else was available to drive it for the offensive which was due to be launched within a short time. The driver eventually agreed to go into attack with the soldiers.

When the attack was finally launched on the 15th of August, 1967 the enemy fled at the sight of this shapeless enormous monster. Even the enemy 106 anti-tank gun which had hitherto bluffed its way through, shooting at individuals for lack of something more spectacular to shoot at, fled with the infantry and armoured vehicles. Led by "Genocide," as our own troops soon christened the armoured vehicle, we rolled into Ikem with the men singing war songs.

As we pursued the enemy towards Obollo Eke, "Genocide" ran into a land mine and was blown into bits, completely putting off our own troops' advance. As soon as the troops recovered from the shock of the disaster, the advance continued but then enemy armoured vehicles re-appeared at the same time as very heavy shelling began. We soon lost all the ground we had gained and even more. The death of "Genocide" was most unfortunate because if it had lived for another 24 hours, we might have pushed back into Obollo Eke at the speed we were going.

But the enemy was again exploiting his success arising out of our disaster. His armoured vehicles surged on, and his shells pounded every inch of ground. Our own troops waited as long as they could for enemy infantry, but they never showed up before we lost the position to armoured vehicles and heavy bombardment. Reinforcement from the First Battalion made no change in the pattern of fighting. Several flanking attacks put in produced only very limited success because as soon as the men exhausted their ammunition they came back to base. The only means then left for us for stopping the ceaseless heavy shelling and the armoured car menace was to get the Air Force helicopters to over-fly the battle zone as often as possible throughout the day dropping bombs on any targets identified. For this purpose, two Biafra Air Force helicopters arrived at my Headquarters on the 17th of August, at 0900 hours. One of the helicopters hit a tree as it tried to land and sustained sufficient damage to demand its being grounded. The other took off to the frontline as heavy shelling was already going on. When the pilot came back, he reported every place calm and his inability to identify any enemy locations or movements. He had not finished briefing me when the sound of heavy shelling and fighting became clearly audible. In anger and utter frustration, I decided to fly with the pilot, identify the targets, and personally throw the bombs out of the door of the helicopter on those targets myself. When we were over the battle zone, the entire area was as silent as a grave. We flew around for over one hour but saw no movement whatsoever. On our way back, we noticed our own troops who were taking advantage of the break in shelling, advancing towards Ikem on both sides of the road. We landed the helicopter near them (this was pretty close to the front), and I ordered them to quicken their advance.

When we came back to my Headquarters, it was about 1500 hours and the weather was getting bad. I was just about to grab a quick lunch with the pilots when the usual cry for the helicopter came from Major Ohanehi, the commanding officer of 14th Battalion. We all trooped out and jumped into the helicopter, but just before we took off, a soldier ran in and said he was sent by the commanding officer to fly with the helicopter and show the pilot the targets. I came down from the helicopter and gave him my place. The helicopter soon took off again, and that trip turned out to be its last one. After overflying the battlefield for 30 minutes, it suddenly exploded in the air and completely burnt out. No one could say for certain, the cause of the accident but it is most unlikely to be as a result of enemy action. It is most likely that someone was trying to throw a primed bomb out of the door and it fell back into the helicopter and exploded.

As soon as this happened the enemy was heard very distinctly crying out loud for joy and then let loose all they had against us. In less than 24 hours, our own troops had seen two major misfortunes — the destruction of "Genocide" and the crash of the helicopter. Everything seemed to be going wrong and morale was very low, particularly when word went round the brigade that I was in the helicopter. Thereafter we held the enemy for another 48 hours of hard fighting before Eha-Amufu main town fell into his hands, while our own troops withdrew behind the river on the outskirts of the town after blowing the bridge.

Several counter-attacks were launched by the 14th Battalion and later by the First Battalion to regain Eha-Amufu without success. The main difficulty with those attempts was that the town is surrounded by a fairly large river on all sides except from the north from where the enemy advanced. With the only bridge across the river damaged, troops had to wade through swift current and quite a few of them were swept away in the process. Before our last attempt, a couple of white men were even seen working on the bridge. We had no alternative but to remain in our defences across the river and watch Northern soldiers and civilians remove doors, windows, roofs, and furniture from all the buildings, for evacuation to the Northern Region.

THE INVASION OF MIDWESTERN NIGERIA

The introduction of Colonel Banjo into the war marked a very rapid decline of Njoku's participation. It also marked the beginning of disasters for the 51 Brigade in particular. All activities of the Colonel were clouded with unnecessary secrecy and mystery and invariably failed totally. This was true of the Midwestern Nigeria operation.

My first knowledge of the operation came from Banjo on the 7th of August, 1967 during a short visit he paid me. That morning he revealed that a lightening operation aimed at capturing the entire Midwestern Nigeria, Ibadan and probably Lagos too, would be launched within 48 hours. For this operation, he wanted my 12th Battalion under Colonel Mike Ivenso to join two other battalions he was already assembling at Onitsha to form a brigade. He hoped to be able to expand each of the battalions eventually into a brigade of the 101 Division. He explained that, until such a time the Division attained its full strength, a large amount of militiamen would be used for holding and garrisoning captured areas during his operation.

His outline plan was to move his forces on three main axis, north, south and west starting from Onitsha. The northern force would establish at Auchi and exploit northwards the best they could, having detached a force to Idah to protect their right flank as well as block enemy lines of communication to Nsukka through the town. Their overall task remained the protection of the northern flank to enable our troops to penetrate into Ibadan and Lagos.

The southern force, he said, would move to garrison the main coastal towns of Warri, Sapele und Ughelli. From there they would strive to foil all attempts by the enemy to land troops in those areas. This force was to be the smallest and would have a lot of militiamen. The main force, Banjo said, would motor to Benin and seize it.

Without any loss of time, they would move on to Ibadan on two axis — through Ore on the new Lagos road and through Okitipupa on the old one. If everything went well, Banjo added, these forces would move to Lagos, after despatching a small force to blow and hold the Niger bridge at Jebba.

In conclusion, Banjo stressed the need for absolute secrecy and pointed out that it was the wish of the Head of State that Army Headquarters, particularly Brigadier Njoku (now promoted), should on no account be told of the operation.

I was most delighted about the whole operation which was perhaps the only way we could score a much-needed victory and restore confidence and morale badly shaken within the rank and file. Admittedly, the troops available for the operation were grossly inadequate for the enormous task before them, but the chances of success were excellent as little or no opposition was expected for some time, provided we moved fast in absolute secrecy.

By last light on the 8th of August, all troops taking part, including the Militia, were already concentrated at Onitsha. After a couple of hours of unexplained delay, Colonel Banjo moved with his troops across the Niger bridge, Onitsha in the early hours of the 9th of August, 1967, and the chase to the various objectives began.

As was expected, Benin was taken early that morning without a single loss of life, amidst frantic jubilations by the entire local population. For reasons best known to him, Banjo conveniently ignored the importance of speed as a principle of war and chose to remain in Benin to "reorganise" the troops that had not yet fired a shot. Much time was lost while the argument raged between Benin and Enugu on who was going to be the Governor of the newly acquired Region and the nature of the broadcast to be made.

Army Headquarters in Enugu had not the foggiest idea of what was happening over there. It did not know about the operation until it started and while the Benin power tussle was developing, Banjo refused to brief any liaison officers and representatives of Army Headquarters. Very soon Colonel Ojukwu began to be left out of the true picture by Banjo in the same way Brigadier Njoku had been all the time. As pressure mounted on Banjo to make a move, he finally did so belatedly on the 12th of August having wasted three days during which he could have occupied Ibadan without firing a shot.

On the Ore Axis, our own troops, led by Colonel Festus Akagha, encountered a feeble enemy force short of Ore bridge and promptly swept it away capturing their stores and ammunition. Colonel Banjo ordered our force to halt there, reorganise and await further instructions. On the Okitipupa axis, the enemy was on the run most of the time but put up a fairly stiff resistance ten miles to the main town. While our own troops sat in their positions, the enemy was marshalling troops from everywhere, including Nsukka, to build up what was to be his Second Division under Colonel Murtala Muhammed, to deal with the Midwestern Nigeria threat. Banjo also had sufficient time to hold daily meetings with the British Deputy High Commissioner in Benin. As a result of these meetings, Banjo soon began to antagonise most of his field commanders openly and subsequently had them arrested one by one. Colonel Henry Igboba who was locked up by Banjo at the time the enemy re-entered Benin, was released and beheaded by the Nigerian soldiers.

To compound the confusion which was developing, the same people who introduced "saboteurs" into the war went round the troops operating in Midwestern Nigeria with their usual story of the presence of saboteurs among the officers. They knew from previous experience that this method was the simplest and fastest way of disorganising a Biafran Army unit.

It worked like magic. Morale of soldiers fell and soon they suspected all actions of their officers, particularly the senior ones and, in fact, began to disobey their orders. Soon the loss of confidence in their officers by the troops become so apparent that command and control was temporarily but almost completely lost. Troops no longer knew who or what to believe and were becoming openly hostile to some of their officers. One afternoon, Colonel Akagha was returning to his Benin Headquarters from Ore frontline when he fell into an ambush at a point where it was impossible for the enemy to be stationed. He lost his command Landrover and all his escorts in the ambush, but managed to escape and make his way to Onitsha, a distance of over 100 miles on foot — a journey that took him over three weeks. Those who had followed the Midwest operation closely could only arrive at the most logical conclusion: that the ambush was organised and executed by our own forces acting under somebody's instructions.

The enemy was now fully organised and had started their massive counter-attack on all three axes. Banjo would not agree to return to Enugu for consultations. With most of the senior field commanders either detained by Banjo or hiding from their angry soldiers, and the remaining few not being completely obeyed by troops, the enemy did not experience much difficulty in pushing our troops steadily back. From Western Nigeria, enemy re-entered Benin on the 18th of September. As a matter of fact, Banjo ordered the withdrawal from Benin when the advancing enemy was 15 miles away from the town. He even ordered against the evacuation of stores, even the military ones, on the pretext that an immediate counterattack would be launched by Biafran troops to regain the town. From Northern Nigeria, the enemy took Auchi and then Ubiaja. Agbor was soon threatened from both the north and the south, thereby forcing our own troops, still at the outskirts of Benin, to withdraw further back to Adoa behind Agbor bridge which they immediately blew up.

As soon as Benin fell, Banjo returned to Enugu having completed his task in the Midwest. He left behind a complete vacuum in the command structure. I was then the Army Commander, and the task of regaining control of the troops in that sector was virtually impossible to achieve. All ranks were still determined to fight to a finish but their efforts were most un-coordinated. Every individual or group of individuals did exactly what was thought right.

It may sound unusual now, but the few officers left behind by Banjo took time off to engage in a bitter tussle for command. Major Wole Ademoyega, Banjo's staff officer, maintained that Banjo handed over full power to him. As such, he was responsible for all operations and accountable only to Banjo. Colonel Ochei claimed command and leadship of the sector on the grounds that he was the most senior officer in the area and also backed by Army Headquarters. It was true Army Headquarters would have liked Ochei to take charge of the operations there, but then Army Headquarters knew very little of this operation which was planned and controlled from State House. There was Major Chukwuka who had his reasons for wanting to assume command of the sector. The most spectacular contestant to the command of the Division was a hitherto unheard of individual called Mr. Joe Achuzia, a militiaman. He was said to be wearing the rank of a Lieutenant Colonel and had assisted in a big way throughout the campaign. The final decision was to be taken by State House and I do not think it was even taken.

The enemy, in the meantime, seizing full advantage of the utter confusion existing within the Biafran ranks, made a move from Warri through Abraka to Umutu where we had removed the bridge on the river there. Our troops at the bridge were able to hold the enemy for a 48 hour bloody battle before we exhausted our supplies and began to pull back. By then the administrative set-up of the 101 Division had virtually collapsed. The network of roads in that area made any attempt at a defensive battle a completely futile exercise because the attacking side could easily run small rings round the defender. Our troops therefore continued to move back until the enemy got to Umunede on the main Benin-Asaba road. Our troops were now stationed at Ogwashiuku and Otutu. From the North, the enemy had pushed into the town of Isele-Uku. Finally the enemy pushing through Ogwashiuku and Otutu, entered Asaba on the 8th of October, 1967. Our troops fell back into Onitsha town and blew the bridge. Those of our troops who got into Onitsha were in complete disarray and disorganised, and in no fit state to halt any immediate attempt by Muhammed to invade Onitsha. Colonel Nwawo was quickly despatched to assemble whatever troops he could find and organise them into a fighting force. While 2 Division was carrying out massive public execution of all adult males in Asaba, Nwawo had the time to do his reorganisation and was thus able to beat back 2 Division's invasion when it came.

Thus ended the Midwestern Nigeria operations. The 101

Division which was created for that operation also died a natural death.

Banjo must have had a change of mind; otherwise the continued success of the operation may have brought the war to a speedy end in favour of Biafra. Despite the unfortunate developments in the course of the campaign, I personally think Biafra did the best thing at the time to have attacked the Midwest. We did it, not to conquer Nigeria but to force her to bring the war to an end and negotiate. It also relieved pressure from our own troops in the northern sectors of the war, particularly at Nsukka from where the enemy withdrew the bulk of the troops with which they initially fought back in the Midwest. If we had had the troops and equipment it would have been easy to clear Nsukka at the time and probably advance into Northern Nigeria.

However, our bold attempt in the Midwest had the unfortunate effect of completely snapping the patience of the British Government. From then onwards, it came out openly to recognise and support Gowon. With Britain went almost the whole world. We were in trouble.

OPERATION TORCH

When Banjo left for the Midwest operations, the command of the Biafran Army was handed back to Brigadier Njoku with a warning from Colonel Ojukwu that unless he achieved some spectacular successes pretty soon, he would lose his command permanently. He was asked to plan an operation to push the enemy in the Northern sector back into Northern Nigeria. To support this operation, Njoku was told he would get the support of three 105mm guns which had just arrived in the country. As an artillery officer I later went to see these guns and found them to be very old guns indeed, of early Second if not the First World War vintage. The guns came absolutely naked. In other words, they had no survey or plotting instruments or even pamphlets or other instructions to enable the gun crew to know what to do with the guns. The gun barrels were badly worn and the recoil system very weak. At the same time, it was also announced that we now had armoured vehicles in the country. When I later saw the armoured vehicles, they were light armoured small vehicles with open tops and tracked wheels. They were absolutely bare with no weapons or equipment inside them. Those of them that moved at all either overheated within 20 minutes or lost their tracks easily. On these vehicles, holes were punctured to allow the use of machine guns. A few had their tops converted locally with thick armour plating and this increased the load on the engine and the rate of overheating and breakdowns. The story spread all over the nation of our new acquisitions and consequent strength and Njoku therefore was told he would have no reasons whatsoever if he failed.

On the 14th of September, Brigadier Njoku held a conference at Ukehe near Enugu to discuss his proposed plan and issue his final orders for the operation. Colonels Ude, Operations Officer in Army Headquarters; Eze, Commander 53 Brigade; myself (now a Brigadier), and other junior staff officers attended the conference. It afforded me the first opportunity of visiting the 53 Brigade area on my left flank and having very useful private discussions with the commander after the conference. Njoku having reiterated his aim as being to push the enemy facing the 51 and 53 Brigades back into Northern Nigeria proceeded to give his execution orders.

53 Brigade would move a battalion through Opi-Eha Alumona main axis to clear Eha Alumona town. From there the battalion would move to clear Obollo Afor and reorganise there. The battalion had, in support, three of the newly acquired "armoured" vehicles. Another battalion of 53 Brigade would move on the Opi-Nsukka road to clear the right half of Nsukka town and then reorganise in the area of Ofoko. The third battalion of this Brigade would move along Nkpologu-Agbo road to clear the left side of Nsukka town and then reorganise in the general area of Okuje and Ibagwa Ani. A fourth but very weak ad hoc battalion, which was quickly assembled, remained in reserve but on readiness to attack Enugu Ezike in the second phase of the operation if the first phase was successful.

The 51 Brigade would move a battalion through Enugu and

Ugwuogo to clear Isi Uzo and Ikem and reorganise there. Another battalion was expected to move through Umalo on the left flank to clear Eha-Amufu from the rear. Thereafter, this battalion would turn left and fight northwards to link up with our own troops who may have re-taken Ikem. The third battalion of the Brigade was to move through Agala to capture Igumale. For this operation I was given an extra 400 men armed with bolt action rifles to replace the 12th Battalion. I named them the 4th Battalion under the command of Lt. Colonel David Okafor. Our prospects were relatively high — at least higher than they had ever been before, considering the armour and artillery support available. Another encouraging thought was the fact that the enemy had thinned down considerably from Nsukka for the Midwest operations, thereby increasing our chances of success. My main fear was that we were taking on by far too much for our strength and resources and I told Njoku this at the conference. My view was that 51 Brigade should marshall the maximum force it could muster and move under my personal supervision and control to Nsukka to support the 53 Brigade operations as the first phase. By so doing, we would concentrate our forces and efforts on a limited number of objectives at a time, and stand a better chance of succeeding. The Army Commander had his very good reasons for rejecting my suggestion. He feared that the enemy could either break through the exposed flanks of 51 Brigade or concentrate even more at Nsukka to neutralise our concentration there. The operation was christened OP TORCH and D-day was fixed for 0600 hours of 16th September, 1967.

In 53 Brigade, the offensive was preceded by the firing of the guns onto the various pre-selected targets with the aid of a prismatic compass that was available. When our guns opened up at their targets at a very slow rate, all Biafran villages near the gun position began to evacuate in the belief that the enemy was shelling as usual. When however word was passed round that it was the Biafran troops shelling the enemy for a change, it soon became a major problem to be able to control the big crowd that gathered at the gun position to applaud the gunners and have a look at the mysterious objects known all over Biafra as "shelling machines." Food and drinks poured into the gun position from the villagers while young women wiped perspiration off the sweating faces of the gunners.

The 53 Brigade attacks went off as planned. On the Eha Alumona axis, our armoured vehicles moved without much difficulty and in their excitement did not even realise that the 15th Battalion they were supporting had not kept to the H-hour. The armoured vehicles soon ran into a barrage of anti-tank fire outside Eha Alumona. The leading vehicle which carried the column commander, Major Megwa was hit and set ablaze. One other vehicle was destroyed and the third managed to escape. Eventually the 15th Battalion moved unsupported under their commanding officer Lt. Colonel Onwuatuegwu (now promoted) but were soon disorganised by the overwhelmingly superior force of the enemy. The enemy thereafter began to push the 15th Battalion back towards Opi junction — a development which threatened the rear of all other troops taking part in the offensive.

Other battalions were doing well and had reached a stage where Nsukka was badly threatened and its recapture from the enemy imminent. It was then that the vital Opi junction fell into the hands of the enemy advancing from Eha Alumona on the 15th Battalion front. The major line of communication with the troops fighting to clear Nsukka was now cut and the reserve force could only attempt to hold a line of defence south of Opi as the 15th Battalion was in disarray. When our forces at Nsukka learnt of the disaster at Opi, they began to pull out through several tracks and foot paths without waiting for instructions, for their resources were exhausted and could not be replenished. Enemy was shelling all villages and advancing towards Enugu. Thus, what had started as a determined offensive in the morning, had turned out to be a retreat by the end of the day. The Biafran artillery had exhausted the 100 rounds that came with the guns and pulled back to Enugu.

My 51 Brigade took off quite well in the operation and before long, moving cross country from the general area of Agala, captured the town of Igumale deep in Northern Nigeria, with little or no opposition. It was easy to move even further North to Utonkon or westwards to Igobido, but mounting administrative and communication difficulties made command and control very difficult. To get to Igumale, our own troops had to trek through 20 miles of extremely difficult terrain, carrying with them their arms, ammunition, and all administrative stores. The most difficult task was the evacuation of casualties from that location using porters. Our troops, to avoid tempting the enemy into a counterattack before we were ready, withdrew to the outskirts of the town of Igumale to await further orders.

In the meantime the First Battalion and elements of the 14th Battalion battled at Eha-Amufu for three days. During that period we pushed the enemy out of the town on two occasions but were each time overrun again by armoured vehicles and artillery bombardment. On the third day, the enemy, using saladine armoured vehicles, and 106 RR guns, demolished almost all buildings in the town to make infantry manoeuvers impossible. We gave up further attempts and reorganised in our defensive positions which were all flooded with water as a result of heavy rains which had fallen throughout the three days of fighting. Due to long and tedious treks involved over a long distance the 4th Battalion started the offensive almost 48 hours late and despite their desperate attempts, they never quite attained their objective. The enemy was then in a position to move reinforcements into Ikem from both Nsukka and Eha-Amufu.

The situation at Nsukka was getting out of hand and further offensives in my sector became meaningless unless that sector was stabilised. The enemy was bull-dozing his way on two axes from Nsukka through Ekwegbe and Ukehe and the resistance being offered by 53 Brigade was no longer effective or impressive. Army Headquarters ordered the despatch of a battalion reinforcement to assist from my Brigade and I moved the First Battalion immediately. A few days later, another Battalion was demanded from me. I withdrew the troops around Igumale and despatched them to Enugu. The situation improved but remained far from being stabilized after the Igumale force tried to re-take Opi from the left flank through Leja. The enemy suffered heavy casualties but retained the initiative. We tried another desperate right flanking move through Uguozo to Idi south of Opi aimed at cutting the enemy's main line of communication. The operation was initially successful until an immediate armour counterattack by the enemy pushed out our troops. A special task force was once more despatched by night through Leja to attack and destroy the enemy and his equipment at Opi. This force was armed with grenades, mines, explosives and other incendiaries in addition to their personal weapons. They displayed such gallantry and bravery and inflicted so much casualty to men and equipment that the enemy punitive bombardments, as a result of that offensive, went on throughout the following day, directed against all towns and villages within range of their guns and mortars. The greatest disaster of that operation was that the well-known poet, Major Christopher Okigbo, one of the bravest fighters on that sector, died trying to lob a grenade into a ferret armoured car. The whole Army in general and the 53 Brigade in particular never completely got over his death for the rest of the war.

Thus, the Biafran soldiers and Militia attacked right, left and centre, day and night to prevent the enemy from making further gains from Opi, the gateway to Enugu. Many civilians who understood the true situation, and the threat it posed on Enugu, came up to the front and joined in the fighting with whatever weapons they could lay their hands on. It was a moving sight and a great display of the will to survive by the people. Needless to say, mere determination could hardly win a battle unless actively supported by the necessary and essential hardwares. For this reason the enemy who had the hardware and perhaps lacked determination was still moving down to Enugu and very soon got into the town of Ukehe, on the 18th of September.

THE UNSUCCESSFUL ATTEMPT TO OVERTHROW COLONEL OJUKWU

At 0600 hours on the 19th of September, Majors Ifeajuna and Alele paid me a visit at my tactical Headquarters located at Nkalagu. Having gone to bed only two hours before then, I was pretty angry to be awakened at that time of the morning. Alele apologized profusely and explained that their mission was vital and urgent but would not take long. Major Alele, who spoke most of the time, first asked me whether I would like to see the war end immediately. I said yes without hesitation. I even added that I would forfeit a year's salary to see such an event happen in an honourable way, in my lifetime. Alele then expressed his profound joy at the fact that my line of thought was completely identical to his. He revealed that he and his group were in contact with British and American government officials who had a peace formula for ending the war.

According to Alele, the only condition demanded by these two countries was the replacement of Ojukwu with somebody else who would do the negotiations, for they did not want to negotiate with Ojukwu. He added that the enemy was waiting to know whether or not we would accept the peace offer before moving into Enugu if still necessary. Speaking about the situation in the Midwest, Alele said it was simply hopeless because the Biafran Army there had completely broken up. He said he expected Benin to fall at any moment, if it had not already fallen. He ended by saying that Ojukwu had to be told to step down on that day because we could not afford to waste the time of an impatient enemy anymore.

I thought the whole story was very exciting and wanted to know if Ojukwu had been given the news, and the answer was that he had not been told. I then asked Alele what would happen if Ojukwu insisted on doing the negotiations himself, and who would take over from him if he agreed to step down. Alele said that Ojukwu would be forced to step down if he showed any unwillingness to do so and would be replaced by my goodself. I pointed out that the whole affair unless properly handled might lead to use of force and bloodshed and would amount to a *coup d'ètat*. If that happened, I explained, we would not only be jeopardising our war effort but would also be risking an internal inter-tribal war within Biafra with prospects of peace with Nigeria farther away than when we started. At this stage, Major Ifeajuna, speaking for the first time, added jovially that he had not quite recovered from the effects of his participation in the January 1966 coup. He said he would rather disappear into the Camerouns, than take part in another coup. He was positive the whole plan would go through peacefully.

167

I rejected the idea of my replacing Ojukwu. My reasons were that nobody, particularly those in the Army, had the foggiest idea of what the government was doing, who our external friends were or from where we got our war supplies. For these reasons, therefore, I argued, it would be unwise for me to assume that impossible responsiblity at that particular time. I also expressed my view that anyone wishing to force Ojukwu out must first ensure he would do better unless he (the new Head of State) wanted merely to surrender and end the war. Above all, I had no intention of being the Head of State who would surrender after a few days.

My suggestion to these officers was that they hand over the matter to Biafran top civilian leaders who were in a position to handle it much better than the Army. I even gave them a list of some civilians they should go and brief at once on their peace formula. I began to grow a bit suspicious of these officers when I learnt from them that even the Army Commander, Brigadier Njoku had not yet been told anything about this. For that reason alone, I called in Lt. Colonel Amadi (now promoted) and after briefing him, asked him to take charge of the Brigade while I went into Enugu to see Njoku. Ifeajuna insisted that I should first call at the ECN flats at Enugu and see Colonel Banjo who, he said, had returned from Midwestern Nigeria the previous night. Naturally, I did nothing of the sort, but rather went direct to Army Headquarters.

On my way to Enugu, I passed a State car carrying Dr. Francis Ibiam and Mr. Christopher Mojekwu, moving in the opposite direction towards my Headquarters at Nkalagu. I was to learn later at Army Headquarters that the gentlemen had gone to see me at my Headquarters. The Army Commander was not in the office and no one seemed to know where he was. I went into the office of one of the senior staff officers, Colonel Patrick Anwunah, and told him I wanted to have a chat with him in private. He insisted that he could only chat with me in the presence of a third person and, having said this, he left his office without telling me the reason why he was adopting that attitude. Eventually, in order to get a hearing from him, I called in both Colonels Nwawo and Nwajei and told them about the discussion I had had with Ifeajuna and Alele. When I finished my account, Anwunah then revealed that he also had information concerning the coup and thought I was a party to it. For that reason, he did not want to get mixed up with me.

I had spent over two hours in Army Headquarters and Njoku was not yet in for work. I was about to go back to my Headquarters at Nkalagu when I was summoned to State House over the telephone by Dr. Ibiam and Mr. Mojekwu. When I got there the gentlemen wanted to know why we were losing ground so fast and what could be done to stop further deterioration unless the Army was tired of fighting. I assured them the Army was doing the best it could against a much stronger enemy and that if we had but 10 percent of the armament at the disposal of the enemy, we could chase him out of Biafra within a few weeks. I knew they were asking those irrelevant questions as a prelude to something they really wanted to know and I could well guess what it was. To save their time and mine too, I told them all about the visit of Majors Ifeajuna and Alele to my Headquarters earlier in the morning, and explained that I had come to Enugu to discuss the matter with the Army Commander. It appeared as if I had hit the main point, for I could see quite easily the bright glow of joy and relief in their eyes and faces. Dr. Ibiam then asked me if I would accept the post of Army Commander if it were offered to me. I said I would prefer to remain with my Brigade. I also pointed out that a vacancy for such a post did not exist in the Army, because we already had an Army Commander. I was then told that the Army Commander was to be fired. The post was again offered to me in a more determined and seemingly threatening voice by Mr. Mojekwu. Frankly with the state of the Army at the time, I accepted it, in order to avoid any misunderstandings that may have arisen if I did otherwise. The three of us then drove to the Premier's Lodge where Ojukwu was then living and there the Colonel confirmed the appointment. I was very anxious indeed to find out the whereabouts of Brigadier Njoku, who I thought may have been killed in battle. I later asked Colonel Ojukwu and he explained that Njoku had become so unpopular that it had become necessary to remove him to a quiet place in his own interest. I moved straight into the Army Headquarters and assumed command of the Army without even going back to my Brigade to bid farewell to my troops and staff. Colonel Amadi was appointed Commander of 51 Brigade in my place.

I did not exactly know for certain that Ifeajuna's peace plan was in effect an attempt to topple Ojukwu until I heard the news that those involved had been executed for an attempted coup. The coup, if that is what it was, had failed but the adverse effect it had on the Army and the war effort generally, was so damaging that Biafra never found its feet again throughout its existence.

From then on, right to the end of the war, every senior Biafran, particularly senior Army officers were assumed to be saboteurs. It was their duty to prove at all times that they were not, and this was one of the most difficult tasks facing all officers throughout the war. One had to bend over backwards and play to the gallery at the expense of military efficiency to achieve any measure of success in this direction. From then on, the entire civilian population, acting out of innocent ignorance, went for the throats of the unfortunate officers in whom they had lost all confidence.

This unfortunate state of affairs was conveniently left unrectified so as to divert the minds of the people from the realities of the war, and to allow them to stick to their wrong impression that we were stronger than the enemy but lost battles due entirely to sabotage.

Only the loyalty of the Head of State was unquestionable in the whole land and as such, he escaped blame for all failures. Still the war effort suffered tremendously to a point where it was too late to do anything about it. In order to complete the purge of the frontlines of "saboteurs," Colonel Eze was removed from command and replaced with Christian Ude. This changeover was a source of great joy to all Biafran civilians whose main desire then was to be told that a saboteur had been identified and got rid of. Eze in particular was not in Ojukwu's good book for allegedly referring to him as "their Governor" before the declaration of Biafra as an independent sovereign State.

THE FALL OF ENUGU

As I sat in my office for the first time in my capacity as the Biafran Army Commander, I was both dazed and confused. The Army was virtually on the verge of disintegration and unless I could personally perform a miracle, it was likely that I had only been appointed the chief undertaker of the Biafran Army and not its commander. Frankly I was not sure whether or not to be grateful to God for putting me into such a high position of honour at the wrong time. The enemy was still pushing the 53 Brigade down to Enugu together with its new Commander Ude. The Brigade had taken a good hiding over a long period without a break and could not be regarded as a fighting force at the time. There was nothing anyone could do for them for no troops existed anywhere to be sent up as reinforcement. From Ekwegbe, the enemy, led by his apparently ubiquitous armoured vehicles, surged on, on Umunko and Ikolo axes and converged on Ukehe. We counterattacked from the flank to take the village of Idi behind Ukehe but initial successes were soon reversed when the armoured vehicles again joined in the battle. As the days passed, our defensive and offensive efforts dwindled rapidly, thereby making it possible for the enemy to take the villages to Enugu one after the other. Okpatu fell, then Ohum, and finally Abor less than four miles to Enugu as the crow flies.

The situation was then too desperate and hopeless to be adequately described. My office was completely jammed with anxious civilians wishing to know what the hell was happening and what I was doing about it. They all had to be briefed and given a hearing if one was not to be bagged for concealing information from the people and thereby acting like a saboteur. From local rumours, that was one of the charges against Njoku whom I had only replaced a few days ago. As a last resort Colonel Ojukwu ordered all provinces to send up all able-bodied men in their provinces, who must be volunteers to defend Enugu. They came in their thousands and at the final count they were 10,000 men in all. Feeding them before they were launched into battle developed into another operation much more difficult than the task they had come to

Biafran families moving out of their homes in a town about to fall into enemy hands

perform for no administrative arrangements had been made for such a large body of men. For instance, by the time they were all fed once, the first batch to be fed were so hungry, they just had to be fed again if they were to be useful to anyone.

Finally they were all transported to their forming up areas at Udi near Enugu where I addressed them together with Dr. Ibiam. A few of them had their own matchets and dane guns and those who had nothing had to be issued with matchets which were brought up in lorries for that purpose. It was now about 2100 hours on the 21st of September and there was not a single civilian leader to help control the mass of human beings surrounding me and apparently itching for battle. The task of issuing matchets to about 10,000 men therefore fell on me, my ADC and seven escorts. The operation was clearly the most tedious I ever embarked upon during the war. It eventually assumed very dangerous proportions when those keen young men began to struggle in the dark to ensure they secured matchets for their offensive. I had to stay and see the end of this if the Army, particularly its commander, was not to be branded saboteurs for their unwillingness to launch willing civilians into battle.

The plan of the operation, Ojukwu had told me earlier, was to move the civilians through Eke and from there swarm the enemy at Abor on two axes, singing war songs, and matcheting all enemy in sight. Frankly, I had little hope about this operation succeeding because I was quite sure those young men, most of whom had never heard the sound of machine gun fire, would run as soon as that happened, or worse still if the enemy shelled. It was futile trying to match determination and matchets against a ruthless enemy using artillery, armour and machine guns. On the other hand, it would have been still more dangerous for anyone to have suggested an abandonment of the offensive.

By 0300 hours the crowd moved in vehicles to Eke and before long it was clear they had begun to advance because the sound of their war songs and yellings were audible from many places. Before 0430 hours, the enemy released a tremendous volley of shells in all directions. The yelling and war songs ceased and the warriors despersed in fright, some straight to their far away villages and others

173

to Enugu. I spoke to some of those who returned to Enugu and they expressed their willingness to fight again if they were absorbed into the Army, trained and issued with weapons.

The enemy was still entrenched in Abor town for the second day running and it was difficult to explain why he had not started shelling Enugu. What I was expecting soon happened when on the 24th of September about ten shells were dropped into Enugu township around the areas of the Police Headquarters and the Government Reservation. From that day on, the enemy shelled various parts of Enugu for three days, causing considerable civilian casualties. It was absolutely impossible to attempt to convince the civilian population that it was the enemy that did the shelling. As far as they were concerned, the Biafran Army "saboteurs" were shelling the town as the enemy according to them was nowhere near Enugu. Some civilians came and reported to me that they had seen the saboteurs inside Ogbete Mines, while others said they were inside Okpara Mines. In that way, over a dozen locations were reported. As an artillery officer who knew only too well the capabilities of the 105 mm gun being used by the enemy, it required a lot of patience on my part to listen to everyone religiously. What was more, I had to despatch troops required for fighting, to investigate each report, to ensure I did not lose my own head for being a saboteur.

On the 26th of September, we put in our last determined effort to destroy the enemy at Abor. From the main axes the 7th Battalion, supported by elements of the 15th Battalion, attacked the town while Colonel Amadi led another force from the 51 Brigade through the right via Iva Valley. It was a good fight which ensued and both sides suffered casualties but our forces failed to move the enemy back. By now, our existing battalions were each no more than a company strength and had lost or damaged a good number of their machine guns which could not be replaced. The following day, therefore, the enemy moved down to Udi (9th mile) junction. At this stage I expressed my fear of Enugu falling into enemy hands to Ojukwu and suggested that the town be evacuated in an orderly fashion, leaving behind only fighting troops and their essential stores. Mr. Mojekwu, who was with us, reminded me that during the Second World War, the enemy was only three miles from Leningrad and was pushed back by the Russians. He did not therefore see the sense in moving out of Enugu with the enemy as far away as nine long miles. In his view everyone should stay and fight to the last man. It was no use explaining to the military historian that, whereas the Russians matched force with force at Leningrad, the Biafran Army had very little to check the enemy with at Udi. The decision however was that Enugu was not to be evacuated, for everyone was going to stay and fight to the last man.

On the following day, despite all attempts the Army was making to stop him, the enemy had made further gains to within five miles of Enugu, and had begun to shell the town with abandon. The people began to evacuate in a hurry leaving all their possessions and those of the government behind. It appeared as if everybody wanted to be the last man. Colonel Ojukwu himself left Enugu on the 26th of September, 48 hours before enemy troops entered Enugu. That night, besides my Headquarters and a skeleton staff, there was nothing left in Enugu. Colonel Ojukwu's instruction that, after his departure from Enugu, a joint Headquarters comprising the Army, the Air Force and the Police should be set up to handle the situation, could not now be implemented, for the Air Force and Police Headquarters had moved away. At least the Police branched in and said goodbye to me before they left — a privilege and courtesy the Air Force never extended to me.

The enemy was in parts of Enugu on the 28th morning and pounding the rest indiscriminately. I went round the town to see what troops there were left and was astonished they were still there in good number but lacked ammunition and food. The civilians who fed the Army and the Head of State who held all ammunition had gone. I met Colonel Amadi by the foot of Millikin Hill on the outskirts of the town still fighting desperately to check the enemy thrust. I gave him quick instructions about the re-deployment and future tasks of his troops and moved on. I later visited the State House and found that it was abandoned intact with three cars locked up outside the main building. The occupants must have left in a hurry. On my way out of Enugu I called at the Food Directorate premises and there all buildings were stacked up with enough food to feed any of the Brigades for at least a fortnight. Other stores contained crates of drinks and cigarettes. My escorts picked up as much food, drinks and cigarettes as they could carry and also the lone Militia sentry who seemed to have been forgotten there.

It was dangerous business getting out of Enugu then, due to the intensity of the shelling, but when I did get out, my ADC managed to send two vehicles to that food store. They moved out a lot of stuff and handed them over to Mr. Mojekwu. By the 29th of September, 1967, the enemy was virtually in full control of Enugu township with no organised force anywhere to check any further moves by him.

To the majority of civilians and some members of the Armed Forces, that was really the end of the war. Morale was so low throughout the nation that an announcement ending the war was expected by many. Disorganisation of civil and military administration was complete and for a fairly long time, what was left of the Army had to devise its own way of administering itself until the civilians got themselves reorganised. During this difficult period, we were very lucky in that the enemy, rather than advance to exploit his success, settled down for a couple of weeks to a methodical and thorough looting of Enugu. This gave us the opportunity to find our feet again to face him once more when he was ready to move.

REFORMATION AND REORGANISATION OF THE ARMY

With the fall of Enugu and the loss of the Midwest, there was really no more Biafran Army except the 52 Brigade in the south, which had not yet seen action. The 53 Brigade and almost the whole of 51 Brigade were in complete disarray and required total reorganisation. Thus, two weeks after my assuming the command of the Army, the same Army ceased to exist as an organised force. My first task was to more or less form a totally new Army if the war was to continue.

The Enugu-Onitsha main road was then undefended. This task I had given to the 15th Battalion under Lt. Colonel Onwuatuegwu.

The author, addressing troops at Agbogugu near Enugu, after the fall of Enugu in 1967.

The author and Dr. Okpara at Army Headquarters, Agbogugu

The Officer pointed out that he had less than 200 extremely tired men left in the battalion and that, until they were granted immediate rest in the rear, his troops would be unable to do anything. I could hardly afford to do that, but with further pressure on the Head of State by Onwuatuegwu, the request was granted. The 7th Battalian relieved them but also pointed out that they were not stronger than the 15th and were equally tired. They had to go there and at least maintain a military presence under Lt. Colonel Adigio (now promoted).

On the Enugu-Awgu-Okigwe road the confusion was even more pathetic. Between Awkunanaw and Akagbe, a distance of about two miles, there were over 4,000 troops milling around without leadership or organisation. Most of them were simply chasing around any senior officers they saw and giving them a good hiding on the grounds that they were all saboteurs. While I was there trying to reorganise the troops with my strong and well-armed escorts, a nervous soldier accidentally discharged a round of ammunition. The 4,000 troops all scattered and began to withdraw in the belief that the enemy was advancing, while some of them thought that enemy agents and saboteurs had already infiltrated their ranks. It took well over two hours to bring the situation back to normal. At the time, unfortunately, Lt. Colonel Nzefili had just arrived to assist me. The soldiers immediately seized him as the saboteur they were looking for, and began to give him a through beating. It required all my escorts, employing all means available to them, to rescue him. He was sent to Awgu hospital and I therefore lost his assistance.

Valuable time was being lost for we could not afford to remain disorganised for any length of time at Awkunanaw which is a part of Enugu town. I therefore recognised the urgent need to have the troops in fighting formations to enable us to defend our ground until we could carry out offensive action against the enemy in Enugu. I therefore spent the rest of 29th September speaking to all the men in groups. I explained to them that the loss of Enugu did not mean the end of the war but merely a temporary set-back which could be rectified with determination. I tried desperately to convince them

179

that there were no more saboteurs in the Biafran Army and that everybody was a true Biafran. I reasoned that the "saboteur tactics" was introduced by the enemy to disorganise the Biafran Army and cause distrust within it. On this issue I am not sure they were all convinced or totally impressed. I told them that if they fought hard enough and recaptured Enugu, the war might end in our favour because the enemy would be too demoralised to continue. Then I went through the reasons why we were fighting and asked whether any of them had any alternative solution. They said no. Finally I asked all those who felt they were too tired to continue, to fall out and go home, so that other volunteers could take their places. Everyone of them stayed put, and soon war songs were being sung loud and clear, and morale was again good. From the crowd, I formed two battalions on the spot. One was deployed in defensive position forward of Awkunanaw and the other advanced into Enugu to make contact with the enemy there. Thereafter all troops of 51 Brigade were sorted out and sent back to the Brigade location at Nkalagu.

While I reformed the remnants of the old Army at Awkunanaw, Colonel Ojukwu, who had also lost all confidence and trust in the Army, was forming a nucleus of a completely new army at Akagbe three miles further back. There, the Head of State had assembled about 400 men, carefully selected from the Port Harcourt Militia and formed them into a special battalion called the "S" Battalion. All ranks were, in effect, civilians and their Quartermaster, Dr. Obunselu, was also a civilian wearing an honorary rank of Lt. Colonel.

On their initial indoctrination, members of the "S" Battalion were told that the regular Army was useless and completely infested with saboteurs. For that reason therefore, they were not to trust or obey any orders coming direct from the Army unless it was cleared by the Head of State, who was to be their commander. They were put on a special diet of eggs, chickens, rice, and fruits in addition to the normal yams and garri.

Word spread through the country that the Head of State had formed a formidable force that was about to clear Enugu and drive away the "vandals" back to the Northern Region. From all over the nation, gifts poured in for the battalion, while young women swarmed their camp to get a glimpse of the heros and pay their compliments to a new army with the true "Biafran Mentality."

Having gathered these freshmen and spoken to them, Colonel Ojukwu left for his new location at Awgu. The task of preparing the battalion for battle fell on me and I was glad I was permitted to teach them elementary weapon training using the discredited instructors of the old Army which were widely accused of suffering from "Nigerian Mentality." As will be seen later, this small force expanded into the "S" Division by September, 1968 and their special nature was a cause of numerous difficulties for the Army throughout the war.

With my Army Tactical Headquarters now stationed at Agbogugu near Enugu we began to make a series of probing attacks on Enugu with the little force available. Very encouraging achievements were made but quite often I had to be at the startline to ensure that those operations went off properly at the right time.

Despite our desperate efforts to became operational once more, our operational and administrative difficulties remained in the main unresolved. For the first time in the course of the war, scarcity of ammunition became an additional problem. With the fall of Enugu and the consequent loss of the airport there, no planes came into Biafra with the necessary supplies for several days. Eventually, when the Port Harcourt airport became operational, the amount of supplies received was so grossly inadequate that ammunition had to be rationed out in rounds to the fighting units right up to the end of the war.

To make our already precarious situation worse, Egyptian piloted Russian Mig planes appeared for the first time to be having real effect on the course of the war. These Egyptian pilots, enjoying complete air supremacy, arrogantly dropped their deadly loads of napalm bombs indiscriminately taking a heavy toll on lives of innocent women and children.

The last and the most tricky problem that confronted me during this period of reformation and reorganisation was the demand for mercenaries by the troops. The soldiers were quite convinced that the enemy at Nsukka had used a large number of white mercenaries who gave the impression of being immortal. According to our soldiers, these mercenaries led enemy attacks, and no matter how much one shot at them, they continued to advance, smiling and beckoning at our own troops who were firing at them. The mercenaries were said to be wearing masks on their faces and bullet-proof jackets.

I was aware that white men were leading some Nigerian attacks at Nsukka and other sectors but they did not obviously have all the powers attributed to them. Yet to neutralise the adverse psychological effect this was having on our troops, it became necessary for us to have our own white mercenaries. I simply loathed the idea of introducing mercenaries into the Army. I later took up the question of procuring mercenaries for the Biafran Army with Colonel Ojukwu and I must say he agreed reluctantly to try to get some. By November, 1967 a number of them arrived in the country and were deployed in Calabar and Enugu sectors of the war. The arrival of six white mercenaries on the Enugu front boosted the soldiers' morale sky-high and they all itched for immediate action, and so one had to be ready to attempt to clear Enugu.

BIAFRA'S COUNTERATTACK TO REGAIN ENUGU

Besides numerous harassing attacks carried out by our own troops against the enemy occupying Enugu, one major but determined attempt was made to clear the town completely of enemy. Troops that took part included the "S" Brigade, which was to put in its first major attack, the 14th Battalion of 51 Brigade, and two battalions of militiamen. The outline plan was to move First Battalion "S" Brigade, through Okpara Mine from Awkunanaw to clear Ogbete complex down to Ogbete bridge close to Enugu General Hospital, for phase one. In the second phase, they would move to clear the General Hospital, the Police Barracks and the Prisons, where they were expected to link-up with the Second Battalion of the same Brigade. Thereafter, both battalions would move, on orders, to the area of the Broadcasting House from where

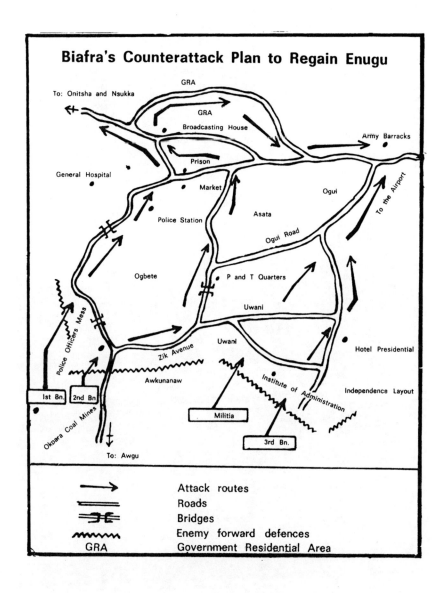

Biafra's Counterattack Plan to Regain Enugu

GRA

To: Onitsha and Nsukka

GRA

Broadcasting House

Army Barracks

Prison

General Hospital

Market

Ogui

To the Airport

Asata

Police Station

Ogui Road

Ogbete

P and T Quarters

Uwani

Hotel Presidential

Police Officers Mess

Zik Avenue

Uwani

1st Bn.   2nd Bn.

Awkunanaw

Institute of Administration

Independence Layout

Okpara Coal Mines

Militia

3rd Bn.

To: Awgu

⟶	Attack routes
=	Roads
⊃⊂	Bridges
∿∿∿	Enemy forward defences
GRA	Government Residential Area

The author addressing troops about to go into battle to regain Enugu

the First Battalion would exploit up the Millikin Hill to the Reform School.

The Second Battalion "S" Brigade was to move on two axes to clear the Police Officer's Mess and Awkunanaw main junction along Zik Avenue. Thereafter the entire battalion would advance on the general axis of Zik Avenue to clear the P and T Junior Staff Quarters and reorganise there. For phase two, the Battalion would move to seize Ogbete market and make contact with the First Battalion in the area of the Prisons across the road in preparation for a combined move to the Broadcasting House. From there the Second Battalion "S" Brigade would sweep through the Government Residential area up to the Army Barracks. As soon as the Militia came up to relieve them at the barracks, the battalion would exploit towards the airport to link up with the 14th Battalion of 51 Brigade who should be moving down that road.

Two Militia battalions were to move on two axes through Uwani to mop up fleeing enemy soldiers. For the second phase they would move through Asata and Ogui sections of Enugu and reorganise along the Kingsway road and then move to the Army Barracks to relieve the Second Battalion "S" Brigade.

The Third Battalion "S" Brigade was to move on the extreme right flank to clear Independence Layout and the Presidential Hotel down to Ogui Road, and then stay there as a reserve force. The 14th Battalion was to move from its location at Emene to clear the Enugu airport. From there it would advance towards Enugu township to link up with the Second Battalion "S" Brigade. After a successful link-up, the 14th would withdraw to rejoin its parent Brigade at Nkalagu.

It was a very ambitious plan which, all the same, had a good chance of succeeding because the presence of the mercenaries gave a tremendous boost to the men's morale. Ammunition was short and the troops had to be taught to shoot only when they could see the brown of the enemy's eyes. In the absence of ammunition pouches, each soldier tied up his 50 rounds of ammunition into bundles of ten each, with bits of haversack provided, and put them into his shirt or pockets. From past experience, we had learnt that loose ammunition broke through pockets and got lost in battle as soon as a soldier ran. For communications, we had two pairs of walkie-talkies with which, it was hoped, Observation Posts Officers would be able to observe the battle from vantage points and report back to the Tactical Operation Centre close to the frontlines. To facilitate control, field commanders were warned against detaching sub-units for odd jobs during the battle.

Finally, the importance of speed was emphasized to enable us to achieve surprise and mix with the enemy before he had a chance of doing any effective shelling. We were thus ready to surround the enemy at Enugu with the infantry and mop him up with the Militia.

Enemy at Ogbete failed to stop our troops when the attack was finally launched on the 19th of November, 1967. When he eventually fell back behind the bridge, our troops of First Battalion occupied Ogbete and thus completed their phase one. The enemy's usually heavy bombardment failed to move them. In the same way, the Second Battalion fought their way gallantly to the P and T Quarters and there fought a two-hour battle to remove the enemy. Even though the shelling was heavy, the formidable armoured vehicles were not yet in sight, and this rendered enemy infantry hopeless. Even the Militia had done extremely well by clearing almost the whole of Uwani right of Awkunanaw. The Third Battalion was also making good progress. By midday it appeared as if Enugu was going to be cleared and rumours to that effect were already circulating even at Umuahia. Unfortunately though, from about 1300 hours all walkie-talkies ceased to function because the batteries had run down and no more replacements were available. From then on, it became difficult to follow the battle closely, despite the efforts of the numerous liaison officers.

At 1600 hours, a Militia liaison officer dashed into my Headquarters and reported that the entire Second Battalion of the "S" Brigade had withdrawn from all grounds they had captured and had moved down to Agbani railway station. From there they intended to catch a train to Umuahia, then capital of Biafra, to see the Head of State and lay some complaints before him. Their main complaint was that they were accusing the Brigade Commander, Lt.

Colonel Frank Obioha, and a majority of the Second Battalion officers of sabotage. They wanted the Head of State, the only one who could give them instructions, to sort it out first, before they resumed fighting, the liaison officer explained. I left the fighting going on and drove to Ndiabo Railway Station to intercept the train and, when the train came in, the whole Battalion was in it.

It took well over one hour of threats to convince the majority of them to come off the train and return to the war front. A few who slipped away and got to Umuahia were arrested and disciplined but irreparable damage had been done. Later, I learnt from the soldiers that they were running short of ammunition and both the Brigade Commander and the battalion officers failed to produce more. By the time I went back to the frontlines, the enemy had moved back into the P and T Quarters and Uwani, and from there moved left and right to cut off both First and Third Battalions, who had not yet known what was happening, due to the non-existence of wireless communications. Supplies to those forward battalions became impossible and soon they were in real trouble.

The only available reserve company put in an attack to re-establish a link with the forward troops but their effort proved futile because, not only were they not strong enough for the task, they also had no ammunition. The Head of State later confirmed to me over the telephone that he too had no ammunition left. I sent an emergency signal to all formations to donate 5000 rounds of ammunition each. Those who could afford it, sent up their quota. By the time any ammunition arrived at my Headquarters, however, the forward troops were already withdrawing in a disorderly fashion through numerous bush-tracks, having lost a lot of weapons. Again it took not less than 48 hours to form an organised force to man our trenches once more. It could have been disasterous if the enemy had attempted to exploit our unfortunate disaster, but rather he was satisfied with regaining all his lost positions.

Thus, we had thrown away Enugu for good as a result of stupid but perfectly innocent ignorance on the part of the Second Battalion "S" Brigade. We had come so close to a major military victory which could have had tremendous political by-products in our favour. We had learnt, I hoped, many lessons despite the failure. One was that ammunition and communications are vital for a successful military operation, no matter how determined one is, for determination will not make a soldier bullet-proof. By far the most important lesson was the question of difficulties attendant upon the introduction of "special units" into an army particularly in a time of war. At the end of Enugu battle, I sent a memorandum to Colonel Ojukwu suggesting that the special nature of the "S" Brigade be abolished and the Brigade be placed under command of Army Headquarters like other units. My argument was that the men of the Brigade were too immature and untrained to fully understand and measure up to the standard expected of them as members of a Special Brigade. I also pointed out to the Head of State that he was too far away and probably too busy with other state matters to command a unit in the field effectively. The Head of State flatly rejected my suggestions and insisted that the Brigade should continue to work directly with him, independent of Army Headquarters. The only concession he gave to Army Hadquarters was that it could give administrative assistance to the Brigade during operations. Even when some of the soldiers and officers who carried out the unauthorised withdrawal were court-martialled, the proceedings and the outcome were kept secret from Army Headquarters.

It took me some time to realise that the "S" Brigade actually existed to counter any mutiny within the regular Army which was no longer completely trusted. I sympathised with the Head of State on this matter, and appreciated the wisdom of his not putting all his eggs in one basket, but I should have thought the best thing to do would have been to have that Brigade in a rear area ready to move to quell any mutiny or coup if they started. But to have them in the frontlines as out-laws, was more damaging to Biafran Army efforts than any enemy action. Unfortunately this system persisted throughout the war and did much damage to the Biafran war effort.

Chapter 9

CIVILIAN INTERVENTION OR HOW NOT TO FIGHT A WAR

The Invasion of Calabar

So far, with the exception of the invasion of Bonny Island, no battles had yet been fought in the south, in the area of 52 Brigade. As already mentioned, out of the two battalions that made up that Brigade, only the 8th Battalion under Lieutenant Colonel Ogbugo Kalu was completely formed. The 9th Battalion in Calabar was still under formation. Colonel Eze having been taken away during the first day of the war, the 52 Brigade remained without a commander and each of the battalions reverted back to the direct command and control of Army Headquarters.

The 9th Battalion, in Calabar, under the command of Major Ogbo Oji, was responsible for the defence of the 75 miles of coastline between Ikang on the Cameroun border and Opobo on the Imo River basin. With its Headquarters at Calabar, the Battalion had two other companies in that town for the defence of Calabar coastline up to and including Ikang. In addition, these companies assisted the Biafran Navy in the task of keeping watch over the high seas with the only patrol boat available. With such a vast area to cover, not more than 20 soldiers could be deployed in any one location, and such places with as many as 20 men were invariably the most likely landing points along the coastline.

A company of the Battalion was stationed at Oron with two platoons on detachment to Egwang. From there a platoon patrolled and defended southwards to Okposo and northwards to Oron, while the other operated westwards to Eket and southwards to cover the coastline between Kwa Ibo River and Okposo. The remaining platoon at Oron, together with the company Headquarters, kept an eye on Cross River and Parrot Island, and at the same time represented the reserve force for the company.

The fourth company of the 9th Battalion was located at Etinam with a platoon each at Eket and Opobo. The platoon at Eket defended the coastline between the Kwa Ibo and the Imo Rivers while the Opobo platoon defended the coastline between the Imo and Bonny Rivers. Looking at a map, the whole deployment appears absolutely ridiculous, necessitating an obvious military question — why not concentrate all available forces in one location and move them together to any area the enemy attacked? My answer is that this was given good consideration but found not to be feasible due to complete lack of wireless communications for early warning of impending invasion. It was therefore better to have a few soldiers on the spot than to come with a strong force too late when the enemy may have been firmly established with an even stronger force. Another point to bear in mind is that as the civilian population fed the Army established in their areas, it was more feasible for the Army to establish as soon as possible in areas they were likely to operate at short notice, in order to have feeding and other administrative arrangements made as early as possible.

The 9th Battalion was armed in the same way as any other Biafran battalion. In addition to their normal bolt action rifles and a few machine guns, the battalion was lucky also to have 4 x 81 mm mortars, a part of the first consignment of mortars received a few days before the fall of Enugu. The only unfortunate limitation to the use of these mortars was the fact that only 100 rounds were available to the Battalion.

That was the military situation in Calabar when the enemy invaded the town on the 17th of October, 1967. The town received heavy pounding from the sea and, together with heavy air support from Russian fighters and bombers which strafed and bombed indiscriminately, the town of Calabar was a hell on earth right from the beginning. In the midst of the confusion created by two hours of bombardment, landing crafts moved in, and soon enemy troops were landing at Atim Bo, Ikang and Esuk Mbai beaches.

Even though Biafran troops at the beaches sank a total of four crafts, the pressure was too heavy for them to withstand indefinitely and eventually they were over-powered during the third enemy attempt. By the time the enemy landed, Biafran rockets, bombs, mines and the indispensable "ogbunigwe" (mass killer) all deployed along the coast, had inflicted alarming casualties on the surging enemy troops. The Biafran soldiers fought with such a determination that not a single soldier withdrew unless he was wounded.

As soon as fighting started on the beaches, firing began in most parts of Calabar town and our troops on their way to the beaches were sniped at. The commanding officer, Major Oji, came under heavy machine gun fire as soon as he left his Headquarters on his way to the frontlines. His left arm was badly shattered and he was immediately evacuated to Umuahia. Thereafter the battalion fought without a commander after only a few hours of battle. As already mentioned, there was no brigade commander either because the Head of State, whose responsibility it was to make the appointment, had not done so. The former Brigade Commander, Colonel Eze, who had gone to help out at Nsukka ended up as a renowned "saboteur" and was therefore ineligible for field command. He was now posted to my Headquarters by the Head of State, as the Chief of Operations Officer amidst pressures if not threats on me from civilian quarters to get rid of him entirely. The alleged saboteurs firing all over Calabar town won the battle through the confusion they created.

While I looked for another battalion commander to replace Oji, one of the young company commanders took over an already hopeless situation. As enemy troops landed and poured into the town, hand to hand fighting developed with our troops shifting from one part of the town to another and laying several effective ambushes. Casualties were very heavy on both sides but was particularly heavy among the civilians who were not spared by Major Adekunle and his troops. By the afternoon, armoured vehicles were landed and were very ruthlessly used in demolishing

191

buildings and inflicting heavy civilian casualties. Before dark, our troops had run completely short of ammunition and withdrawn to the outskirts of the town to the area of the Hope Wadell Institute.

The Head of State unfortunately had no ammunition in his store, so that, while I tried to raise ammunition loans from all other field formations, rattles, similar to those used by football fans but scientifically constructed to produce the same sound as machine guns, were despatched to our troops. With these, they would simulate machine gun fire from time to time to discourage the enemy from advancing. In the meantime our troops prepared their defences and constructed armour traps. A counterattack was even planned as soon as the promised ammunition and reinforcements were received. I must say the rattles deceived the enemy for the day, the only problem being that as soon as they were sounded, the enemy reacted with heavy shelling.

On the following day, Lt. Colonel David Okafor took over the command of the 9th Battalion. In addition, some ammunition was despatched, enough to go round 30 rounds per weapon at the least. No counterattacks could be launched because the promised reinforcement had not yet arrived. In the meantime, with the rattles and frequent fighting patrols into the town, the enemy was kept busy shelling.

On the 20th he resumed his offensive northwards from Calabar. On the first day of this offensive in spite of the usual lavish support, our own troops held their ground firmly. Twice we lost two lines of defences, but each time we quickly regained them, with less than 350 men against the enemy brigade. Enemy troops came in waves, with each wave fighting for two hours against the same Biafran troops who had to fight without a break all day. On the second day, when the enemy offensive began after an all night shelling, our troops soon ran completely out of ammunition again. The men were very tired and their strength had been reduced to about a company of 200 men. There were no more mortar bombs left in that sector of the war.

A bit of difficulty arose over the movement of the 7th Battalion to Calabar even though they had been warned for some time. When the 7th withdrew for a rest, their automatic rifles were withdrawn and issued to the 15th which was being despatched to 51 Brigade at Nkalagu. Now that the 7th was due for deployment the only weapons available were the usual bolt action rifles in use with most other Biafran field units. The soldiers of the 7th rejected these weapons and insisted on having their usual automatic rifles before they moved to Calabar. After my long address made up of a medley of threats and persuasions, the troops left rather late but with the promise that they would get automatic weapons soon. There was no question of disciplinary action against them because most soldiers were very keen and only acted foolishly at times as a result of misguided enthusiasm or pathetic ignorance due to little or no basic military training.

With Lt. Colonel Okafor in Calabar commanding the 9th, and Lt. Colonel Adigio going down there with the 7th to join him, the need to create a Brigade Headquarters for the two battalions arose. I therefore submitted a list of qualified officers for consideration to the Head of State and he was doing just that.

By the time the 7th Battalion got down to fighting, the enemy had already pushed the tired 9th Battalion ten miles outside Calabar township, for the trick of the rattles seemed to have been discovered. The two battalion commanders, working independently but in close cooperation and understanding, rallied their troops into a series of desperate counterattacks particularly as the 7th came down with a big ammunition consignment of 40,000 rounds of rifle ammunition, 200 rounds of artillery shells and the same number of mortar bombs. Using also our locally manufactured products, the enemy was hit so hard that while he retreated with his armoured vehicles towards Calabar, our troops followed closely on his heels chanting war songs under a rain of mortar and artillery shells let loose by the angry enemy.

We had regained four miles before we were hit by the usual ammunition shortage. While the troops dug in and laid ambushes deep behind enemy lines, frantic but futile efforts were made to secure ammunition from somewhere. When the enemy therefore counterattacked, this time with the full weight of his air support, our troops had no alternative but to start retreating again. Within a few

193

days Odukpani had fallen and the enemy was still advancing towards Aya Abam. Enemy jet planes completely covered all lines of communications to our front troops by day, thereby making supplies and evacuation of casualties impossible in daylight. Heavy casualties were inflicted by these planes on soldiers, militiamen and civilians who, in anger, tried to engage them with rifles and dane guns, in the absence of anti-aircraft guns.

While enemy pressure mounted, the Commander of 7th Battalion, Colonel Adigio, developed an acute stomach ulcer and was replaced by his second-in-command, Major Omerua. Shortly after, the soldiers in desperation, accused Colonel Okafor of keeping back ammunition meant for fighting and refusing to issue it to them. I knew this was going to happen sooner or later, and all the signal messages sent to that sector from Army Headquarters to confirm officially that there was a shortage of ammunition failed to save the situation. Word went round Biafra that a new saboteur and the main cause of failure in Calabar, had been found out. The nation, while giving thanks to God for this discovery, demanded nothing but Colonel Okafor's head. I remember a top Biafran Government official during his visit to my Headquarters at Agbogugu in December, 1967 telling me that he was working on having Okafor publicly executed. I put the true facts before him and Okafor retained his head at least to the end of the war amidst public protests. As usual I, as the Army Commander, came under public criticism for condoning sabotage. Okafor left the sector and was replaced by his second-in-command, Major Odigwe. I was glad the Head of State as a soldier knew the facts just as much as I did. Yet the Biafran public must not be told that we had practically nothing with which to fight our battles. If they had known, their logical reaction would have been to call for an end to the war against the government policy of fighting to the last man.

With enemy pressure on the increase and all experienced officers ousted by vigilant Biafrans, the need to appoint a Brigade Commander to supervise the young Battalion Commanders became very urgent. Colonel Akagha was the most qualified officer available for the post at the time and I put him up to Colonel Ojukwu for consideration. Colonel Akagha, who had just been released from police custody, was of very low morale. Apparently, after his escape from the ambush in Midwestern Nigeria, he returned to Biafra only to be accused by all of sabotage. He and his wife were chased and hounded by a section of the population until the police finally bagged him for a couple of weeks. His story that he had spent two weeks walking back through the bushes from the area of Benin to Biafra was not believed by those outside the Army. Rather, it was said he had spent those two weeks in enemy camp, even though looking at him, it was obvious he had gone through hell. It was therefore with great reluctance that the Head of State approved this appointment and it was also with considerable amount of fear of getting into trouble again that the Colonel left for Calabar. When Akagha got to his new sector, he set up what was called the 56 Brigade. The situation was still very grave despite the impressive efforts of the young Battalion Commanders. Akagha quickly reorganised the new Brigade and forwarded his plan to me for dealing with the enemy. That plan unfortunately could not be implemented due to acute shortage of ammunition which was far from adequate even for a meaningful defensive operation. As the situation became hopeless and intolerable, Akagha sent the following emergency signal to me:

> From: 56 Brigade
> To: Tactical Army Headquarters
> Info: Defence Headquarters, Commander-in-Chief
>
> Commander for GOC. Situation this sector definitely out of hand if not hopeless. Not a single round of ammunition held while enemy pressure continues ceaselessly for the past 48 hours. We intend to stay on and make the supreme sacrifice. Please help before it is too late. We who are about to die, salute you.

Admittedly the signal was moving, and a few of my staff tried to conceal the tears in their eyes, but then there was nothing I could do unless of course they wanted more rattles. The situation there was further complicated by the mercenaries who had just arrived in that sector. After operating for 48 hours, these mercenaries began to realise the overwhelming odds against the Biafran Army. Their courage oozed and they took fright. Some of them even began to admit that they lacked what it takes to fight on the Biafran side. The leader of the mercenaries then decided that our troops should withdraw over 50 miles from Aya Abam to behind the Cross River at Ikot Okpora. There he said, we would defend the riverline with the little resources available until we were ready for a fight. They revealed that on their way to the front, Colonel Ojukwu had told them that jet planes, heavy artillery and mortars, machine guns and limitless amounts of ammunition were expected to arrive soon in Biafra. They therefore argued that it was unwise to suffer unnecessary casualties before the arrival of the new consignment.

The Brigade Commander and his Battalion Commanders who had heard this type of story several times before did not even want to consider the withdrawal plan at all for they knew nothing of the sort was ever going to come into Biafra. I also ordered them not to withdraw. The mercenaries grew very angry and quarrelled with the Battalion Commanders. They told the troops about their withdrawal plan and split their ranks with some wanting to withdraw while others refused to do so.

When the mercenaries took the case to Defence Headquarters, all the Battalion Commanders in the Sector were removed and replaced by others who would obey the mercenaries. In addition, Calabar operations were handed over to the mercenaries with instructions to deal with the Head of State. Colonel Akagha was allowed to stay on, but only to assist with the administration of the Brigade. The discredited Battalion Commanders, Omerua and Odigwe arrived in tears at my Headquarters for another posting.

The situation created by these mercenaries in the Calabar sector of the war completed the disaster there. There were then no field commanders on the ground, leaving behind only tired soldiers split into two camps and without ammunition. I thought the situation was serious enough to demand an immediate discussion between Colonel Ojukwu and myself.

Because the telephone line between my Headquarters and the State House was faulty, I drove the 60 miles to Umuahia from Agbogugu to see the Head of State. There at Umuahia, the Principal Staff Officer at the Defence Headquarters, Colonel Emmanuel Nwobosi, after checking with the State House, announced that the Head of State and the Commander-in-Chief of Biafran Armed Forces, Colonel Chukwuemeka Odumegwu Ojukwu did not want to see me because I had not booked an appointment to see him. He knew what I had come to discuss.

In the end, the mercenaries led the Biafran soldiers in a type of withdrawal yet unknown in Biafra, through a distance of 50 miles in a most disorderly manner. As soon as our own troops moved across to the west bank of the Cross River at Ikot Okpora, the enemy moved up quickly and occupied the east bank, and then began to shell us heavily day and night. The mercenaries could no longer wait for the promised planes, armour, artillery and mortars and, in frustration, they abandoned their positions in mass and left Biafra.

A point the mercenaries did not seem to have considered when they decided to withdraw to Ikot Okpora was the effect it would have on our troops further North in parts of Ogoja Province. The Ogoja force under Colonel Ochei covered from the area of Ikot Okpora northwards to Iyahe bridge and westwards to the Cameroon border. With the enemy at Ikot Okpora their entire rear was open, so that when eventually the enemy advanced unchecked further north to Obubra, the Ogoja force was cut off completely and virtually disintegrated.

Thus, the entire Calabar Province was lost to the enemy, not because of his valour or competence, but because of a series of self-inflicted wounds to our command structure there — wounds which were made ulcerous as a result of poor administrative and tactical support and unnecessary protocol. As expected, the people selected their scapegoats and reacted violently against them. Colonel Akagha was moved out of the sector and Colonel Ochei lost his command. The people of Biafra were appeased temporarily but an irreparable loss had again been sustained. From then on, I considered the very presence of mercenaries in Biafra a threat to our survival as a nation.

FIRST INVASION OF ONITSHA

The fall of Enugu at the end of September, 1967 and also Calabar shortly after, left Biafra an anxious and demoralised nation. The struggle by the Army to survive was becoming increasingly difficult with a good number of its senior officers already discredited. Second Division, which had been mopping up Asaba since it got in there on the 8th of October, had within 48 hours completed its task of killing off most of the young men and violating the women folk, and was ready to continue its advance.

At Onitsha sat what was left of the Midwest Expeditionary Force which had been quickly reformed into three weak battalions, the 11th, the 12th and the 18th Battalions, each with about 400 weapons. The 18th Battalion, under Major Nsudoh, was responsible for the defence of Onitsha town and about four miles north and south of it. The 11th Battalion defended the riverline from Atani to (Akri Ogidi) Ndoni while the 12th under Colonel Ivenso was based at Otuocha and was responsible for the defence of the area between Nsugbe and Idah in Northern Nigeria. The Calabar operation, which was still going on at the time, had taken up almost all the available ammunition in the country and only very little ammunition was held by other sectors including Onitsha. However the Research and Production Board had worked very hard to solve the problem of ammunition shortage by making available to the Army a good quantity of their products most of which were deployed at Onitsha. Along the banks of the Niger, "ogbunigwes," Biafran rockets, "foot cutters" and other mines of all sorts, were deployed in addition to Biafran-made hand grenades which were available to the soldiers in good quantity. To ensure a water-tight defence with minimum use of small arms, two six pounder anti-tank

Samples of Biafran made weapons used during the civil war

guns and one 105mm artillery gun available were also deployed in the sector.

On the 4th of October, the shelling of Onitsha became unusually heavy and before midday all civilians inside Onitsha had evacuated having suffered a considerable amount of casualties. The pattern and intensity of the shelling clearly indicated that an attack would follow from Asaba across the River Niger.

Before long, our speculations about a possible invasion were confirmed when between eight and ten boats of various sizes were identified on the Asaba bank of the river. Soon the Armada sailed and the invasion of Onitsha was about to begin. Biafran soldiers sat quietly and patiently in their bunkers and waited for the boats to come within effective killing range of our weapons. The lone artillery gun in the meantime, tried to engage the boats with direct fire, but packed up after firing six rounds out of the twenty rounds available to it. At mid-stream, the invading force split into two — one force continued to move down towards the Onitsha market beach while the other wheeled off towards the ferry point in the area of the Prisons.

At this stage the order to open fire was given, and within thirty minutes of opening fire, four enemy boats had been sunk, but that did not stop the rest from continuing the advance, particularly towards the ferry point. In the meantime, three more boats left Asaba and began to move down to Onitsha to join the fighting. Very soon the leading boats carrying enemy heavy equipments had got close enough to make possible accurate use of those equipments. From the boats, enemy Panhard and Saladine armoured cars, together with several 106 mm guns, opened up a heavy barrage on our bunkers, some of which began to crumble.

Our six pounder guns had exhausted their ammunition leaving our troops with nothing with which to deal with the considerably large and armour-plated enemy boats which now sat defiantly facing us and blazing away without a meaningful retaliation from our side. When the pressure became unbearable, our troops began to withdraw into the Onitsha hinterland and thus by midday, the whole riverline had been abandoned to the enemy.

While we reorganised in the area of Saint Charles College, the Seminary and Boromeo Hospital, the enemy landed in Onitsha and quickly spread all along the riverline. The first evidence we had to show that the enemy had landed was that the Onitsha Market, the largest of its type in Black Africa was ablaze, together with various other places. The full implications of the occupation of Onitsha at that particular time by the enemy were obvious to the Army. That meant that all routes leading into the "Ibo heartland" would have been completely undefended thereby making further resistance by Biafra difficult. While our own troops reorganised with our Headquarters now set up at Ogidi six miles away, the enemy swarmed the whole of Onitsha up to the Dennis Memorial Grammar School. A quick counterattack was planned and launched with two strong companies which had been assembled. These companies, each with a Landrover mounted with a machine gun in support, were led by Joe Achuzia, a volunteer Militia Officer, and Major Nsudoh, a seasoned regular.

By 1330 hours, the companies moved down and quickly cleared the Denis Memorial Grammar School complex and thereafter split into two in pursuit of the frightened enemy soldiers. With Achuzia advancing on the New Market Road axis and Nsudoh doing the same on the Old Market Road, the enemy was in complete disarray and were scampering all over the town in large groups. As Biafran troops again approached the riverline, hundreds of enemy soldiers were seen trying to get into fleeing boats, and it was particularly sad to see several of them drowning in the Niger in their attempt to escape.

On the New Market Road axis, Achuzia soon reoccupied his trenches despite the intense heat generated by the blazing Onitsha Market close by. When our troops on the New Market Road got to the ferry point, they discovered to their utter amazement that the enemy had just off-loaded and was about to put into action a Panhard armoured vehicle, the first of a fleet waiting to be off-loaded. The armoured vehicle, which was not yet in a position to fight, was immediately attacked and taken intact while a sizeable

201

group of Nigerian infantry men around it scattered in many directions without a fight.

As the story of the Biafran success inside Onitsha spread, those Biafran troops who had earlier been dislodged and were still reorganising outside Onitsha moved back in strength to join in the mopping up operation. By 1700 hours we were once again completely in control of Onitsha. Enemy losses were so much that rather than quote casualty figures, it is sufficient to say that the invading Nigeria's Second Division was almost destroyed. The only comparison to this destruction could be found in the Battle of Obollo Afor.

SECOND INVASION OF ONITSHA

Barely seven days after the first enemy invasion of Onitsha it became clear that the second one would come any day. For ten days there was a non-stop air bombardment of the town beginning at dawn each day and lasting till dusk. The Russian war planes strafed and bombed until neither life nor buildings were left in Onitsha; thereafter the planes resorted to attacking livestock. All the same, our troops, then in high morale, were quite comfortably relaxed in their trenches and keeping a round-the-clock vigil over the River Niger. In my view I considered the air bombardment a diversionary measure in preparation for an invasion which, if it did come, would be from somewhere else other than from Asaba. There were some officers who thought that Colonel Muhammed would not be daft enough as to attack Onitsha again, and therefore regarded the raids as a kind of punitive measure by Nigeria to make good her losses. Whatever it was, we were not taking any chances, for each night after the raids, we continued improving our defences with fresh mines, rockets and the indispensable "ogbunigwes." An attempt was made by the Science Group to completely electrify the coastline, but this idea was dropped due to lack of time and necessary stores.

With all the ammunition and weapons captured during the first enemy invasion, we were much stronger than ever before. The newly acquired armoured car sat confidently under cover near the Catholic

Cathedral at the ferry point, and each morning most of the soldiers went on a pilgrimage there to ensure that it had not been stolen. No one could stop them. On the morning of the 20th of October, the Nigerian Armada of approximately ten boats was again sighted sailing down the Niger from Asaba in exactly the same fashion as in the first invasion. As the Commander of the Onitsha troops (now called the 11 Division), Colonel Nwawo, went from trench to trench to alert the troops, he found quite a lot of them playing cards and chanting in complete disregard of the approaching enemy vessels. The soldiers in their over confidence explained to their commander that they did not intend to bother themselves until the enemy got to the usual killing ground. The soldiers were later ordered to take up their positions and as soon as the boats were in mid-stream, we opened up with all we had.

The six pounder pounded away hitting one boat after another and sinking them. The most exciting incident was the sinking of a boat by a Biafran-made rocket. Apparently, when the rocket was fired it flew away towards the boats trailing behind it very heavy smoke. Halfway to the boats, the rocket veered right and then right again and appeared to be flying back directly to our trenches thereby causing a considerable amount of panic. All of a sudden the rocket did a complete turnabout, and raced towards the enemy boats and before it had a chance to turn off again it hit one of the boats which was more than 200 metres away from the one it was aimed at. Hit by the powerful warhead the rocket was carrying, the boat began to smoke and finally explosions were heard as the boat tilted on its side. Screams of both the wounded and the frightened were distinctly audible and many soldiers were seen jumping into the river. Dozens of other rockets which were fired, clearly missed their targets but the one hit scored was enough to put the fear of the Lord into the hearts of the enemy.

After two hours of battle, six boats had been destroyed or put off action and the rest were sailing home to Asaba the fastest they could, having suffered more casualties than in their first attempt. This second defeat of the enemy at Onitsha more than reassured us of our ability to hold the town indefinitely against any attacks on it from across the river. The Biafran Science Group war products along the river bank had done so well and were so effective that they were nicknamed "the shore battery."

The Onitsha successes brought with them the introduction of active politics within the Army and the use of military campaigns to political advantage in Biafra. This came about as a result of the Commissioning of Militia Officer Achuzia into the Regular Army. Following the commendable role played by Achuzia during the two successful Onitsha campaigns, I approved the recommendation by Brigadier Nwawo (now promoted) to have Achuzia commissioned as a Major in the Regular Army. Hardly did I realise at the time that I was making the greatest mistake of my military career by so doing.

Achuzia realised as soon as he got into the Army that the two vital requirements needed by an officer to win the admiration and respect of the people of Biafra were publicity and playing to the gallery. He, in short, saw the vital need for doing and saying what the people wanted to see or hear whether those things impeded the war effort or not. Like a few others, he discovered the magic of speeches of glorious intentions among the Biafran Public, even if these were not followed up by action.

As soon as he was commissioned, Achuzia got the approval of the Head of State to go and clear Nsukka with two rifle companies! This was obviously a waste of time and ammunition, but he was asked to do so for publicity reasons. He infiltrated his troops through Otuocha-Adani and Nkpologu into Nsukka and carried out three raids. One of these raids was against the army barracks there, and the others against Opi junction and Ukehe. Soon afterwards the news was flashed throughout the whole country that Achuzia had not only cleared Nsukka, but was holding the road to Enugu thereby cutting off the entire enemy force at Enugu. By this Achuzia had become a national hero while civilian pressure mounted on me to arrange to mop up the stranded enemy inside Enugu. The aim of that exercise was to discredit the regular officers and give the Biafran civilians the impression that the Biafran Army had all they needed to win the war, but lacked expertise and loyalty. These civilians therefore began to argue, quite logically too, that if a civilian like

Achuzia could achieve such a success after two weeks in the Army, and the regulars could not do the same, then something must be wrong with the Biafran Army. While all Biafran information media were still echoing the news, Achuzia and his men were already back in Onitsha.

Thereafter the anger of the civilians against the "Nigerian officers" in the Biafran Army was on the increase. It was then that Colonel Aghanya visited Onitsha to congratulate the officers who took part in the recent successful operations. While he was at Onitsha there was an air raid during which Aghanya ordered the soldiers around him not to engage the planes with rifles; otherwise they would only be attracting them. As soon as the planes left, the soldiers arrested Aghanya for preventing them from shooting down the jets which they claimed flew so low. When he tried to get away, a burst from a machine gun was fired by a soldier close to him as a warning. He was eventually stripped to the pants and given a good beating. Brigadier Nwawo who wanted to intervene, was accused of collaboration and to save his life, Nwawo was smuggled out of Onitsha in disguise. He returned the following day to resume his command. In the meantime Aghanya was being taken to Awgu by the soldiers who insisted on taking him before the Head of State. The Commissioner of Police for Onitsha saved Colonel Aghanya when he successfully convinced the soldiers to release the officer at Awka; by then he had been well beaten. Seeds of disintegration had at last been introduced into the Army.

THE THIRD INVASION OF ONITSHA

Preliminary Battles around Nsukka

By the end of November, 1967, there was sufficient intelligence information to show that there was going to be a third invasion of Onitsha, this time from Nsukka. When, however, the enemy Second Division began to move up to Idah from Midwestern Nigeria, it was obvious the offensive was indeed going to take place. We followed the progress of their moves and concentrations daily, but had absolutely no counter measure capabilities. Another invasion of the Midwest at the time by us could have at least halted the move but we lacked the means and the strength required to do that effectively. There were even no troops available to strengthen our defences in the area of Nsukka. I therefore deployed militiamen in such places as Agbo, Nkpologu, Orobo, Abi and Adani, to check infiltration and give the Army timely warning. Immediately behind the Militia in the area of Udi was the 53 Brigade which was already over-stretched trying to confine the enemy to Enugu. To the left flank of 53 Brigade were some elements of the 12th Battalion of 54 Brigade whose task was solely to guard the Northern approaches to Otuocha.

That state of affairs persisted until late December, 1967 when Colonel Muhammed began his long march to Onitsha. The news of the new move reached my Headquarters then at Agbogugu, through Militia sources who claimed that the enemy was advancing in strength from the area of Nsukka, through Agbo towards Nkpologu. This was closely followed by another information that another enemy force was advancing along Abi axis towards Nibo. When those reports were later checked by the Army, it was confirmed that at least a brigade of enemy infantry, supported by a minimum of four armoured vehicles, artillery and heavy mortars, was indeed advancing southwards in that sector. No further confirmation was needed to show that Colonel Muhammed's Second Division was indeed on the move to Onitsha which had eluded them for so long. The militiamen also reported hearing enemy soldiers cry out "Anicha sosai" (Onitsha without delay) as they attacked their locations over 80 miles from the final objective.

I held a quick conference with Nwawo and Ude, Commanders of 11 Division and 53 Brigade respectively and gave them tasks. 53 Brigade had the task of establishing a very strong defensive line behind a small bridge north of Ukpata. From there they were to send a force further north towards Nkpologu to make contact with the enemy. In the meantime the Brigade was to prepare other major defensive positions along the riverline at Umulokpa where the enemy was not to be allowed to pass under any circumstances. The usual mines, rockets and "ogbunigwes" were laid, trees felled and traps for armoured vehicles dug all along the likely enemy approach routes. Colonel Ojukwu made a generous grant of 480 bolt action rifles and a new battalion was formed on the spot to reinforce the weak defences. All the mercenaries who were still in the Enugu sector were ordered to join the 53 Brigade under their leader, Captain Le Rois. They took with them six brand new 81mm mortars specially issued to them for this operation by the Head of State. For these mortars the mercenaries managed to wrench 300 bombs from Ojukwu.

For 11 Division, two companies of the 12th Battalion, were ordered to move up through Umueje to Adani and from there to Ukpabi-Nibo and Nkpologu if possible. If they managed to get there, they were to link up with 53 Brigade. It was also the task of 54 Brigade of 11 Division to defend the Umueji-Adaba road, and also to construct an impregnable defensive line behind the Anambra River at Umueje. In addition, the Brigade was responsible for covering all road and tracks leading westwards from Umulokpa. These tasks were obviously too much for the forces available but that was the best that could be done under the circumstances.

Even before our troops were in position, the enemy, as yet unchallenged, was already inside Nkpologu and advancing further south on two axes to Adani and Ukpata. 53 Brigade first made contact at Uvuru south of Nkpologu and there a very bloody battle, which lasted for almost a whole day, was fought at the end of which we were forced back to our second line of defence at Ukpata. That first encounter showed quite clearly that Muhammed was advancing with a very formidable force, perhaps stronger than the whole of the Biafran Army put together. It was noticed that behind that formidable force came a convoy of heavy road construction equipments, which were used for clearing the roads and reconstructing the bridges immediately.

By the time the enemy advanced up to Ukpata our troops had collected themselves better. An extremely bitter battle raged for two days ceaselessly with the enemy attacking in waves with armour support and lavish artillery and mortar bombardment. During that period our numerous road obstacles played a major role in preventing the armoured vehicles from moving very freely. On the third day, however, we were forced to withdraw due to shortage of ammunition, lack of reinforcement and fatigue. Before withdrawal, our troops had trapped an armoured vehicle in a ditch but had no means of destroying it. Several attacks were put in to capture and recover it, but these failed because of the heavy fire coming both from the armoured vehicle itself, and from enemy troops on our flanks. The 53 Brigade was now beaten back to Umulokpa, the last major defensive location on the left flank of Udi.

Meanwhile, on the Adani axis, the 12th Battalion had done very well to prevent the enemy from advancing farther than Ukpabi-Nibo. It even appeared at one stage as if we were pushing the enemy back to Nkwelegwu near Nkpologu. Despite its achievements, the 12th Battalion was still in danger of being cut off below Adani from the Adaba road. To avoid this major disaster, most of the troops deployed along the Adani-Nkpologu axis were pulled out for the defence of Adaba road to their flank. If our troops had on the other hand advanced through Adani to Nkpologu we should have also cut the enemy off at Umulokpa, but for obvious reasons, that could not be done. For an operation of that nature, strength both in manpower and equipment backed fully by good administrative support was vital and those were exactly what we lacked. The enemy was equipped to fight indefinitely without re-supply whereas no Biafran force could last for more than a 24-hour battle if it was not re-supplied on the normal daily basis. I have already mentioned the futility of long-range penetration operations without wireless communications, for control is bound to be lost as soon as the operation starts. For the above reasons and many others, we simply had no alternative but to dance defensively to the tune of the enemy.

To discourage the enemy from advancing further from Umulokpa so that we could have the time to be fully prepared for him, I decided we should invest all the ammunition we had into a spirited attack on his locations. Two companies of 12th Battalion were ordered to move from the left flank to seize Ukpata and destroy the small bridge there being used by enemy vehicles. From there, they would advance northwards to Uvuru. 53 Brigade was also ordered to move a force on the right flank to capture Adaba and thereafter move to link up with 12th Battalion at Ukpata. While these minor attacks were going on behind the enemy, the Special Task Force Battalion (STF) formed with the 480 bolt action rifles given by the Head of State, would attack enemy concentration at Umulokpa.

When we moved into this offensive we did very well initially, inflicting very heavy casualties on the enemy, but the presence everywhere of armoured vehicles made the capture of ground very difficult. Even when considerable ground was captured it was impossible to hold it for any length of time. This offensive ended after 48 hours and had served a useful purpose in a way.

BATTLE OF AMADIM OLO — DECEMBER, 1967

Shortly after our offensive, Colonel Muhammed launched the first major offensive of his move, aimed at capturing the vital Umulokpa bridge and the adjoining Olo town. The preliminary bombardment which started by 0530 hours was so heavy that by 1130 hours over 5000 shells had been fired against 100 rounds of Biafran counter bombardment. Major Obioha, commander of the nearby "S" Brigade, gave the number of shells fired by the enemy at 1130 hours as 8000 rounds. The shelling continued till 1400 hours when the enemy put in his first assault obviously expecting the location to have been abandoned. It was not, but then almost half of the men in STF Battalion, which was defending the bridge, had already been evacuated to Achi Military Hospital, suffering from shell shock or what was known in Biafra as "Artillery sickness."

This new development not withstanding, the remainder of STF Battalion under the formidable Major Olehi, assisted by a battalion of 53 Brigade, commanded by Captain Nweke, succeeded in beating back waves of enemy assaults. A ding-dong battle went on for several days around the bridge which we had earlier destroyed. Several times the enemy crossed the relatively shallow river without his armour, but each time he was beaten back with heavy losses. This battle, which was consuming over 50 percent of all resources available to the entire Biafran Army, was becoming by far too expensive to sustain and subsequently the quantity of ammunition available dwindled rapidly.

As a result of the massive shelling on the first day, the leader of the mercenaries, Captain Le Rois, an excellent and brave officer, was seriously wounded on the left leg. The other mercenaries grew panicky and decided to stop fighting until they had been to Umuahia to see Colonel Ojukwu and appoint a new leader. Everyone may have welcomed their departure if they had not taken with them all the mortar barrels issued to them for the operation. We were thus unable to fire off the few bombs we had for several days. The mercenaries never showed up again in the northern sector and, in fact, almost all of them left the country like their Calabar counterparts.

Increasing ammunition and other difficulties forced our troops to withdraw from Umulokpa bridge to Olo town on the 7th day of fighting. Christian Ude, the Brigade Commander, began immediate preparations for a counterattack as soon as ammunition was available and weapons found for unarmed men within the Brigade. Unfortunately, the usual distrust of soldiers for their "Nigerian officers" began to develop again. The soldiers were convinced that the two battalion commanders, Olehi and Nweke, had hidden away all the ammunition for the battle in order that Nigerian troops would win.

In preparation for a possible counterattack, Captain Nweke left his front positions one morning at 0430 hours, accompanied by three escorts, to do a preliminary reconnaissance in accordance with accepted military procedure. As he re-entered his defensive locations at 0730 hours feeling very happy with himself for a job well done, he was stopped and arrested by some of his troops, most of whom were not yet six weeks in the army. Led by the Company Sergeant Major whose nickname was "One man, One bullet," the soldiers accused Nweke of having gone across to the enemy to confer with him. They thought their suspicions about the officer withholding ammunition had been proved. Nweke's desperate attempt to explain to them what he had gone to do, and how important a reconnaissance was before an attack, failed to impress his men. They had already made up their minds to execute him on the spot, because they feared that the Army Headquarters would do nothing about it in the same way it had done nothing to punish all saboteurs captured on previous occasions. Major Olehi, the other battalion commander, got to the scene before the execution and tried to plead for his colleague's life, but was soon accused of the same offences and awarded the same punishment — death. Immediately Captain Nweke was shot dead, Major Olehi dashed into the bush and escaped under heavy machine gun-fire. Thus, all the battalion commanders in the area had been removed by their men who then sat there waiting for the enemy, without their commanders. The stage was therefore set for Muhammed's next move.

The irony of this unfortunate incident is that the two officers were hand-picked from other brigades in an attempt to organise the best resistance against Colonel Muhammed's move to Onitsha. Captain Nweke came from Calabar sector at the request of Colonel Ude, while Major Olehi, who had become famous for his Obudu and Obollo Afor exploits, was sent there by me. No replacements were immediately available; even when they were, the officers selected were too scared to go there. Those who committed the murder, I think, got the logical punishment but had done an irreparable damage to the national war effort.

It was indeed at that stage that I thought a separate operation was necessary within Biafra to try and remove the "saboteur mania" which both the Army and the civilian population were suffering from at the expense of the war effort. I visited many units and war fronts and spoke to the troops on this subject. Many believed but many others took it with a pinch of salt. There were even a few who grew suspicious of me. I also asked Colonel Ojukwu to intervene and save the situation by doing the same himself or with government information agents and agencies. He flatly refused to do anything of the sort because, according to him, the Army was losing ground daily and he was not going to conduct a campaign to save its face. He explained that the only solution was for the Army to start winning with the resources it had, and the "saboteur mania" within the country would cure itself before long. In short, it was better for the public to regard all members of the Army as saboteurs, so that individuals and groups of individuals would have a task of proving themselves loyal by achievements in the field.

This situation which looked like blackmail was quite frightening. The Divisional Commanders and I knew very well that we in the Army were already performing near miracles by checking the enemy as well as we had done so far. I could no longer wait for the grass of Biafra to join in the fight. All that was needed now were arms and ammunition.

THE LOSS OF UDI

Barely 24 hours after the murder of Captain Nweke by his troops, Muhammed's Second Division offensive took off again in a grand style, on two main axes — Olo-Umueze-Mgbagbu Owo and Ngwo-Nsude-Udi. The Brigade Commander, Colonel Ude, was completely helpless without battalion commanders to fight for him. He tried to command each battalion in turn but it did not work out well with the two battalions fighting serious battles at the same time. The soldiers fought hard to prove that no more saboteurs existed among them but their efforts lacked co-ordination. When the Brigade was finally overpowered at Olo, and the enemy reached Amadim, 12th Battalion of 54 Brigade rallied into yet another attack on Adaba to cut the enemy supply line. Their effort was commendable but the objective was not attained because the enemy had left two armoured vehicles in that location, in anticipation. 53 Brigade even tried once more to take Umulokpa bridge from the flank and failed.

Three days later the enemy had pushed into Mgbagbu Owo, but intercepts showed that he had suffered very heavy casualties among whom was a battalion commander. Military policemen and white mercenaries were always noticed lined up behind the advancing enemy troops to drive them on and prevent them from running back. Thus, whenever we broke the enemy advancing column, it was quickly reformed and was very soon advancing again. On the Ngwo-Udi road, which was an excellent road, the encmy advanced much faster with heavy support and equipments using bull-dozers and graders to remove obstacles on the road or construct diversions. Soon the enemy was at Udi and the position of our own troops on the left flank at Eziama became untenable.

53 Brigade was by now an extremely worn out Brigade with an average strength of 300 armed men in each of its three battalions. What had kept the Brigade going in the midst of tremendous odds, posed by the enemy's overwhelming strength and the internal witch hunting, had been their extraordinary courage and determination. As his troops dug in around Amokwe, two miles south of Udi, Colonel Ude was still in high spirits and optimistic that by the time Muhammed got to Onitsha we would destroy his Division. His optimism and high morale did not last long for soon his own people of Udi accused him of sabotage for abandoning Udi to the enemy. As usual, when the story spread, extremists demanded his execution, while the moderates wanted him dismissed from the Army and publicly disgraced. Many delegations visited me to press for his removal from the Army before he did more damage. The delegation from Awka Province (my home province) threatened to hold me responsible if I allowed Colonel Ude to continue his withdrawal exercise through Awka Province. Almost all delegations believed that Ude was there simply to show the enemy the way to follow, and for that reason they threatened to kill him if he passed through their towns or provinces. An ultimatum which I got from the Awka delegation was that if Ude must remain in command of troops, he should be well advised to withdraw eastwards through Achi and not Ugwuoba and Awka. It was pointless trying to explain the true position, particularly with regard to the scandalous disparity in strengths of the opposing forces. In any case, if one tried to do so, he would definitely be guilty of demoralising the people. More important was the fact that no delegation was prepared to run the risk of being convinced against the popular belief of the people who

sent them and the nation at large, for fear of being branded themselves. It was a vicious circle.

Colonel Ude was not altogether demoralised for he knew he was merely taking his turn in a game which was bound to affect all senior officers sooner or later. In his view, it was better sooner than later. The fear among senior officers to fight in the frontlines increased daily, not because they were afraid to die for what they believed in, but for fear of being branded as saboteurs and worse still, dying as "saboteurs," with no one to shed a tear for them. The senior officers who enjoyed any measure of peace and perhaps respect were only those who worked in rear Headquarters and para-military organisations. For that reason, we soon got to a stage where it was difficult to employ or deploy trained and experienced senior officers in the frontlines.

The loss of Udi posed many tactical problems, particularly with our troops deployed around Enugu. The enemy, on the high grounds of Udi, was now looking down at our troops. In addition, our left flank was badly exposed and the rear was threatened by the presence of a five-mile motorable road from Udi to Ozalla directly behind us. Before then, the enemy's First Division at Enugu had made many fruitless further attempts. At Emene, ceaseless battles had raged for days in an attempt by the enemy to dislodge our 14th Battalion from Emene bridge close to Enugu Airport. When our own troops destroyed with mines, two armoured vehicles, one of which was recovered, the enemy gave up. At Awkunanaw we also managed to absorb ceaseless enemy onslaughts. Whenever we were pushed out, we managed to regain our trenches. We were now confident we could repell any direct attack from Enugu.

In January, 1968, two days after the fall of Udi, the "S" Brigade was moving a small force from Ozalla on the Udi road to cover their rear, when they suddenly encountered a strong enemy force led by an armoured vehicle already advancing on that road. It was rather late for us to do anything effective and, after a short but fierce battle, Ozalla fell into enemy hands. The situation was truly grave. Not only was the entire "S" Brigade cut off, but the 14th Battalion at Emene was hemmed in on all sides by the enemy with only a withdrawal route westwards. My Army Tactical Headquarters at Agbogugu was now less than three miles away from enemy location with absolutely no troops to defend it or the road leading to it. Very soon, a few troops were assembled to defend the Ozalla riverline, the bridge having been blown. This was possible because the enemy was kept very busy by both the "S" Brigade and 14th Battalion which were desperately fighting their way out, for the next few days.

The 14th Battalion under the command of Major Opara fought brilliantly and for three weeks prevented an enemy link-up between Ozalla and Emene. When the link-up was eventually achieved by the enemy, the 14th Battalion was still in positions along the sides of the road to make the use of the road by the enemy virtually impossible for many months to come.

It was during these battles by the 14th Battalion that the only mercenary left in the northern sector and, perhaps in the whole of Biafra, by the name of Steiner, came to public notice. A report prepared for me by Opara showed that it was Steiner who prepared and sited the land mine that blew the first enemy armoured vehicle to shreds at Emene. For his impressive performances and initiative, Steiner was granted a commission into the Biafran Army with the rank of a Lieutenant. Shortly after, Steiner put up a proposal to me to the effect that if he were given 100 men, he would give them a quick special training and then use them to attack and destroy the Enugu Airport with all the Russian jets there. The Head of State later prepared him for the operation and Steiner from then on reported directly to him. Steiner's operation was launched and, according to all Biafran information media, he completely achieved his mission.

While announcements of Steiner's achievements were being made, enemy jets which had taken off from Enugu Airport were pounding the nearby Agbani Railway Station. All the same Steiner had made his name and the sky was his limit. Soon afterwards, he retired with his small force to Madonna High School at Etiti near Umuahia, for reorganisation. Eventually, Steiner's force grew into a Brigade and later a Division under the direct control of the Head of State. Many new mercenaries flocked back into Biafra to join

Steiner's army, which assumed the name "Commandos" in commemoration of their expedition to Enugu Airport.

The Loss of Awka

In the meantime the enemy force from Udi had linked up all round with their counterparts inside Enugu, thereby controlling up to a radius of at least 15 miles from Enugu in all directions. The Commander of "S" Brigade, Obioha, was discredited and sacked and Onwuatuegwu appointed in his place by the Head of State. As mentioned earlier, to prepare our forces in Onitsha for the battle with enemy Second Division they were reorganised into 11 Division under Brigadier Nwawo with 54 and 57 Brigades under command.

While the enemy was exploiting his capture of the strategic town of Udi, I re-allocated tasks to the Brigades to ensure that Colonel Ude's life was not endangered by his being forced to withdraw further south beyond Oji River. The task of containing the enemy south of Oji River was given to 54 Brigade based at Onitsha, more than 50 miles away, while Ude and his 53 Brigade were to defend the Oji-Achi road eastwards.

Finally, in the second week of January, 1968, the enemy Second Division made a move southwards, from Udi, on two axes. One force moved from Umudim with a view to capturing Amokwe and Oji River, while the other moved towards Aguobu so as to burst out at Ugwuoba through Obinofia.

Most uncharacteristic of Nigerian troops, the Second Division completely avoided the use of the main tarmac road from Udi to Oji, which we had completely mined. Thus, when the attack commenced, we were completely taken unawares for the defences on the routes chosen by the enemy were weak. Oji fell to the enemy before 1400 hours after a battle lasting over 8 hours. Further to the left on the Aguobu-Obinofia axis, the 54 Brigade was now engaging the Second Division for the first time on hard ground having thoroughly beaten that Division twice on the River Niger. The Brigade did very well indeed by destroying two armoured vehicles at Obinofia but then continued to inch his way into Ugwuoba, forcing our troops to destroy the bridge there, over River Mamu. The enemy soon linked up Ugwuoba and Oji.

Since the battle of Olo, we had packed up our mortars and artillery because there were no shells or bombs to fire. Indeed, the difficulty posed by shortage of ammunition was getting out of hand to the extent that some formations were now not receiving more than an average of one round per rifle per day. For instance I arrived at Ugwuoba shortly before it fell. Before then our own troops had stopped fighting for over two hours due to complete shortage of ammunition. When I presented a box of 1600 rounds of ammunition I had in my Landrover to the Battalion Commander, Major Nsudoh, he virtually kissed my hands and then quickly disappeared with it to revive the fighting. The Brigade Commander, Colonel Ivenso, who watched the ceremony speechless, simply sprang to attention and gave me a real smart salute, in appreciation of my invaluable donation.

The Mamu bridge obstacle was a major one and, in fact, the only natural obstacle along the 90-mile route between the Northern Region of Nigeria and Onitsha. I was confident we would tie down the enemy there indefinitely, provided that the men had just enough ammunition to prevent the enemy from repairing the bridge. That did not appear feasible. It could have been better still if we could have afforded one shell every 30 minutes on the bridge, but that was wishful thinking.

For many days, the enemy attacked ceaselessly and shelled without a break, but our own troops sat calmly in their trenches as they once did on the banks of River Niger against the same force, which we now knew to bark much more than it could bite.

On the morning of the 17th of January, our troops suddenly pulled out from their trenches near the Mamu bridge and withdrew, in mass. As I moved towards the front line with Brigade Commander Ivenso, the troops we met coming back looked genuinely frightened. They reported that the enemy had fired a type of gas which was choking them in their trenches and they had found it impossible to stay on. Even though all soldiers reported the same thing, I was

217

definitely not in a position to form an opinion on that matter. What concerned me most as the Army Commander was that we had lost the vital Mamu bridge, and thus the very last obstacle on the route to Onitsha. I just could not see how we could ever again stop the enemy from achieving his objective which was now less than 30 miles away. It was pretty difficult to convince the Biafran troops to go anywhere near the bridge unless they had gas masks, which were not available anywhere.

By the evening of the same day, the enemy column was advancing from Ugwuoba along the three-mile stretch into Awka town. I moved with Ivenso towards the advancing enemy with a small reserve force available, but the shelling in the area of the valley less than a mile from Awka was so heavy the movement of troops was very risky. As we looked down the straight road we could see the enemy advancing in very large number led by armoured vehicles. While the men began to construct their defences, I went back into town and was indeed lucky to have got out of that hell created by flying bombs and shrapnels. With the enemy less than two miles away from Awka, and shells falling less than half a mile away, life was pretty normal in the town with shops and markets open, as the sound of shelling in the valley was not yet audible in town. There were hundreds of young men assembled to go "combing" for saboteurs around the town, for they had not yet realised that the enemy was virtually on top of them.

I had a great urge to speak to a few of the local leaders around and advise that women and children be evacuated together with all other essentials, but then, that could have had very disasterous consequences. Even though Awka is my town, I could easily have been accused of causing panic and forcing the people out of their homes to facilitate the entry of the enemy. In short, I could have been a saboteur who, like Ude at Udi, helped the enemy to capture his home town. For those of us in the Army, we were fighting two wars of survival at the same time — one against Nigeria and the other against the over vigilant Biafran public intoxicated by the "sabotage" propaganda. In order to overcome the temptation of speaking to my own parents and relatives about the situation, I gave instructions to my ADC to prevent them from coming too close to me when I saw them hanging around with an anxious crowd.

Biafran soldiers fought desperately to prevent the enemy from entering the town until the afternoon of the 19th of January when the town came under heavy bombardment. The confusion that followed could hardly be described as men, women and children ran about under a rain of shells. Many died and the survivors abandoned the town intact. Many young men who were still "combing" for saboteurs were caught and executed by the enemy. It was simply impossible for the Biafran Army to engage the enemy in a meaningful battle inside the town for we had neither the men nor the means to fight in such a built-up area against an enemy equipped with armour and various highly destructive heavy weapons. Our own troops pulled out completely from Awka main town and began to establish a defensive line along the Ngene Ukwa River forward of the Awka Prisons. The complete destruction of Awka town which eventually took place was therefore done by the enemy at a later date, in his own chosen time.

ENEMY ENTERS ONITSHA

The fall of Awka marked the beginning of civilian intervention in the Biafran Army command structure and procedure. Before then, the civilians were quite satisfied with rendering assistance as well as criticising those they thought did not do well enough. Now, a good number of them moved in and virtually took command of the troops. They included professional and medical doctors, engineers, economists, lawyers, politicians, etc. One economist assumed all powers of command and control of the 11 Division from then on and reported directly to Ojukwu. When I met him in his Headquarters at Abagana six miles from Awka on the 21st of January, the economist gave me his outline plan for reorganisation. He intended to sack Colonel Ivenso, commander of 54 Brigade because, according to him, the Colonel was too tired to think and plan properly. He was going to use Brigadier Nwawo, the 11 Division Commander, for

219

administration, because, according to him, the Brigadier was already spending too much time on administration and spending too little on operations. As replacements, the new civilian commander of 11 Division appointed Major Nsudoh as the commander of 54 Brigade on promotion to the rank of a Lieutenant Colonel. He also appointed Major Achuzia the "Division Operations Officer," in short, the effective Division Commander. It is true that Achuzia campaigned for it, quoting as his qualifications his Nsukka exploits and his participation in the Korean war, but the appointment was a serious military error. The irony of it all was that Achuzia was now commanding a Division after three months of commission into the Biafran Army, and what was more astonishing was the fact that his administrative officer was Brigadier Nwawo who brought him into the Army in the first place.

The blame for this disaster cannot be put on the civilian commander who was acting in good faith given his scanty know-ledge of military affairs. But for anyone being a "soldier," to have given his approval to such appointments just to please the public was, to say the least, unwise. The economist and many civilians in high place simply worshipped Achuzia and he knew that, and exploited their ignorance of military affairs to the fullest personal advantage, politically. Achuzia, in fact, laid down conditions for his acceptance of the command of 11 Division. One of them was that neither Nwawo nor the Army Headquarters should be allowed to interfere with, or plan his operations. The conditions were all accepted and from then on, the Army Headquarters could only render administrative assistance to 11 Division while the new special command set-up did the fighting, occasionally under the supervision of Army Headquarters.

In order to fully understand the next phase of the Onitsha battle, one should first understand the tactics of the new commander of the 11 Division. For reasons best left unsaid, the new commander of 11 Division never prepared operational orders before going into battle. As a result, when a battle developed, each formation under him waited for him to come round and tell them what to do. That meant that he had to work very hard indeed, with very few results to show for it, particularly if he was fighting on more than one axis. With this brand of tactics he was always faced with a tremendous problem of control whenever he was put in charge of anything much larger than a company in the field. Yet he had a whole Division on his hands, and no trained senior officer to help him. He was an officer of extraordinary personal courage who was willing to sacrifice everything to achieve his objective. His method of fighting was unorthodox to the extreme.

That was the 11 Division that tried to stop Muhammed and his Second Division when they eventually pushed from Awka. Achuzia and his troops fought the best they could but the enemy pushed them quite swiftly to Abagana, in a matter of a few days, with really no organised resistance or counterattacks. The whole Division was by then without an effective commander and the troops were in complete disarray.

At midnight on the 24th of January, 1968 when the situation had become hopeless and there was a possibility that the enemy would make a dash for Onitsha the following day without opposition, Colonel Ojukwu telephoned me. In effect he was saying that the situation was so bad that I ought to go down and command the troops myself if Onitsha was not to fall into enemy hands the following day. He threatened that if Onitsha fell, he would "throw in the towel." I did not want to do that this time but was prepared to despatch my Operations Officer, Colonel Eze, to go and assist. Ojukwu approved that. For further assistance, Ojukwu said he was getting in touch with Colonel Sokei, the Air Force Commander in Port Harcourt, to ask him to go down and work with Eze.

Eze himself was fully aware of the risk he was taking by being thrust into a hopeless situation because he was already a well-known national "saboteur." Nevertheless he was quite willing to go if that would save the situation. Courageous freelance fighters like Colonel Aghanya, who always went to fight wherever the situation was bad, were soon all there to render assistance. In the meantime, Achuzia faded away naturally.

When the seasoned officers got to that sector, the enemy was already in the village of Dunukofia, 14 miles from Onitsha and two

221

miles forward of Abagana. The soldiers were quickly reorganised and firm defences constructed. Counterattack plans were worked out and for a fortnight, very heavy fighting went on without gains or losses of ground, except that the enemy was finally pushed back the two miles to Abagana. Very little ammunition was available and most of the fighting was done with locally produced Biafran war products. During that fortnight, there was a period of four days when not a single round was issued to the troops, yet Muhammed's Division was stopped from advancing, with all the senior Biafran officers staying with their men in the trenches, and firing Biafran-made rockets, mines, bombs and so on.

Enemy morale was definitely falling rapidly, and our troops were more confident. A special force, under Major Emmanuel Okeke, an Engineer Officer, was despatched with local rockets, mines and grenades, to the rear of the enemy. Their task was to locate and destroy enemy armoured vehicles in their parking base at night. The operation was successful and the "tank hunters" reported two armored vehicles destroyed. However, Major Okeke was wounded and two of his men killed. Thus, the enemy was confined to Ifite Ukpo junction on the outskirts of Abagana until the 12th of March, a total of three weeks.

On the 13th of March, 1968, in our confidence completely unsupported by ammunition or other essential war equipment, the Ministry of Information, acting on someone's instructions played for the enemy Second Division through powerful loudspeakers, some recorded threats. In this broadcast, the enemy was told that he was completely surrounded preparatory to annihilation, unless he withdrew back to Northern Nigeria, immediately.

This broadcast, good for our troops' morale as it may have been, was not done with the knowledge of the Army Headquarters. As a result, there was no military follow-up action. The broadcast must have driven Colonel Muhammed mad for the following day he let loose with all he had on our own troops. He did that either because his pride and that of his Division had been badly hurt, or perhaps simply to ensure that his force was not wiped out as threatened. It dawned on him that unless he broke through to Onitsha only 14 miles away as soon as possible, he could get into real trouble before long. In panic and desperation therefore, the enemy Second Division fought like a wounded lion and broke through our defences. By last light on the 14th of March, we were again in trouble with the enemy again in control of Dunukofia, and leaving our troops disorganised without ammunition.

On the morning of the 15th of March, all the senior officers were assembled under a tree at Afor Igwe Ochie market at Ogidi only a mile away from the enemy location, to work out a counter-attack plan using our usual local war products. While the conference was going on, two mortar shells fell close to them. Colonel Sokei, the Air Force Commander, whose heart was pierced by a small piece of shrapnel died later in the hospital. Brigadier Nwawo and Colonel Eze were also fairly seriously injured and were treated in hospital. Thus, the whole command structure again collapsed and Achuzia took up his command again with the assistance of Colonel Udeaja, a tough Engineer Officer, who had instructions to do only what Achuzia wanted him to do. Meanwhile, as Eze was recovering from his wounds, he was very much in the news again. Rumours spread very fast throughout Biafra that it was "saboteur" Eze who killed Colonel Sokei. To appease the angry Biafrans, the Colonel was laid off active military duties for a long time and was not permitted to return to Army Headquarters as the Principal Staff Officer. Colonel Nwawo who was a "collaborator" was also laid off for a period.

From then on, we just had no answer to the enemy show of force. He pounded every inch of ground and surged on with his armour. Even then, our troops, who were still fighting brilliantly in the belief that all "saboteurs" had been removed, held the enemy for 20 days before he finally made the last 14 miles to Onitsha. The Second Division of the Nigeria Army entered Onitsha on the 25th of March, 1968 after four months of intensive battles from Nsukka, their scandalous amount of casualties notwithstanding. In making his final dash to Onitsha, Muhammed had left all his administrative support at Abagana. It was therefore vital and urgent that we prevented him from bringing that support to Onitsha if we were not to get into very serious trouble soon.

With 11 Division Headquarters now at Oba, two ad hoc battalions, each of about 350 men, were quickly assembled within 24 hours for use in re-establishing our presence between Onitsha and Abagana. One battalion was moved on Abatete-Eziowelle route to take Ifite-Ukpo junction and from there move back towards Abagana. The commander of that battalion was Major Uchendu, a very capable and extraordinarily brave man. The other battalion moved through Obosi to take Nkpor junction just outside Onitsha town. From there they would try to link up with Abagana 14 miles away. Small ambush parties were located at Ogidi and Umunachi to deal with unexpected enemy movements. Within 48 hours of the start of this operation, we were completely in control of the 14 miles of road between Onitsha and Abagana, with a part of the enemy Division now isolated inside Onitsha town itself, without a line of communication except across the River Niger.

IMMEDIATE COUNTERATTACKS TO REGAIN ONITSHA

The Nigerian Second Division — Abagana Disaster

On the 31st of March, the enemy Second Division main force at Abagana finally made a move towards Onitsha. It was a formidable and extremely terrifying force moving in a convoy of 96 vehicles carrying stores and men. In front of this convoy were a saladine and a ferret armoured car, while two other ferret armoured cars brought up the rear. The first reaction of the Biafran troops immediately they saw the convoy was to take fright and run for cover in desperation. I was at 11 Division Tactical Headquarters at Oba when the information came that another Division of the Nigerian Army was moving from Abagana into Onitsha. According to the information, the enemy force was so strong that we stood absolutely no chance of halting it. The enemy move started at 1600 hours and by 1800 hours the entire convoy and enemy soldiers with it had been destroyed. This is how the battle was fought.

When the convoy approached our troops around Ifite-Ukpo

junction, Major Uchendu very wisely allowed the advance party of armoured vehicles to pass. He then attacked the main convoy from the front, middle and rear. The leading lorry was knocked out and blocked the road, and was quickly set on fire. None of the vehicles, thereafter could move forward, and being very bulky, could not turn about on the narrow road. The armoured vehicles in front could not make their way back; neither could those behind move up, for the whole road became completely jammed up with vehicles. Our troops then completely surrounded the 96 vehicles loaded mainly with ammunition and stores, and prevented the troops in them from dismounting. The enemy was helpless and in less than one hour, all the enemy soldiers were either killed or had escaped, leaving us with all the vehicles and their stores. Major Uchendu feared that a very desperate counterattack would be launched by the enemy almost immediately, which he was definitely not strong enough to beat off. To ensure that his almost unbelievable catch was not recovered by the enemy, he ordered that all the vehicles and their stores be set ablaze.

While the vehicles burnt, a counterattack of a strong company led by two ferret armoured cars was launched by the enemy from Abagana. Biafran troops were too happy and excited to abandon the vehicles at any cost. After one hour of very desperate battle, the enemy company was virtually destroyed together with one of the armoured vehicles. The rest fled back in the direction of Abagana town. The expected enemy counterattack had come and gone and we were now faced with the task of trying to put out the fire so that we could salvage some ammunition and stores. At that stage only six lorries had not burnt, and the amount of ammunition recovered from them was more than the Biafran Army got in any period of two months.

In the meantime, the advance party of the convoy, consisting of the two armoured vehicles and three soft-skin vehicles, were bull-dozing their way to Onitsha. Colonel Udeaja was however at Ogidi with a company of soldiers to receive them. Again the armoured cars which were going as fast as they could, were allowed to pass, and then the other three vehicles were attacked. The first

225

The destruction of Nigeria's Second Division convoy at Abagana by a Biafran ambush party

A burnt ammunition vehicle in the Nigerian Military convoy which was destroyed at Abagana in 1968

vehicle was hit but managed to escape, but the other two were halted. The armoured vehicles did not even attempt to turn round to help, but rather accelerated forwards. We recovered the valuable ammunition and other military stores in the vehicles and then set them ablaze. In the end, besides two armoured vehicles and a lorry, the entire enemy Second Division force, estimated at a brigade strength, which set out for Onitsha on that memorable day, was completely destroyed.

Muhammed's Second Division was in Onitsha at last after three major disasters since his first attempt in October, 1967. It was still to be seen whether his sacrifice was worth the prize. It was quite humourous to all who knew that Achuzia, who was not even in his Divisional area during the battle, took journalists to the scene of battle the following morning to explain to them how he fought the battle. He impressed them and they christened him "Hannibal" on the spot. In a matter of days he ensured that his name was on the lips of every Biafran.

Biafran Commandos' Counterattack to Regain Onitsha

It was my view that the disaster suffered by the enemy in his futile bid to reinforce his troops in Onitsha could be exploited with a good measure of success. The very indiscriminate and ceaseless shelling being carried out by the enemy from Onitsha was a good enough indication that he was very frightened in there. In the hope that 11 Division had once more reverted under command of Army Headquarters, I ordered Achuzia to move a battalion to re-occupy Onitsha bridge head and the Fegge quarter of Onitsha if he ever hoped to clear Onitsha. But I soon found out that he was still taking direct instructions from the Head of State and to emphasize his independence of Army Headquarters, he preferred to attack enemy strong points at Boromeo Hospital and Saint Charles College. For several days he chased around in those areas and ended up each day with nothing other than heavy casualties.

In the meantime, the enemy settled very strongly in Fegge and, in fact, established his Headquarters there, before Achuzia finally realised the tactical importance of that area of Onitsha. A few attempts made thereafter to clear Fegge and the bridge head failed rather woefully. The Head of State, determined to see Onitsha cleared at once, decided to try the Commando Brigade, which Major Steiner had been forming since he left Enugu in December, 1967. It was a test battle for Steiner and his new brigade, and from the publicity given to this new formation, everybody thought the clearing of Onitsha was simply a question of time.

Because the Commandos were to operate under the control of the Head of State, they had special treatment in the issue of ammunition and the allotment of support for the battle. Each of the 1000 men in the brigade had 200 rounds of ammunition for his bolt action rifle. In addition, the brigade had two 105 mm artillery guns with 200 rounds of shells, four 81 mm mortars with 300 rounds, and one bazooka gun carried personally by Steiner himself. What the brigade had for the fight was an all-time record for a single operation and was, in fact, what would normally be issued to any other Brigade in a fortnight, in the best of times.

I left my Headquarters very early in the morning and took up a good position to watch the Commando attack on D-day. Our guns and mortars pounded away on their targets until their shells were exhausted. Then there was heavy small arms fire from both sides for well over two hours without any troop movements. By midday the whole front was quiet and remained quiet for the rest of the day. When later I saw Steiner, he said he was going to Umuahia to report to Ojukwu on the operation. That apparently turned out to be the end of the Steiner operation to clear Onitsha. I frankly did not know what actually happened, and I still do not know. I guess the operation must have failed.

The loss of Onitsha was a military as well as an economic and social disaster for Biafra. On the tactical side, Nnewi and the much advertised Ibo heartland were now badly threatened. We had, as already mentioned, lost the Onitsha market, probably the biggest in Black Africa, and with all that it contained. That market while it existed and functioned was the main source of supply to the Army

229

and the civilian population alike. With the added loss of the Onitsha Textile Mills, the Army's clothing problem worsened. Above all, the people of Onitsha now joined the refugee population, thereby worsening the already serious refugee problem of the country. So much time, ammunition and efforts had already been put into preventing the enemy from capturing Onitsha and all to no avail. With our limited resources, we had performed well throughout the five months of operations which the enemy had to undertake to get there. For this we were proud. We could however not waste any more time in Onitsha because the few supplies the Army had were needed for fighting much stronger enemy Divisions in other sectors where they were now launching massive offensives. We were satisfied with building solid defences around Onitsha in the hope that enemy Second Division was too tired to carry out any serious attacks for some time. To some extent we were right.

THE INVASION OF ABAKALIKI

While the enemy Second Division was pushing to Onitsha, his First Division was making a determined thrust from Eha-Amufu southwards, against our 51 Brigade. In December, 1967, shortly after the return of the bulk of the brigade from Enugu where they had assisted in the defence of the town, the enemy attacked Eha-Amufu bridge. The Brigade, tired and depleted as it was, fought very hard for four days before it lost the bridge head to the enemy. For that battle, the 51 Brigade had only the First Battalion to fight with because the 14th Battalion was still committed in Enugu while the 4th Battalion had virtually ceased to exist. When the enemy therefore pushed the tired 51 Brigade out of Nkalagu Cement Factory, I despatched the fresh 15th Battalion under Onwuatuegwu to assist, to give the First Battalion a chance to have a rest. The 15th carried out a series of counterattacks against the enemy in the cement factory with very limited success. Their failures were mainly due to the fact that the enemy was stronger. The Battalion also lacked the type of determination usually found in Biafran Army units in the field. The soldiers of 15th Battalion were over-petted

230

by their Battalion Commander whom they adored and worshipped. As a result, efficiency suffered, for military orders were discussed and debated and not issued. The 51 Brigade Commander Amadi informed me that the Battalion often changed dates and timings of brigade operations at will without authority, if only to please the soldiers. Whenever the Battalion eventually went into an operation, they were always behind H-hour and when their operations started, they never lasted more than 30 minutes of exchange of fire. This was exactly what cost us Opi junction and subsequently Enugu, because the same 15th Battalion failed to move in time. Amadi, who was aware of this fact, preferred to fight with only one battalion rather than have the undisciplined 15th Battalion around his Brigade area. I turned down his request and the 15th Battalion stayed on.

Thus, one morning in February, 1968, the enemy launched an attack against the 15th Battalion from Nkalagu Cement Factory, along the Eha-Amufu-Abakaliki road. There was practically no resistance according to the Brigade Commander. As a result, in less than two hours the enemy had gained over seven miles and occupied the vital Eha-Amufu-Enugu-Abakaliki junction. Colonel Amadi was extremely bitter over the incident and insisted that the Battalion be removed from his sector for several reasons. He dreaded the politics involved in dealing with Onwuatuegwu who, he said, he could not be found anywhere around his Battalion location during the enemy push. He also feared that his gallant First Battalion would soon be contaminated with the lax discipline of the 15th and that would mean the end of his Brigade. I still refused to remove the 15th Battalion because I wanted them to have another chance. In any case, I had no replacement for them.

Later the 15th Battalion not only got Amadi deeply embroiled in real politics, as was the case with Eze in Nsukka, but also contaminated and ruined with their laxity the First Battalion, the oldest and the best fighting unit in the whole of the Biafran Army. Onwuatuegwu himself, like Achuzia, loved publicity and was getting quite a bit of it already, with full assistance from high places.

With the 15th Battalion in disarray, the First again moved to occupy the front trenches around the junction so as to give the 15th a

231

chance to reorganise and stage a counterattack. Two hours after the attack went in, Onwuatuegwu sent a sitrep which read something like this:

> Our gallant troops, in a lightning offensive, attacked and quickly drove the enemy out of the vital Nkalagu junction, causing very heavy casualty on the enemy. Own troops held all captured ground for one hour, thirty minutes and forty-five seconds before being forced out due to a heavy enemy counter-attack as well as shortage of ammunition. Own casualties negligibly low, morale sky high.

I was taken in by this report which sounded like a good start at last for the 15th until Colonel Amadi drew my attention to the unusually accurate timing of Onwuatuegwu's period of occupation of his objective under extremely hazardous conditions of the battlefield. I then became suspicious and from 51 Brigade Headquarters where I was, I sent a signal to Onwuatuegwu which read something like this:

> Reference your sitrep, congratulations. Your battle timekeeper required this Headquarters as soon as possible for debriefing.

As I expected, no timekeeper turned up and no further reports about the battle were received. In the meantime, a 51 Brigade liaison officer who watched the battle came in to report. He explained that shortly after H-hour our troops opened fire from their trenches for about 45 minutes. The enemy replied, until we stopped firing, when he also stopped and everywhere became quiet again. He stayed there for yet another three hours and nothing more happened.

I had had more than enough of the 15th Battalion and therefore decided to withdraw and disband it before it caused further damage to the Army. The Battalion was immediately withdrawn to Awgu, completely disbanded, and Onwuatuegwu appointed the Commanding Officer of the School of Infantry. I then assembled a

battalion of recruits under Colonel Ohanehi, armed them with the
15th Battalion weapons and despatched them as 26th Battalion to 51
Brigade as a replacement for the 15th.

Unfortunately, I had not acted fast enough on the problem of
the 15th Battalion for by the time they left the 51 Brigade area, they
had already done irreparable damage to the Brigade during their
two weeks stay in that sector. During that period, they had succeeded
in convincing men of the First Battalion that it was futile fighting
without automatic weapons. They urged the First Battalion to press
for automatic weapons to be issued to all soldiers in the Battalion
because, according to them, the Head of State had already made the
weapons available but their Brigade Commander, Amadi, a
"saboteur," had hidden away the weapons. As a further proof that
Amadi was a saboteur, they argued that whereas the 15th Battalion
always had light casualties, units under Amadi invariably had heavy
casualties. The 15th Battalion did not stop there. They went on to
explain to the First that the 15th had already had a rest period like
many other battalions, and urged the First to demand theirs as of
right.

By the time the 26th Battalion arrived in 51 Brigade, stories of
Colonel Amadi's sabotage activities had spread throughout the
entire Biafran Army. The First Battalion then refused to fight until
they were granted a fortnight's leave and issued with automatic
weapons on their return. Amadi's pleas to them to stay on and fight
with what they had until the situation improved, failed to convince
any of them. I ordered their withdrawal to Afikpo. There I addressed
the men and granted them seven days collective rest in that town
before going back to the front. They wanted nothing but to go for a
rest in their respective villages. If I had ordered them back to the
front, they would not have fought well and may have caused even
more damage to the Army. I had no alternative but to grant them
leave.

Thus, Colonel Amadi found himself overnight commanding
two recruit battalions in which most of the men were yet to fire their
weapons for the first time. In front of him was the Third sector of
enemy First Division and behind him, inside Abakaliki, was a big

233

demonstration by men, women and children demanding his removal and execution as a newly found saboteur.

From then on, as at Nsukka, Calabar, Enugu and other places, there was a scapegoat to take the blame for all subsequent disasters, thereby diverting the people's attention from the fact that the government just had to find a way of increasing the strength of the Army if we were to tackle the enemy more effectively. The Provincial Administrator for Ogoja, Mr. Mgbada tried to convince his people that Amadi was an efficent and loyal officer and almost lost his own life as a collaborator. He had however made history for being the first civilian to risk his life defending a nationally acclaimed "saboteur." The stage was thus perfectly set for the enemy when he began his push to Abakaliki from Nkalagu junction, with Amadi having an additional task of dealing with a highly hostile Biafran population, itching for his blood.

The enemy pushed our recruits slowly towards Ezillo bridge. Those recuits, yet unspoilt by local sabotage politics, gave the advancing enemy the first real battles he had had since his move towards Abakaliki. All the way the ammunition situation was simply hopeless and the men quite frequently had to stay in their trenches without ammunition in the hope that they would engage the enemy in a hand-to-hand combat when he made his final assault on our defensive locations.

That was exactly what the 26th Battalion did at Ezillo bridge even without bayonets. During that memorable Ezillo bridge battle, while the 26th Battalion engaged the enemy in an exchange of blows, · Captain Okoye, the D Company commander, crawled with two soldiers through the right flank and lobbed a grenade into a ferret armoured car which was advancing slowly and cautiously towards our trenches. He killed the occupants and halted the armoured vehicle. While he was trying to dash back across the road into the bush, he was caught in heavy enemy machine gunfire which shattered his right leg. He was recovered by his escorts but eventually lost that leg. Ohanehi, the Battalion Commander, was in the trenches trading blows with enemy soldiers until a stray bullet grazed his chest. In the end, the enemy first assault on Ezillo bridge was successfully beaten back with very heavy casualties on both sides.

The enemy shelled throughout that night so heavily that a mild earthquake was felt all the way to Abakaliki town still more than 20 miles away. We knew we had dealt a severe blow on the enemy during the day, but no one imagined it was as bad as that. That was what went through my mind when I issued to 51 Brigade 50 rounds of artillery shells and 100 mortar bombs, which represented the entire Army reserves.

Fighting started quite early the following morning with the enemy shelling with abandon. Both Brigade Commander Amadi and all his officers not engaged in essential administrative duties, were inside the forward trenches for that all-important battle and to control the rate of expenditure of ammunition by soldiers. The first wave of attack came in at 0730 hours and was repelled in less than thirty minutes. At 0900 hours the second wave made up of completely fresh enemy troops came in and was beaten back after two hours. Just as the enemy was falling back the second time, two fighter-bomber jet planes appeared over the battlefield. We were completely caught on the hop and lost a lot of vehicles and some men on rear administrative duties. Those planes from then on stayed almost permanently in the air over us, and inflicted very heavy casualties, particularly on the civilian population inside Abakaliki town, in addition to destroying many buildings. Movement on the roads to the frontline within a radius of about 20 miles was impossible in daytime.

In the trenches our troops were almost completely spent in strength and ammunition when the third enemy assault came at 1400 hours. With ammunition exhausted, a withdrawal was ordered. We could ill afford another hand-to-hand fight which had proved quite expensive the last time, and would be even more so now that the enemy had advanced with his armour well forward.

After the withdrawal from Ezillo bridge, we were never again in a position to check enemy advance effectively; neither could we stage a meaningful counterattack. Thus, the enemy occupied Agaga and then Ezamgbo shortly after, despite our gallant efforts to stop him.

The loss of Abakaliki in addition to disorganising the 51 Brigade brought with it some tactical complications. All our troops in Ogoja area along the Alama River and the Iyahe bridge were severed from the rest of the Brigade. It took some of them days and others weeks to rejoin the Brigade. The problem of our troops in the area of Effim was even more difficult for there was no withdrawal route from there except by infiltration. They were therefore ordered to remain there and fight a guerrilla warfare. They did so till the end of the war, and effectively too, judging from their reports. As a result of the loss of Abakaliki, the enemy was able to link up with his troops at Ogoja and thus became strong enough to continue his push southwards almost without delay. In his effort to exploit his Abakaliki success the enemy moved down through Nkwoagu to Amuzu before he was halted at Akpoha bridge.

Perhaps the greatest disaster attendant upon the loss of Abakaliki was the fact that it was by far the greatest food-producing area of Biafra. In addition to this, several tons of food were abandoned in the town by the Food Directorate, probably through no fault of theirs.

THE LOSS OF AFIKPO

A complete reorganisation of both the 51 and the 55 Brigades became necessary after the loss of Abakaliki. The 55 Brigade, having been dislodged from its operational area around Obubra and Ikom as a result of the loss of Ikot Okpora, also fell back to the area of Afikpo on the Western bank of the Cross River. The Brigade, now under the command of Major Agbogu since Colonel Ochei was removed as its Commander, had less than a total armed strength of 600 men. During the reorganisation which followed, 51 and 55 Brigades were placed under the command of Amadi and became known as the 13 Division. The two Brigades were later made up to an average strength of 1000 armed men each.

While this reorganisation was going on, the 3 Marine Commando launched yet another attack from across the Cross River with a view to landing on Ndiba Beach to take Afikpo town. During the four days of battle which ensued, the greatest menace turned out to be the indiscriminate way the enemy used his air support. The beach was bare and desolate and any movement attracted the planes. The jets were so ruthless that on one occasion, two of them attacked and completely destroyed a wounded soldier who was walking back across the beach to receive medical treatment. Our trenches were thoroughly strafed and bombed using both high explosives and napalm bombs.

Thus, on the fourth successive day of the battle, we had no alternative but to withdraw from the beach during the night, for none of the sandy trenches was still standing. Next morning, the enemy landed on the beach with his heavy equipment. Before last light on the same day, after an all-day battle, he succeeded in entering Afikpo town. In less than 24 hours the presence of armoured vehicles in the town was felt and sounds of destruction were clearly audible. During the first week of enemy entry into the town we launched three counterattacks which, though effective, failed to push the enemy out of the town.

As usual, the people of Biafra raged with anger against Amadi and his officers in particular, and the whole Army in general. Even the gallant recruits of 51 Brigade were now beginning to call their Division Commander a saboteur. The usual cry for heads re-echoed all over Biafra as a just reprisal for the disaster.

At that time also one of the greatest disasters of the war occurred. The Nigerian Government changed her currency. It would appear that no arrangements had been made in Biafra to counter that move which had been anticipated in Biafra for a long time, even by laymen. Everyone was too busy keeping watch over the Army and its numerous saboteurs to think about such irrelevant matters. However, that simple financial operation by Nigeria cost the people of Biafra over 50 million pounds.

That loss contributed more than anything else to the loss of the war. If that amount had been realised and invested towards the

237

execution of the war, the story today may well be quite different. However, the people of Biafra were too preoccupied with the immediate task of repelling the enemy invasion to fully understand the extent of this total and irreparable disaster. In short, they did not realise that they had virtually lost the war for which they had sacrificed and were still to sacrifice so much.

Chapter 10

THE OVERRUNNING OF THE SOUTH IN THE FACE OF BIAFRA'S DESPERATE RESISTANCE

THE LOSS OF ANNANG AND UYO PROVINCES

All our forces in Calabar, Uyo and Eket Provinces were regrouped during the month of January, 1968 to form the 12 Division under Colonel Akagha. The 12 Division had the 55 and 56 Brigades under command initially, but when the tactical situation made it impossible for the 55 Brigade to remain under the control of 12 Division, the 58 Brigade was formed to replace it. The 56 Brigade under Colonel Simon Uwakwe, was based in Arochukwu while the 58 under Colonel Ifeanyi Aniebo, who had just come back from a mission abroad, was based at Uyo. The new 58 Brigade in particular was nothing more than a weak battalion made up of remnants of units that took part in the Calabar battle. In March, 1968, the enemy commenced a massive daily air bombardment of the entire area between Oron and Ikot-Ekpene. No towns, villages or important institutions were spared by the planes. The Mission Hospital at Itu came under a particularly heavy and daily air bombardment until it finally collapsed with all its patients inside it.

On the 6th of April, 1968, the enemy began a heavy artillery bombardment of Oron beach. In addition, throughout the day, two jet bombers ran shuttles from Calabar to off-load their bombs on Oron beach-head at thirty minute intervals. During the first 48 hours of battle our troops at Oron, supported by a reserve company from Uyo, foiled four enemy attempts to land a brigade on Oron beach. Three enemy boats were sunk by our lone artillery gun firing directly at the boats before the enemy planes discovered the gun position and destroyed it. On the 9th of March the enemy landed at Oron and from then on, no one including the Brigade Commander Aniebo, really knew what was happening until Ikot-Ekpene, 50 miles from Oron, also fell.

However, within hours of enemy landing, there was firing in many towns and villages between Oron and Uyo. Thereafter, wherever our troops tried to deploy in the area, they fell into an ambush. That confusion continued until the 11th when firing started inside Uyo town and we soon discovered that the "enemy," whoever he might be, was there. In short Uyo had fallen! Our own troops were pulling back in disarray, absolutely unable to establish a defensive position anywhere along the route. Having lost complete control of his Brigade with no prospects of regaining it, Colonel Aniebo was dismissed from command and summoned to appear before the Head of State, Ojukwu. He arrived at the State House with a "Verey Light" Signal pistol which was mistaken for a lethal weapon by the State House security men. For that, he appeared before a special tribunal which sentenced him to jail where he remained until the end of the war.

While this confusion was going on, Ikot-Ekpene fell on the 12th of April barely six days after the Oron Landing. Thus, the enemy had covered a distance of over 50 miles within that short period without a fight, for no one actually saw him all the way. What happened is quite clear. Before his offensive, the enemy had stationed local collaborators in all towns and villages along his route. His landing at Oron was a signal for those various groups to dress up in Nigeria Army uniforms and operate in accordance with an agreed plan and timing. For the enemy it was a clever and resounding success which left the whole of Biafra stunned with surprise and disappointment. Before then, no one had imagined that any part of Biafra could be a party to that degree of collaboration with the enemy, despite our minor domestic differences. If that confusion had continued for another 48 hours, Umuahia or Aba or perhaps both could have fallen into enemy hands. The only reason the enemy could not continue in that fashion was that, beyond Ikot-Ekpene, he could no longer enjoy the cooperation of local inhabitants. The enemy was now in Ibo heartland.

When the enemy reached Ikot-Ekpene, Umuahia, 35 miles away, and Aba, 29 miles away, were both badly threatened, and we lacked an organised resistance on any of those axes which were completely jammed with thousands of refugees. In a desperate move, Colonel Ivenso, the "saboteur" of Onitsha sector, was sent to replace Aniebo. Very soon there were complaints and the Head of State was forced to remove him after a few days. He was then posted to Army Headquarters as the Adjutant General. It was at this point that Colonel Aghanya, acting on his own initiative, collected a platoon of 30 men and with it inched forward on the Aba-Ikot-Ekpene road until he got to Uwa bridge just outside Ikot-Ekpene. He prepared and blew the bridge and established some defences behind it. As soon as Major Olehi, one of the battalion commanders cut off behind enemy lines during the confusion, rejoined his troops, he took over the defence of the bridge from Colonel Aghanya. Olehi's unit, which started as a battalion inside Uyo Province and came out of it as a weak platoon, soon grew up into the famous and formidable 58 Brigade of the Biafran Army.

On the Ikot-Ekpene-Umuahia road the situation was even more explosive because there, most of the officers were still not out of the confusion and there was therefore nobody immediately available to reorganise the troops and establish defences. At that stage, Major Oji, who was still undergoing treatment at Queen Elizabeth Hospital, Umuahia following his battle injury at Calabar, volunteered to leave the hospital in order to go and command the troops along Umuahia-Ikot-Ekpene road. His left hand was still in very bad shape and there was still a good chance of its being amputated. Oji however put so much pressure on the Head of State that he allowed Oji to go eventually.

Major Oji collected a company of armed men from several administrative units around Umuahia and advanced towards Ikot-Ekpene on the 14th of April. On his way he also collected and reorganised all troops he could find and marched with them. His force was of a weak battalion strength when he came in contact with

241

the enemy six miles to Ikot-Ekpene town. A two-hour fierce battle took place before the enemy withdrew into Ikot-Ekpene town. Oji's battalion moved to within half a mile from Ikot-Ekpene and there established a strong and permanent defence. This force later grew into the 62 Brigade and Oji became its first Brigade Commander. Thus, at the end of Annang-Uyo battles, the original Biafra 58 Brigade under Colonel Aniebo had split into a new 58 Brigade under Major Olehi and the 62 Brigade under Major Oji.

Civilians all over Biafra and particularly those around Aba and Umuahia, were naturally very angry with the people of Uyo and Annang provinces for the role some of them played in the collapse of those provinces. As there were still Annang villages for up to ten miles from Ikot-Ekpene towards Aba and Umuahia, there was genuine fear in the minds of many people that a repetition of the disaster was not only possible but probable.

Civil Defence Organisations from Umuahia and Aba, acting on orders from sources unknown to me or Army Headquarters, carried out an exercise to "comb" out saboteurs in the area of Ikot-Ekpene. During that exercise some over-zealous civilians, particularly along the Umuahia road, in their search for saboteurs, burnt down a few thatched houses belonging to the Annangs. Even though the Army did not know the exercise was going to take place until it actually started, the leaders of Annang and Uyo provinces held Major Oji fully responsible for all the damage done to their villages by the Civil Defence. They argued that Oji was in a position to have put a halt to the acts of destruction if he had wanted to do so. From then until the very end of the war, Ojukwu came under ceaseless pressure from the injured leaders to remove Oji from the Army and punish him. The Head of State resisted the pressure successfully till the last fortnight of the war when he gave up. It was then that Oji was sacked from the Army to please those leaders who had not realised at that late hour that the war was about to end. If a competent authority had explained to Annang leaders the reasons for the combing exercise and apologised for the excess, the whole incident may have ended quite happily. But rather, it was thought that by doing so, what was left of Annang and Uyo loyalty might be lost.

THE INVASION OF PORT HARCOURT

Soon after landing on Bonny Island in August, 1967, the enemy exploited as far north as Asanamafo. Colonel Kalu's 52 Brigade later launched a major offensive in December, 1967 to clear the enemy from the island. Advancing from the general area of Bodo, the Brigade re-entered Bonny Island from two axes. Both the Biafran Navy equipped with homemade gunboats, and the Biafran Air Force equipped with a lone B26 aircraft and two helicopters, gave their maximum support throughout the operation. While the Navy shelled selected targets in Bonny from the Bonny River, the Air Force attacked the Nigerian Warship, *NNS Nigeria*, which was reported hit several times.

On the whole, the operation went extremely well resulting in the recapture of over three-quarters of the island before a command crisis developed on the battlefield between the two battalion commanders on the spot. This crisis arose over the tactics to be adopted in clearing the rest of the island, and resulted in one of the commanders pulling out his battalion from a flank to another location from where he thought he would operate more effectively. The enemy, already desperate soon moved into the exposed flank in strength and succeeded in cutting off the bulk of our troops. Thereafter, control became difficult and our two battalions pulled out of Bonny once more. Even though subsequently the two battalion commanders were severely disciplined by me, there was nothing anyone could do to rectify the situation. The enemy however, suffered heavy casualties as a result of this operation.

The failure of the Bonny offensive encouraged the enemy to show more aggressiveness in the creeks. He made several spirited attempts to move up the channel into Port Harcourt but each time the Biafran Navy not only foiled the attempt but succeeded in destroying and damaging several of his warships. West of Bonny, we still controlled the entire coastline of Biafra but to the East we controlled only up to Imo River, having lost the rest during the Calabar and Oron-Ikot-Ekpene battles. What we had left was still too extensive for the Biafran Navy to cover effectively, their gallant efforts and extraordinary bravery notwithstanding.

243

Enemy's First Abortive Attempt — The Battle of Onne

On the 2nd of April, 1968, the enemy boats successfully slipped through Bonny River without detection by our Navy and landed a brigade at Onne waterside where we had only a platoon deployed in a defensive role. Soon after, whatever the 52 Brigade as well as the Navy and the Air Force could muster from Port Harcourt was immediately despatched to the area. A pitched battle raged all day, and at the end of the first day's battle, we were able to confine the enemy to the beach.

By early morning on the 3rd of April the Biafran Navy with all its home-built armoured plated warships moved into Bonny channel. There they found many Nigerian ships waiting for the beach to be cleared to land their stores. The Biafran Navy immediately went into action and before long chased and scattered the enemy warships. Five enemy boats were sunk, three captured and the rest driven into the open sea. The Air Force with all its helicopters and a DC3 aircraft ran shuttles from Port Harcourt to Onne dropping homemade bombs out of doors of their planes on the enemy. The Biafran Air Force raids were effective.

The enemy weakened but stayed on. We also weakened and it appeared as if there was going to be a stalemate which we could ill afford. It was at that stage that an obscure mercenary turned up with a company of men and a locally-made armoured car and offered to clear the enemy from Onne. Once at Onne, mercenary George and his force fought so well that, at the end of a four-hour battle, enemy defences began to crack. Not long after, the enemy broke up completely and fled in many directions. As the enemy fled and fired indiscriminately, a stray bullet hit the brave George on the head and he died at once. All Biafrans, who had come to love and respect him, mourned his death for several days.

A large quantity of stores was abandoned by the enemy at the waterside. Enemy stragglers were almost everywhere and it took us many days to remove the menace they created. Items captured in this battle included large quantities of rifles, bazookas, anti-aircraft guns, about 300,000 rounds of ammunition, food, clothing, and so on. The destruction of the enemy at Onne was total and very similar to the fate of the Second Division at Onitsha in October, 1967. It was indeed a great achievement on our part to have cleared Onne; otherwise it would have taken the enemy only a few days to move from there into Port Harcourt.

Enemy's Second Invasion and the Fall of Port Harcourt

The success at Onne made everybody in uniform in Port Harcourt a hero to the people. Thereafter special dances called "jumps" were arranged for the Army once a week and Army officers moved into air-conditioned apartments. Port Harcourt, at the time with a population of almost a million people, was both the largest and the most densely populated town in Biafran hands. It also held the 52 Brigade Headquarters as well as the Headquarters of the Biafran Air Force and Navy, and the Port Harcourt Militia with over 5000 militiamen.

Since the outbreak of the war, I had not visited the South due to tremendous enemy pressure all over the Northern sectors. With the Onne battle and stories of luxurious life among soldiers in Port Harcourt, I thought the need had arisen for me to go down there to reorganise and re-deploy the units more effectively after studying the ground with the Brigade Commander. I was pretty certain the enemy in his normal way would have another go at Port Harcourt and unless we were careful we would be caught with our pants down, still celebrating the Onne victory.

I was fully aware of the fact that, if a serious battle developed in Port Harcourt, as in any other area, I, as the Army Commander would have to go there and fight it. It was therefore, in my best interest that I should know the ground pretty well in advance in all sectors in order to be able to go anywhere and take over command at a very short notice. For the above reasons, I got in touch with Colonel Ojukwu on the 10th of April and told him about my intention to pay a three-day visit to Port Harcourt to sort things out. He said the visit was unnecessary because he was taking care of Port

Harcourt effectively from Umuahia. In his view, I could not afford to leave the Northern sectors for any length of time. Perhaps he was right.

While I was having lunch in my Headquarters at Awgu on the 20th of April, 1968, General Efiong telephoned to say that the enemy had commenced a massive push towards Port Harcourt, and that Colonel Ojukwu wanted me to go down there and take over command of the operations. I was livid with anger, but then, I had a duty to perform, and so I left immediately for Port Harcourt. At Umuahia, I called on Efiong who gave me a general briefing on the situation. Later I got a more detailed briefing from Kalu at his Brigade Tactical Headquarters in Okrika, near Port Harcourt.

The enemy had attacked from across the Imo River in two places, and had already succeeded in landing troops from Opobo at Kono and Obete further north. At Kono, I was told we had a battalion of 300 men commanded by Captain Nebo who, until a fortnight before, was my ADC. At Obete we were said to have a company commanded by a certain Lieutenant. In each of these areas, the enemy attack was massive and our own troops were not holding their own very well. Colonel Kalu was then thinning out troops from all other areas under his command for use as reinforcements, but I knew that practice had not worked too well in any other area. What we required was a fresh and strong force with plenty of ammunition. I discussed the situation at length with Kalu and left necessary instructions on what could be done at once before I left to see Ojukwu at Umuahia. I briefed the Head of State in detail and stressed the need for us to have plenty of weapons and ammunition to help us check the enemy move before it was too late. I got 450 bolt action rifles and about 100 rounds of ammunition per weapon.

When I got to Port Harcourt the following morning the enemy on the southern axis was at Buan, three miles from Kono and our troops were in the process of launching a counterattack. This counterattack only succeeded in inflicting casualties on the enemy but was not strong enough to dislodge him.

At Obete our counterattacks, which came both from Okpantu

road and Sime Lucken, succeeded in pushing the enemy out of Obete completely and back across the river. Before long, the enemy attacked again there, supported by jet planes and succeeded in landing again at Obete, and then began to advance towards Okpantu, in spite of our constant counterattacks. Thus, for four days, daily fierce battles went on, at the end of which the enemy had inched his way to Kwawa in the south and Okpantu town in the north.

On the fifth day, enemy armoured vehicles and heavy artillery crossed the river and appeared on the battlefield. Thereafter, things began to be difficult for us and, indeed, it became clear to me that unless a miracle happened, the enemy would eventually get to Port Harcourt sooner or later. Our primary duty became to inflict as much casualty on him as possible and thus delay his entry for as long as possible. Major Nebo was soon wounded and was replaced by Major Odigwe and yet the men were more determined and fought even more relentlessly. As weapons and ammunition filtered in daily, we made up our losses and tried to improve on our fighting strength in order to perform that miracle required to save Port Harcourt. As time went on, the disparity in strengths of the opposing forces appeared to be widening in favour of the enemy. Our chances of success further diminished when the enemy fielded only his armour, artillery, and mortars while reserving his infantry. Each time we attacked enemy infantry from a flank, he fled but soon sent his armoured vehicles to clear the location.

Thus, the situation deteriorated slowly until the enemy occupied Kani Babbe in the south and Maribu in the north. At that stage the Port Harcourt civil leaders thought Kalu was "tired." Colonel Ojukwu saw in this an opportunity to hand over the situation to Achuzia, his political officer. Achuzia came down from Onitsha and Nwawo was permitted to take care of 11 Division in his absence on a temporary basis.

Achuzia arrived in Port Harcourt in a grand style with his normal pomp and pageantry. He had with him a force of 250 armed men. The news of his arrival brought high hopes to the already despairing civil population of Port Harcourt. To the civilians who

247

came to the Tactical Headquarters to meet him on his arrival, Achuzia announced his intention to destroy the enemy within 48 hours provided that no one interfered with his operations and that Kalu was removed from Port Harcourt. At the end of the big civilian applause for him, I briefed Achuzia on the situation, and then he dashed off to the southern axis where the enemy was fighting to get into Wiyakara. He joined in the bitter fighting to push the enemy back, but the enemy eventually got into the town before nightfall. From Wiyakara he went to the northern axis, and while he was there Maribu fell after a gallant effort by our troops against scandalously overwhelming odds.

Achuzia came back that night to the Tactical Headquarters, a very tired, frustrated and disgusted man. He told me that our troops fought extremely well but were still losing ground because he thought there were saboteurs. That word "saboteur" simply made my heart skip a beat. I did not want a single civilian in the Port Harcourt area or even a junior rank within the Army to hear that word "sabotage" mentioned, particularly by a senior officer, otherwise the whole operation would collapse within a very short time, giving way to a witch-hunting exercise against "saboteurs." I seriously warned Achuzia against the use of that word ever again, citing for him numerous examples of the amount of damage it had already done in other areas. I emphasized the need for planning, which I was prepared to do for him. I encouraged him and tried very hard to convince him that we lost simply because the enemy was by far stronger than we were, and not as a result of sabotage. I then produced and discussed with him, the details of my plan and operational orders for the following day. How much of that he understood I do not know, but I had also prepared two fresh but weak battalions for the offensive. One of the battalions came with him from 11 Division while the other was formed locally with militiamen.

In outline, I wanted the 11 Division Battalion to move on the southern axis through Bori and Zakpong to clear Kani Babbe at the rear of the enemy. On the successful completion of that task, the Battalion, while ignoring the enemy at Wiyakara but ensuring the safety of their rear, would move fast to retake Kono waterside, thus cutting the enemy line of communications in the south. To assist the Kono operation, our own forces already on the ground were expected to attack Wiyakara using the Bori road to ensure that our troops moving to Kono were not taken from the rear by enemy troops at Wiyakara. On the northern axis, the militia Battalion was expected to move through Umuaba to the area of Banori and Ka Lori and from there clear Maribu and Okpantu and them move back to Obete waterside. Our own troops, already on the ground at Umuabayi, were to assist with the clearing of Maribu.

As I have already said, I was not sure how much of those orders Major Achuzia understood but all the same he raised his objections. He preferred to move all available forces on the two main axes to take the enemy frontally, so as to save time and avoid complex manoeuvres. By tradition, Achuzia received his orders only from the Head of State, but the Army Headquarters could make suggestions. All I could do therefore under the circumstances was to point out that, with the enemy's usual bombardment and numerous armoured vehicles, a frontal attack would gain nothing but casualties.

When Achuzia started his operations the following day, the first report that reached me was that the enemy was pushing to Azuago in the north and Notem in the south. I left the Tactical Headquarters and visited both fronts only to discover that my plan had not been implemented. Achuzia apparently had put everybody on the two main axes as he had indicated, and the enemy had broken our resistance in less than four hours. Before our troops could be reorganised for use again in the absence of reserves, the enemy had entered Bori in the south and Umuabayi in the north.

In the absence of Kalu, I found myself virtually stranded in Port Harcourt with Achuzia and not a single trained senior officer in the whole area. I could not move the Army Tactical Headquarters at Awgu to Port Harcourt because there were several other formations it had to control. I therefore sent personal messages to various well trained senior officers in rear units ordering them to come down and help out. Soon after, Colonel Morah, the Chief Paymaster, took over the administration and reorganisation of the worn out troops.

249

Colonel Olisakwe, the Commanding Officer of Pay and Records Office, took charge of the issue of arms and ammunition when they were available, Colonel Orogbu, the Chief Signals Officer, in the absence of wireless sets, gave troops their final briefings and took them up to their forming up places. Invariably he always stayed on and fought with them for a while before coming back. It was at that time that Orogbu tried to give me a lecture on the indispensability of wireless communications in modern warfare. I made it clear, probably in anger, that the Biafran Army was far from being modern and that the sooner he trained his signallers to shout their messages clearly over a distance of four miles, the better. I reminded him that our fore-fathers had done that quite successfully, and failure on his part to do the same would amount to incompetence. He never discussed wireless communications with me for the rest of the war.

Colonel Achuzia wanted Colonel Eze sent for as well, but I refused to do so because Eze was a very controversial figure. Having ended up both at Nsukka and Onitsha as a "saboteur," his very presence in Port Harcourt would start the civilians talking once again. Achuzia and Eze had never worked together amicably in any sector, and I saw no reason why they would do so in Port Harcourt sector. Eventually Achuzia succeeded in getting Eze down through direct arrangements with Colonel Ojukwu. "Saboteur" Obioha, the former commander of "S" Brigade was also down to assist and I gave him the command of the northern axis. In addition, I withdrew the strong 14 Battalion from its location at Agbani and put it on the northern axis. To strengthen our defences in the south in the absence of troop reinforcements, the Bomu oil fields were prepared and set ablaze.

These elaborate preparations and efforts paid off well for some time because when subsequently the enemy pushed, we were able to engage him for several days without any loss of ground. Eventually our supplies began to dwindle, and so did our strength. Thus, the enemy broke through in the south at Bori and began to advance towards Yehe. Similarly in the north, after several days of fighting, the enemy also broke through at Umuabayi and moved up to Obeakpu, while in the south he had reached Deyor Chara.

The threat to Port Harcourt was now real. In addition, the loss of Afam Power House which supplied electricity to most of Biafra was almost a certainty. The oil refinery at Okrika which supplied all the fuel required for fighting the war, was now ten miles away from the frontline. At that stage, I called in the leaders of Port Harcourt and some heads of government departments and corporations and briefed them on the situation. I advised that while the Army continued its efforts to check the enemy advance in the hope of eventually pushing him back, all essential stores and equipment in Port Harcourt, required for the continuation of the war should be evacuated at once. In order to drive the point home, I told them how much we had already lost in such places as Enugu, Calabar and Onitsha. They saw with me but failed to carry out those instructions because they were afraid of a possible hostile public reaction towards any attempt to implement such instructions.

Moreover, Achuzia had also instructed the Militia and the Civil Defence to prevent anyone from leaving Port Harcourt, because he was going to ensure that the enemy did not get into the town. By now, someone had told the public of the presence of saboteurs who wanted Port Harcourt abandoned to facilitate enemy entry.

From then on, Port Harcourt grew rather lawless. Everybody set up his or her own road block somewhere in the town, and searched for saboteurs. People had their property seized if it appeared they were leaving the town, while others were beaten up for one reason or the other. In other words, the usual atmosphere that preceded the fall of a major town had been created, and no one again talked of the enemy, but saboteurs.

On top of all that, the enemy continued to push against the brave resistance of the Biafran Army. Soon Wakama, in the South, fell into enemy hands, thereby forcing me to move my Tactical Headquarters from Okrika to Umuchitta on the main Port Harcourt-Aba road. On that day also, the enemy entered Obunku in the north, and I went up there to assist Colonel Obioha in working out a counterattack plan in an effort to save the vital Afam Power House. As I moved with Obioha towards the forward trenches and bullets whizzed past us in various directions, we came across two frightened

251

and rather excited natives who told us that enemy was already moving on our right flank along a road which would bring him to Okoloma, well to our rear. I had no intention of allowing myself to be captured alive and I told Obioha so, and advised that we went back to Abiama so that from that safe point, we would arrange to deal with the new development. Obioha thought I should go back alone, while he remained to sort out some points. He probably did not believe the story of the natives. I later went back and shortly after, the enemy took Afam from the rear and Obioha was not seen or heard of again.

14th Battalion, which had been reorganising at Abiama since their first battle, went into an immediate counterattack. It was a very good battle and both sides mixed and fought freely. It was indeed the first occasion the enemy 3 Marine Commando Division had fielded a unit whose infantry was truly willing to fight. There was no shelling, there was no armour, just the infantry on both sides slugging it out quite happily. Unfortunately the Biafran Army luck never lasted for long on any occasion. All of a sudden, confusion broke out among our troops and many of them began to pull back. They complained that every soldier in the battlefield, including those supposed to be the enemy, was wearing "14" on his uniform. They therefore concluded that we were fighting saboteurs and not the Nigerians, and that had made identification in the battlefield difficult. I realised immediately what had happened and tried to explain it to our troops without much success. I explained that the enemy formation we were fighting at Afam was the 14 Brigade of the Nigeria Army which was entitled to wear the number "14" just like the 14th Battalion of the Biafran Army.

It was too late, for the entire 14th Battalion including their Commanding Officer, Colonel Opara, had been accused of being saboteurs and should all be executed. Members of the 14th Battalion therefore took fright and disappeared in various directions to escape death from our own side. In the end I had no other alternative than to disband the 14th Battalion. The following day as I was going to Aba from Port Harcourt at 1800 hours, my staff car came under heavy fire at Obigbo junction, four miles away from the known enemy location at Afam. It turned out that the enemy had moved into the junction with the disappearance of the 14th Battalion.

Despite the confusion at Afam, our troops in the south were still fighting with determination, even though the enemy had once again begun to employ massive air support in his bid to capture Wakama. Colonel Ojukwu sent 1000 bolt action rifles to me and asked me to find the men and arm them as reinforcement. The only manpower available in Port Harcourt were the militiamen, most of whom had not handled a weapon before. I went to their camp in town with Colonel Eze, and, with the assistance of Mr. Onwudiwe, the local Militia commander, we organised 1000 militiamen into sections, platoons and companies and then ran a quick weapon training course for them. Finally they were grouped into two battalions. Commanders at all levels were appointed on the spot based on the recommendations of Mr. Onwudiwe and the two battalions were ready for battle.

I ordered one of the battalions to move through the left of the main axis to attack Nonwa Kebara behind enemy main concentration. On the successful completion of that task, one company would move further east to Deyor Chara which was now virtually empty, while the rest of the battalion would swing back and attack Wakama from the rear. While that was going on, the other battalion was to move through our tired troops on the main southern axis to attack Wakama using both the main road and the oil pipe line.

Those militiamen fought very gallantly indeed, and succeeded in checking enemy advance for several days. They even succeeded in clearing Nonwa Kebara but could not hold it for long. Colonel Ojukwu was so happy about this that he asked me to promote Achuzia to the rank of a Lieutenant Colonel. A day later when Colonel Ojukwu wrote a memorandum to Achuzia, he started it off with "Dear Colonel." Achuzia immediately put on the rank of a full Colonel and never quite forgave me for telling him that he was promoted to a Lieutenant Colonel when the Head of State wanted him promoted to a Colonel. Achuzia did not know that it was perfectly normal to address a Lieutenant Colonel as "Colonel," and I did not have the time for explanation.

253

On the 23rd of May, 1968, the Militia's gallant resistance cracked in the face of ceaseless enemy armoured thrusts, extremely heavy air bombardment as well as heavy artillery and mortar concentrations. Soon afterwards, Okrika fell and we lost the Oil Refinery there. Port Harcourt town was now completely exposed to the enemy. For eventually giving way under enemy pressure, all militiamen in the Port Harcourt sector were branded saboteurs. A good number of them were rounded up and dealt with ruthlessly, while their leader, Mr. Onwudiwe, went into jail where he remained until the end of the war. Even at that stage, the Colonel still prevented all civilians from leaving Port Harcourt even though the enemy was now at Okrika and Aletu in the south, and at Obigbo in the north.

On the 24th, the enemy shelled Port Harcourt all night and inflicted very heavy casualties on civilians. This brought about the greatest civil disorganisation and confusion since the beginning of the war. There were people who still maintained that the shelling was being done by saboteurs, but the road blocks were removed and people began to move out of town rather late. Everyone just wanted to get out of town as quickly as possible and save his neck. As a result, not a pin was evacuated. In the meantime, the enemy moved from Aletu and Obigbo and converged at Umukoroshe just outside Port Harcourt main town. Colonel Achuzia stayed back in town with his escorts and tried to engage the advancing armoured vehicles. He soon came out when he was almost run over by an enemy saladine.

After the fall of Port Harcourt, 52 Brigade Tactical Headquarters was located at Igrita along Port Harcourt-Owerri road. From there, several attempts were made by the Brigade to re-enter the town. Many times both the Port Harcourt Army Barracks and the Airport were cleared but each time they were soon lost again. There was a combined Army and Navy operation to land troops on the Port Harcourt harbour through Rumechie. The operation which was carried out with two local gun boats, one of which had a six-pounder and the other a 105mm gun, started very well initially. During the battle that followed, we sank two enemy boats before one of ours was badly hit. The other also came under heavy fire and as soon as the enemy jet planes appeared as well, it turned back. At the end of that operation Nigeria announced that General Efiong and myself had been killed during the operation.

Later in July, 1968, the enemy got as far as Igrita. I thought Achuzia was too tired to continue and succeeded in persuading Colonel Ojukwu to have him posted to Army Headquarters for staff duties until he had had some rest. The Navy Commander, Captain Anuku, who, in the meantime had no water on which to operate, took temporary charge of 52 Brigade.

The loss of Port Harcourt was one of the biggest setbacks of the war. Apart from the adverse effects it might have had on the Kampala Peace Talks, it was a military as well as an administrative disaster for Biafra. Because of this loss, both the Air Force and the Navy ceased to be operational for quite some time. The Militia ceased to be effective and was rather despised by the people. The Science Group lost the bulk of their stores and equipment so vital for the production of their war products which had kept the Army going. We had lost the Oil Refinery and most of the oil wells, not to mention the big departments stores. There was to be no more electricity in Biafra with the loss of Afam. Even the ammunition required to continue the war could not come in for several days until Uli Airport was commissioned.

The most revealing thing captured by our own troops during the Port Harcourt battles was the enemy brigade operational orders, captured at Onne. These orders must have been written by a gossip who not only was rude to Biafran Officers, particularly Brigadier Kalu, but also talked glibbly about all aspects of Nigerian life including her history, geography, religious customs and so on. Those orders also stated very clearly that the aim of the Nigeria-Biafra war was purely to capture the entire oil industry in Biafra and place it under the control of Lagos. In the ten-page orders, it was very remarkable to note that not a single word was put in for unity and One Nigeria. The enemy objective seemed to have been achieved through the fall of Port Harcourt, at great cost in enemy lives including some expatriate officers like Captains P. Boylen, R. Leigh, L. Darrel and Deane Symonds, who were all said to be British — a

255

fact I cannot swear to. Biafra could have been perfectly happy if the Nigerians held on to the oil and stopped the war; rather a change of aim occurred and the war continued.

EFFORTS BY THE ARMY TO SURVIVE THE ONSLAUGHT
OF THE "BIAFRAN REVOLUTION"

The newly-introduced "Biafran Revolution" was by now sweeping through Biafra, and had already swept many top civilians and military officers into jail for "offences" against it. The very continued existence of the Biafran Army became badly threatened as a result. By June, 1968 the Biafran Army had virtually lost the services of most of its senior officers who were either in jail or branded saboteurs by the people of Biafra. To recapitulate, Nwawo and Ivenso were branded during the Onitsha battles and were now lying virtually fallow. Eze was first branded at Nsukka and was later confirmed at Onitsha and was resting at Umuahia. Kalu got the plaque at Port Harcourt and was still floating. Akagha was branded at Calabar but was still hanging on to his 12 Division much to everybody's annoyance. Saboteur Amadi of Abakaliki was also still in command of 13 Division in the midst of threats to his life from Biafran sources. Also, during that month, the enemy pushed the 53 Brigade through Achi and eventually captured Awgu. For that reason, Ude, the Brigade Commander, who was first branded when he lost Udi, was confirmed as a saboteur and replaced by Colonel Nwajei. The above "sabateurs" represented the cream of the Nigeria Army when they were a part of it. They were not only trained in the best military schools all over the world but had each held his commission for upwards of 12 years.

"Sabotage" epidemic notwithstanding, it remained my duty to ensure that all major field units were commanded by the best available officers. During that month of June there was an urgent need to find commanders for the 11 Division in the absence of Achuzia and a replacement for the unpopular Akagha of the 12 Division. There was also a need to remove Amadi from 13 Division before it was too late. For that reason, the Head of State, Colonel Ojukwu, selected the very best officers for these appointments. He posted Nwawo to 13 Division, Eze to 12 Division and Amadi to 11 Division. Even if I had been consulted, I could not have produced a better solution.

Public reaction in respect of Amadi and Eze was swift and immediate as soon as the two of them assumed their new commands. There was panic in Awka and Onitsha Provinces when Amadi got to his new Headquarters at Nnewi. Some people even began to evacuate their homes when some mischievous individuals spread the story that Amadi's real name was "Ama-adi" which in Ibo language means "we will not survive." Several delegations, some of them led by "intellectuals," came to see me and, I think, went to see the Head of State too to demand the immediate removal of Amadi from command of 11 Division. I asked them to give Amadi a chance and I am glad that the Head of State was also completely adamant on that issue because he wisely realised that, politics apart, it required an officer of Amadi's calibre to save Nnewi, his home town. The pressure to remove Eze was equally strong but not quite as sustained as in the case of Amadi. Eze also stayed on in the end.

At the end of that political battle with the civil leaders over the new appointments, I called in the two officers to discuss military battles. I ordered the two of them to take their Division into immediate operations which must produce results good enough as to give them temporary relief from civilian pressures. Amadi was ordered to attack Onitsha immediately he had completed reorganising his Division. Eze was ordered to clear Ikot-Ekpene as soon as possible. I procured some ammunition for the offensives and the two officers left, determined to prove to all Biafrans that they were not saboteurs but victims of a rather strange system.

11 Division: Amadi's Special Bid

Prior to his offensive, Colonel Amadi thoroughly reorganised the 11 Division which was left completely devoid of any form of

257

military system by Achuzia. He also constructed and developed such a formidable defensive system that it was impossible for the enemy to have broken through. There was such a complex network of tunnels and communication trenches in his front that it was possible for one to visit every single soldier in 54 Brigade front without the visitor ever surfacing above the ground. In addition, a ditch three feet deep and six feet wide was dug along the whole bank of the Idemili River behind the front trenches and filled with crude petroleum, ready to be set ablaze if the enemy broke through the main defences by any chance.

Finally Amadi attacked Onitsha with his 54 Brigade, which was now being commanded by Major Ohanehi who came with Amadi from the 13 Division. The Brigade attacked from three points. One force moved along Enugu-Onitsha road to seize the Boromeo Hospital, the Seminary, and Saint Charles College. Another force moving along the general axis of Aba-Onitsha road went for Christ the King College. The third force had the task of moving through Obosi to take Dumez quarters. Link-ups were to be carried out after the initial tasks had been completed, in preparation for a further thrust into Onitsha town.

On the whole the operation was not a success insofar as it failed to clear Onitsha, but it was far from being a total failure. On the Enugu road axis, the enemy infantry fled and sent up their armoured vehicles as soon as we attacked. As the leading saladine armoured vehicle approached us slowly and cautiously it blazed away with all its armaments. Then Cpl. Nwafor of B Company, 29th Battalion of 54 Brigade took careful aim with the only anti-tank rocket available in the entire Brigade. His compatriots around him prayed. He fired. He hit the saladine and stopped it. He killed the crew. The subsequent joy and excitement over that achievement was such that it threatened the continuation of the operation itself. But to complete our joy on that axis, an armoured personnel carrier which was behind the damaged enemy saladine, in its attempt to turn back, fell into a ditch-trap and the occupants got out and fled.

Our troops then moved into Boromeo, Saint Charles and the Seminary and there started a defensive battle with whatever ammunition they had left, while attempts were being made to recover the captured armoured vehicles. Both vehicles were finally recovered but Corporal Nwafor himself died during the recovery operation. In his memory, the saladine armoured vehicle which he secured for the Biafran army was christened "Corporal Nwafor." Thereafter, both vehicles performed magnificiently well in all sectors of the war until they were either damaged or recaptured by the enemy. Also, along the Aba road axis, even though we failed to gain any ground we succeeded in trapping yet another saladine. The trap into which it fell was so deep we could not recover it. It was subsequently cannibalized on the spot and, with the parts obtained from it, Corporal Nwafor was kept on the road for well over 18 months.

While the battle at Onitsha was going on, the 11 Division also despatched a force through Atani across the Niger to Midwestern Nigeria to re-occupy places abandoned by Nigeria's Second Division in their bid to capture Onitsha. Colonel Kalu, just out from Port Harcourt with nothing to do, was placed in charge of that force which later grew into the 63 Brigade. Once across the Niger, the special force moved northwards and westwards to take Asaba, Ogwashiuku, Ibusa and Oku. Many enemy stores and equipment were captured, but most of them that could not be brought across the River Niger into Biafra were destroyed. At the end of a series of counterattacks by the enemy in the Midwest, our troops fell back to the general line of the Asse River. We had therefore succeeded in re-establishing Biafran military presence in that Region once again.

The Biafran civilian population in general, and those around Awka and Onitsha provinces in particular, were very happy with the achievements of Amadi and his 11 Division. No one exactly praised Amadi, but he was free from public molestation for some time. Later a very well attended memorial service was held at Umuoji near Onitsha in commemoration of the death of Corporal Nwafor, the soldier, and the birth of "Corporal Nwafor," the saladine armoured vehicle. As "Corporal Nwafor" sat confidently with melancholy elegance and dignity outside the church, men, women and children worshippers filed past him to pay their respects before going into the church. During the service, two enemy jet-bombers attacked the church and the rest of the village. The priest asked all worshippers to remain calm in their places during the raid and the congregation did just that. There was not a single casualty inside the church. The one man killed outside the church was the only person who ran out of the church in defiance of the priest's instructions. The end result of Amadi's test operation was that he got from the Head of State a promotion to the rank of a Brigadier. Nwawo who also took over command of 13 Division successfully was promoted.

12 Division: Eze's Special Bid

The final plan for Eze's "confidence" operation was rather ambitious for he requested for permission to conduct other limited offensives prior to his main attempt on Ikot-Ekpene. His aim was to draw enemy out of Ikot-Ekpene to defend those areas that would be attacked initially and also to try to capture more ammunition and weapons to enable him to make a good impression at Ikot-Ekpene when the time came to attack the town. Good as his plan and reasons were, I still harboured a fear that he was taking a risk ammunition-wise. For if he failed to draw the enemy out of Ikot-Ekpene as well as capture ammunition through his diversionary attacks, he would be forced to cancel his main operation and remain a saboteur in the eyes of the people for the rest of his life. Colonel Eze was prepared to take the risk because, according to him, "he that is down, needs fear no fall."

The first operation was a battalion offensive designed to capture all enemy-held towns and villages across the Imo River, south of Aba. By so doing we would appear to be threatening Port Harcourt, thus forcing the enemy to send in reinforcements from somewhere. A Special Task Force Battalion under a keen and gallant officer called Nweke, crossed into Umuabayi from Akwete. Soon afterwards the Battalion captured Umuabayi, together with the enemy ammunition and food dump located there. Not every-thing captured could be brought across the river but that which was brought back included 100,000 rounds of ammunition, 50 bicycles, 3 battery charging machines, 4 wireless sets, 2 typewriters, 300 rounds of 105mm shells, 2 anti-aircraft guns and ammunition, a few weapons, and fairly large quantities of food and clothing. The Battalion, in addition, captured a few more villages in the area before the enemy counterattacks developed momentum and strength. During the enemy counterattack on Umuabayi, our troops destroyed a saladine and an armoured personnel carrier (APC). The saladine was eventually recovered by the enemy, but we again cannibalized the APC and took away the useful and movable parts for the maintenance of the one captured at Onitsha. After ten days of operations Captain Nweke and his Battalion crossed back into Akwete proud but very worn out.

While the Umuabayi battle was going on, Eze's second diversionary offensive was being carried out by the 61 Brigade under Major Okeke. The operation was aimed at pushing the enemy at Nkwok as far back towards Opobo as possible and also to threaten or take Opobo if possible. The Brigade plan was to advance from Azumini to clear Nkwok, thereafter to move a force to clear Obiakpa and straddle the Aba-Opobo main road. Another force was to move northwards to attack Ntak-Afa, Ikot Okoro and other enemy pockets in the area, so as to remove all enemy presence on our aside of the Kwa Ibo River down to Etinam. The third and the main force, was to attack Ekefe-Mbioso and Ibesit and after clearing those areas to move to burst out at milestone 18 on the Opobo road.

Initial moves were successful and very encouraging and before long many objectives had been taken. Ikot-Okoro and a few other villages were cleared in the North and our own troops were within a mile of Obiakpa junction. Forces going south towards Opobo cleared several villages on their way up to, and including Ibesit. As we expected, the enemy soon moved in for his counter, but fortunately from Ikot-Ekpene. We lost a good deal of the ground gained to the enemy but whatever we had left, together with the luring away of the enemy from Ikot-Ekpene, made that operation a worthwhile exercise. So far Eze's calculated risk was paying dividends and with high hopes and morale, Eze took his Division on the final stage of his "confidence" test.

261

The Offensive to Clear Ikot-Ekpene

Both the 58 and the 62 Brigades were now geared up for the Ikot-Ekpene offensive. Judging from the amount of ammunition captured at Umuabayi, the 12 Division would have had no ammunition difficulties for a pretty long time, but that unfortunately was not the case. The bulk of the small arms ammunition was of a calibre that could not be fired by any weapon in use within the Biafran Army. Those that could be fired were taken over by the Army Headquarters and shared to all units, apart from a small extra quantity given to 12 Division as her prize for the successful offensive. However the Division could be said to be in good spirits because it was holding more ammunition than it had ever held at any one time since its formation. The outline plan for the offensive was as follows:

For 58 Brigade, the First Battalion was to move from Ikot Ebak to capture Ikot-Nturen-Ukana on the Abak road. Having made arrangements to protect its rear, the Battalion would move on to clear Nsiak, Abak-Oko and then Ibiaku on the Ikot-Ekpene-Uyo road. Thereafter it was expected to exploit its success to a limit of Ikpe-Nung-Inyang town and from there to be prepared to advance to Uyo. THE Second Battalion of the Brigade had the task of moving northwards from Ikot-Ntuan-Ukana to clear Ibibio State College on the outskirts of Ikot-Ekpene town. Having done that it would move to clear the left half of Ikot-Ekpene town. As soon as Ikot-Ekpene had been taken completely, this Battalion would move, on order, to Ntuan-Ukana to reorganise and be prepared to clear Ikwak, when instructed to do so. The Third Battalion remained in its location in defensive position, as well as a reserve force for the Brigade.

The 21st Battalion of the 62 Brigade was to move from Ndiya-Etuk to clear Ukpom-Uwana, Ikot-Nyoho and Ekpene-Ebam on the Ikot-Ekpene-Itu road. It was to move from there to establish a link with the 58 Brigade on the Uyo-Ikot-Ekpene road. A successful completion of that task would seal off enemy troops inside Ikot-Ekpene town. The 22nd Battalion of the Brigade was to move from Ndiya-Etuk through Itak-Ikot to clear the right half of

Ikot-Ekpene. The 23rd Battalion remained in a defensive role and acted as a brigade reserve force as well.

The operation started well and progressed very fast. Almost on all axes the enemy was on the run after a short-lived resistance. Soon the First Battalion of 58 Brigade was astride the Uyo road and the Second had swept through Ibibio State College into Ikot-Ekpene town. In the uncontrollable excitement of the chase, the Battalion cleared the entire town, instead of clearing only the left side of it as ordered. This was because troops of 62 Brigade who were to clear the right half of the town, were yet to arrive. This exceptionally good battalion was under the command of Major Archibong, one of the bravest officers I have ever met. Eventually the 22nd Battalion of 62 Brigade also moved into the town. Even though the 21st Battalion of 62 Brigade could not advance further than Ukpom Anwana, we had completely cleared Ikot-Ekpene and up to a minimum radius of six miles.

Wireless intercepts showed that the enemy was badly disorganised and was evacuating from Uyo to Oron. We had not the amount of ammunition required for another immediate move; otherwise, judging from the state in which the enemy was, we could easily have taken Uyo. Our ammunition state was such that we could not even beat back a determined immediate counterattack. We held our ground and waited for ammunition.

Immediately Ikot-Ekpene fell, I went into the Prisons there and what I saw still gives me nightmares from time to time. I saw several hundreds of Zombie-like creatures — men, women and children, lying, sitting or squatting in the midst of others who were dead. The living ones were completely reduced to skeletons and could not talk. I was seeing for the first time what I later knew to be kwashiokor, which was not yet noticeable in Biafra-held territories. Frankly, I took fright, and so did a majority of Biafrans at the thought of what would happen to the "majorities" in the hands of the Nigerians, if the much-talked-about "minorities" got nothing but slow and painful death by starvation. I believe that any foreign troops from anywhere in the world, occupying Ikot-Ekpene or any other town in

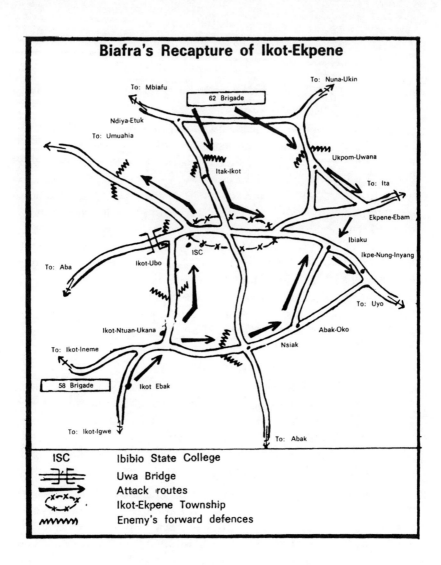

Biafra's Recapture of Ikot-Ekpene

To: Mbiafu

62 Brigade

To: Nuna-Ukin

Ndiya-Etuk

To: Umuahia

Itak-Ikot

Ukpom-Uwana

To: Ita

Ekpene-Ebam

Ibiaku

Ikpe-Nung-Inyang

ISC

To: Aba

Ikot-Ubo

To: Uyo

Ikot-Ntuan-Ukana

Abak-Oko

Nsiak

To: Ikot-Ineme

58 Brigade

Ikot Ebak

To: Ikot-Igwe

To: Abak

| ISC | Ibibio State College |
| Uwa Bridge |
| Attack routes |
| Ikot-Ekpene Township |
| Enemy's forward defences |

Biafra, would have shown much more sympathy toward the vanquished.

We were still waiting for ammunition when the enemy completed his reorganisation and launched a massive counterattack heavily supported by artillery, mortars and jet bombers and fighters. We gradually withdrew to our former defences, disappointed but not exactly demoralised. For apart from large quantities of stores, equipment and food we captured, we had proved to all Biafrans that, given adequate supplies, the enemy could be removed from any Biafran town he occupied, without much difficulty. The most significant item captured in that battle was a brand new 105mm artillery gun which looked as if it had not been fired at all. Thus, Colonel Eze completed his tests and passed them by all standards. For some time he was free from molestation and was soon promoted to the rank of Brigadier by Colonel Ojukwu. Above all, the relatively good results achieved both at Onitsha and Ikot-Ekpene, through these special "confidence operations," gave the Biafran Army another lease of life.

Biafran children suffering from **kwashiokor** in a refugee camp.

Chapter 11

BIAFRA'S FIRST COLLAPSE — SEPTEMBER, 1968

THE INVASION OF ABA — RUDOLF STEINER'S BLACKMAIL

During the month of July, 1968, the enemy had moved up
northwards from the south quite considerably. The end result was
that he was now controlling all important towns along the bank of
Imo River such as Obigbo, Igbo, Chokocho and Ozuzu-Odufo. On
the main Port Harcourt-Owerri road, he had pushed up to
Umuakpu, 22 miles south of Owerri. At the same time he was
occupying Ebocha along the Ahoada-Oguta road. The Biafran 52
Brigade on the Owerri road and the 60 Brigade on the Ahoada road
were not stronger than a weak battalion each as a result of weeks of
continuous battles without reinforcements. Captain Anuku, the
Biafran Navy Commander, ably supervised operations in that sector
on my behalf, but it was still necessary for me to visit the sector daily
to deal with major operational problems. To get over this problem, it
became necessary to establish a joint Headquarters for 52 and 60
Brigades and to appoint a commander if there was going to be any
co-ordination. The obvious choice as the commander of the new
Division was Navy Captain Anuku, not only because he was already
supervising operations in that Sector satisfactorily, but also because
he was a seasoned and experienced officer trained in Dartmouth,
England. Achuzia told me he wanted the command and was going to
contest for it. I warned Anuku about it.

Achuzia came into my office one afternoon from 14 Division
and reported that there was near mutiny there because of Anuku's
high-handedness. He insisted that unless I went there and intervened the situation would get out of hand.

When I got to 14 Division Tactical Headquarters at Umuagwo, near Owerri, many people had already gathered to give evidence against Anuku, each one reading out his charges and complaints. Mr. Okeke and Mr. Agwu, Ojukwu's special representatives in the Division, charged Anuku with high-handedness, poor leadership, inefficiency, and maltreatment of those of lower ranks both civil and military. Several others gave evidence, but no one put in a good word for Anuku who now sat in a complete daze. I sent for Colonel Ugokwe, the 52 Brigade Commander, and when he turned up and began to read out similar charges against Anuku, Anuku broke down. I suspended the case.

Though I was quite certain Anuku was merely a victim of a water-tight conspiracy, it was all the same no longer possible for him to remain in the Division. I was determined to ensure that Achuzia on the other hand never got the command of the 14 Division. When I discussed the matter with Ojukwu at Owerri two days before he left for Addis Ababa, he decided to take Anuku with him and approved the appointment of Colonel Ben Nwajei of 53 Brigade, as the first commander of the 14 Division. Nwajei, who had been in command of 53 Brigade for a relatively short time had not then lost a battle and was still completely undefiled as far as sabotage was concerned.

While I was with the Head of State, I explained the very grave threat to Owerri and Aba as a result of enemy recent moves. I pointed out that only a considerable amount of reinforcements and plenty of ammunition to 12 and 14 Divisions could prevent a major military disaster. As none of those things were immediately available, I recommended that the Commandos, who had been at rest for the past four months, since their bid to re-take Onitsha in April failed, should be ordered back into action at once. Colonel Ojukwu asked me to go to the Commando camp at Etiti and make overtures to Steiner and see what I could get from him. It was becoming increasingly evident that nobody in Biafra appeared to be in effective control of Steiner.

As Major Steiner sat on his throne in the Commando Officers' Mess surrounded by almost a platoon of fierce looking soldiers, Taffy Williams, another mercenary and Steiner's Chief Aid, ushered me in. I later retired into Steiner's office with him and there, on bended knees I put my case to him and asked for his assistance. He agreed to help, provided that a white Mercedes car which he once saw in my Headquarters was delivered to him, because, according to him, he had no car for any operations. I promised to give him the car and Steiner began to make preparations to move the Commandos to Owerri, almost at once. That was the 19th of August, 1968.

By last light on the 20th Steiner's troops were all concentrated at Holy Ghost College, Owerri. That night, Steiner, who was promoted to the rank of a Colonel by Colonel Ojukwu before his departure to Addis Ababa, was happy enough to permit me to discuss his future operations with him. He had two battalions and soon we agreed on a plan for them. One was to remain with 14 Division and assist with the operations going on around Omanelu. The other was to go to Owazza near Aba to assist the 12 Division. From there this Battalion would cross the Owazza bridge, capture Chokocho and destroy the bridge there, so as to cut the line of communication of the enemy force moving on that axis towards Okpuala. I had wanted the Commandos to move northwards from Chokocho towards Okpuala, to take the advancing enemy from the rear. Steiner preferred something more dramatic and chose to move southwards to attack Igrita and possibly Port Harcourt. It was too minor a difference in tactics between the two of us to cause friction, and so he had his way. The D-day for the Chokocho offensive was fixed for 1600 hours 22 August, 1968.

By the end of the day on August 21st, Taffy Williams and his battalion were already in position around Owazza, less than two miles away from the bridge which they would assault the following day. At midday on the 22nd, enemy force of company strength, attacked the bridge head supported by 106 mm guns, bazookas, and 105 artillery guns which were firing at point-blank range across the river. Our bunkers were crumbling slowly and the men inside them were finding it increasingly difficult to stay on. I ordered Williams and his Battalion of 850 armed men who were close by to move in and round up the enemy company of less than 150 men, without delay. Major Taffy Williams refused to do so. He argued that it was

269

the duty of 12 Division (or to use his words, "the infantry") to keep the bridge open and secure for his crossing which was going to take place in less than two hours time. He said he would not deviate from Colonel Steiner's operational instructions without due clearance from him. While Eze tried to scout for men to help at the bridge, I set out with Williams on a fruitless search for Steiner. In the meantime Taffy Williams' Battalion sat quietly in complete indifference less than two miles from a crucial battle. By the time I came back to Aba that night, Eze had not found any troops and the enemy had crossed the Owazza bridge, thus forcing the Commandos to move back as well, without a fight.

Early in the morning of the 23rd, Williams said he had obtained Steiner's permission to attack, but he would not be ready to do so until 1600 hours. I pleaded with him to try and make it earlier otherwise by the time he had chosen to attack the situation would have changed so much that his Battalion would be grossly inadequate and ineffective against the enemy. To drive home my point, I showed him an enemy intercepted message received during the previous night. In this intercept Adekunle had urged a number of his formations in the south to move as quickly as possible across the bridge during the night.

Williams did not budge an inch, and while he waited for his attack at 1600 hours, the enemy put in his own at 0800 hours. The Commando Battalion, yet unprepared for a battle, pulled back into Aba town to "reorganise," according to Williams. Within 24 hours from then, the enemy having brought across all his heavy equipment, seized the Asa junction and was probing towards Aba and Akwete.

For the next seven days the 12 Division tried to confine the enemy to Asa junction using troops thinned out mainly from Ikot-Ekpene sector and a few other areas. Ammunition shortage at the time was simply scandalous and any soldier was lucky if he had five rounds of ammunition in any one day. Taffy Williams' Battalion held quite an appreciable amount of ammunition — at least 20 rounds per man — but no one could get them to attack or to surrender the ammunition. Aba was then in grave danger and its fall became a question of time. While the enemy pushed the 12 Division back slowly towards Aba town, Colonel Steiner himself turned up at Aba on the 28th of August with another force of 450 men to bring the strength of the Commandos in Aba to a total of 1300 armed men. He set up his Tactical Headquarters close to mine and promised to launch a massive attack on the 30th to clear the enemy from the entire Owazza complex once and for all. He wanted to clear Asa and Owazza through the right flank. To assist Steiner, I ordered the 12 Division to collect all available ammunition from units under command and use it in assaulting Akwete through the left flank so as to link up with the Commandos at Asa.

12 Division commenced the operation at 0600 hours on the 30th as planned, and progressed as well as could be expected. At 0900 hours, I learnt that the Commandos had not started their operation. On my way to their frontlines to find out the reasons for the delay, I saw Colonel Steiner outside the Aba market, and somewhere around the market the Commando band was playing and marching to their popular number "Up with the Commandos," to the joy of all. With Steiner, was Mr. Fredrick Foresythe, a former BBC man in Enugu, who had remained in Biafra since the outbreak of the war, after he had announced that the BBC "dismissed" him for filing news items favourable to Biafra. He was now acting as Steiner's interpreter. Others around Steiner were Major "Taffy" Williams and the rest of the mercenaries. Mr. Foresythe, as the interpreter, explained that all the mercenaries had taken a unanimous decision earlier not to go into action until all their outstanding salaries were paid. Mr. Foresythe added that it would be grossly unfair of anyone to expect the mercenaries who only fought for money to go and do so without getting it. At that stage, Williams, a Welshman, said quite frankly to me that blackmail was a perfectly legitimate weapon of a mercenary if he was to get his pay regularly. In Katanga, he continued, they had used it on several occasions with excellent results against Tsombe for whom they had fought. I sent an emergency message to Colonel Ojukwu and asked him to try to settle the pay of these people quickly to enable them to take part in our efforts to save Aba. This was done a few days later, when it was absolutely too late to do anything to

save Aba. Later on, I sent for Foresythe and accused him of being a spy. I threatened to get soldiers to get rid of him before long unless he voluntarily left Biafra. The fellow was so frightened that he spent almost two hours trying to convince me of his innocence. To get rid of him, and not because he had convinced me, I withdrew my charge against him and shook hands with him. He continued to stay in Biafra but I never saw him again.

The 12 Division offensive on the 30th soon fizzled out as a result of acute shortage of ammunition. From that date, not a single round of ammunition of any description came into Biafra. For that reason Aba sector got nothing — absolutely nothing, in the way of ammunition. This horrible state of ammunition went on for four days, until midnight of the 3rd of September when the enemy began a massive bombardment of Aba township and the environs. My Tactical Headquarters, still located in Aba, came under monstrous artillery barrage as Brigadier Eze and I worked out a plan for the following day. I went under my office table and from there telephoned Colonel Ojukwu at Umuahia to give him an idea of what was happening and to plead for ammunition. He said I just had to hold on somehow until he could find ammunition, which he said he did not have at the time. By 0600 hours on the 4th October, 1968, enemy infantry began to move into Aba unchallenged, while our troops moved out of it to within a distance of two miles radius of the town. Morale was very low generally. Eze and I worked all morning to reorganise and re-deploy our troops after I had been promised that ammunition would soon be available to enable us to fight to regain the town.

At about 1130 hours that morning, some senior Biafran Government officials came to see me at Umu-Aro near Aba where I was setting up a temporary mobile Army Headquarters. Those who came included Mr. Okeke, the Inspector General of Police, Mr. Akpan, the Chief Secretary, Mr. Ugwumba, and several Provincial Commissioners and Administrators. They said Ojukwu had sent them to investigate a report he had to the effect that our troops did not fight well in Aba because their officers had abandoned them. I did not believe that Ojukwu in the full knowledge of our difficulties in the Aba sector since the enemy crossed the Imo River could have ordered such an investigation.

I decided to go and see Ojukwu at Umuahia. At Umuahia, I told Ojukwu that our people were so ignorant of the military situation that an immediate action was necessary to rectify it before any more damage was done. I suggested that thenceforth, I should be allowed to attend the weekly Executive Council meetings so as to personally brief the Biafran leaders on the military situation. Alternatively, I requested that the minutes of each meeting should be forwarded to me to enable me to know what was going on, and to determine how much the people knew about the war they were fighting.

Colonel Ojukwu rejected these proposals and told me that I was raising the very issue which had brought a quarrel between him and Brigadier Njoku, as a result of which Njoku went into detention. It was the first time I knew for certain what Njoku's offence had been.

Less than a week after the fall of Aba, Colonel Onwuatuegwu, the Commander of "S" Brigade operating near Awgu, came to see me at my mobile Headquarters which was then stationed at Umuoba near Aba. With him was his Principal Staff Officer and His Excellency's Special Representative for that Brigade, Mr. Okonkwo, who, until the outbreak of the war was the District Officer for Enugu Ezike near Nsukka. Onwuatuegwu said he had been mandated by Ojukwu to form a new Division to be called the "S" Division, with which he was to clear Aba. The purpose of his visit therefore was to receive from me all it took to form such a Division. He revealed that he was expected to take over the weapons of the Commandos, who would then pull back to their base at Etiti for rest, regrouping and reorganisation. This last fact was soon confirmed by Steiner who had even started to pull out from some of his defensive locations without being properly relieved. From the already battered 12 Division in particular, and the rest of the Army I collected vehicles, clothing, fuel, and other available items and equipment and, together with about 1200 recruits sent in by the Training Depot, an ad hoc "S" Division was established in less than a week. During that week, Steiner had grown impatient and left for Etiti with all his merce-naries, leaving instructions with Biafran officers under his command to bring back the men when the takeover was completed. However, as soon as Steiner left, his men thought the withdrawal had begun and therefore started pulling back in a rather disorderly fashion. It required tremendous effort to recover the bulk of their weapons, with which the new "S" Division formed two armed battalions.

In my first plan of operations for "S" Division and the 12 Division to clear Aba, the "S" Division had the task of moving through Ugba junction (Umuivo) along the Aba-Owerri road to clear Ngwa High School as their first step towards clearing Aba town. 12 Division had the task of clearing Ogbo Hill on the Umuahia road, preparatory to a re-entry into the town. On three consecutive occasions, the 12 Division started the operation at H-hour only to find that "S" Division could not make it for one reason or the other. While "S" Division fiddled, the enemy struck out at them and moved into the strategic Ugba junction and indeed began to advance towards Umuahia through that road. A timely intervention by the 12 Division halted the enemy move and pushed him back to Ugba junction. I thereafter made "Corporal Nwafor" available to "S" Division and ordered the Division to clear Ugba junction soonest. When on four different occasions the D-day for the offensive was postponed by the "S" Division for various excuses, I moved my mobile Headquarters back to Okigwe in disgust, to join my main Army Tactical Headquarters. I did not want to get involved in the political storm that normally accompanied operations by Achuzia and Onwuatuegwu. My departure from Aba sector brought to an end for a very long time all meaningful attempts to clear the town.

TOTAL DESTRUCTION OF ENEMY TROOPS AT OGUTA

All enemy attempts to cross the Ebocha bridge in his bid to invade Oguta proved abortive. The Biafran troops of 60 Brigade, stationed at the bridge, beat the enemy back as often as he attacked, until there was a stalemate. On the 9th of September, however, our troops there reported seeing what appeared to be enemy boats moving up the Orashi River towards Oguta. When this report was investigated with an Air Force helicopter the following day, it was discovered that there were six enemy boats already at Ezi-Orsu, less than four miles to Oguta town. The alarm was given, and the Biafran Navy went into action with its lone boat mounted with a six-pounder. This boat had been lying idle on the Oguta Lake for some time. In the subsequent battle the Biafran Navy destroyed two enemy boats before it received a hard hit and had to limp back to the Lake. By first light on the 11th of September, my mobile Headquarters moved to join the Navy Headquarters at Oguta. The town of Oguta appeared absolutely normal for the civilian population was not yet aware of the explosive situation.

My first rude shock on arrival at Oguta came with my discovery that the Navy had no troops at all stationed in Oguta except for a few administrative elements and, with all army units of the 60 Brigade now by-passed by the enemy, there was no one to fight in defence of Oguta. When all of a sudden Oguta town came under heavy bombardment, which was quickly followed by massive air raids, the few Naval ratings assembled by Captain Anuku found it difficult to stay in their locations along the Lake. No trenches had been dug because no one ever dreamt that Oguta could be threatened or was going to be threatened at such a short notice. It was now too late to dig trenches because, besides the heavy artillery and mortar bombardment going on, the Russian jets strafed and bombed individuals who dared to move around.

The situation was so hopeless that I had to brave a trip from Oguta to Owerri to try to get some troops from Nwajei's 14 Division. Twice on the way a jet fighter attacked my car unsuccessfully. At 14 Division I wrenched from Ugokwe's 52 Brigade a strong company of 250 armed men and the Brigade's only anti-tank weapon, regardless of Ugokwe's protests for losing so much. Unfortunately, by the time this reinforcement got to Oguta with me, the enemy had entered and occupied the town. The troops of the 52 Brigade were then used for establishing initial defences along Oguta-Mgbidi road. When the Biafran Air Force and the Navy eventually found some men and deployed them along Oguta-Uli road, the enemy was reasonably well contained inside Oguta town itself.

With Uli Airport six miles away, the only Biafran link with the outside world, the situation was so grave that unless it was rectified at once, the war could come to an abrupt end within a short time. In preparation for a counterattack, I ordered Amadi of the 11 Division to send up an infantry battalion. By first light on the 12th Amadi had brought up 300 armed men himself, being the best he could do immediately while the rest were to follow when assembled. The Navy and the Air Force had about 100 armed men each and the 250 men of 14 Division were still there. All added up to a sizeable force for a counterattack. The Head of State made available more ammunition than we ever dreamt of for operations of that nature. The outline plan was to move in 14 Division troops assisted by the Navy on the Mgbirichi-Oguta road to take the left half of the town including the Lake. 11 Division force, assisted by the Air Force, would move along Uli road to clear right of the town. The H-hour was fixed at 1600 hours on the 12th of September to give the field commanders sufficient time to do their reconnaissance and issue detailed orders to their troops. I left the area of Oguta at 0700 hours to go and deal with other urgent matters and also to prepare for the operation.

Achuzia, who was also delegated to assist with the operation later came to see me at 1300 hours looking extremely worn out and dejected. He revealed that the counterattack I planned on Oguta for 1600 hours had already taken place and failed woefully. He narrated how Colonel Ojukwu came to the sector at 0900 hours shortly after my departure, and ordered an immediate counterattack to be controlled by him personally. Not only had the operation failed and the Head of State returned to Umuahia, all the ammunition including 300 rounds of 105 mm artillery shells we had saved up for the operation had been exhausted. Colonel Nwajei and Captain Anuku who, together with Achuzia, had commanded the troops during this futile operation, were now re-organising what was left of their troops. Achuzia still maintained that we could clear Oguta.

At the end of his story, I ordered Achuzia to return to Oguta and inform all commanders to prepare to repeat the operation at 1700

Salvaging a Nigeria Army anti-aircraft weapon from Oguta Lake after the Nigerian troops had been driven out of the town

hours, and this time properly. Shortly after Achuzia left I received
the following signal message from Colonel Ojukwu:

> C-in-C for GOC. Oguta operations. Army efforts at
> Oguta appear fruitless. There is no basis for Achuzia's
> optimism. Nwajei only hopes while Anuku is hopeless.
> You will take the situation personally in hand and report
> progress. Acknowledge.

The second attempt to clear Oguta on the 12th started promptly
at 1700 hours in accordance with the original plan. Achuzia, Anuku,
and Nwajei displayed such determination and gallantry during the
battle that by 1845 hours, all our troops had converged on the banks
of Oguta Lake, having cleared the town completely. It was sad to
watch enemy soldiers who had missed their boats jump into the lake
rather than stay on and be captured. Much equipment and clothing
were salvaged from the boats which we destroyed, including a 40mm
Bofor anti-aircraft gun marked "Royal Electrical and Mechanical
Engineers" (REME) and a Panhard armoured vehicle which was
immediately christened "Oguta Boy." When I telephoned Ojukwu
at Umuahia later that night to give him the good news, he found it
almost impossible to believe me.

During the 24 hours the enemy was in occupation of Oguta our
defences around Ebocha bridge had disintegrated and our own
troops had withdrawn completely, thus enabling the enemy to
link-up all the way from Oguta to Port Harcourt. The clearing of the
enemy from Oguta was therefore a small fraction of the task of
removing the overall enemy to Uli Airport and the recovery of
Egbema oil fields. The enemy was now at Ezi-Orsu only four miles
away and not only was Uli Airport still threatened from there, but
we were yet to recapture the Egbema oil fields which were the only
remaining source of crude oil for the entire Biafra. There was
pressure on the Army from all quarters to regain the oil fields, as the
nation was already feeling the pinch of their loss. What people did
not realise was that we did not even have enough ammunition with
which to prevent the enemy from re-entering Oguta or making a
possible successful move to Uli Airport.

When enemy threat increased together with the local pressure, Major Asoya, the commander of 60 Brigade came to see me to demand ammunition with which to clear Ezi-Orsu and Egbema. I gave him whatever I had, which was grossly insufficient, and told him to go to Defence Headquarters at Umuahia and ask for more if he thought he had a chance of succeeding. When he got to Umuahia, Ojukwu ordered him to return to his unit location without delay.

The Head of State discovered, shortly after his order to Asoya, that he was still in Umuahia and put him under close arrest for disobedience. Ojukwu then summoned me to Umuahia and after briefing me on Asoya's obstinacy, asked me to look for a new Brigade Commander for 60 Brigade. But when Asoya, who was still around, explained that he was waiting for his vehicle which he had sent somewhere in town to collect brigade stores, I convinced Ojukwu to forgive him.

He subsequently got some ammunition for his operation. Asoya had a company of 200 men for the operation but both the Air Force and the Navy were kind enough to make available to him a Company of 150 armed men each. I took down with me "Corporal Nwafor," and with my mobile Headquarters just outside Ezi-Orsu, Asoya and I launched the men into battle.

The men of 60 Brigade, fighting with an armoured vehicle for the first time, were by far too excited to think of danger. "Corporal Nwafor" was simply wonderful and so were the soldiers. Soon Ezi-Orsu fell and the push towards Egbema oil fields began. At the end of a five-hour continuous battle, we had recaptured Egbema oil fields and pushed the enemy down to Okwuzu. We could easily have continued to Ebocha, but we had to preserve some ammunition for possible counterattacks. Casualties were evacuated by porters throughout the operation but it was worth it, for once again, oil was flowing in Biafra. I really wonder now how many people in Biafra realised how close we were to the end of the war when we lost Oguta and Egbema. For his bravery and determination, Major Asoya, who a few days before was about to go into detention, was promoted to the rank of a Lieutenant Colonel.

THE INVASION OF OWERRI

I was at 14 Division Headquarters at Obinze near Owerri on the morning of the 13th of September to congratulate Nwajei again and celebrate with him the recapture of Oguta. We had not even had a round of laughter yet, not to talk of drinks, when Mr. Ohanu, a Police Commissioner, came in to report that the enemy was attacking our troops in strength at Awarra. According to Ohanu, the Company of soldiers we deployed there was already being pushed back quite rapidly by an enemy force estimated at brigade strength and supported generously by armour, artillery and heavy mortars. A liaison officer was immediately despatched to the scene and on his return, he not only confirmed the police information, but added that the enemy had already occupied the town of Asa.

There was not much anyone could do immediately to strengthen our resistance, as we had practically exhausted our human and material resources in pushing the enemy out of Oguta the previous day. Before long, the enemy was in Ohoba town and was still advancing from there towards Avu and Obinze on the outskirts of Owerri. With resources available to it, which were mainly local science products, the 14 Division managed to delay the entry into Owerri of the enemy until the 18th of September.

Colonel Nwajei moved his Headquarters to Atta and there a delegation came to see him to find out why he had lost Owerri. Nwajei told them rather in anger, that he lost the town because he had no ammunition to fight with. He told members of that delegation that unless something was done to rectify the deplorable ammunition situation in Biafra, there could be many more losses similar to Owerri in the near future. Some members of that delegation later went to Umuahia to see Colonel Ojukwu, and there they told him that Nwajei was demoralizing the civilian population. The Head of State promptly removed Nwajei from command of 14 Division and indeed from all military duties. The officer was later attached to the civilian Fuel Directorate, while Colonel Kalu of Port Harcourt was brought in to command the 14 Division.

Kalu took over command of the 14 Division at a time when the enemy's brigade move on Chokocho-Okehi-Okpuala road was being intensified. Shortly after Kalu took over, Okpuala junction fell into the hands of the enemy, thus exposing the whole of Mbaise to the enemy. We still had no answer to enemy moves because he soon linked up Aba and Owerri and began a two-pronged advance into Mbaise. He moved on both the Olakwo-Obiagwu road and the Okpuala-Uvoro road with a view to converging on the main Owerri-Umuahia road at Inyiogugu, 17 miles east of Owerri.

In the absence of ammunition and reinforcements, and with little or no prospects of getting them in the immediate future, the situation was very grave and almost too hopeless to be described properly. If the enemy got to Inyiogugu, not only would the bulk of 14 Division around Owerri town be rendered useless and disorganised, there would not have been a single soldier available to stop him from moving from Inyiogugu to Umuahia, the then capital of Biafra.

The 63 Brigade which was now facing the enemy had already fought for almost six weeks without a break, and was therefore both tired and very much depleted. What was left of the 63 Brigade was completely reorganised, and that included the removal of its brave but tired commander, Major Okilo, and his replacement with Major Ihenacho, who was before then an exceptionally good Battalion Commander with the 53 Brigade at Inyi near Enugu. Ihenacho, being from Mbaise, had an additional advantage of knowing the ground pretty well. A battalion of "S" Division was ordered to move from Aba to reinforce the 63 Brigade, but by the time the battalion was in position the enemy had pushed to within a mile of Inyiogugu main junction. Alarmed at the situation, Colonel Ojukwu sent the following signal message to Kalu and sent me a copy:

> Your role in the Port Harcourt disaster is still fresh in the minds of the people. You cannot, repeat cannot therefore afford to disappoint the nation a second time. You will clear the enemy completely from Mbaise within 24 hours or submit to me your resignation from the Biafran Army.

Obviously, Kalu could not beat the deadline and when he wanted to forward his resignation to Ojukwu, I advised him against it; he remained in the Army until the end of the war.

In the meantime we had started a determined counterattack against the enemy using 63 Brigade on one axis and the "S" Division battalion on the other. For six days we had sufficient ammunition to maintain our position, in addition to launching a total of four unsuccessful attacks to dislodge the enemy. On the 7th day of the battle for Inyiogugu, the enemy grew so desperate that on two occasions that day, he almost succeeded in pushing us out of our defences. On the first occasion, most of our defences had fallen when the few remaining Biafran soldiers exploded an "ogbunigwe" on the surging enemy infantry. About a company of them lay dead or wounded and the rest of them withdrew. After two hours of what appeared to be retributive shelling of our locations, the enemy re-grouped and again attacked. This second time, the last "ogbunigwe" held in the Brigade, broke up the assault and inflicted almost as many casaulties as in the first assuault. The enemy again withdrew, this time into dead silence.

One hour later, we began to advance again on two axes and were surprised to find the enemy running back in a disorderly fashion. Thereafter, the enemy never again resisted our advance effectively, and the rate of our advance depended entirely on how much ammunition we had. Before long, we were soon back on the main Aba-Owerri road at Olakwo and Okpuala, and shortly after, we regained full control of that road between Olakwo and Owerrinta bridge, near Ugba junction.

We continued to push the enemy southwards slowly but quite steadily. From Olakwo, we soon regained control of all towns and villages in Ngor complex right down to Elelem. Similarly, from Okpuala junction we had pushed right down to Amala again. We could easily have exploited our success in this sector right down to Chokocho if we had had sufficient ammunition. Even the little ammunition available was then more urgently required in other areas of the 14 Division. The enemy inside Owerri was trying to push out of town in all directions. On the Owerri-Okigwe road he had already exploited up to Orji bridge, four miles from Owerri. From there he launched a major attack in the direction of Mbieri and Orodo with the aim of getting to Orlu and Nkwerre. We succeeded in halting this move less than a mile from Mbieri and, following a series of counterattacks lasting several days, he was pushed back to Orji bridge. On the Ihiala road, he soon got as far as Ogbaku from where he spread northwards towards Oguta again. In that move, all towns and villages on the left of Owerri-Ihiala road to as far north as Izombe, fell to the enemy. Both Oguta and Uli Airport were once more threatened. As soon as 60 Brigade was able to stabilise the situation by pushing the enemy slightly back from Izombe to Obudi, we had no choice but to leave Owerri sector as it was in order to face a new but very serious threat which was developing in the North against the town of Okigwe.

THE INVASION OF OKIGWE

Since Brigadier Nwawo took over the command of the 13 Division, the Northern Sector had been reasonably quiet, except for the battle of Awgu which was fought by the independent 53 Brigade, then under Colonel Nwajei. The 13 Division now had under it the 51 and 55 Brigades which had been reduced to battalion strength and were commanded by Colonels Christian Ude and Agbogu respectively. There was also the "S" Brigade, operating independently along the Okigwe-Awgu road, under the command of Major Atumaka. The Brigade was a part of the "S" Division at Aba and was under the direct control of the Head of State.

The 13 Division was stretched to its limits as a result of the vast area it had to cover, thereby making its defences rather weak. The 55 Brigade was responsible for the defence of the entire area between the Cross River around Afikpo and Akeze where the Division Headquarters was located. The 51 Brigade defended from Akeze westwards to the main Awgu-Okigwe road. Both "S" Brigade and the 53 Brigade operating independently were responsible from that road westwards to the area of Ugwuoba, where the 53 had a link with

283

11 Division. I had been away from my main Tactical Army Headquarters at Okigwe for over five months fighting the battles of Port Harcourt, Ikot-Ekpene, Aba, Oguta and Owerri and only returned on the 19th of September after the fall of Owerri.

On the 21st of September, two days after my return, a strong enemy force estimated at battalion strength, moved from Nkpololo on the Oji-Awgu road and attacked the 53 Brigade Company located along the riverline at Agunta. Soon after this, our troops got dislodged after a bitter and determined effort, and the enemy crossed the river. By the time a company reinforcement which I raked up got to the battle area, the enemy had completed the crossing of all his troops and equipment and advanced to Mbala.

As fighting raged at Mbala, another report was received over the wireless that the enemy was also attacking our troops in strength at Ndiaboh on the right of Okigwe-Awgu road. According to the report, "a pregnant woman was also in the battle area but had not delivered any babies." That meant that an enemy aircraft which was yet to drop its bombs, was in the battle area. The significance of the use of air support by the enemy was that it was always a clear indication of a long drawn-out major move by the enemy. Later that day, Okigwe town itself came under heavy air bombardment.

Despite gallant performances by the Biafran Army which resulted in heavy losses to the enemy in men and equipment, the enemy still advanced through Ndiaboh to Obilagu Red Cross airport where we did not even have any military presence. By occupying the Obilagu airstrip situated along Okigwe-Afikpo road, the enemy had blocked the only motorable road between the 13 Division and the Army Headquarters if not with the rest of Biafra. Over three-quarters of the entire Division including the Commander and his Division Headquarters were thus cut off. All that was left of the Division on the Okigwe side with which to continue the battle were elements of 53 Brigade numbering about 200 armed men, and their Brigade Commander, Colonel Ude. A determined effort by the 13 Division to re-establish a link fizzled out as soon as the little daily ammunition ration the Division had finished. Thereafter, the only alternative left to the Division was to withdraw through various tracks the best they could, leaving behind almost the entire Division's heavy stores which could not be lifted by porters and soldiers. It would have been hopeless attempting to send any ammunition to the Division even if we had had the ammunition because it would have taken over 12 hours to deliver an average daily quota of 5000 rounds on foot — a quota which would hardly have influenced the situation. At Mbala, the situation was being checked more effectively, even though the enemy was gaining ground slowly towards Okigwe.

Colonel Achuzia requested directly, and got the permission of the Head of State, to attempt to clear Obilagu airstrip in an attempt to prevent the 'enemy from getting into Okigwe town. In addition to whatever troops there were on the ground, Achuzia brought with him a weak battalion of Commandos. Achuzia and his troops fought extremely well for 48 hours but, despite their courage and determination, we lacked the punch required to clear an enemy as well equipped as the Nigerians. At the end of the operation, Achuzia went back to Umuahia together with the Commandos, leaving Ude once again to continue the battle. On the 29th of September, while we battled for the airstrip, the enemy at Mbala had captured the vital ground at Ngodo, thus forcing the "S" Brigade deployed around Awgu to withdraw all the way to Okigwe. Later that day we made a desperate attempt from Lekwesi and Ogbabu simultaneously to seize Isuochi in an attempt to cut off the enemy at Ngodo, but that failed. We therefore began to dig trenches and make other defensive preparations against enemy final assault on Okigwe. On the 30th of September after a fierce battle lasting all day, the enemy eventually bull-dozed his way into Okigwe town from Ngodo through Ihube with a concentration of artillery, mortar and armour. All Biafran troops fought to their very last round of ammunition before they pulled out of Okigwe town. For unknown reasons, the enemy entered Okigwe with vengeance, as a result of which they burnt down most of the houses and killed everyone they saw including a British couple working with the international Red Cross.

The 13 Division was disorganised to the point of being almost disbanded and, for some time, there was no form of defensive arrangements of consequence around Okigwe. Achuzia came to see me on the 2nd of October at my mobile Headquarters at Ihube near Okigwe. He said he had the mandate of the Head of State to take over the command of 13 Division from Brigadier Nwawo. According to him, authority had also been given to him to change the name of the formation to 15 Division, because "13" was an unlucky number.

The Head of State later confirmed all that Achuzia said. In addition, there was an order to make all officers in the former 13 Division, from the Division Commander down to the Company Commanders, drop a rank each for losing Okigwe town through inefficiency. I was present throughout the battle for Okigwe and knew only too well that we lost because the enemy was by far stronger and not because we were inefficient. If nothing but inefficiency lost us Okigwe town, there was no reason why I should not drop a rank as well. I took no action on that instruction but when Achuzia took full command of the 13 Division, he reduced in ranks some of the officers. The Head of State then posted Brigadier Nwawo to Army Headquarters as my Chief of Staff and removed Colonel Ude entirely from the Army and gave him a job with the Rehabilitation Committee. I made an attempt to explain Ude's case to Colonel Ojukwu but was warned to steer clear. Thus, Colonel Ude, one of the best trained military officers in Black Africa received his final knock-out blow with the fall of Okigwe, having gallantly withstood all the heavy blows aimed ceaselessly at him since the fall of Udi. Though I tried very hand to retain Ude in the Army, the officer himself was completely convinced that I sacked him because I did not like him. Somebody may have told him that; but his training and experience were such that I needed him throughout the war if I had had my way.

Special attention was given to Achuzia by the Head of State and I also gave him a lot of supplies to enable him to rebuild his 15 Division quickly and clear Okigwe as he had promised. On the 10th of October, the day of the attack, Ojukwu and I were at the 15 Division Tactical Headquarters at Ihube to watch the battle. It was launched supported by "Corporal Nwafor." There was no clear cut plan, and it therefore failed. It was repeated the following day and again failed more woefully. Ojukwu admonished Achuzia and later left in anger for Umuahia. Achuzia then summoned a conference of all his brigade and battalion commanders. During that conference which I attended as an observer, he told his commanders about his intention to launch a third attack on Okigwe. He wanted all formations to advance from their locations at H-hour into Okigwe town to capture it. He warned that he would deal ruthlessly with any commander who failed to attain his objectives. No orders were issued, neither were discussions held on the questions of ammunition supply, administrative support and so on. I unsuccessfully tried to bring those vital omissions to Achuzia's notice.

Just before H-hour, most of the field commanders who were pretty sure they could never attain their objectives with what they had, abandoned their troops and fled for genuine fear of what might befall them if they failed. Some of those run-away commanders took refuge in Defence Headquarters, Umuahia from where they were posted to other units. Prominent among those officers were Major Igweze and Obi. Igweze, who joined the 15 Division a week before the operation, came on posting from Ikot-Okpara where he had displayed so much gallantry with the 56 Brigade. He was later appointed the Commander of the 52 Brigade which he commanded very well during the successful battles to clear Owerri town. Obi later became the commander of the 12 Commando Brigade which did very well during the last stages of the war.

The Okigwe Administrator later told me how he had driven to the frontline on the day of the operation, and how, as he approached the troops in his car, which was similar to Achuzia's staff car, the soldiers were all diving into the bush and running away. At first the Administrator had thought it was an air raid but later found out that the soldiers thought he was Achuzia coming up to carry out his judgment. The end result of all this confusion, was that the offensive never was launched and a considerable number of our troops deserted their trenches in fear of Achuzia. Following this incident, Achuzia became known as "air raid" throughout Biafra.

During the second week of October, Colonel Onwuatuegwu, a

political rival of Achuzia's, volunteered to the Head of State to clear Okigwe if given as much support as Achuzia got for his attempts. His request was granted and he got as much as Achuzia, if not more. In addition to whatever ammunition he was given, he also had 850 bolt action rifles with which to arm a fresh battalion of recruits for the offensive. The decision for Onwuatuegwu to clear Okigwe was taken between Onwuatuegwu and Colonel Ojukwu without the knowledge of Army Headquarters. I was only called in to intervene when the Head of State had failed after repeated attempts to get Onwuatuegwu to start the offensive. When I got to the scene, it was clear to me that Onwuatuegwu needed not less than 14 days to organise his force sufficiently to launch a meaningful attack independent of 15 Division. All he had in his Tactical Headquarters in the way of personnel were himself and Mr. Okonkwo, and I did not have the necessary time and resources required to build him up into an effective fighting formation as I had done for him at Aba when the "S" Division was being formed. Onwuatuegwu, having failed in his task, was eventually ordered back to his "S" Division at Aba, leaving behind at Okigwe the new battalion he had formed, which thereafter reverted under command of 15 Division.

Onwuatuegwu's politico-military gimmicks at Okigwe were not altogether a waste of time because both himself and the Army as a whole benefitted from it. During the period of just under a week of his absence from "S" Division, Brigadier Eze was able to rally both the "S" and the 12 Division into a determined operation which not only cleared the Ugba junction, but pushed the enemy seven miles back into Aba.

No other planned attempt was made to clear Okigwe for the next six or seven weeks. By the end of November, during one of my routine visits to 15 Division Tactical Headquarters, Achuzia revealed to me that he was finalising plans to launch an attack once more to clear Okigwe. He was so sure of succeeding that I wondered if the enemy had not evacuated from Okigwe for unknown reasons. The normal crowd of civilians that regularly surrounded Achuzia became uncontrollable with anticipatory joy as Achuzia explained that he required no external assistance as far as supplies were concerned. That was because, he explained, he had discovered within his Division enough ammunition for the operation. When he told me how much ammunition he had, I was quite surprised he had as much, even though it would not have been more than the "first line" scale for a rifle Company in a modern army. It was a Sunday morning, and Achuzia said that his operation would be launched the following day at 0600 hours. I promised to be present. Before my departure from 15 Division Headquarters, Achuzia wanted me to promise that I would give him the command of 11 Division as his reward for clearing Okigwe after a successful completion of his operation. I gave him the necessary assurance.

On the following morning, I got to Achuzia's Headquarters at 0900 hours and not only had the operations not started, but he was still in bed suffering from a severe hangover. When I succeeded in waking him up, he gave me many reasons why the operation had not been launched and had to be postponed till 1600 hours the same day. The operation did start at 1600 hours but did not last more than 30 minutes before it fizzled out and everywhere was quiet again. That was the end of Achuzia's operation.

Before long it was clear that Achuzia's honeymoon with the 15 Division was over. He had completely lost all interest in the Division in favour of his new fancy Division — the 11 Division. It was now almost impossible to find Achuzia in his Headquarters or operational area during the day, thus forcing me to go to his Headquarters and sit in for him any time anything developed in his division during his absence. After persistent pressure from me on the Head of State, I succeeded in getting Achuzia removed from the command of 15 Division in December, 1968 and in his place, Colonel Ohànehi who had been commanding the 54 Brigade at Onitsha was appointed the Commander of the 15th Division. Within a period of one month, Colonel Ohanehi had reorganised and brought up the Division to normal Biafran standards.

The rapid loss of Aba, Owerri, and Okigwe all in one month simply broke the will of the Biafran people to continue the war. The social problems, particularly with respect to refugees, was much more than the country could handle adequately. The food problem was acute and it appeared as if the majority of the people simply wished for nothing but to see an end to the war at all costs.

To divert the people's attention, a planned rumour soon began to circulate throughout Biafra that a new group of saboteurs had been discovered. Those on the list included the Chief Justice, Sir Louis Mbanefo; the Inspector General of Police, Chief Patrick Okeke; Dr. Nnamdi Azikiwe; Dr. Kenneth Dike and myself, the General Officer Commanding the Army. This ruse succeeded for, while the people speculated on how best they could deal with us, they temporarily forgot the recent reverses of the war. This incident also re-established full confidence between me and my senior field commanders who, prior to that time, had often wondered why all senior army officers had been branded saboteurs except their General Officer Commanding.

Chapter 12

BIAFRA'S ATTEMPTS TO REGAIN THE INITIATIVE

OPERATION HIROSHIMA

Despite the temporary appeasement of the people through the "scapegoat" tactics which never improved the battle situation, the need to do something practical to improve the desperate war situation still existed. I had my eyes on Owerri where the enemy, according to reports, had thinned out considerably. At the same time, but unknown to me, Colonel Ojukwu also had his eyes somewhere else — Onitsha. When therefore I was invited by Ojukwu to Nnewi near Onitsha on the 13th of November to attend an operational conference for an attack on Onitsha, the current rumours that the Commandos were about to clear Onitsha town were confirmed as far as I was concerned. The Head of State had attached so much importance to absolute secrecy with regard to this operation that all preparations for it were kept secret from Army Headquarters until the very last minute. Unfortunately Steiner, who had nothing to gain by operating in secrecy, gave his operation maximum publicity. When his troops moved to Nnewi, they went with their brass band and held a number of parades in the town to entertain the people before launching the operation. Eventually the enemy knew so much about the impending operation that occasionally they would shout out to our men in the trenches "when are you going to start your operation, or have you given it up?"

At Nnewi, on that 13th day of November, a plan, which had previously been arrived at between Ojukwu and Steiner, was discussed and finalised. It was a big job trying to get Steiner to attend the final conference because he thought he was too busy to attend any more conferences on the operation. When he did attend eventually, he rejected both the D-day and the final plan. After a lot of persuasion and cajoling, Steiner agreed to a plan as modified by himself and also accepted the 15th of November as the D-day. The operation was named Operation Hiroshima.

Even though essentially a Commando operation, the Hiroshima plan made room for maximum participation of 11 Division in whose operational area the offensive was going to be launched. The outline plan was to move a Commando force, assisted by elements of 54 Brigade, along the Onitsha-Enugu road to clear Boromeo Hospital, the Seminary and St. Charles College. Thereafter the combined forces would move through Onitsha inland town to clear all areas left of the New Market Road (inclusive) down to River Niger. From there they would swing left to link up with other friendly forces at Fegge Quarter. Another commando force was expected to pass through the defensive lines of the 11 Battalion of 54 Brigade at Nkwelle, to attack and clear all areas inside Onitsha between the River Niger on their right and the Onitsha General Hospital on their left, and then move deep down to the New Market road, which would be their maximum limit of penetration. For that move, the 11th Battalion stood by in readiness to assist in exploiting success only. In the way of assistance, elements of 54 Brigade were given the task of clearing through Ukawood down the road to the bridge head and the Textile Factory. From there they were to move to link up with the Commandos in Fegge.

When the operation began on the 15th of November, enemy resistance was stiff from the beginning for the element of secrecy and surprise had long been lost. After clearing Ukawood, the 54 Brigade elements could go no further, and spent the next two or three days slugging it out in the area of Ukawood, with no significant changes on either side. On the Enugu Road axis, enemy resistance stiffened after we had managed to clear Boromeo and the Seminary. Thereafter, enemy counterattacks came in rapid succession accompanied by fierce and ruthless shelling. By the third day when we began to experience severe shortage of ammunition, we pulled back to our trenches after one of the most bitter battles ever fought around Onitsha. On the Nkwelle axis, the operation was abandoned after two successive but spirited attempts by our troops to occupy the Government Reservation Area had failed.

Thus, Operation Hiroshima came to an end on the third day without improving the tactical situation at Onitsha. It was not possible for us to continue on account of shortage of ammunition. However, if we had had the ammunition, it would have been pointless continuing, in view of the fact that the enemy was fully prepared for us. The Commandos suffered fairly heavy casualties in the same way as the enemy did, but probably deserved much better results judging from the amount of effort they put into the battle. However, the Commandos learnt a few useful lessons from the operation. They appeared to have learnt the importance of secrecy with regard to a planned military operation because from then till the end of the war, I never heard their band play before an operation. The Commando unit which operated through Nkwelle learnt that there is always a need to use a covered approach to one's objective in the battlefield. Twice they had moved from Nkwelle through an open field to attack the Onitsha GRA and on those two occasions, they came under effective artillery and mortar bombardment. Frequent open confrontations between Ojukwu and Steiner before, during and after Op Hiroshima were clear indications that the Head of State had lost control over Steiner. Yet, if the Commandos were to contribute gainfully towards our winning the war, it was imperative that Steiner be removed and replaced by, preferably, a Biafran. Already Commando troops had been trained to consider themselves as something special and to disobey instructions from all persons outside the Commando formation. By early December special foreign assistance arrived in Biafra to remove Colonel Steiner and Brigadier Nwawo, my Chief of Staff, was appointed to take command of the Commandos. He completely reorganised it and retrained all the soldiers in accordance with generally accepted military tactis and procedures. He restored normal military discipline and the formation was formally named the Commando Division and placed under command of Army Headquarters for the first time.

THE DESTRUCTION OF ENEMY AT AGULU

Op Hiroshima left the Commandos in a state of complete ineffectiveness militarily. With their strength greatly depleted on account of the Hiroshima casualties, in addition to the command vacuum created by the sudden departure of Colonel Steiner, and complete shortage of ammunition, what was left of the Commandos constituted more of a menace than an asset in the Onitsha front. The Hiroshima operation in fact created difficulties for 11 Division. Not only did they expend a considerable amount of ammunition which they did not plan for, but new axes had been opened as a result of Hiroshima which stretched the Division to the breaking point in their attempt to cover up. These difficulties notwithstanding, the 11 Division continued for several days after Hiroshima to launch limited attacks on various parts of Onitsha to keep the enemy there busy. These minor attacks were producing such good results that I was even contemplating another major effort to clear Onitsha quite soon.

On the 25th of November, however, the enemy, moving from Awka, launched a brigade group attack on our Agulu defences. He found practically no difficulty in dislodging a company of Biafran troops deployed in a defensive role there. Moving thereafter without opposition, he swept through Agulu to Adazi junction and from there, was poised for Nnewi and Uga Airport. We had no immediate answer to this move and it is still hard to guess why the enemy did not continue his unimpeded march to any destination of his choice in Biafra. I drove to the 15 Division being the nearest to my Headquarters and ordered Achuzia, then the commander, to organise and despatch a battalion of 450 men to Agulu before first light on the 26th to assist in checking the enemy advance. Achuzia, always itching for new battles and detesting stale ones, promised in his usual excitement to send 750 men whom he intended to

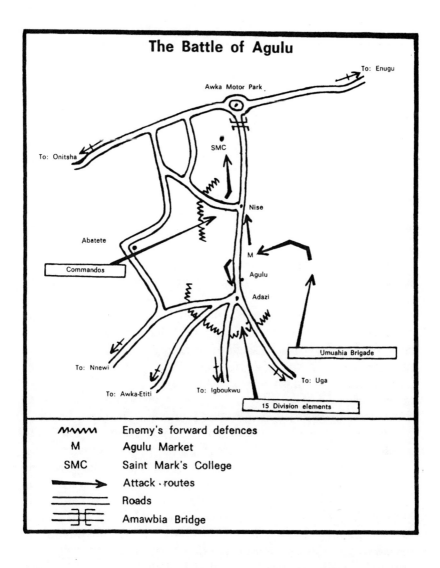

The Battle of Agulu

To: Enugu

Awka Motor Park

To: Onitsha

SMC

Nise

Abatete

Commandos

M

Agulu

Adazi

Umuahia Brigade

To: Nnewi

To: Awka-Etiti

To: Igboukwu

To: Uga

15 Division elements

ᨕᨕᨕᨕᨕ	Enemy's forward defences
M	Agulu Market
SMC	Saint Mark's College
➔	Attack · routes
═══	Roads
╪╪	Amawbia Bridge

command himself. With the strength of his Division at the time, I very much doubted whether he could muster the 450 men I asked for, but his offer of 750 men gave me joy with doubts. Achuzia followed up his promise with a glorious signal message to 11 Division, which he copied to the Head of State and the Army Headquarters to the effect that he was going to bring down a strong force of 750 men to smash the enemy located at Agulu and Adazi. Later, after my short discussion on the situation with Colonel Ojukwu at Umuahia, he made available to me his reserve force of 500 men stationed at Umuahia. The force was often referred to by everyone as "Umuahia Brigade" and was commanded by a Major Njoku. By the time I got back to Nnewi, Amadi had also organised a battalion from the remnants of the Commandos and prepared it for battle.

On the following day, the 26th, the "Umuahia Brigade" was in position but not a single soldier from Achuzia's 15 Division had arrived. For that reason, I decided to go ahead with the operation using whatever was available starting at 0600 hours on the 27th. The outline plan was communicated to Colonel Ojukwu for his information, but he was already very impatient and angry with what he called an unnecessary delay. By that plan, the "Umuahia Brigade" was to move through the right flank to clear Agulu Market, thus cutting the main line of communication of enemy troops in Adazi. Thereafter, the "Brigade" would swing right towards Nise. The Commando Battalion was expected to move through the left flank to capture Nise Market and junction, and then swing left to clear St. Mark's College and Amawbia bridge. The 15 Division Battalion, if and when it arrived, were to be joined by the few troops already on the main axis to attack enemy forward concentration at Adazi with a view to linking up with the "Umuahia Brigade."

Even though Colonel Ojukwu thought my plan amounted to "shadow boxing" and wanted all available forces concentrated on the main axis for an immediate frontal attack by last light on the 26th, I decided to stick to my plan and also to carry it out at first light on the 27th.

While Amadi and I held discussions in his Nnewi Headquarters with local leaders to finalise details of civil administrative support for the operation, Colonel Achuzia came in. He announced that his troops had arrived and he was under Ojukwu's orders to launch an immediate attack. All he wanted, he said, was to take away the ammunition for the operation from Amadi. He added that there was no time left for "Sandhurst planning." All the civilians, around appeared quite impressed by him and from the look on their faces, nothing short of an immediate attack could have satisfied them. I checked back Achuzia's story with Ojukwu over the wireless and he confirmed it.

Having collected his share of the ammunition, Achuzia left for Ekwulobia from where he was going to launch his attack while rumours went round Nnewi town that Achuzia was about to drive the enemy away. Two hours later, I drove up to Ekwulobia front with Brigadier Amadi to watch the battle. The whole area was absolutely quiet and there were no troops around, except for about 150 men of Achuzia's 15 Division. The young company commander with these troops revealed that Achuzia had visited them earlier and distributed some ammunition and instructed them to await further orders from 11 Division. According to this officer, Achuzia had since then returned to his Headquarters at Ihube near Okigwe. While the young officer spoke, a top civilian administrative officer came up also to report that Achuzia had removed almost all the fuel made available to him for the evacuation of Ekwulobia if the need arose. According to the civilian, Achuzia said he needed the fuel for emergency operation, but was later known to have taken all or most of it away to Okigwe. That inexplicable action of Achuzia posed fresh problems with regard to the impending operation. Not only did he fail to attack as he had promised the public, the Army had lost to him both ammunition and fuel for the operation. When the Head of State was told what Achuzia had done, he gave up further attempts to get the operation started before first light on the 27th.

The attack was finally launched on the morning of the 27th after a preliminary bombardment carried out with one 105mm artillery gun firing 100 rounds and two 81mm mortars that fired 150 bombs. "Umuahia Brigade" took Agulu Market and moved quickly

297

to the major road from where they encircled all enemy troops still left in the market. In less than thirty minutes, the encircled enemy got disorganised and scattered in many directions. Having completed their mopping up in the area of the market, our troops moved down towards Nise town opposed by a solitary enemy saladine armoured vehicle. With no anti-tank capability available to us for dealing with the saladine, we had no alternative but to by-pass it. Finding itself by-passed and ignored, the armoured vehicle turned round and fled to rejoin the retreating infantry. The Commandos also moved very swiftly to capture Nise junction having inflicted very heavy casualties on the enemy there. When we fought our way to St. Mark's College, we found enemy resistance there extremely stiff, as a result of further enemy reinforcements moved in there from Awka. After a series of attempts to clear the College had failed, Biafran troops dug in all around it. Our force on the main axis consisting of a collection of troops from various formations, greatly encouraged by the all round successes on all flanks, attacked the main enemy concentration at Adazi with extraordinary determination and courage. Contrary to all reasonable expectations, the enemy panicked and soon became disorganised and ran away. Biafran troops gave a chase, wrestling and trading blows with those they caught up with.

By 1600 hours, enemy resistance in all areas had ceased and local civilians had moved in to carry out their usual "combing" exercise. Enemy stragglers who were all over the place constituted a real menace and a security risk. Soon afterwards, most of the Biafran troops left the battle area and went down to Nnewi to celebrate the victory and it took a pretty long time to get them back to their defensive positions. If the enemy had carried out an immediate counterattack, it could have had disasterous consequences for us in the absence of those troops.

The Agulu victory was a very important one indeed for Biafra because if the enemy had gained another two miles in any direction from their location at Adazi, not only would Nnewi and all the surrounding towns have fallen, the 11 Division would have been written off. The battle also convinced the Head of State of the need for planning an operation before its execution no matter how pushed for time one is. He was also beginning to understand, at least for the time being, that a flanking move by the infantry whenever possible, was better than a head-on collision against armour. For a considerably long time, the enemy in the whole of Onitsha sector remained quiet and this made it possible for the 11 Division to reorganise fully and have a bit of rest which they very much needed.

Shortly after the Agulu success, Colonel Ojukwu invited General Efiong and I to Umuahia for a presentation of honours and awards. There, in the State House, he sat alone barefooted in his living room, with a lot of medal ribbons lying around him. He showed us a long list of Biafran honours and awards and the corresponding medal ribbons, and then went on to explain that the medals were yet to come. He then awarded me the Army Cross (AC) and the Distinguished Service Cross (DSC). General Efiong also won some awards which I cannot remember. Before we left the Head of State, General Efiong asked him which committee had decided on the details of those national honours and awards. Colonel Ojukwu answered "Well, the usual committee — Mr. Chukwuemeka, Mr. Odumegwu and Mr. Ojukwu." His full name being Chukwuemeka Odumegwu-Ojukwu, he was merely telling his Generals that the effective Biafran committee on that matter was himself alone. It explained to both of us so many things we had not fully understood.

Since the entry of the Second Division of the Nigeria Army into Onitsha in March, 1968, all its attempts to advance inland in any direction had been foiled by the 11 Division. Indeed the enemy was finding it increasingly difficult to control the whole of Onitsha town effectively. That was probably why the enemy First Division stepped in to render assistance to the Second Division in December, 1968, shortly after the Agulu disaster. On the 24th of December, 1968, therefore, the First Division started a massive operation from Abagana, designed to link that town once again with Onitsha. Such an achievement would not only have cut off the entire 57 Brigade of the Biafran Army stationed at Otuocha, but would have meant the loss of the last major food-producing area left in Biafran hands.

299

After several days of heavy fighting, the enemy, massively supported by artillery, armoured vehicles and jet planes, succeeded in closing the 13 miles gap between Abagana and Onitsha, despite his heavy losses in men and equipment. A situation which could hardly be tolerated for any length of time in Biafra was thus created and therefore necessitated the suspension of all other operations so as to effect an immediate rectification.

On the 26th of December, 11 Division went into a spirited counterattack, and at the end of a three-day bitter battle costing the Army almost all its entire resources, we regained Nkpor junction, the Ogidi Rest House road junction, and the Umudioka-Ogidi (Afor-Igwe) Market. When those three areas were later linked up, we were soon controlling 8 miles of corridor to Otuacha and the 57 Brigade once again. Thereafter, fighting to retain the 8 miles continued almost every month till the end of the war. We still hung on to three miles of it at the time the war ended and that achievement represented one of the greatest displays of courage, determination and gallantry of the war by Biafran troops.

When it became obvious to the enemy First Division that their operation to close the Onitsha corridor was proving futile, it began yet another fresh move to overrun the entire 57 Brigade operational area at Otuocha. For several days the enemy attacked on two axes with lavish air support which, with napalm bombs, wiped out several towns and villages in that area from the face of the earth. Because of long distances involved and the fact that it had to get its ammunition on daily basis like all other formations, the 57 Brigade, more than any other formation, lacked the ability to fight a sustained battle. The situation was such that by the time the 11 Division's daily ammunition quota got to Nnewi from Umuahia and then was sent up to 57 Brigade after the internal re-distribution within the Division, the enemy had invariably ended the day's move with little or no opposition. The ammunition could however be used for counter-attacks only, but it was never enough for dislodging the enemy. Thus, after several days of good fighting whenever there was ammunition, the enemy captured a good part of Otuocha with our troops still hanging on to Nkwelle and Umunya areas until the end.

300

BIAFRAN ARMY OFFENSIVE TO CLEAR OWERRI

Our minor successes on the Owerri front since the clearance of Oguta and Egbema oil fields, had been encouraging enough to tempt me into doing something better organised on a larger scale. In addition to pushing the enemy back all the way from Inyiogugu to Amafor on the left flank of Owerri, we had also, on the right, pushed him further south from Egbema to Ebocha bridge. As a result of these successful flank operations, the enemy inside Owerri thinned out quite considerably to protect those flanks. Having taken these facts into consideration, I decided to start an operation to clear Owerri town.

At this time, our troops around Owerri included the 60 Brigade under Colonel Asoya, which, with a strength of about 1000 armed men, had the responsibility of defending the whole area between Owerri-Ihiala road and Owerri-Port Harcourt road. There was the 52 Brigade roughly of the same strength, under Colonel Chris Ugokwe, whose responsibility it was to defend from Owerri-Ihiala to Owerri-Umuahia road. The Third Brigade of the 14 Division, the 63 Brigade under the command of Colonel Lambert Ihenacho, protected the entire Division left flank stretching from Owerri-Umuahia road down to the Imo River. In addition the "S" Division sent up a battalion reinforcement which was concentrated in Emekuku near Owerri, for the proposed offensive. This battalion, called the 68 Battalion, was under the command of Major Ikeji and was to operate independently but in support of the 14 Division. With the forces available and our limited resources, I did not expect to immediately drive the enemy out of Owerri. I however realised that if we could prevent him from getting reinforcements and supplies, we could in our own time, wear him down gradually until he lost the will to fight. The overall plan for dealing with Owerri was therefore geared towards achieving that aim.

The task of surrounding Owerri and gradually destroying the enemy inside it was going to be a gigantic one, and would take a very long time, considering the fact that ammunition supply to the troops was normally small and most irregular. For that reason, the whole operation was divided into three major phases. The aim of the first phase was to box in the enemy on all sides as much as possible into Owerri town, and sever all his routes to the rear except for the Owerri-Port Harcourt main road. It was necessary to leave that major line of communication open for the enemy, otherwise we would scare him too soon, and compel him to take necessary precautions before we were fully prepared to deal the final blow. For that phase, 52 Brigade was to push enemy back in all its areas of responsibility to within one mile from Owerri. Its special tasks during that phase were to clear Egbu, Orji and Orogwe. 60 Brigade was to clear all areas right of Port Harcourt-Owerri road and then maintain a strong defensive line all along the side of that road from Irete on their left to Umuakpu on their right. In addition, the Brigade was to deny the enemy the use of Elele-Umudiogu-Ubimi road, thereafter. The 68 Battalion of "S" Division had the task of moving through the left flank of 63 Brigade to clear all areas held by the enemy on the left side of Port Harcourt-Owerri road between Naze and Umuakpu. The 63 Brigade was to remain in its defensive positions but prepared to provide reinforcements for places where they were needed for exploiting success.

On the successful completion of the first phase, we expected to see the enemy concentrate heavily inside Owerri town, and thereafter having as his only link to the rear the main Port Harcourt road. On our side, we expected to find our troops who were widely despersed in defensive locations, better concentrated and in a position to operate more effectively. If and when that happened, it would then be the signal for the beginning of the second phase of the operation.

In the second phase, the sole aim was to move swiftly in strength with all that was available and seize the Port Harcourt road between Avu and Umuakpu, and thus seal off Owerri. During that phase 60 Brigade was to move to take Obinze and Avu and link up both towns and exploit southwards to Mgbirichi where they would join up with 68 Battalion elements. The 68 Battalion itself was expected to seize the thinly defended towns of Umuakpu and Umuagwo and, having linked them up, was to move northwards to Mgbirichi to make

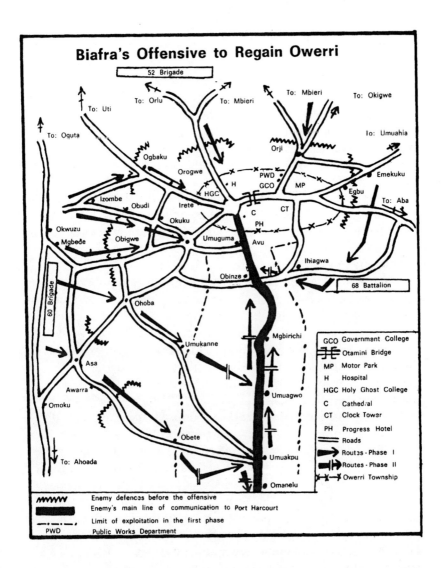

Biafra's Offensive to Regain Owerri

52 Brigade

To: Uti
To: Orlu
To: Mbieri
To: Mbieri
To: Okigwe
To: Oguta
To: Umuahia

Ogbaku
Orji
Orogwe
PWD
GCO
Emekuku
HGC
H
MP
Izombe
Egbu
Obudi
Irete
To: Aba
Okuku
C
CT
Okwuzu
PH
Mgbede
Obigwe
Umuguma
Avu
Ihiagwa
Obinze
68 Battalion

60 Brigade
Ohoba
Mgbirichi

Umukanne

Asa
Umuagwo

Awarra
Omoku
Obete
Umuakpu
To: Ahoada
Omanelu

GCO Government College
Otamini Bridge
MP Motor Park
H Hospital
HGC Holy Ghost College
C Cathedral
CT Clock Tower
PH Progress Hotel
Roads
Routes - Phase I
Routes - Phase II
Owerri Township

Enemy defences before the offensive
Enemy's main line of communication to Port Harcourt
Limit of exploitation in the first phase
PWD Public Works Department

303

contact with 60 Brigade. It was clearly obvious that if the second phase was successful the reaction of the enemy inside Owerri would be very violent indeed. For that reason, the task of 52 Brigade during that phase was merely to prepare troops to beat back enemy counter-attacks both in 60 Brigade and 68 Battalion areas.

The third and final phase of the operation was to descend on the encircled enemy inside Owerri and destroy him while preventing him from breaking through southwards. For the final phase, the 60 Brigade was to clear the right half of the town up to the clock tower. The 52 Brigade was to tackle the left side of the town while the 68 Battalion was to defend the Port Harcourt-Owerri road and flanks right and left of it.

It was a very ambitious plan based entirely on optimism, for its success depended mainly on the amount of material and administrative support that would be made available. With the scarcity of food, troops were expected to harvest wild cassava, yams and vegetables and augment the Food Directorate supplies. It was in their interest that they did all they could to clear their objectives if for no other reason, but to be able to harvest abandoned crops in enemy held areas. On the issue of ammunition, which was what mattered most, the Head of State promised and later issued the following ammunition to all troops taking part for the first one week of the operation — 50,000 rounds of small arms ammunition, 200 rounds of 105 mm artillery shells, 300 rounds of mortar bombs, 20 rounds of anti-tank rockets, grenades and other smaller items. 14 Division Commander Kalu, wanted the whole ammunition for a period of one week issued to him in bulk to ensure that his operations were not interrupted by frequent ammunition shortages. Ojukwu turned the request down and preferred to issue on daily basis to ensure that the week's quota was not exhausted in less than a week. Ojukwu later told me that he did not even have that amount of ammunition, but had based his allocations on what he expected to receive every night during the week of the operation.

On the 3rd of December, the 63 Brigade launched a two-pronged limited offensive against Elelem and Eziama as a part of a diversionary plan to occupy the enemy's attention. The main Owerri offensive started in earnest in all sectors at 0700 hours, 5 December, 1978. 60 Brigade moved with a battalion each on three fronts. On the left, a battalion moved to clear Izombe and Obudi. From there, while a part of it moved to clear Ogbaku on the Ihiala road, the rest of the battalion moved to Ofogwe. From the centre, another battalion moved from the area of Okwuzu and Mgbede and took Obigwe and, shortly after, were in full control of Okuku. This particular move was so swift that the enemy Battalion Headquarters at Obudi did not realise for some time that it had been cut off together with most of the battalion sub-units. Thus many enemy soldiers and vehicles which were either moving to Obudi or returning from there fell into our hands in the area of Okuku. The third battalion of 60 Brigade moving on both Ohoba-Umukanne road and Asa-Awarra road, took Umuakpu quite easily. Thus, in the first three days, the 60 Brigade had completed their tasks in the first phase, resulting in the clearing of several hundreds of square miles of enemy occupied territory.

68 Battalion was equally successful in clearing all enemy held areas left of the Port Harcourt road down to Mgbirichi, thus establishing a permanent link with the 63 Brigade. The 68 Battalion success left us completely in control of all areas southeast of Owerri town down to Owerrinta bridge to a depth of about ten miles from the Aba-Owerri road. The 52 Brigade facing the enemy forward concentrations made only small gains as expected. Once or twice they cleared Orji but lost it again. At the end of one week, the first phase was considered to be over and the results, particularly in 60 Brigade area were very encouraging.

A considerably large quantity of arms and ammunition was captured, even though most of the weapons were damaged and the bulk of the ammunition was of a calibre useless to us. Because of the rapidly decreasing quantity of ammunition available to us for the operation, I decided to execute the second phase with only one brigade fighting at a time, and as soon as its objectives were completely attained, the next brigade or formation would start. For that reason, the 60 Brigade started off by clearing Avu and Obinze while other formations remained in defence. Both towns fell and

305

were linked up but by the end of the day we had lost them again following an enemy armoured assault on both towns from Owerri. For a couple of days, we put in a series of attacks on both towns but the enemy invariably managed to push us out despite his loss of an armoured personnel carrier, a ferret armoured car and many men during these battles.

The enemy in Owerri, had very good reasons to be desperate because the International Team, which observed atrocities, was trapped inside Owerri town and had to be got out if they were to continue "observing." After about seven days of unsuccessful operations against Avu and Obinze, I became quite sure that we would not succeed in sealing off Owerri from that area. Avu was too close to the enemy concentration in Owerri and therefore attracted a swift and immediate counterattack from him any time the town was threatened. It therefore became necessary to look for a point along the Port Harcourt road which would be far enough from Owerri to discourage the enemy from journeying all the way from Owerri to counterattack. Even if he did that, it would be after we should have had enough time to dig in properly to resist his attack more effectively. In that case, he would be overstretching himself. In a modified plan for phase two, the 60 Brigade therefore moved further down to attack and capture Umuagwo and Umuakpu from Umukanne on their right, while 68 Battalion was to attack Obinze.

The operation started on the 6th of January with immediate tremendous success. The enemy at Umuakpu and Umuagwo was quickly rounded up and destroyed and his stores and equipment captured. The going was so easy for us at Umuakpu that our force that took it moved further down and also took Omanelu, thus threatening Elele 35 miles south of Owerri. Due to difficult terrain, the 68 Battalion was rather slow moving up to Obinze but later, with the assistance of our troops who had moved northwards from Umuagwo through Mgbirichi, Obinze was also taken. Throughout the battle there was very little reaction from the enemy inside Owerri except when we tried to move from Obinze to Avu. Then he grew very violent and we went back to Obinze.

By the end of the day we were controlling over 20 miles of the road which was before then the last link between Owerri and Port Harcourt, thereby having the enemy brigade at Owerri completely surrounded. In order to ensure that the enemy on both sides of the corridor did not link up ever again, we used several hundreds of civilians to render that stretch of road absolutely impassable using mines, ditches and heavy trees felled across the road. Thereafter, the 68 Battalion which had grown gradually and been renamed the 68 Brigade, took charge of the defence of the Port Harcourt road (inclusive) westwards to 63 Brigade, while the 60 Brigade defended eastwards to Orashi River.

From the 8th of January, 1969, the enemy began his counter-attacks to reopen the road. These attacks, which came from the Port Harcourt end, persisted for several months unsuccessfully until we cleared Owerri town itself.

For the success of the third and final phase, which was to clear Owerri town itself, our greatest hope lay not so much on our strength as on the happy thought that if we attacked the enemy in Owerri with determination for long, he would run out of ammunition and give up further resistance. For that reason, the prevention of the enemy from breaking through into or out of Owerri was even more important at that stage than trying to clear the town in a hurry. The troops taking part were now getting increasingly tired despite their high morale, due to the steadily deteriorating state of supply and administrative backing generally. Sickness in the war front was on the increase as a result of hunger and exposure, but we had no other alternative but to continue with the operation to the end.

On the 15th of January, therefore, the final phase began. 60 Brigade moved to clear the Holy Ghost College, the Cathedral and the Progress Hotel. On the successful completion of those tasks the Brigade was expected to wheel right and mop up the enemy up to the Clock Tower, and the neighbouring Motor Park. The minimum the Brigade was expected to achieve was at least to get to the small bridge on the Otamini River adjacent to the Holy Ghost College and blow it up. That achievement would prevent the enemy from using his vehicles beyond the centre of the town in any attempt by him to move southwards.

As soon as we struck, the enemy in the Holy Ghost College and the Cathedral fled into Owerri town centre, abandoning large quantities of ammunition, food and clothing. Instead of keeping up with the chase down to the Otamini bridge and from there into the town, Biafran troops, hungry and naked, halted to eat and evacuate enemy abandoned food, and also to change into the newly captured uniforms. In the confusion and excitement thus created, it was virtually impossible to retain control of the men to enable us to push on, despite desperate efforts in this direction by all senior commanders. While this confusion persisted, the enemy quickly counter attacked, and took good advantage of the confused and disorganised state of Biafran troops to dislodge us from the captured grounds. We were soon back in our trenches after having lost all gained grounds.

For the next one month, we launched several attacks a week, still hoping that the enemy there would eventually run out of ammunition. In the meantime, from the direction of Port Harcourt, enemy daily attempts to break through to Owerri had developed into a major brigade operation. From Elele, the enemy was pushing northwards desperately for several weeks on both Omanelu-Umuakpu and Elele-Ubimini-Awarra roads. We fought him back with equal determination, but he was still gaining ground slowly but steadily. By the end of March, the enemy was at Umuakpu on the main axis and at Asa on the right flank. That was a considerably alarming situation for us because Asa was less than 20 miles from Owerri.

Meanwhile, inside Owerri, the enemy was clearly in trouble after over two months of complete isolation within the town. All wireless intercepts confirmed that fact. Reconnaissance reports also showed that the enemy was so short of food that he was compelled to kill most of his Biafran prisoners of war and civilian detainees inside Owerri because there was not sufficient food with which to feed them. After two months of daily promises of a link-up by Port Harcourt had failed, the enemy resorted to air dropping of ammunition and food. What was left under enemy control in Owerri was so small that most of what was dropped fell into Biafran hands.

Any Biafran unit around Owerri which wanted something dropped for it by the enemy, only needed to clear a bit of bush, spread a white sheet of cloth over the clearing, and he would get a drop. Unfortunately, due to the gross inefficiency of the enemy air-drop operations, the very large quantity of ammunition we acquired through it was almost all damaged and therefore useless to the Army. Gun powder was however laboriously extracted from the damaged ammunition for use by the BOFF and other civil defence organisations. As a result of enemy air drops, the 14 Division was for some time fairly well fed and thus became fitter for its operations.

On the 15th of March, following a detailed review of the Owerri operations, during which much consideration was given to the pathetic and desperate state of the enemy in Owerri, Colonel Ojukwu and I decided to put in a last spirited effort to clear the town. Fresh supplies were said to have come into Biafra a few days before by air and Colonel Ojukwu was willing to make generous grants in support of the effort. Besides issuing ammunition he made available 960 bolt action rifles. These weapons he said, would be used to reinforce the "S" Division so as to enable them to move two more battalions and the Division Headquarters from Aba to Owerri for the operation. It was hoped that, in the long run, the whole of "S" Division, wherever they were, would concentrate in Owerri. In discussing a possible plan for the operations with the Head of State, I wanted the "S" Division to move to the area of 68 Brigade and from there, attack the enemy in strength from the rear. My argument was that the enemy was weakest there, and would be caught unaware if we attacked for a change from his rear as opposed to the usual frontal or flanking attacks.

The Head of State on the other hand wanted all available forces concentrated at Emekuku, and from there they would attempt to "smash" through the main road into Owerri to capture it. It was quite clear to me after 15 months of hard fighting experience that we stood very little chance of success if we attacked frontally because we lacked the punch necessary to break through Nigeria Army defences frontally. In the end, however, Ojukwu's plan was adopted.

The "S" Division troops under Colonel Onwuatuegwu, initiated the move and after several days of daily encounters, we failed to move the enemy while, at the same time, the ammunition available for the operation was running out rapidly. I was neither satisfied with the efforts of the Division as a whole, nor with the effectiveness of the Division Commander. He was often absent from his Division operational area during operations and, as a result, his troops lacked effective leadership and never kept to any timings. Worse still no detailed military instructions could be passed to his Division Headquarters in his absence because most of his staff were civilians with no military training or, at best, the usual four weeks training at the Biafran School of Infantry. For reasons best known to him, he seemed to prefer it that way.

With such a bad situation, Achuzia, who was often eager to prove his fighting ability, sought directly and obtained Ojukwu's permission to take over a part of "S" Division and clear Owerri with it. Onwuatuegwu did not like that arrangement but had to obey the order. When Achuzia arrived, Onwuatuegwu reluctantly gave him his "S" Brigade under Major Atumaka but refused thereafter to co-operate with or render any further assistance to him. In less than 24 hours, Achuzia had broken through and cleared Egbu town and advanced to within a mile of Owerri town centre.

Achuzia's success was achieved with heavy casualties on our men. Thus, when Achuzia wanted the rest of the Division placed under him so as to continue the offensive, the two officers began to quarrel to the extent of drawing pistols against each other. Even though all this happened in my presence, I had to take the two officers to Umuahia to see Ojukwu under whose direct command they were placed for the operation.

Ojukwu ruled that Achuzia should take command of the entire "S" Division for a week's intensive operations while Onwuatuegwu took a rest. All subsequent operations by Achuzia did not succeed and resulted in very high casualties on our side including the "S" Brigade Commander, Major Atumaka. The Head of State therefore called off the operation, withdrew his material and administrative support, restored Onwuatuegwu to his command, and asked me to start all over again, this time using my own plan. Other major battles developing elsewhere made that impossible for some time.

Early in March, 1968, the British Broadcasting Corporation announced that the Nigeria Army was about to start its final offensive into the "Ibo heartland," in an attempt to bring the war to an end. With that announcement, the BBC also put forward possible plans which could be adopted to achieve that aim. Broadly in accordance with the BBC plan, Nigerian troops began to concentrate in Onitsha and Awgu. The troop concentration at Onitsha was called the "Nnewi Task Force." As the Nigeria Army usually put in one major effort at a time, it was difficult for anybody to forecast accurately which of the concentrations was going to carry out the major attack. The only clue we had was again from the BBC which revealed that the Nigeria Army wished to capture Umuahia as a wedding present to Gowon.

While the speculations were on, the Nnewi Task Force at Onitsha struck first on the 17th of March as if they were about to move to capture Uli Airport, as suggested by General Alexander of Britain, who considered such a move to be the quickest way of ending the war. So far, each time the Nigeria Army was about to embark on a major offensive, the British Parliament normally met to discuss the war and that always provided a diversion for the world. When, therefore, that Parliament began to meet in an emergency session, we knew we were in for another rough time. The enemy came in waves from three points inside Onitsha, and for 14 days attacked our positions ceaselessly. The 11 Division, particularly the 54 Brigade, successfully stopped the Nnewi Task Force from gaining an inch of ground during that very bloody fortnight. Enemy casualties, particularly as a result of "ogbunigwes," were very high, and threatened the very existence of the Nigerian Second Division. If not for the fact that the enemy was initiating another major move in the north, we may have been able to clear Onitsha once and for all

311

during that month. The move against Umuahia had commenced and we needed all we had to check it.

The emergency session of the British Parliament was followed by a visit to Nigeria of a British Foreign Office Minister. Shortly after, the Prime Minister of Great Britain himself, the Right Honourable Mr. Harold Wilson also visited Lagos to discuss the progress of the war as well as Nigeria's future plans and intentions. His visit marked the very peak of the war and, quite frankly, frightened most Biafrans out of their wits, particularly with the rumours going around that the Honourable gentleman had brought plans for a physical intervention of the British Army. The Nigerian revolution, which led to the war started a few days after Mr. Wilson's visit to Nigeria in January, 1966. It was therefore reasonable for anyone to expect something terrible to come out of this particular visit.

While the Prime Minister discussed whatever it was with Gowon, the enemy First Division started its major offensive to capture Umuahia on the 27th of March. The attack came in from two completely different areas for the first time. In one area near Okigwe on the left, a Biafran Company under 15 Division was attacked in their location at Amokwe near Okigwe. In another area on the right, elements of 55 Brigade, located in the area of Owutu near Afikpo, were attacked in strength. If not for the very heavy shelling which preceded those attacks, they appeared to be merely insignificant daily raids, judging from the tiny villages being attacked. With the very heavy shelling which went on throughout that day, very little information on what was actually happening came into 13 Division Headquarters due to complete lack of wireless communications with the frontlines.

On the 28th of March, after the return of 13 Division Commander Ohanehi from the scene of action, the first information came in. The enemy had moved down from Uturu and attacked Umunekwu, thereby by-passing our company location in the area. From there, the bulk of the enemy was advancing eastwards, out of 13 Division operational area, and there was no force to stop them. The little force quickly assembled by him, had put in a good fight throughout the previous day, but was not only too weak and tired to check the advance effectively, but had also completely run out of ammunition. The enemy was therefore moving towards Uzuakoli which apparently was within a gap that existed between the defences of 64 and 55 Brigades. Colonel Ohanehi also revealed that the enemy attack on the right was directed against Owutu and Ngusu from the area of Akanazi. From all indications, it appeared as if both enemy forces were fighting to link up around Ahaba north of Uzuakoli.

With the above information, I went to see Colonel Ojukwu at Umuahia, having made available to 15 Division all that the Army Headquarters could muster. I learnt from the Head of State that he had already despatched a recruit battalion to the area of Uzuakoli under Colonel Akagha to try to check the hitherto unchecked advance, while arrangements were being made for effective counterattack forces. He wanted me to go over there and take charge of the battalion and its operations. I met Akagha and his battalion at Umuezike, north of Uzuakoli as they prepared for battle. That particular battalion was so green that most of them had never touched a rifle before, and none of them, including myself, had seen before the type of rifles they were issued with.

Despite their eagerness to advance against the enemy, I insisted that we had to find out more about the weapon and then teach the men how to use them before arming and sending them forward. Colonel Akagha, my ADC, and I took away three of these weapons to an obscure corner where we fiddled with them until between us we learnt enough to teach the men. Thereafter we formed up the officers and their men into weapon training squads, and gave them a thirty minutes instruction on the use of their weapons.

The battalion of 480 men was then regrouped into two task forces and given assignments. One group was asked to move through Ahaba to Ovim and Isiukwuato with the sole aim of making contact with the attacking enemy and checking his advance. The other group had a similar task of moving through the same Ahaba town to check enemy advance on the right in the area of Amokwe. No sooner did the two task forces leave their assembly area at Umuezike than they made contact at Ahaba with the rapidly advancing and completely unopposed enemy.

As fighting developed there, it was obvious to me that what I had just sent up would hardly stand for long against enemy armour and artillery battering. I therefore sent for the 8 Commando Brigade which had been reorganised and was retraining in the area of Nnewi. When the Brigade eventually arrived under their new commander, Major Ananaba, they numbered only 450 fighting men. In the same manner, I sent a passionately worded signal to all other formations which were already overstretched to send a battalion of 450 armed men each for the defense of Umuahia which, to most Biafrans, represented the last meaningful symbol of a Biafran nation. Both 11 and 12 Divisions abandoned their defences in various areas to meet the demand, but the others could not do so without completely collapsing.

By the 29th, Achuzia had crossed into Biafra from Midwestern Nigeria where he was operating and obtained Ojukwu's permission to assist. His political rival, Onwuatuegwu, on hearing about Achuzia's action, abandoned his "S" Division in Owerri front and turned up with a Company of men. He also sought and obtained Ojukwu's permission to assist.

Colonel Okwechime, the Adjutant-General, left the Defence Headquarters and joined the frontline team to assist with the administration of the fighting troops. All other Division commanders came up to see me at Uzuakoli to find out what they could do to help save Umuahia. Hundreds of civilian leaders, both men and women, braved the dangers of the battlefield as they poured into my Tactical Headquarters to be given assignments. That was the Biafran spirit for the impending Umuahia battle which, to many, was to be the last major battle of the war. Everyone wanted to be associated with that battle and this made control very difficult if not impossible.

On the 30th of March, before the troops coming from various places arrived in the battle area, the enemy was pushing towards the town of Uzuakoli with heavy fighting raging in the village of Umuezike less than four miles from Uzuakoli main town. In the meantime, all available troops were being reorganised into three fighting forces in the concentration area at Umuokpara. The first of the three forces came under Achuzia and had a task of clearing Uzuakoli, which we were sure we would lose before we were ready to begin operations. The second group under Onwuatucgwu was to defend both flanks in addition to being prepared to assist Achuzia in his efforts to clear the town. The third force was a slightly reinforced 8 Commando Brigade under Ananaba, whose task was to defend the main Uzuakoli-Umuahia road.

The enemy was in full control of Uzuakoli by the time we got ready to launch an attack. Achuzia's force moved on both sides of the main Uzuakoli road to seize objectives inside the town. On the left they were expected to 'clear from the area of Umuogwugwu eastwards to the centre of the town and exploit northwards to Umuezike if possible. Important objectives within that half of the town which the force was expected to clear included the Railway Station and Staff Quarters and the town market square. The remainder of Achuzia' force, moving through the right flank under the command of a Major Okafor, a crack ex-Police Officer, was to clear the right half of the town and exploit as far north as Eluelu road junction. Thereafter, their task was to garrison the entire Uzuakoli town and act as reinforcement for Achuzia's force in any subsequent attempt to continue the advance northwards.

There were to be two diversionary attacks during the operation. A company, under Major Ginger, was to attack Umuezike through Uzuakoli Leper Colony while the Commandos on the main axis, supported by the captured armoured car "Oguta Boy," were to launch a company attack on the town through the main axis. With over 1000 rounds of mortar bombs and about 500 artillery shells available for the offensive, we had by far more ammunition than we had ever had for an operation since the outbreak of the war. For this operation also, all civilian organisations in the area of Umuahia cooked and brought in food and, at times, insisted on taking it to the front trenches to ensure that the fighting men got it.

On the 2nd of April, the offensive began after the heaviest artillery and mortar bombardment ever fired by a Biafran force. The enemy counter-bombarded with even greater ferocity and for the

315

first time he was using self-propelled artillery guns which let out rapid volleys of four shells at a time. Our troops on the left soon disorganised the enemy who were already dazed by our unusual rate of shelling. After an hour's chase around the town, all the objectives on the left of the town were recaptured while the enemy fled northwards in the direction of Umuezike. Progress on the right flank was considerable slow as a result of a very bloody battle which was going on there.

Eventually however, enemy resistance there was also broken. As he ran away northwards, all Biafran troops including the Commandos with the "Oguta Boy," moved in and occupied Uzuakoli town once again. The combined pursuit of the enemy out of town continued up to Uzuakoli bridge where the enemy quickly reorganised and stood his ground.

For the next three days the Nigerians counterattacked massively with armour while scandalously shelling the entire neighbourhood very heavily. On the 6th of April, our troops began to fall back into town again in the face of enemy heavy pressure. Heavy fighting soon resumed inside Uzuakoli town once more. On the 8th, "Oguta Boy" was hit and later destroyed by enemy anti-tank gunners. Even though the entire crew escaped, the Reconnaissance Squadron that evening held a short memorial service which was well attended by many sympathisers, to mark the death of "Oguta Boy." The loss of "Oguta Boy," which was the only armoured support available to us in Uzuakoli, turned the scale swiftly in favour of the enemy. His armoured vehicles soon swarmed the whole town and began to chase around without opposition particularly in the total absence of anti-tank weapons on the Biafran side. We were soon forced out completely from Uzuakoli town to our former defences by the end of that day.

On the 10th of April, the enemy, eager to maintain momentum and to exploit his recent success to the maximum, launched another attack in a southerly direction in an attempt to advance further towards Umuahia from Uzuakoli. After the usual thorough pounding of our forward trenches with artillery and mortars, the enemy infantry advanced along the major road led by a ferret armoured car, which was closely followed by an armoured personnel carrier. In the meantime, the self-propelled long-range artillery guns were engaging all day all towns and villages between Uzuakoli and Umuokpara six miles from Umuahia. My Tactical Headquarters at Amcke, five miles from Uzuakoli was shelled throughout that day from 0900 hours until 1700 hours. My driver and some of my orderlies who had to run errands during the battle were soon knocked out, together with the vehicle itself. At 1100 hours that day, I remember Onwuatuegwu coming to see me to put in some demands and receive instructions. He stood outside my bunker in his usual high spirits laughing and beaming out "yes, yes, yes..." For five minutes I tried to convince him to come into the trench as the Headquarters was under heavy artillery bombardment. He preferred to stay outside because, according to him, he was in hurry. Soon the whistling of the next volley of shells was heard, and Onwuatuegwu grabbed his orderly by the neck and the two of them rolled into the trench and ended up on my laps. The shells burst close to the entrance of the bunker. That was the nature of the shelling which was going on, on the 10th of April, 1968 at Uzuakoli sector.

In the meantime, as the enemy force advanced, 8 Commando Brigade opened fire on them. As soon as the leading ferret armoured car got within point blank range of the "ogbunigwe" mine, the explosive was triggered off. The armoured vehicle was lifted high and thrown into the side of the road and the shock of the explosion killed the crew. The armoured personnel carrier immediately moved up and began to blaze away at our troops with the numerous heavy machine guns it carried. It was soon knocked out with the lone anti-tank gun we had — a gun which had a quota of two rounds. Having knocked out the two enemy armoured vehicles enemy troops fled back into Uzuakoli town pursued hotly by Biafran troops. Both armoured vehicles were recovered by our own troops and were soon commissioned back into battle. The ferret armoured car fought under the name "Uzuakoli Boy" while the armoured personnel carrier became known as "Ndidi," which in Ibo language means "patience."

From the 11th of April the enemy called in massive air support and rendered all movements by day between Uzuakoli and Umuahia absolutely impossible. Even Umuahia itself, still 14 miles away from the fighting lines, came under severe air bombardment with napalm, high explosives, and demolition bombs. Enemy pressure from Uzuakoli mounted daily until the 19th of April when he finally broke through our defences and was soon at Ameke less than six miles to Umuahia township. As soon as that happened Colonel Achuzia sought and obtained Colonel Ojukwu's permission to go back to his formation in the Midwest. Colonel Onwuatuegwu thereafter took full charge of operations, and soon afterwards my usual difficulties with Onwuatuegwu's operations began. I found it difficult to locate him or any of his senior officers in their operational area during the day. As a result, the troops, fighting virtually without leadership, performed badly due to lack of co-ordination. It also appeared as if Onwuatuegwu's interest, since the departure of Achuzia, had shifted back to Owerri, and he was even taking to his Division in Owerri some of the ammunition issued to him for Umuahia battle.

By the time I fully appreciated the extent to which Onwuatuegwu's interests had changed, it was rather too late, for the enemy was already at the outskirts of Umuahia township. Colonel Asoya was brought up from 60 Brigade, Owerri to take over command of Umuahia troops from Onwuatuegwu. The day Asoya arrived, after a short briefing in my Tactical Headquarters inside Umuahia, he moved forward to conduct a reconnaissance. Three miles outside Umuahia, he came face to face with the advancing enemy and there were no more Biafran defences. Apparently Onwuatuegwu and his troops had left for Owerri without being properly relieved when Asoya arrived to take over from him. Asoya stopped his Landrover, and using his escorts as the crew, he began to shell the advancing enemy with a 60mm morter which he had in his Landrover. The enemy was forced to halt and deploy. Together with a company of men who were despatched to the scene as soon as I learnt of the situation, the enemy was prevented from entering Umuahia for the next 48 hours.

The enemy finally entered Umuahia town on the 22nd of April

almost a month after he began his operation to capture that town. It had been indeed a gruelsome battle particularly from Uzuakoli. If our intelligence reports are anything to go by, the enemy casualties for that operation were fixed at over 10,000 dead and wounded. On our side, we were too exhausted to attempt to clear Umuahia town immediately. All we could do for a long time was to assume strong defensive positions and carry out raids against the enemy in that town. As a result of those effective raids, the enemy was never really in complete control of Umuahia town until the end of the war more than 18 months later.

Many Biafrans regarded the loss of Umuahia as a logical end of the war. So many highly placed civilian friends of mine spoke to me in confidence about their disapproval of continuation of the war that I began to have the impression that some crafty person had misled the people into believing that I alone could stop the war. However, I made sure I told those friends of mine that only the civilian authority which gave the mandate for Independence of Biafra could stop the war. The Army, unless it is rebelling, existed only to defend the state and her interests. Many civilians in a position to do so, began to send away their families from Biafra. It was pretty certain we were going to collapse in a question of weeks if not days, but for the completely unexpected recapture of Owerri three days after we lost Umuahia.

THE RECAPTURE OF OWERRI BY BIAFRAN FORCES

By the 14th of April, it had become obvious judging from the situation on the ground, that Umuahia was going to be lost. It was also clear that such an event would destroy completely the will of the Biafran people to continue the war. It was then that Colonel Ojukwu told me of the need to revive the Owerri operation on the off-chance that we might score a victory there to counter-balance the loss of Umuahia. The idea was to share the few resources available into two to try and clear what was left of Owerri before it was too late. The whole idea was a calculated risk worth taking if the Head of State who alone knew what ammunition the nation had, thought so.

319

On the 18th of April, therefore, the Owerri operations were reopened. As I was still at Umuahia, I did not know exactly what was available for the offensive. However, the plan of the operation which was sent to me for approval, showed that the 60 Brigade was again to clear the right side of the town up to the Clock Tower and including the Holy Ghost College, the Catholic Cathedral and the Progress Hotel. The 52 Brigade, now under Major Igweze, was to have another go at Orji and the northern part of the town, down to the Public Works Department and the Government Secondary School. Elements of "S" Division under command of 14 Division in the absence of Onwuatuegwu, who was still at Umuahia, had the task of advancing through Egbu and Nekede into Owerri, as far as to the motor park.

Right from the very start of this operation, it was clear the enemy was beginning to feel the bite of his over four months of isolation inside Owerri town. Everywhere his resistance was stiff but shortlived and mainly sustained with armoured vehicles. From the four corners of Owerri, our troops gradually closed in, and even began to set up road blocks in parts of Owerri. Yet in the part of the town the enemy occupied, it was still impossible to break through the armour barrier. That was the situation when I returned to Owerri front in the evening of the 23rd of April, 1969, following the fall of Umuahia the previous day. The first report I got on my arrival was that the enemy at Owerri had lined up all his vehicles facing southwards, in a manner suggesting a withdrawal. After a very lengthy discussion of the situation with the Divison Commander, I decided it would be better to allow the enemy to leave the town and then attack him somewhere out of Owerri, at a point where we still stood a chance of destroying him. I thought that for us to put in everything we had against the enemy inside the town could result in our exhausting our limited resources without success, and then run a risk of losing a large part of the town which we already controlled. For that reason, a battalion of 60 Brigade was despatched to Umuguma to wait for the enemy. To encourage the enemy to start the move we began to shell his convoy at a very slow rate with the little quantity of bombs we had. During the month of March, the enemy had on two occasions similarly lined up his vehicles to withdraw from Owerri. On each of those occasions, we had attacked him and it had resulted in his redeploying to defend himself and successfully too. This time we were not going to attack him and therefore hoped that he would not change his mind.

During the night of the 24th of April the enemy began to move out of Owerri to the uncontrollable joy of all. Once out of town, a Biafran company was put on their trail to harass them and hasten the withdrawal. At Umuguma, the major battle began on the morning of the 25th and the enemy suffered very heavy casualties indeed. Many vehicles carrying women, children and enemy casualties were allowed to proceed on their journey southwards unmolested. After 24 hours of heavy fighting the enemy shifted further down to Avu, only to face another biafran force waiting for them there. After barely four hours encounter at Avu, the enemy moved again further south to Ohoba and there linked up with his counterparts advancing from the south. Thereafter all attempts to move him again failed, in the same way as did all his attempts to move back from there into Owerri.

The Owerri victory revived the dying Biafra. All Biafrans who a few days before wanted nothing but an end to the war, now pressed for a continuation of the struggle to the end. The Umuahia disaster was soon forgotten and the only quarrel civilian military tacticians had against the Army was that they allowed the enemy to escape from Owerri instead of destroying him there completely. Inside Owerri the enemy left a considerably large amount of ammunition of different calibres, but he managed to take away almost his entire heavy equipment including armoured vehicles and artillery pieces. The town was completely ravaged and not a single building was habitable without major repairs. All vehicles not taken away by the enemy were overturned and burnt by him. Mass graves were discovered all over the town and the victims appeared to be civilians and prisoners of war. All the same, the enemy force at Owerri which was the 14 Brigade under a young Calabar officer called Utuk, was easily the best fighting unit fielded by Nigeria throughout the war. Right from Port Harcourt, and particularly at Afam, it had become

Civilians returning to Owerri after its recapture from the enemy in April, 1969

Biafran top commanders at Isu watching a parade to mark the 2nd anniversary of Biafra's independence in 1969. Standing left to right: Colonel E. Udeaja (parade commander), Wing Commander W. Ezeilo (Air Force Commander), Colonel S. Ogunewe (Military Aid to Head of State), Major General P. Efiong (Chief of Defence Staff), General C. Ojukwu (Head of State), Major General A. Madiebo (Commander Biafran Army), Mr. P. Okeke (Inspector General of Police), Captain F. Anuku (Navy Commander).

obvious that the Brigade was a force well led. Inside Owerri, they fought with extraordinary courage, flexibility and determination. The withdrawal of the Brigade from Owerri was tactically tidy and well planned and executed. Without doubt no other Nigerian Brigade could have withstood for more than a month the punishment the enemy 14 Brigade absorbed with patience for over four months. Only that Brigade could have got out of Owerri under the circumstances.

The Head of State put out a long list of promotions to commemorate the recapture of Owerri. He himself became a General while Okwechime, Eze and Kalu were all promoted to Brigadiers. Various others were promoted except Onwuatuegwu, the darling of the people, who was left out of General Ojukwu's list. That omission became a national political issue. "Jet 77," the government sponsored propaganda company of Onwuatuegwu's "S" Division, accused the Army Headquarters of not promoting Onwuatuegwu because it hated him. The "Jet 77" produced hand-outs for the public in which they revealed that the "S" Division under Onwuatuegwu had cleared the Ugba junction and Owerri and, on each occasion, the gallant Onwuatuegwu got nothing in return but humiliation from the GOC of the Army.

I was not worried by this propaganda which I knew was just one of those false rumours deliberately released against various individuals from time to time in order to control their popularity with the masses. I often disagreed with Onwuatuegwu in the same way I disagreed occasionally with all other commanders under me. To talk of an Army Commander in war loving or hating officers under his command is being childish in the extreme. In such a game involving human lives, a commander's aim is to end it successfully as soon as possible. Onwuatuegwu, as an individual, being the godfather of my first son and the officer closest to my family, knew I was putting the welfare of the people before family ties and friendship.

After the fall of Umuahia and the recapture of Owerri, General Ojukwu in May, 1969, took two significant decisions for reasons best known to him. Thereafter I was allowed to see the Head of State on military matters at any time of the day or night without booking for

324

an appointment in advance — a privilege I had not enjoyed before then. Again the Head of State decided to set up a Joint Planning Committee chairmanned by himself, with the Chief of Staff, General Efiong, and the Commanders of Army, Navy and Air Force as members. In addition, I was given the privilege of controlling for the first time, a small fraction of the national ammunition holding, but the bulk of it still remained under the control of the Head of State.

All those privileges and changes were in effect an eye wash, designed to satisfy civilian and military pressures, which had existed since the beginning of the war, in favour of the establishment of a war council. Civilians now had the impression that not only did we do joint planning, but also that the Army Commander controlled all ammunition. The Joint Planning Committee met once a week from May, 1969 to the end of the war but not one of the 14 operational plans which it produced was ever carried out. The committee planned all the time without knowing what was available; and invariably at the end of each plan it discovered that there were no resources for such a plan which would then be discarded and a new plan produced. The Planning Committee under Brigadier Okwechime worked like that until the end of the war. However we looked forward to JPC meetings because they were held in the State House, one of the very few places in Biafra where one could get a glass of cold beer.

Chapter 13

BIAFRA'S RAINY SEASON OFFENSIVES — 1969

For the enemy, the rainy season was a rest period either because he disliked being wet or, more likely, because his heavy equipment got bogged down on muddy roads. When the rains started, therefore, there was general calm in most of the fighting fronts. This was followed by intensive friendly overtures and fraternisation on the part of the enemy towards our forces. Fully aware of the pathetic administrative support available to Biafran troops, enemy soldiers in all fronts began to exploit the situation to their advantage. For a start, the enemy began to shout from their trenches to our troops requesting for a complete truce and cessation of all hostilities in the frontlines whether or not Ojukwu and Gowon wanted it that way. Then they began to throw cigarettes tied to stones, drinks and other gifts into no man's land. At first our soldiers ignored those gifts, but before long, they began to crawl out of their trenches to take them whenever and wherever they were thrown, and this, out of desperation. Encouraged by that, the enemy soldiers began to pay visits to our trenches with their gifts which were obviously invaluable to Biafran soldiers.

Before long Biafran soldiers in many fronts began to cross into enemy lines to attend frequent food and drinks parties. It looked as if the war, which the Nigerians had failed to win with military hardware was about to be won by them with gifts, without the civil or military authorities being aware of it. The intensive and universal fraternisation going on came to the notice of the authorities only when a considerable number of Biafran soldiers were arrested by the enemy at the end of a party given by him.

Despite the acute shortage of necessary ammunition and other supplies, the only solution to the problem appeared to be a resumption of offensives on all fronts, however limited. All formations were therefore instructed to save up ammunition for offensives and then request for extra assistance from Army Headquarters as soon as they were ready with a plan. As a result, during the rainy season of 1969, all Biafran Army formations in the field executed limited offensives with encouraging results in places.

REPUBLIC OF BENIN BRIGADE:
CAPTURE OF THE ITALIAN OIL MEN

Biafran units in Midwestern Nigeria; known in Biafra as the Republic of Benin (ROB), won the right to be the first to start operations. Following a series of reconnaissance patrols in that Region, it was discovered that the oil fields in the area of Kwale were being tapped by a large number of expatriates who dressed up occasionally in military uniform. Nigerian soldiers were observed to be stationed in the oil fields but not in strength. We were immediately tempted to drop our previous plan to clear Okogbele and Okoanala and move up to Asaba, in favour of seizing the oil fields. Our chances of success were good because, despite our weak strength and poor resources there, the terrain was very difficult, the like of which the enemy hated to operate on as the use of armoured vehicles was almost impossible.

On the 8th of May, 1969, our troops attacked enemy locations along the Asse River and dislodged the enemy without much difficulty and thereafter succeeded in crossing the river. The following morning, we continued the advance towards Kwale oil fields without firing a shot as there was no opposition after the enemy deployed along the river had fled. The march was made in such silence that our troops were inside the oil fields before anyone there knew of their presence. The Nigerian troops still left in the area ran away in all directions, firing indiscriminately as they fled. The numerous expatriates who were completely caught with their pants down, soon came running out from their living quarters and caravans with their rifles and pistols. The majority of them surrendered as soon as they realised the situation was hopeless but there were a few who opened up fire on Biafran troops.

The news of the tremendous success of the operation which was meant to be a limited raid, came as a surprise to both Colonel Achuzia at his Headquarters at Oraifite near Onitsha, and to me at Army Headquarters, Isu. I immediately instructed Achuzia, as the commander of the Midwestern forces to go to the scene of battle and ensure that all prisoners were returned to Biafra without molestation. Later, I inspected the prisoners at Oraifite as soon as they were brought into Biafra across the River Niger. Most of them claimed to be Italians but all were in good spirits. One of them, a Lebanese who spoke English fairly well after thanking me on behalf of the others for the good treatment they were getting, remarked "those Nigerian soldiers with us are very rude. They did not even tell us before they ran away."

The extraordinary restraint and discipline displayed by Biafran troops during that operation by not killing the entire 18 oil men on the spot was very commendable. Despite the fact that most of those oil men were caught with firearms — a situation which was highly provocative — the Biafran troops merely disarmed them without brutality. That was the subject of a congratulatory message which I later sent to the troops concerned. If those oil men had been operating in Biafra and were caught by Nigerian troops they would have been stone dead before the "Observers" could have done anything about it. The fate of the British Red Cross couple who were captured at Okigwe and slain by the Nigerians, was a good enough indication. That minor operation which was of very little tactical importance, not only stopped further oil production in that area until the end of the war, but also became the most important operation of the war with regard to international politics and diplomacy.

SPECIAL TASK FORCE (STF), AROCHUKWU — JUNE, 1969

The Special Task Force stationed at Arochukwu, was a Biafran formation which has not yet been mentioned in this narrative. It was formed after the fall of Umuahia for effective control of all Biafran forces operating in the areas of Arochukwu, Bende and Ohafia. The STF, under the command of Colonel Simon Uwakwe, operated independently under the direct control of Army Headquarters. Before long, the formation proved to be very reliable and formidable, despite the problem of very long distances over very bad roads between it and Army Headquarters — a problem which made supplies to, and liaison with the formation irregular.

Those difficulties notwithstanding, the STF was able to halt enemy attempts to advance further south from Abriba and Ikot-Okpara. I paid a visit to the formation in June, 1969 to launch it into an offensive, having received an indication that they were ready, and being fully aware of the need for an immediate offensive there to put an end to the very intensive fraternisation going on between our troops and the enemy. Moreover, civilians in that area were beginning to complain aloud against apparent neglect and lack of interest towards the area by the Biafran Government, resulting in little or no Biafran military activities there. To demonstrate to the civilians the willingness of the Army to continue fighting with whatever was available to it, I decided to assault Abriba. Shortly after an impressive but touching reception accorded to me by the local leaders, I off-loaded my Landrover of the few boxes of ammunition I had brought up as extras for the operation and presented them to Colonel Uwakwe.

When the offensive subsequently started, we pushed the enemy back a mile towards Abriba town but failed to clear the town itself. We however inflicted heavy casualties on the enemy and that not only stopped all fraternisation in that sector, but discouraged the enemy from attacking our troops for a very long time.

12 DIVISION OFFENSIVE TO CLEAR ABA — JUNE, 1969

Since the fall of Aba, the 12 Division had done nothing but minor limited offensives within the limits of its resources. The subsequent withdrawal of the "S" Division from that sector to Owerri had made prospects of any meaningful offensive there rather poor. In his eagerness to launch an attack like all other formations, Brigadier Eze applied and got my permission to go for Aba township. The enemy had moved away many of his troops in Aba for Owerri battles and, provided we had the means, it was possible to clear Aba, or at least put an end to the fraternisation going on there.

Our tactic for the Aba offensive was very similar to the one we had used in clearing Owerri — to surround the enemy and either destroy him or lead him out of town. Even though such a method was going to be much more difficult to implement in Aba sector where there were numerous roads, it still remained the only way that Biafra could remove the enemy from any town. Biafra's 65 Brigade under the command of Lt. Colonel Omerua was in control of all areas west of Aba-Port Harcourt road down to Owazza, with the exception of the strategic town of Ogwe. The Brigade therefore had a good chance of encircling Aba if it were given adequate support and supplies.

In the first phase of the operation, the 65 Brigade was to attempt to sever all links between Aba and the south. To do that, a battalion of the Brigade was expected to move from Obokwe to seize Ala-Oji on the Port Harcourt main road. From there the battalion would move northwards to clear Ohabian on the outskirts of Aba. The second battalion, and by far the strongest of the lot, was to move through Umudike to clear the enemy stronghold at Ogwe and Obiga before advancing southwards to seize the Asa junction and then the Imo Bridge. A third force was to move from the area of Umudike through Asa junction to clear Akwete and all other smaller villages in the area down to Azumini bridge. A fourth force from the brigade was to clear the Owazza oil fields and exploit down to the bridge behind the oil fields. The 58 Brigade had a standing force on the alert as reinforcement only in extreme emergency. As soon as the 65 Brigade had completed its tasks, the 61 Brigade under Lt. Colonel Joseph Okeke was to conduct an offensive to clear the enemy from all positions held by him east of the Aba River, down to Azumini. The final phase of the operation was to assault the enemy inside Aba town with all available forces. Here again, just as with Owerri, only one brigade could operate at any one time because of acute shortage of ammunition and other essential supplies.

The offensive met with stiff resistance right from the start as the enemy, who had learnt his lesson from Owerri, appeared to have known exactly what we were up to. At Owazza, however, we scored maximum success when the enemy was completely put to rout with heavy casualties inflicted on him. We seized the entire oil fields and advanced down to the bridge beyond. Ala-Oji and several other objectives were taken but were lost shortly after, due to acute shortage of ammunition. The operation which was planned to last a fortnight ground to a halt after three days because ammunition did not come into the country each night as we expected. I understood the planes broke down or something similar to that. The whole exercise became embarrassing when the enemy discovered we lacked ammunition and made a joke of it. Each time we attacked them, they would withdraw with remarks like "you Biafrans will soon finish your ammunition and as soon as that happens, we shall regain all our lost ground." Invariably the enemy kept his word every evening throughout the period of the offensive.

I was forced to call off the offensive in the end. Even though we had cleared Owazza oil fields and still held them, the overall result of the effort was disappointing. Above all we had clearly exposed our weakness and difficulties to the enemy in that sector. Thereafter, he was no more in doubt about our inability to fight a sustained battle due to lack of ammunition.

It was mainly for that reason that the enemy selected the Aba sector as the starting point for his final offensive in November which brought about the collapse of Biafra. On our part, we had learnt an important lesson to the effect that our system of planning battles in Biafra with arms and ammunition still outside the country was ridiculously unreliable. The offensive put an end to fraternisation between our troops and the enemy for only a short time, for barely a month later rumours of a resumption of the practice began to reach my Headquarters again.

14 DIVISION OFFENSIVE TO CLEAR OHOBA — JULY, 1969

Having cleared Owerri town, the 14 Division was easily the most popular Biafran Army formation. That also meant that it was the best administered unit in Biafra because of large donations of food and sometimes fuel from the public, particularly those who were occupying the newly captured Owerri town. As a result of its constant high morale and the universal support it enjoyed, the 14 Division was always eager and itching to go into action any time ammunition was given to it. Enemy continued presence at Ohoba constituted a threat to Owerri and the Division was given the last chance to remove that threat.

Since his defeat and expulsion from Owerri, the enemy had entrenched himself in the town of Ohoba 14 miles away despite more than three months of desperate efforts by our forces to get him out from there. With life in Owerri town back to normal, heads would have definitely rolled if the enemy got in there again whether or not the Army had ammunition. It was to avoid that, that an operation to clear Ohoba was planned in July, 1969.

The intention was to block, at a point somewhere north of Elele, the enemy's only line of communication to Ohoba. Biafran troops were already in various locations on both sides of the route which ran from Elele through Ubimini and Awarra to Asa and Ohoba. The 52 Brigade was to go for Asa and Awarra while the 60 Brigade was to tackle Ohoba town after it had been cut off as a result of the fall of Asa and Awarra. Ambush parties armed with specially designed extra large "ogbunigwe" flying mines, were stationed at various points along the southern approach route to Ohoba, to prevent or minimize the amount of enemy reinforcements that could get through to Ohoba during the battle. The 14 Division Strike Force Battalion was given the task of clearing both Ubimini and Egbeda and affecting a link-up of both towns with Asa and Awarra. If all objectives were attained, we would have the enemy at Ohoba at least ten miles inside our territory and his final destruction would have been a question of time.

The offensive, as was the tradition of 14 Division, started with a bang and before long the first two villages of Ohoba town — Umunwoko and Umuwayi — were overrun, with the enemy hanging on to the last village. That last village should have been cleared at the same time with the others but it was later discovered that the Biafran Company Commander who had that task had earlier signed a non-aggression pact with his enemy counterpart, as a result of which no action took place there. What our troops and the enemy did in that sector was to remain in their trenches and exchange fire so as to give the impression that a battle was going on there.

In the meantime, other Biafran forces operating against Ohoba had converged at the centre of the town lead by "Corporal Nwafor." As the advance into the last village was in progress, "Corporal Nwafor" fell into a ditch. Soon after, the Biafran saladine armoured car came under a barrage of anti-tank guns and all of a sudden from nowhere, an enemy saladine showed up for the first time since the battle began. Our troops were soon forced to fall back to the first two villages, abandoning "Corporal Nwafor" to the enemy from whom we got him about a year before. The shock caused by the loss of "Nwafor" was very much felt by the entire Army, particularly in the 14 Division.

Elsewhere, Asa was completely cleared as well as parts of Awarra. In addition, the force at Asa was able to advance three miles northwards towards Ohoba. Some of the enemy troops at Ubimini fled towards Port Harcourt and others in the direction of Awarra when Biafran troops advanced into the town of Ubimini. From there we were able to exploit northwards towards Awarra for a distance of four miles. In effect, we had bottled up the enemy both at Ohoba and Awarra. His counter-attacks were swift and immediate and very heavy and for this, he used massive reinforcements from Ahoada. After ten days of very heavy and continuous battles, the enemy succeeded in reopening his line of communications to Ohoba before we could deal adequately with his forces in that town.

This operation was not altogether a waste of time and supplies for we had, during that fortnight, inflicted heavy casualties on the enemy. In addition, the enemy was forced to move out almost his entire troops on the Ahoada front for this battle, thus reducing the threat to the vital Egbema oil fields, the only source of crude oil under Biafran control.

THE EBOCHA OFFENSIVE — JULY, 1969

The entire Biafran population continued to be anxious to see Ohoba cleared, but I was sure it would amount to a waste of valuable ammunition and time for the Army to continue such an operation against a very massive enemy concentration drawn into Ohoba by our recent offensive there. As a result of this offensive, we appeared to have increased the threat to Owerri in the final analysis, and unless an immediate counter-action was taken, it was very likely that the enemy would be tempted to use his Ohoba concentration in invading Owerri sooner than he had planned. For that reason, I made immediate arrangements to attack Ebocha and move swiftly down to Elele, in order to force the enemy to move back to that sector his forces which had moved from Ebocha to Ohoba. Such an operation, if successful, was bound to bring about an immediate and violent reaction on the part of the enemy because not only would Port Harcourt itself be threatened, all enemy troops between Umuakpu and Ohoba would be sealed off by the presence of Biafran troops in Elele.

A joint Military-Naval operation was eventually planned, aimed at capturing Ebocha, Omoku, Ahoada and Elele and reoccupying parts of the Rivers Province. The Biafran Navy, using their last locally-made gun boat, was to move along the Orashi River to provide artillery support on each objective for the advancing infantry. The operation started after several postponements during which all hands were on deck in the search for sufficient engine oil for the Naval gun boat. When the boat eventually limped her way from Oguta to the start-line at Ebocham the troops' morale became uncontrollably high. At H-hour, the boat bombarded Ebocha bridge and town with the 30 rounds of artillery shells allotted for the objective. Before the defending enemy at the bridge head knew what

335

had hit him, the Biafra troops rushed the bridge, completely disorganised the enemy troops, and set them running backwards in utter confusion. The success there was so total and the chase so fast that by the end of the day we were completely in control of Obrikon seven miles away from Ebocha. On that first day, we were in such a hurry to gain maximum ground that we completely ignored all enemy stragglers who were unable to catch up with the speed of the retreat.

From Obrikon, enemy resistance became better organised and much stiffer. All the same, we continued to make steady progress southwards towards Ahoada. After four days of bitter fighting we recaptured Omoku town. As soon as the town of Obido was taken and our advance continued to Ogbogwu, the Navy landed at Kreigani to refit and reorganise. The physical condition of the civilian population at Omoku was pathetic and only comparable to the condition of the natives of Ikot-Ekpene when the town was recaptured in April, 1968. All civilians — men, women and children — were kwashiokor cases even in their home which was "liberated" over a year before. Very soon some food was organised for the town and massive celebrations began in the midst of massive enemy air raids which killed a considerably large number of people.

As we anticipated, the enemy was now moving massive infantry reinforcements as well as heavy equipment into Ahoada from Owerri. The skies were now dominated by Russian jets which dived to attack even individuals including pedestrians, cyclists, and people in their farms. The planes searched for our gun boat each day from dawn to dusk, but failed to find where it was carefully concealed under some low trees on the bank of the river. Just before we moved into Ogbogwu, the enemy began his massive counterattacks supported generously by artillery, armour, and jet planes. We soon began to yield to the massive pressure and, as we pulled out of Omoku, the natives wept bitterly. The gun-boat, which had developed engine trouble as a result of bad oil, was also leaking in one or two places. It just about made the journey back to Oguta. In less than a week, we were back to our start-lines behind Ebocha bridge having lost all the ground gained during the operation.

The operation was again a success in a way because it had made Owerri safer by forcing the enemy to disperse his strong troop concentrations in Asa and Ohoba which were very close to Owerri. Without this operation, Owerri may have fallen into enemy hands before the end of August, 1969 and that may have ended the war earlier. Thereafter, we kept up regular alternating offensives at Ohoba and Ebocha to discourage the enemy from concentrating to attack Owerri or Egbema oil fields.

"S" DIVISION OFFENSIVE TO THREATEN OR DISRUPT PORT HARCOURT — JULY, 1969

Both the Head of State and I, judging from the past performance of the "S" Division as a special unit, were of the opinion that it was necessary to reorganise the formation on the same lines as other Biafran Army units in order to achieve some measure of good results from the unit. After the recapture of Owerri by Biafran troops, General Ojukwu recommended the removal of Colonel Onwuatuegwu from command of "S" Division. He was replaced by Colonel Asoya, who immediately got rid of the entire staff of the Division who were almost all civilians and replaced them with trained army officers.

Thereafter, the Division for the first time since its formation, came under the control of Army Headquarters. Both the removal of Onwuatuegwu as commander and the removal of other civilians from their staff appointments caused a considerable amount of public resentment. The Army Headquarters absorbed a good part of the blame, but with the satisfaction that at last the "S" Division had been turned into a military unit from the political organisation which it had been. By July, 1969 after two months in command of "S" Division, Colonel Asoya had turned it into one of the best fighting military formations in Biafra. The propaganda wing of the unit — the "Jet 77," was disbanded after the men had been made to understand that the best propaganda for a unit in a time of war was for that unit to ensure it achieves regular victories in the battlefield.

337

The men of "S" Division began to realise that a soldier fought when he was ordered to do so and not when he felt like it. Most important of all, the importance of adhering to H-hour was fully understood for the first time by all ranks within the Division.

A series of minor battles designed to train the "S" Division had produced good results and proved that the Division could undertake a major offensive like other Biafran Army field formations. Between April and August, 1969, the Division had cleared many villages southwest of Owerri resulting in the liberation of several hundred square miles of food-producing areas which, in addition to absorbing a lot of refugees, became one of the greatest sources of food supply for the Army and the nation as a whole. By the beginning of July the Division had established its forward defences along a line running east to west through Umuakpu-Apani-Ibiama-Omodome and Abara on the Ogochia River.

After a long and tedious preparation due to administrative difficulties and the problem of long distances over unmotorable roads, the "S" Division was finally ready to start an offensive to capture Umuetchem oil fields and from there threaten or at least disorganise Port Harcourt. 68 Brigade was to take the oil fields and then move through Chokocho bridge to Igrita. Such a move, if successfully carried out, would isolate all enemy troops operating against the Biafran 63 Brigade at Amala. A battalion of "S" Brigade had the task of moving from their location at Umudema to clear Agwa. After ensuring the destruction of Isiokpo bridge to their rear, the battalion was expected to fight its way to clear Igrita and join up with elements of 68 Brigade also moving into that town. The Division Strike Force Battalion was to move through Agwa to Aloa and Isoba from where all villages around Port Harcourt would be shelled. This force was also to assist in clearing Igrita from Aloa if it became necessary.

Having quickly brushed aside minor enemy resistance in villages on its way, the 68 Brigade was soon fighting a pitched battle with the enemy led by white men inside the oil fields. The enemy withdrew towards Chokocho bridge after several hours of bitter fighting. Our troops continued the advance until we came near the bridge where another pitched battle began. This time the enemy was very heavily reinforced with fresh troops sent from Port Harcourt and Amala, and this made further gains on our side difficult.

In the meantime the battalion of "S" Brigade had taken Agwa and was on the outskirts of Igrita town 14 miles away from Port Harcourt. Aloa was also taken and very heavy fighting had developed all around Igrita with the enemy fielding a force by far stronger than we had anticipated. The major setback to what might have become our most brilliant operation of the war was the failure on our part to gain immediate control of Isiokpo bridge. As a result, almost all the reinforcements and heavy support which the enemy needed to fight back with came from Owerri and Ahoada sectors through the Isiokpo bridge. That development forced our troops at Aloa to withdraw to Agwa, not only to ensure that they were not cut off, but also to defend the rear of friendly forces still fighting at Igrita. Fighting went on for several days without progress on both sides until we were forced to call off the expensive exercise when we could no longer afford the ammunition for it.

The operation achieved a good number of encouraging results. Besides putting two armoured vehicles out of action through traps, we had moved sufficiently down towards Port Harcourt to force most of the oil men to flee to Lagos and the local civilians to start going into hiding. Most important of all was the fact that Umuechem oil fields were never again exploited for the rest of the war. Our new positions meant that the enemy line of communication between Port Harcourt and Owerri was unsafe for him almost all the way.

15 DIVISION – AUGUST, 1969

Since its re-formation in September, 1968, the 15 Division had not fought a major battle and had spent most of its time on raids into Okigwe town and other villages nearby which were under enemy occupation. The nearest it ever got to a major confrontation with the enemy was in April, 1969 when the enemy passed through its extreme right flank during his advance to Umuahia. This long period of relative calm, was beginning to cause a great deal of anxiety and apprehension among the civilians of that province. By July, 1969 rumours were already going around the area that the 15 Division Commander, Colonel Linus Ohanehi was so incompetent that the war was going to end through his sector. Even though this rumour was started by an officer who wanted to regain command of that Division, the damage had been done and the need had arisen for the Army to do a limited operation there to re-assure the people.

We had let the sleeping dog lie in Okigwe sector due to lack of ammunition, but with the rumours, Colonel Ohanehi, a well-trained, hardworking officer, became very anxious to be given a chance to prove himself. A decision was therefore taken by the Joint Planning Committee to conduct an offensive with the 15 Division to clear Okigwe. An ambitious plan produced by that committee was later rejected by the Head of State as being over involved and too expensive for the Biafran Army. I was therefore obliged to work out a much simpler plan for the offensive, the overall aim still being to surround Okigwe town and then destroy the enemy inside it. To do that, the 69 Brigade under Lt. Colonel Oparaji had the task of moving a battalion through Ngodo to Lokpauku from where they were expected to clear both Leru and Ihube villages. The capture of Ihube junction would block the Awgu-Okigwe road as well as all approaches to Okigwe from the north and the northwest. 64 Brigade was to provide a force to move on the right flank through Umunnekwu village to clear Ugba junction, thereby blocking off the Afikpo road and other western approaches. With Okigwe town thus sealed off, the intention was to attack and clear the town with two battalions moving in from the south and the east.

The Division had serious initial difficulties which made the operation unlikely to succeed. Ammunition, food, fuel, transport and weapons were very short indeed; three of the battalions for the operation were armed with nothing other than sten machine guns, each with a magazine of 30 rounds and no reserves. By the time the hungry soldiers walked long distances to their start lines, they were too tired to go into operations but, despite that, they looked forward to the offensive and were determined to make it a success.

The operation started on the 10th of August at 0600 hours. Before 0700 hours, men of the 69 Brigade had swiftly descended on Leru Village from left and right of the town. The enemy detachment there was put to complete rout and ran away in many directions. From Ihube, the enemy brought down on Leru an extremely heavy mortar concentration which inflicted more casualties on enemy troops than on Biafran troops. In the meantime, enemy artillery began to bombard all surrounding Biafran villages within a radius of four miles as a punitive measure, but the Biafran troops at Leru were advancing dauntlessly toward Ihube, their main objective.

At Ihube, the enemy was more prepared but the Biafran troops also still held sufficient ammunition to give him a good fight. For two hours, the battle for Ihube raged under the personal control of Colonel Ohanehi. Finally the enemy gave up the fight and fled when a Biafran platoon went through the left of the town, overran the enemy Tactical Headquarters, and set it ablaze. Casualties were very heavy on both sides, particularly on the enemy side. We dug in at Ihube while frantic efforts were being made to find food and ammunition for the troops.

From the right, a giant size "ogbunigwe" flying mine quickly disorganised the enemy frontlines at Umunnekwu which shortly after fell into our hands. Over a platoon of enemy troops were rounded up still dazed and suffering from shock as a result of the explosion. As Biafran troops moved on towards Ugba junction, the lone 105 mm gun the 15 Division had, tried desperately with the 50 rounds available to it to silence a battery of enemy guns and mortars. By midday, our own troops were completely in control of Ugba junction after the enemy had run away in the direction of Uturu airstrip. However, the weight of enemy artillery and mortar concentration on Ugba junction was such that it was impossible for Biafran troops to stay anywhere near it. Our troops therefore had to abandon the junction and move back a distance of 400 yards from it to dig in.·

The attempt to clear the town itself was considerably successful. Our troops, advancing from the eastern side of the town, broke through enemy defences after four successive assaults. Before long, chanting Biafran soldiers had occupied the right side of the town including the entire administration centre. The enemy then concentrated all his armour in the southern part of the town facing Umuna, as a result of which little or no progress was made by our own troops attacking from that direction to clear the left side of Okigwe. Our failure to clear the left side of the town made the position of our troops already inside Okigwe untenable. Subsequently we had to withdraw from the town but to a new defensive location much closer to the town than our former defences. During a week of enemy counterattacks which followed, the only ground we lost was our position at Ihube.

We had to stop the offensive when we began to experience acute shortages both in ammunition and administrative items, for during the advance from Umunnekwu to Ugba junction, two Biafran soldiers collapsed and died of hunger. We were, however, so close to Okigwe town after the offensive that from our front trenches it was possible to identify the ranks won by enemy soldiers inside the town. That made the enemy irritable as a result of which he shelled our locations and all surrounding villages very heavily at the slightest provocation. The people of Okigwe province became more relaxed and happier.

11 Division — Operation Do or Die

The continuous struggle by 11 Division to keep open its route to 57 Brigade at Otuocha had gone on fairly successfully for over 18 months. Early in September, 1969, the enemy again carried out a major operation which succeeded in linking up his locations at Abagana with his troop inside Onitsha, thereby completely isolating the Biafran 57 Brigade. That had happened quite frequently during the war, but each time it had been quickly rectified with immediate and invariably successful counterattacks. When however, the enemy closed the gap this time it was obvious that he meant to close it for good, because after a whole week of bitter battles we were unable to move him out. In the meantime, the 57 Brigade, completely without ammunition, was being harassed daily from the north by the enemy.

On a few occasions, we successfully delivered ammunition and other supplies to 57 Brigade by using porters who travelled in a transport to Inyi. From there they trekked across country to Ugwuoba and then crossed the main road cautiously into Ebenebe where they were met by people from 57 Brigade. The journey lasted several days and required a large number of men if they were to carry an appreciable quantity of ammunition, petrol, and medical supplies. It soon became obvious that the only solution to that problem was to do everything possible to reopen the major link to Otuocha and the 57 Brigade because, above all, the enemy was becoming aware of what was going on. For that reason, I took a decision to launch a major offensive once more with the 11 Division to reopen what had come to be known as "the Onitsha corridor" and also to penetrate into Onitsha as far as possible so as to discourage the enemy Second Division from interfering in the fighting.

There was clearly a need to reinforce the 11 Division if it was to make a good impression during the offensive. As I had neither reinforcements nor weapons, I instructed Achuzia's ROB Brigade close by to make available 500 weapons to 11 Division for the offensive. Achuzia preferred to bring down 500 armed men under his personal command for the operation rather than send weapons. I accepted that in the absence of a better alternative, but fully conscious of the implications of getting Achuzia involved in a major operation. 11 Division Commander Brigadier Amadi refused bluntly to have anything to do with Achizia in connection with the operation and preferred to carry out the offensive without assistance. He finally accepted Achuzia's assistance when I threatened to initiate courtmartial proceedings against him. Thus, Achuzia was to bring down his troops and operate independently in support of 11 Division for the duration of the offensive. The desperate nature of this operation and the fact that it simply had to succeed earned for it the name "Operation Do or Die."

In addition to the normal Biafran bolt action rifles, a considerable amount of heavy support was secured for the Division in an attempt to improve the chances of success. This included one six pounder anti-tank gun with ten rounds, two specially designed super heavy mine throwers — "Marshals" — with five mines each, two 73mm anti-tank guns with two rounds each, one 82mm mortar barrel with 100 bombs and one 107 anti-tank gun with four rounds of ammunition. That was easily the largest arsenal we had ever assembled in any one place during the course of the war.

The overall aim of Operation Do or Die was to re-establish the corridor between Onitsha and Abagana through which we communicated with the 57 Brigade and Otuocha, the largest food-producing area still under Biafran control. The entire 11 Division was to be involved in the operation including the belea-guered 57 Brigade. The 66 Brigade under Major Osuagwu had the task of assaulting three objectives simultaneously with its three battalions. The "Tiger" Battalion went for Uzoma Maternity at Ogidi; the 78 Battalion was to clear the Iyienu Hospital, while the Third Battalion was to clear the Afor Igwe Ofu Market. Having achieved those objectives, the 78 Battalion was to remain in position while the other battalions were expected to link up and fight their way astride the main Onitsha-Enugu road towards Abagana. The 54 Brigade, by far the strongest and the best fighting formation within the Divison, had the task of breaking through enemy concentration at Nkpor junction. Thereafter two of its battalions were to move on both sides of the main road towards Onitsha to clear Boromeo Hospital, the Seminary and St. Charles College. The third battalion was to wheel right from Nkpor junction and fight its way to link up with the 78 Battalion of 66 Brigade at Iyienu Hospital. Achuzia's force was given the task of assaulting Dumez Quarters at Onitsha, primarily to dissipate enemy efforts from Onitsha. If, however, he succeeded in clearing his objective he was to continue his advance into Onitsha very cautiously while maintaining very close liaison with 54 Brigade troops on his right.

It took quite some time to persuade Achuzia to carry that assignment which he considered too minor to be worth the effort he had put into the moving of his troops from the Midwest Region to Onitsha for the operation. He wanted a much more exciting task like clearing Onitsha Textile Mills, the bridge head and the Fegge Quarters. Besides the local propaganda value, such an operation would have achieved nothing on the ground for obvious reasons, besides being a complete waste of valuable ammunition.

After a series of postponements while we waited for the arrival of Achuzia's troops, I ordered the operation to commence at 1400 hours on the 18th of October, even though only 300 out of the 500 men expected by Achuzia were in position. It was always my firm belief throughout the war that any enemy location not dislodged by a Biafran offensive during the first 20 minutes of our attack could not be dislodged again. Our success depended entirely on surprise and good tactics rather than on strength, and usually after 20 minutes of battle if the enemy was still around, only strength counted thereafter.

We put this theory to maximum use in launching this operation. At exactly H-hour, every support weapon under 11 Division was blazing away at its target. The flying mines, the "Marshals," mortars, artillery, and some anti-tank guns were all firing. The noise was dreadful, particularly when all machine guns joined in the preliminary bombardment.

After ten minutes the infantry moved to their various objectives. As the 54 Brigade under Colonel Nebo moved into Nkpor junction, very confused fighting began. Enemy and our troops got so mixed up that one could not easily identify one's enemy at first sight in the confusion. The situation was much worsened by the fact that several enemy soldiers in the battlefield were suffering from severe shock as a result of the heavy explosions during the Biafran preliminary bombardment. These enemy soldiers did not know where they were, or what was happening and therefore constituted a nuisance by wandering about in the battlefield with their weapons slung on their shoulders asking innumerable incoherent questions.

Very soon the enemy began to withdraw from the junction, some towards Onitsha and others towards Ogidi. Our troops pursued in both directions, past Boromeo Hospital, the Seminary, and Saint Charles in the direction of Onitsha, and also down to Iyienu Hospital towards Abagana. In withdrawing from Nkpor junction, the enemy left behind a strong 106mm anti-tank team closely protected by a saladine armoured vehicle. It was a clear

345

indication that an immediate counterattack was imminent. A fierce duel developed between the enemy 106mm gun supported by the saladine and the Biafran six pounder gun. After one hour's slugging match, the six pounder received a direct hit from the saladine. It was badly damaged and most of its crew were killed and others fatally wounded. The enemy saladine and 106 gun thus remained at Nkpor junction unable to rejoin their troops in any direction.

The battle in 66 Brigade area was one of the bloodiest of the entire war. In all locations enemy counter bombardment was fierce. Nevertheless, the three Battalions of 66 Brigade fought courageously every inch of the ground to their respective objectives before last light on the 18th.

The following morning when all battles resumed at 0500 hours, enemy fire power had more than doubled and our casualty rate was very high. By 1000 hours we had lost the objectives we had captured the previous day and it appeared as if the enemy was even pressing on into our defensive lines. Having checked his advance, the 66 Brigade launched yet another attack to regain its objectives. The fighting was bitter and casualties on both sides were extraordinarily high; yet before 1500 hours we were once more controlling the Iyienu Hospital, and, consequently, a corridor of six miles.

On the 19th, the enemy began a massive attack by 0530 hours from both the Abagana and Onitsha ends of the corridor. As enemy shells poured down like heavy rain on our locations, Biafran troops replied with fairly heavy concentrations of home-made flying mines, rockets and mortars. By midday the enemy had put in three waves of attacks each from Iyienu and Onitsha and had been beaten back with very heavy casualties on both sides. Shortly after the third wave of attack, two Russian jet fighter-bombers appeared in the battle area in support of the enemy. The jets bombed and strafed our locations and all surrounding towns and villages heavily and meticulously and that hampered our efforts considerably. However, the most notable achievement of the enemy planes on that particular day was the attack on a funeral procession at Oba near Onitsha. After a thirty minutes onslaught on the procession by the two planes, over twenty mourners were dead and the corpse itself which was abandoned by mourners on the main road, was completely shredded into tiny bits by several hits of canon fire.

The enemy was making significant gains towards Nkpor junction from Abagana end but our troops around Onitsha remained unruffled but in grave danger of being enveloped from the rear by the advancing enemy. By last light the enemy had gained control of Nkpor junction once more but was unable to link up the last two miles from there to Onitsha because of the numerous obstacles created along the road by Biafran troops.

We went into yet another determined attack on the 20th, being the third day of battle, in an effort to clear the Nkpor junction and prevent a link-up with Onitsha. The Biafran troops used everything ever manufactured for war in Biafra. The "Marshal" was fired as well as the flying "ogbunigwe. " Biafran rockets of all ranges and capabilities flew to all directions where the enemy was located. Even petrol bombs were thrown or fired for the first time. The enemy once more began to withdraw to Ogidi and the chanting but worn-out Biafrans gave chase, capturing a considerably large quantity of equipment. Before midday, we were again controlling Iyienu Hospital and six miles of corridor and thus re-establishing contact with the 57 Brigade. Three Russian jets soon swooped in and began one of the most destructive air raids of that sector of the war. Using napalm as well as high explosive bombs, the planes destroyed hundreds of lives, houses and other valuable property, particularly vehicles within a radius of five miles from the battle area. A Biafran army ambulance carrying 15 wounded soldiers was burnt to ashes with all the casualties inside it as a result of a napalm bomb dropped on it by one of the enemy planes at Obosi.

When the planes departed it appeared as if both sides were too tired to continue the battle. Enemy intercepts showed that he had suffered very heavy casualties during the three days of fighting and was also very tired. He even expressed the fear that he was unable to hold his positions at Ogidi if we attacked again unless he had immediate reinforcement.

On our side. I knew we were equally tired and completely short of all calibres of ammunition. In other words we were unable to

347

continue even if we had wanted to do so. Even though Achuzia's determined efforts against Dumez achieved absolutely nothing except high casualties among his men — a fact which enraged him to the extent of waging a lengthy political war against the entire Biafran Army — the operation was a success because it had opened once more a direct route to 57 Brigade and the food-producing area of Otuocha. Viewed from any angle, that operation was indeed an "Operation Do or Die." for many did, and many died.

Chapter 14

THE FINAL COLLAPSE

Early in October, 1969, the British Broadcasting Corporation announced a "final push" by the Nigeria Army against Biafra. At first the announcement was regarded as one of many such announcements of "final pushes" already made by the BBC-since the beginning of the war. When, however, intensive international radio debate developed over the tactics to be adopted by the Nigeria Army no one in Biafra was left in any doubt that the final "final push" was about to commence. On the one hand, General Alexander of Britain, a member of the "neutral" International Observer Team who at that stage was disenchanted with the Nigeria Army field commanders to the extent of accusing them of incompetence, extravagance and operating without co-ordination, insisted that the immediate capture of Uli Airport, the only link Biafra had with the rest of the world, was the quickest way of bringing the war to an end. On the other hand, the British Broadcasting Corporation preferred simultaneous offensives by Nigeria on all fronts with maximum use of the newly acquired Russian 122mm artillery guns, whose capabilities, judging from figures released by the BBC, were truly frightening.

The Biafran Army, which could not do anything to improve on its fighting strength or administrative support in preparation for the coming enemy offensive, settled down to fortifying its defences as the next best alternative. Even though previous enemy "final pushes" only achieved limited success before they were checked, the fact still remained each final push meant a loss of ground for Biafra and an increase in hardship and suffering for the people. I therefore hated "final pushes" immensely, particularly the one which was about to take place. The Biafra Army was, however, more determined now than at any other time during the war to prevent any further loss of ground even if it meant fighting with tooth and nails and erecting human barricades before enemy armoured vehicles. There was absolutely no ground left anywhere in Biafra we could lose and still continue the war. While all Biafran Army field units remained vigilant in case the BBC plan was adopted, the Biafran Air Force deployed each of their two newly formed battalions at Uli and Uga airstrips as a precautionary measure against the possible adoption of General Alexander's plan. Before the third week of October, enemy preliminary and apparently diversionary offensives began on all sectors of the war. In the area of Biafra's 11 Division, Onitsha, the enemy attacked the 57 Brigade in strength in a desperate attempt to squeeze us out of our positions at Otuocha and affect another link-up of Abagana and Onitsha. The Brigade fought and resisted the enemy attempts very well under Lt. Colonel Akonobi. The battles there were still going on fairly well, and none of the enemy objectives had been completely achieved at the time the war ended.

On the Owerri front defended by the 14 Biafran Division, the enemy moved along Omoku road and from there began a determined and sustained offensive to cross the Ebocha bridge in order to seize the Egbema oil fields and, subsequently, Oguta and Uli Airport. After five weeks of continuous battles, the enemy gave up his attempts, having achieved nothing through that operation. While he was trying to cross the Ebocha bridge, the enemy on that front was also attacking all villages around Asa and making, at the same time, desperate efforts to break through to Owerri town from Ohoba. All these attempts were foiled by Biafran troops with little or nothing to fight with except extraordinary bravery and determination. Even when the enemy attacked all locations of the Biafran "S" Division, his offensives were promptly and effectively checked.

The first major offensive of the final push was directed against the 53 Brigade of the 15 Division located at Awlaw, during the last week of October, 1969. It was an estimated brigade group offensive, fully supported by armour, artillery, mortars and jet planes. The initial weight of the attack when it came in, and the swiftness with which it moved, produced the type of rude shock that could only have been absorbed by the Biafran 53 Brigade under the command of the tough, courageous and iron-willed Lt. Colonel Nsudoh. For even though our trenches around Awlaw were overrun by the enemy, the situation remained perfectly under control but highly explosive in view of the fact that we had only two rifle companies immediately available on the ground for containing the enemy.

Having gained control of Awlaw, the enemy began to advance towards the vital Umueji junction from where he could either move northwards through Ufuma, or southwards through Ajalli, to Uga Airport. A week of very bloody battles followed during which our troops lost no further battles or ground and indeed on a few occasions we regained our trenches at Awlaw for short periods. As fighting went on daily with no signs of stopping, our resistance appeared to be weakening as our fighting strength and support diminished daily in the face of a rapidly increasing enemy pressure. From all indications it appeared as if the battle of Awlaw was the beginning of the major operation of the enemy's "final push."

With a reinforcement of 450 armed men drawn from all Biafran field formations, the 53 Brigade launched their first major counter-attack against Awlaw. Air support for this effort was given by three Biafran Air Force Minicons (Biafran Babies). In less than 24 hours after our counter-offensive was launched, we had regained all lost ground and had begun to exploit as far as our resources would permit. The low flying sneaky "Biafran Babies" completely took the enemy by surprise and, in addition to inflicting heavy casualties on his exposed men in rear areas, the planes also destroyed considerably large quantities of enemy heavy war equipment and stores lined up in the open along the Inyi-Awlaw road. Thereafter heavy fighting continued in the area from time to time until the enemy gave up fighting completely at the end of five weeks during which he had gained nothing. From intelligence reports and enemy intercepted messages, it was clear the enemy had suffered very heavy casualties

351

A Biafran war casualty waiting to be evacuated, by head porters, to the rear for medical attention.

A Biafran war casualty being evacuated from the war front

to the extent that an inquiry had to be ordered on the conduct of the operation by the Nigeria Army Headquarters in Lagos.

We had beaten the enemy very soundly at Awlaw and for that reason should have been glad. Rather, I was personally sad and anxious over the fact that we had used the entire Army resources, particularly ammunition, to do that. During that operation, the 53 Brigade went through hell due to an almost total lack of fuel. The men walked several miles from their various locations to get to the battlefield, and all casualties were evacuated to the hospitals by porters over equally long distances. Most of the serious cases died on the way to the hospitals or even before the porters arrived to pick them up. My sadness and anxiety therefore arose out of the fear that if we were attacked immediately anywhere, it would be virtually impossible for the Army to offer any more resistance unless fresh and substantial supplies were quickly made available. That was exactly the picture I painted to the members of the Joint Planning Committee during its meeting at the State House, Owerri, in the middle of November, 1969. At that meeting the Head of State asked me to inform the Army that if we held the enemy back till the middle of December, he was promising a complete and dramatic victory by Biafra over the Nigerians by January, 1970. The members of the committee were, however not told the secret behind the impending Biafran victory. But for people who had lived through the war with their morale built up and sustained by the Head of State, with parables suggesting that miracles were about to take place in favour of Biafra, that promise was unlikely to be believed.

MILITARY AND POLITICAL SITUATION IN 12 DIVISION PRIOR TO THE COLLAPSE

Biafra eventually collapsed as a result of the collapse of Biafra's 12 Division. With the appalling state of tactical and administrative support then available to the Biafran Army, any other field formation within the Army would have collapsed under the weight of the enemy attack which collapsed the 12 Division. In order to fully understand the implications of the enemy final attack against the 12 Division, it is necessary to discuss in some detail the state of the Division and its major problems at the time of the final offensive against it.

After the fall of Umuahia, the seat of Biafran Government and all administrative Directorates moved across the Imo River to the areas of Etiti and Owerri. The rest of the civil population also moved with the government and the Directorates. The first major problem that confronted the 12 Division was acute shortage of manpower because each Division recruited its men from local civilians within its operational area. Thereafter the maximum strength of any brigade within the Division at any given time was 800 armed men and indeed some brigades in that sector had, on some occasions, been reduced to a strength of 250 armed men. The situation was at its worst in August, 1969, when I observed during a battle in Azumini sector that a certain battalion of 71 Brigade which was carrying out the offensive had three officers and 23 armed men. As a result of desperate efforts by my Headquarters, it was possible to raise the average strength of all brigades within the 12 Division to an average of 599 armed men each at the time of the final push. By any standards, that would still be regarded as a very weak strength for a brigade engaged in war, particularly if that brigade is armed entirely with bolt action rifles against armour.

At that stage, it would have been an understatement on the part of anyone to talk of poor administrative support for the 12 Division or any other Biafran field formation for that matter. The fact was that such support had long ceased to exist because, with the exception of ammunition, each formation had to support itself almost entirely besides whatever other assistance I could personally render. The average quantity of petrol supplied to 12 Division per day was 50 gallons between September and December, 1969. Most of it was received from the fuel refinery set up and operated by the Army Headquarters in order to assist field units. Other Biafran formations were luckier than 12 Division with regard to fuel because they were nearer the civilian source and could therefore maintain a daily supply average of about 100 gallons of fuel through constant and ceaseless personal contacts. Moreover, those units which were near enough to Egbema oil fields stole crude oil by night and refined it secretly in order to keep a few essential unit vehicles on the road. That act was against Biafran Government orders and could not be practiced by far away units without detection by the authorities. 12 Division, in particular had no petrol that could be spared for long journeys to collect crude oil, particularly as it was not absolutely sure of succeeding.

In addition to complete lack of fuel for the Army, there was now absolutely no engine oil available anywhere in Biafra, thus making my efforts to find fuel look ridiculous. By September, 1969, there were over 180 vehicles in the 12 Division which could not be used because they lacked fuel or oil or both. Not a single brigade of that formation could afford to keep more than two vehicles on the road, but as a result of a desperate appeal for engine oil which I made to General Ojukwu, I received ten gallons of oil with which five vehicles were put on the road for a few days.

By September, 1969, the problem had got out of hand in the entire Army. With 12 Division in particular, the ammunition situation was simply hopeless. I had, after the fall of Umuahia, created an ammunition sub-depot close to the Division at Mbawsi to facilitate the delivery of ammunition to Aba and Arochukwu sectors of the war. The sub-depot could never function effectively for many reasons. To start with, the main Ordnance Depot near Owerri which received its ammunition supply daily, could not afford to send ammunition in bulk to any sub-depot. That meant that all Biafran formations wherever they may be were expected to send a vehicle each night to the Ordnance Depot to collect their daily ammunition quota. The 12 Division in particular could definitely not afford the fuel for daily collection of ammunition and therefore often failed to do so, at times, up to a whole week, thus leaving the Division without a round of ammunition for long periods.

The Ordnance Depot could render no assistance towards solving the problem by moving the 12 Division quota daily to Mbawsi sub-depot because it also had no fuel for such moves. For some time I undertook the responsibility of forwarding the 12

Division ammunition every night using my command Landrover, but soon I discovered I could no longer afford the fuel for it, and as soon as I gave up, the problem remained unsolved.

We had by now reached a stage where any soldier who was sure of one good meal in two days was indeed lucky. This problem, which was common to the entire Army, was again more pronounced in the 12 Division. The reasons were that after the fall of Umuahia no Biafran banks operated on the East bank of Imo River in the operational area of the 12 Division. For that reason there was no cash in the area for the purchase of the little, but extremely expensive food items that were still available for sale in local markets. Attempts to draw money from banks in other areas failed because those banks gave priority to units and other organisations operating in the areas where they were located, in view of the very limited amount of cash they held at any given time.

The insurmountable hardships facing the Army were being exploited for personal benefit by certain unscrupulous individuals through spiritualism. Many spiritualist organisations sprang up in the area of 12 Division, Aba, for the purpose of exploiting an Army which desperately wanted to win a war but had no practical means of doing so. Many officers and men, realising that we lacked the material force to prosecute the war successfully, resorted to spiritualism and prayers as the only alternative way of winning the war. This practice which began within the ranks of the "S" Division soon after its formation in September, 1968, had assumed disasterous proportions by the middle of 1969. In July, 1969, the commander of 12 Division, Brigadier Eze, made a request through me to the Head of State asking for the removal of all spiritualists from his operational area. As an alternative, he wanted all spiritualists and all allied practices banned in his sector in order to prevent soldiers from indulging in them to the detriment of our war effort.

To my knowledge, no effective action was ever taken to check this development. Consequently, all ranks of 12 Division became so deeply engrossed in the practice that only their spiritualist, "Doctor Wise" could give most units of the Division the final go-ahead for any battle. Thus, "Doctor Wise" became to all intents and purposes, the effective Commander of the Division.

The situation improved considerably as a result of various talks I gave to units of 12 Division against the practice, but the general influence of spiritualism persisted until the end of the war. When a military administration was set up for Aba Province in August, 1969, the Administrator, Lt. Colonel Ben Gbulie, arrested "Doctor Wise" and put an end to his practice. Documents recovered from the "Doctor" showed that his followers included top civil and military leaders. Before long, the Head of State ordered his release and the "Doctor" resumed his practice which thereafter continued to the end of the war.

The political situation in Aba and Annang Provinces was so bad and confused that no Biafran Army unit could have done better than the 12 Division with the resources available. For political reasons I do not know, the people of Aba were by now becoming disenchanted with the war. As a result, the 12 Division got less support and goodwill from the local population than units in other areas got. For an Army which depended almost entirely on the support of the people, that state of affairs made the efficient operation of the 12 Division very difficult. The attitude of the people changed from quiet indifference to open hostility when the only Military Administrator in Biafra was installed in that province. Thereafter the 12 Division lost almost all the civilian support it had enjoyed in that area for a long time.

There was also a political problem existing between the Government and the people of Annang in the 12 Division operational area. The problem arose as a result of the civil defence operation in Annang province after the fall of Ikot-Ekpene in April, 1968. As pointed out before, the entire blame for the operation was conveniently allowed to rest on Lt. Colonel Oji who was now the Principal Staff Officer (Operations) in 12 Division Headquarters.

By September, 1969, the demand by the Annangs that Oji should not be allowed to operate in Annang Province had reached a stage of constituting a major political problem. In addition, since the 1968 civil defence affairs the relationship between the Annangs and their Umuahia and Aba neighbors had remained strained. This unfortunate political situation adversely affected military operations. I had resisted for over 14 months all pressures designed to prevent Oji from operating with any unit east of the Imo River because, being the only trained officer on the staff of 12 Division Headquarters, his removal would have meant a speedy collapse of the Division. By October, 1969, I was still resisting successfully.

Who Destroyed Biafra's 12 Division — Nigeria or Biafra?

The decision by the enemy to attack 12 Division in strength was probably taken as a result of a very accurate and detailed report which the enemy was said to have obtained from a Biafran officer who defected in September, 1969, after he was punished for an offence. A copy of this report was later brought back to 12 Division by a Biafran Army agent operating with the enemy; and it was such as would tempt any Army into launching an immediate offensive. The 12 Division of the Biafran Army, lacking in manpower and administrative support, and beset with political, social and spiritualist problems, was neither fit to initiate an offensive nor to absorb the shock of one launched against it. Enemy attack on the Division at Eberi on the 18th of November, 1969 merely helped to bring to the notice of the people of Biafra the true situation existing in that sector of the war. The enemy moved from the area of Owazza oil fields with heavy ground and air support and attacked our positions at Eberi in strength. The news of the attack reached 12 Division Headquarters at Mbawsi 24 hours after it started and took almost two days to get to the Army Headquarters. The reason for this delay was because the 65 Biafran Brigade which was being attacked, lost its only wireless link with the Division Headquarters during the first wave of enemy air attack. With absolutely no fuel in the Brigade area for carrying the message in a vehicle over a distance of 35 miles to the Division Headquarters, it took a runner 24 hours to get there. The Division Commander, Brigadier Eze, had to go down there to take charge of the operations because the Brigade Commander, Lt. Colonel

Omeruo was admitted into hospital with hepatitis two days before.

The situation was already hopeless when Eze arrived there. Biafran troops had completely exhausted their ammunition after only four hours of fighting and were pulling back together with several thousand civilian refugees. All casualties sustained by our troops in the past 24 hours remained unevacuated as there were neither vehicles nor fuel with which to do so. Evacuation soon started with Brigadier Eze's command Landrover, the only vehicle in the entire area. A thick cloud of human beings drifted slowly northwards towards Ugba junction. At least once every one hour, enemy jets swooped over them bombing and strafing intensively and leaving behind heaps of mutilated and charred corpses of men, women and children scattered all over the road. No one took cover anymore. No one cared for cover. The corpses, however, blocked the roads and evacuation of casualties with the only available Landrover was rendered almost impossible.

The entire small arms ammunition reserve of 8000 rounds available to the Division was brought down to the battle area by the Division Commander. With that ammunition, the majority of 65 Brigade soldiers who were still hanging on in the hope that assistance would be sent, were prepared for battle. More assistance came from the 58 Brigade which now had less than 500 armed men. Thereafter, Biafran troops fought desperately with an average of ten rounds of ammunition per man per day in an attempt to halt or at least to delay the enemy advance. After a series of bitter and cruel encounters, the enemy recaptured the Ugba junction.

The fall of Ugba junction posed tremendous problems to the Army and constituted a dangerous threat to the continued survival of the Biafran nation. As an immediate remedy, I ordered the 14 Division to assume responsibility for the defence of Okpuala bridge in order to safeguard their left flank. I also moved a battalion of the Commando Division out of their defences at Umuahia to Ugba junction in an attempt to halt the enemy advance there. These arrangements made it possible for the battered and tired 65 Brigade to pull out completely for a rest and reorganisation. Regrouping and redeployment was slow generally because, apart from the overwhelming administrative difficulties, movement by day for our troops was rendered almost impossible by enemy aircrafts operating in the area.

While we were trying desperately to stabilise the situation around Ugba junction, the enemy struck in strength from Ikot-Ekpene along the Aba road. Massively supported by jet planes, artillery and mortars, he attacked the 58 Brigade forward locations near Uwa bridge on 25th November. The 58 Brigade, part of which had gone to Eberi as reinforcement, was now reduced to a total fighting strength of about 350 men. The Brigade however fought desperately for over five hours to prevent the enemy from crossing the bridge. By noon, the enemy had crossed and before last light had moved up to the area of Ohanze bridge. This development posed a difficult problem for me because, above all, the entire 61 Brigade, spread out over a large area in the Azumini sector, was now threatened with a complete seal-off. Lack of any form of communications made it impossible to alert and redeploy the Brigade quickly. 58 Brigade's determined counterattacks had no chance of success for the formation lacked the necessary ammunition and strength.

When fighting got to Nwaigwe bridge less than 14 miles to Aba, we destroyed the bridge so as to prevent an enemy link-up with Aba before we could receive the much needed ammunition. On the 30th of November, while heavy fighting was still going on in the areas of Nwaigwe bridge and Ugba junction, the enemy, with his usual support, launched yet another massive attack. This time, he moved from Aba township and attacked Ogbor Hill along the Aba-Umuahia road. Biafran troops there, none of whom had more than ten rounds of ammunition, withdrew as soon as they had exhausted their ammunition. The enemy from Aba thus crossed the Aba bridge and began to advance along Umuahia road. Within a short period of ten days, therefore, the enemy had launched three major attacks against the 12 Division which was now fighting almost bare-fisted.

It was at that stage that the Biafran public first became fully aware of the ugly situation in the area of the 12 Division and, as I expected, they were very angry. Everybody wanted the Division

Commander, Brigadier Eze, removed. Even though the Head of State kept quiet, I simply refused to take such an action as I had no other Division Commander who was likely to beat the enemy back without ammunition and other essential support. To further confuse an already confused situation, the Annangs renewed with more vigour and determination their demand that Oji be removed from the 12 Division. In short, what all Biafran civilians were agitating for without realizing it was that 12 Division, or at least its Headquarters, be disbanded at a time when the enemy was squeezing the formation to death from three directions. When General Efiong, who was under heavy pressure from the Annangs, intervened in favour of Oji being removed, I posted Oji to the nearby Commando Division at Umuahia. Brigadier Eze was thereafter left virtually alone to man his Division Headquarters in the absence of a trained officer to replace Oji. However, I was there throughout the battles to assist.

During the Joint Planning Committee meeting on December 13, 1969, General Ojukwu gave the following instructions:

1. That 12 Division Headquarters be disbanded and Brigadier Eze be posted to Army Headquarters as the Chief of Staff.

2. That 12 Division operational area be split into two sectors each with an independent headquarters to be equipped with assets of the disbanded 12 Division Headquarters.

3. All actions to be completed by last light of December 15, 1969.

I made it quite clear to all members of the Committee at this meeting that our difficulties and subsequent set-backs were caused by our basic weakness in strength and complete lack of administrative support, rather than by incompetence on the part of anyone. I then warned members seriously against any attempt to embark on such a major reorganisation of the 12 Division at a time when the enemy was mounting daily pressure on the Division from all directions; otherwise we might lose complete control of the situation.

I was told I was talking with too much passion to be objective and the reorganisation was to go ahead as ordered.

I left State House, Etiti after the meeting at 0200 hours on the 14th of December and moved straight back to 12 Division Headquarters and there ordered its disbandment. In its place, sectors 90 and 94 Headquarters were created. Sector 90, under the command of Colonel Onwuatuegwu, became responsible for the defence of the area stretching eastwards from Aba-Umuahia road on its right, to Ikot-Ekpene. Sector 94 under the command of Colonel Okeke, former commander of the 61 Brigade, took charge of the defence of the area from Aba-Umuahia road (inclusive) westwards to the Imo River.

Thus, on the 16th of December, 1969, the day Brigadier Eze and his 12 Division Headquarters ceased to function, enemy locations were: Ugba junction on the right, Abayi village near Aba to our front, and Nwaigwe bridge along Aba-Ikot-Ekpene road to our left. I gave instructions to Brigadier Eze to distribute the entire stores of his 12 Division Headquarters to the new Sector Headquarters before his departure to Army Headquarters to assume his new appointment.

While he was working on that assignment in the village of Umumkpeyi near Mbawsi, a despatch rider brought a message from State House telling Eze that his continued stay in that Sector of the war was an impediment to Biafran war efforts in the area. The message ordered him to leave the area immediately or face the consequences. Brigadier Eze left immediately for Army Headquarters without knowing what his offenses were. The situation was so fluid at the time that the enemy overran Umumkpeyi before an alternative arrangement could be made to distribute or even evacuate the stores.

My mobile Army Tactical Headquarters, which was comprised of my ADC and ten other soldiers, was left with the task of controlling and administering the two sectors that were once 12 Division. That task was, to say the least, humanly impossible. The majority of the units under the 12 Division had no opportunity of knowing that their Division Headquarters had been disbanded. For

363

that reason, they searched endlessly for their Headquarters and invariably ended up in mine. The new Sector Headquarters could not form on the ground and the commanders used their Landrovers as their headquarters. The responsibility for the procurement and supply of food, fuel, ammunition, transport and all other items required by the men to continue the struggle, rested squarely on me. Where Army Headquarters could not produce those items, the Army set up road blocks and got them from the public. The situation was now simply chaotic because even the civil administrative support for the Army had finally broken down completely and there was nothing the Head of State could do about it.

In the midst of that confusion, the enemy was moving in against an uncoordinated and greatly reduced Biafran resistance. In the area of Sector 90 the enemy launched yet another major attack along the Umuahia main road from the direction of Ikot-Ekpene. As a result of the relatively fast progress he was making, the entire Special Task Force, operating in the area of Arochukwu under Colonel Simon Uwakwe, was in danger of being completely cut off. In addition, the enemy was steadily gaining ground from Aba towards Mbawsi and Umuahia. However, with the enemy still at Ugba junction, the Sector 94 area was much more stable. This achievement was as a result of the brilliant and courageous performance of a Commando Battalion reinforcement which I moved in there under the personal command of Colonel Oji. For several days, all enemy attempts to advance southwards from Ugba junction met with complete failure.

That was the situation on the 20th of December, 1969 when the State House sent another order to me at my Ihie-Mbawsi Tactical Headquarters to the effect that Oji must leave the East bank of Imo River on that particular day before last light or face grave consequences. The Commander of the Commando Division, Brigadier Nwawo, who was sharing the same Headquarters with me at the time, broke down when I read out the State House order about Oji. Rather than lose Oji at a time like that, Nwawo preferred to resign his commission, and indeed was getting ready to go and inform the Head of State of his intention. I stopped him from doing so in his own interest and gave him 24 hours rest in a quiet place, while I took temporary command of his Division. Oji was immediately withdrawn from Ugba junction where he was engaged in a bitter battle. He packed quickly and disappeared to the commando base at Etiti. He never stopped asking "What do they say I have done?"

The climax came on the 21 December when State House sent yet another written instruction to me through Mr. M.C.K. Ajuluchukuwu. The instructions said among other things: 12 Division must now be disarmed or destroyed. This instruction is to be carried out to the letter. Report progress." In my reply, through the same Ajuluchukuwu, I explained to State House that I had no force available for the destruction of even the little that was left of the 12 Division. If I had had such a force, it would have been better to have been employed in destroying the enemy that was pushing 12 Division around in all directions.

Unfortunately, the State House had also passed the same instructions about the destruction of the 12 Division direct to the Commandos at Umuahia and they were already implementing the instructions to the letter. The Commandos poured out of their trenches around Umuahia and completely flooded the 12 Division operational area and began to disarm and destroy the Division. They set up road blocks all over the area, arrested all ranks of the 12 Division on administrative duties in the rear, and removed their weapons, stores, equipment and vehicles. Within 24 hours of this special commando operation, the 12 Division ceased to exist as the majority of its officers and men fled across the Imo River to escape the wrath of the Biafran Commandos. There were even senior officers of the Division who came into my Tactical Headquarters to seek protection. The Commando Division, in its attempt to destroy the 12 Division, had abandoned its defences and disorganised itself considerably. In short the advancing enemy, without any military action, had defeated two Biafran major formations and was then in a position to move in any direction with little or no opposition.

The systematic destruction of the 12 Division by the State House which commenced with the disbandment of its Headquarters, then the removal of its trained officers, was now complete with the routing of its rank and file. All the same, the enemy was moving in

365

from all directions without opposition. His advance was slow because all roads were completely clogged up with refugees.

Enemy first attempt to advance from Ugba junction after the removal of Oji was successful. I had no other officer immediately available to take over the command of that front and the troops remained without a commander. From the south, east and west, the enemy moved down in the direction of Umuahia. By midday on the 24th of December, the enemy was near enough to Umuahia to force the Commando Division to pull out of its trenches around the town. Over half a million people were now moving down to Udo bridge at Mbaise, which was the only exit from 12 Division area. Before 1600 hours on that day enemy had linked Aba and Umuahia. It required my entire escort party of 15 men, pulling and pushing for almost two hours, to get me across the bridge to Mbaise. I believe some enemy troops had completely mingled with the crowd around the bridge head and I might have been led away by them if I had not discarded everything on me that would have given away my rank and position. The only defence on that road was a machine gun team I sited along the bank of the river near the bridge before I left the bridge head to see General Ojukwu and brief him on the situation.

I saw General Ojukwu at about 2100 hours. After my briefing, he swore that the war would continue to the last man and that the Udo bridge at Mbaise must be blown up before the following morning and that he was going to make the necessary arrangements himself.

After a short conference with my staff at the Army Headquarters at midnight, I drove to 15 Division Headquarters to try to get some troops, however few, to be used in establishing a defensive position at the bridge head before morning. While I was there, enemy artillery guns were carrying out some harassing fire all around the 15 Division Headquarters; yet the men sang their Christmas carols unruffled. They sang of the love, glory and power of God. "We shall understand it better by and by" they sang. I just wondered. I however managed to squeeze out a platoon from the Division and moved them down to Udo bridge before morning. By 0630 hours on the 25th of December, the bridge was blown, under arrangements made by Ojukwu. As was usual in Biafra, after a major disaster someone had to be responsible. The deliberate rumours that soon began to circulate placed full responsibility for the calamity on Eze. Public anger against this officer was almost uncontrollable. I must have received over 200 telegrams from citizens of Biafra acting in ignorance, demanding that Eze be thrown out of the Army in disgrace. There were many others who wanted nothing less than his head. The military-minded ones among them admonished me for "promoting" Eze to the "rank" of Chief of Staff as a reward for his recent failures. I was in complete sympathy with all those who sent me telegrams on that issue because I believed they were fully entitled to know what was happening. I was however not in a position, neither was it my duty, to get the public informed.

The campaign against Brigadier Eze and the Army was unfortunate and achieved nothing except to divert public attention from the realities of the war. I was of the view that, at this stage, the public should begin to know the truth and I had always made this view known to the Head of State since the fall of Aba. Nevertheless, as a reaction to public mood and pressure, Ojukwu dismissed both Brigadier Eze and Colonel Oji from the Biafran Army without consulting me, his Army Commander. To ridicule them, Eze was later made a Fire Officer while Oji became a Police Officer. The people were appeased and happy for they had won their long war against Eze and Oji. One sometimes wonders if they would have felt so happy if they had known the true story, particularly the fact that Eze received apologies in private by those who disgraced him in public, in order to keep the war going.

Enemy link-up of Aba and Ikot-Ekpene with Umuahia also isolated the STF at Arochukwu. Within 48 hours after this isolation, the unit ran out of all supplies. All attempts to supply them using porters, as was the case with the 57 Brigade at Otuacha, failed because this time, the porters had to go through over 50 miles of enemy-held territory. Seizing advantage of the situation, the enemy attacked the formation from the South through Idoro-Ikpe and from the North through Abriba-Elu road. The STF fought on gallantly until the 6th of January, 1970, when my Headquarters lost wireless contact with them.

Looking back on the fate of Biafran 12 Division, I have always wondered who was really responsible for its destruction and the consequent collapse of the people's resistance. The questions will always be asked: "Who destroyed 12 Division of the Biafran Army — Nigeria or Biafran military and civil forces? Why did it become necessary to send the Commando Division to destroy the 12 Division, thereby neutralising the two forces and rendering further Biafran resistance impossible? Why was it that the State House was unable to resist public pressure to remove such a well-trained officer as Eze from his command and to have him disgraced? Yet in the Nnewi war front (Ojukwu's home town), there was a heavier and more sustained pressure from the people to have Brigadier Amadi removed. There everyone realised (unlike in Eze's case) that no adequate substitute existed in Biafra. The people of Nnewi soon got tired of demanding the removal of Amadi from their area. Thus, Amadi remained there and defended Nnewi successfully to the end of the war. If such civilian pressures in all other sectors of the war had been similarly treated on merit, the military achievements of Biafra may have been better.

THE LAST ACT

Except at the initial stages, the enemy contributed very little to the destruction of the 12 Division and to the self-inflicted disorganisation of the Commando Division. He was therefore able to maintain the momentum of his advance without stopping for rest or reorganisation. When the enemy linked up Aba with Umuahia, 12 Commando Brigade was completely cut off and only the 4th and the 8th Brigades of that Division managed to cross to the west bank of the Imo River. These two brigades, then very much depleted, engaged the enemy in bitter battles around Umuahia for three days without much success. This was to be expected in a place where the enemy 3 Marine Commando Division from the south had linked up with elements of his First Division operating in the North.

The collapse of the Commando Division at Umuahia exposed

the rear of Biafra's 15 Division in Okigwe sector and also gave the enemy complete control of all areas East of the Imo River as far north as Umuahia. The 14 Division was now attempting to take up the responsibility of the disbanded 12 Division as well and, by so doing, had become over-stretched and by far too weak to fight effectively anywhere. The enemy therefore found little difficulty in moving northwards from Umuahia towards Okigwe using the exposed right flank of the 15 Division. Following four days of battles, the whole of 15 Division pulled back behind the Imo River as well. The 73 Brigade, under Colonel Ginger, which was still fighting successfully in the area of Uzuakoli also had to pull back to avoid being cut off. Like the Commandos at Umuahia, all attempts by the 15 Division to fight their way back to their trenches around Okigwe town failed.

With very little space left in Biafra, all displaced Divisions could no longer settle down completely anywhere. That, added to the fact that all administrative machinery in Biafra both military and civil had ceased to exist, rendered both the 15 and the Commando Divisions completely unoperational. With the disbandment of the 12 Division and apart from the STF at Arochukwu, only the 14 Division at Owerri and the 11 Division at Onitsha were holding their positions, and were still capable of fighting if well supported. As the situation continued to deteriorate, General Efiong and I held a discussion in my office on the 3rd of January, 1970 to re-examine the situation and make fresh recommendations to General Ojukwu. We arrived at a decision to ask Ojukwu to hold a meeting of top civilian leaders during which I would brief them thoroughly on the situation to enable them to take a firm decision as to whether or not to continue the war. In arriving at that decision, we also took into consideration the fact that some leaders of Onitsha and Okigwe Provinces were already holding dialogues on the question of sending a joint delegation to Ojukwu to request that the war be stopped.

General Efiong later informed me that the meeting had been arranged for 2100 hours on the 5th of January, 1970. Contrary to my expectations the Head of State had invited over 40 army officers and only five civilian leaders for what now appeared to be a military seminar rather than a serious meeting to discuss the fate of millions of people. With such a big crowd, many people were unlikely to talk frankly for fear of subsequent public reaction. The Head of State insisted that everybody present should speak but not for more than five minutes. These limitations notwithstanding, everybody who spoke said in effect that the war should be called off unless we were sure of a definite miracle in our favour very soon. Ojukwu summarised by stressing that the war must continue to the last man, and for as long as he was alive. In order to convince those present that he meant to fight on, General Ojukwu read out his plans for the complete reorganisation of the Army and for future offensives. He revealed his plan to move 4000 armed men into Midwestern Nigeria under Colonel Achuzia for an offensive to overrun that Region. As the Army Commander I knew that such a plan was sheer fantasy in Biafra, at a time when it was almost impossible to raise 200 men in a month not to talk of weapons. Yet we all listened very patiently. Soon afterwards, the story of the planned invasion of Midwestern Nigeria spread like wildfire everywhere, and the morale of the people rose considerably. But for all senior officers who watched what I knew to be the final show, morale was very low indeed when the curtain fell.

On the 7th of January the enemy, with massive ground and air support, launched an attack against the 63 Brigade location at Amala. The Brigade, already very much stretched in an effort to cover some of the 12 Division locations, fought surprisingly well to hold the enemy in check for about four hours before collapsing under the weight of the attack. Thus, for the first time in 15 months, Biafra's 63 Brigade under Colonel Lambert Ihenacho was losing ground, and very fast too, because there was no assistance anyone could render to it. Before long, the advancing enemy got to Okpuala junction and there split into two — one force continued to move northwards into Mbaise while the other moved westwards to Owerri through the exposed left flank of the 14 Division. I still had a reserve force of 200 armed men in my Headquarters but no one, including the Head of State, could provide a vehicle and fuel required to move them down to assist the 63 Brigade. This Army Headquarters reinforcement began to walk the 22 miles to Okpuala through Owerri.

The following day, 8th of January, the reinforcement force made contact with a strong enemy force in the area of Olakwo bridge eight miles from Owerri. We fought very well but by last light the enemy was already at the outskirts of Owerri and was shelling the town. That meant that the bulk of "S" Division deployed over 25 miles south of Owerri had been cut off without them realising it. In the absence of wireless communications, transport and fuel, a message which was sent to the Division frontlines would have taken not less than four days to get there.

Owerri was evacuating and that meant the disappearance of the last semblance of the Biafran Government. The evacuation was still going on when the enemy entered Owerri on the 9th of January, 1970. As a result of the congestion on all roads caused by refugees moving out of Owerri, military operations anywhere within ten miles from Owerri was impossible. Even in that confusion, enemy jet planes were bombing and strafing all areas around Owerri ruthlessly.

I had just returned from Owerri war front on the 9th of January, 1970 and was holding a conference with my staff to work out immediate probable moves of the Army Headquarters when General Efiong came in at 1600 hours to see me. He looked reasonably cheerful when he told me that General Ojukwu would like to see me at once at Nnewi, his home town.

General Ojukwu's house at Nnewi was full of luggages piled high both inside and outside and there was a big crowd of relatives and close friends. The fact that Ojukwu was in military uniform, which was a very rare occurrence, made me rather suspicious and worried. In a short briefing, General Ojukwu told me in the presence of General Efiong, that the Biafran Cabinet had taken a decision to send a "peace mission" abroad the following day, the 10th of January, 1970. According to him the mission, which would include Dr. M.I. Okpara, the Political Adviser; Mr. N. U. Akpan, the Chief Secretary to the Government; and myself, the General Officer Commanding the Army, would be led by him personally. The

371

"peace mission" he added, would be away for five to seven days and only a suitcase each was required by each member of the mission. In my absence he said, Brigadier Amadi was to act as the Army Commander. He did not have to say more for me to understand that he had finally admitted that the war was lost, even though I would have expected him to have the courtesy of taking me into full confidence at that stage, for a change.

In spite of the short notice and the extreme vagueness surrounding the "peace mission," I was still able to brief a good number of my senior field commanders on the new development, making it clear that the mission was unlikely to return to Biafra for some time. I was also able to speak to Wing Commander Ezeilo, the Air Force Commander, and Captain Fred Anuku, the Navy Commander, about this peace mission and advise them to endeavour to come out of Biafra in their own interest, as soon as Ojukwu was gone. The military officers I spoke to were very glad I was going out on the "peace mission" because they were sure that if indeed there was still anyone interested in restoring peace to Biafra, I would tell them the true military situation in Biafra for a change.

The 10th of January was very chaotic. The enemy was pushing in all directions from Owerri. By 1400 hours he had got to Amaraka on the Okigwe road, only four miles from Army Tactical Headquarters at Isu. On the Owerri-Ihiala road, the enemy had got to Awomama and crossed the Njaba bridge, thus threatening the Uli Airport. The whole of Mbaise had been overun and Colonel Ogunewe, Ojukwu's Military Assistant, came to see me to report that his entire family at Mbaise, his home town, was missing. At that stage the enemy moved everywhere without opposition besides the delay brought about by the movement of millions of refugees on the roads.

As Isu and Nkwerre began to evacuate, I moved down to Nnewi to see the Head of State once more and brief him on the situation. At last, and for the first time during the war, he appeared terrified. He wondered if we had not left our departure rather too late and if we would still make it. He advised me to come to the airport with my full escorts because he had been reliably informed that certain people were planning to stop us from leaving Biafra. For that reason I went to the airport with more escorts than I ever used throughout the war. At that stage, I was no longer sure of the nature of our "peace mission.": my doubts had been confirmed and I realised that we were escaping Biafra for good.

By 2000 hours, the threat to Uli Airport was such that no one was sure it could be used again. While alternative arrangements were being made for a possible use of Uga Airport, the Biafran Air Force confirmed that Uli could still be used. As a precautionary measure, General Ojukwu travelled incognito in a Peugeot 403 car to the airport while someone else who could pass for him in darkness, travelled in his official car. Ojukwu's Peugeot car was packed in a nearby jungle for over five hours until the plane was ready to take off at 0300 hours on the 11th of January, 1970. Thus, General Efiong was left behind to play the last honourable, but sad and difficult task of undertaker for Biafra, which we had all fought very hard, but without success, to create and preserve as the last sanctuary for the then oppressed peoples of Eastern Nigeria.

III

EPILOGUE

Chapter 15

EPILOGUE

WHY WE LOST THE WAR

Mao Tse Tung's dictum that "power comes out of the barrel of a gun" finds its most obvious illustration in the outcome of the Nigeria-Biafra conflict. For when we reached the stage where the Nigerians had the guns and we had not, they simply overran our territory and we were defeated. It was not really as simple as that or was it? Why did we ever reach the stage where we no longer had the guns? It is in trying to answer this question that we can discover why we lost the war.

While international opinion had been conditioned by the incessant propaganda of the news media of certain great powers to expect the collapse of Biafra as an inevitability, we, the people of Biafra, convinced of the justness of our cause, never doubted for one moment that justice would prevail eventually and victory would be ours. This faith in our ultimate victory was what kept Biafrans slugging on for three years in spite of heart-breaking set-backs, to the astonishment of the whole world. We felt that having been so unjustly treated, humiliated and massacred, God and international opinion could not stand idly by and allow us to be exterminated in our homeland. Unfortunately for our innocently naïve people, political and military logic do not follow sentimental lines. It was therefore in ignorance of this basic fact of life that we made several grievous mistakes which contributed so much to our defeat. It is therefore necessary that we examine some of the more important of these mistakes in order to learn from them. Indeed, it is to the eternal glory of the Biafran common man that, despite these numerous

377

grievous mistakes, mistakes that could have caused any other people as unequipped as we were to collapse much sooner, the Biafran resistance endured for three long years.

In the first instance we could have prevented the war by effectively challenging the counter coup of July, 1966 promptly rather than allow it to gain momentum. If that had happened, we would not have had a war to lose in the first place. Gowon's counter-revolution having gained momentum, I believe it was still not impossible to have delayed the war itself by clever political and diplomatic manoeuvers, if we had had a more capable leader or, better still, a collective leadership.

As discussed earlier, when the coup started on the 29th of July, 1966, Southern Army officers, lacking effective leadership and co-ordination because of General Ironsi's political naïvety, went in confusion into hiding in the hope that things would soon sort themselves out instead of challenging the move about which they had ample information and warning.

Certain of these Southern officers, exasperated by continuous Northern Nigeria's agitation for secession, were more inclined to allow the coup to take its full course if that would bring the much desired peace to that part of Africa. Little did they realise that interested outside powers had other things in mind. Encouraged by the apparent unwillingness or inability of all Southerners to fight back, Gowon, who was already evacuating all Northerners to Northern Nigeria in preparation for the secession of that Region from Nigeria, became emboldened and therefore added to his counter-revolution, pogroms, and later a total war. These could have been avoided if General Ironsi had taken appropriate counter-actions during the preparatory stages or through a quick intervention by all military personnel of Southern Nigeria origin, as soon as the counter-revolution started. We realised the need to resist only when we had our backs against the wall, but by then it was by far too late.

After the pogroms of 1966 and the punitive Decrees of early 1967, a war could hardly have been avoided entirely but could have been delayed through careful and skillful political manoeuvers without a loss of face and without compromising the security which the people of Eastern Nigeria wanted so much. Such a delay could have given us time to prepare for an effective resistance that could have brought us victory in the early stages of a war. Naturally and quite justly too, we got so completely carried away by our total conviction in the justness of our course, and our belief in the existence of a fair and just world conscience, that we took it for granted that justice would be done and our rights recognised just by bringing our case to the notice of the world. We therefore made no alternative arrangements or necessary preparations for an armed show-down with Nigeria. By the time we discovered rather belatedly, that world conscience is really not that effective in international politics, we were already in serious trouble.

In my opinion the most important reason why we lost the war, apart from the question of foreign support for Nigeria, was the existence of a crisis of confidence in Biafra throughout the war. This crisis existed within the Army, between the Army and the civilians, between the Army and the government and, indeed, between the Biafran government and some of the foreign supporters. The initial detention of Dr. M. I. Okpara, former Premier of Eastern Nigeria soon after Ojukwu became Governor, the wartime unexplained mass detention of top ranking Biafran Army officers and civilians, and the appointment of Colonel Banjo, a Yoruba, to lead the invasion of Midwestern Nigeria in 1967, were the more blatant manifestations of this lack of confidence. It was because of the lack of mutual trust by people pursuing the same aim, that Ojukwu dispensed with the inner confidence of military experts and highly experienced political leaders who could have perhaps helped him save our people from the greatest calamity that ever befell them. Even our foreign friends were not given sufficient information to enable them to plan and render a more meaningful military and diplomatic assistance to Biafra. Thus, within and without Biafra, ignorance of the true situation was universal with the disastrous consequences this had for the people of Biafra.

It is my view that Biafra never had a government but merely operated under a leader, and that Biafra lost the true aims of the revolution soon after it started. Thus, on the civil side, we had a Consultative Assembly and a Cabinet which existed to listen to glorious speeches of "achievements" and impressive future plans and intentions. The most important function of those bodies still remained that of giving fresh "mandates" to the Head of State whenever he required them. On the armed forces side, we had the Joint Planning Committee, which came into being rather too late, merely to satisfy the long outstanding demand of the people for an organised and collective planning of the war. The Committee worked without necessary facts and achieved absolutely nothing. In short, what Biafra needed most but never had was collective leadership. Over concentration of powers into one hand is bad enough in peace time, and should never be allowed in time of war when mental strains affect good judgment. As Ojukwu once said to Efiong, Biafra's effective policy-making body consisted of Chukwuemeka, Odumegwu and Ojukwu — in short, himself alone. All the same, it is my candid opinion that if the committee had been expanded to include a few more people, better and more flexible decisions would have been taken for the benefit of all. Moreover, in struggles of this nature, there is always the tendency for a lone but powerful leader to try to make his name. Biafra was not an exception. A few officers were more interested in making their names politically than fighting the war. A few succeeded and boasted about it even though they succeeded at the expense of the success of the war. Projecting a name to the world, though occasionally necessary, cost a lot of money which could have been put into better use by Biafra.

The Head of State, being a soldier and suddenly a politician, found himself, therefore, in a unique position he could easily exploit if he so desired, particularly at a time of a popular national revolution. He was the champion of both the Army and Government, and it was easy for him to separate the two organisations completely and act alone on their behalf. The situation thus created was that each time a major decision was taken in Biafra, the Army thought the civilians were responsible for it while the civilians thought the reverse was true. In effect, as it turned out later, only one man took all these decisions. As a result it was difficult for any one person to know enough facts about the situation to render a meaningful advice even if he had the opportunity to do so. By the time this fact was known, it was too late for anyone to have done anything to rectify it.

Judging from the little information available to me through local rumours and radio stations concerning the situation in Nigeria, I was convinced by May, 1967 that there was need for a firm stand by the people of Eastern Nigeria against Gowon's Lagos Government. The Consultative Assembly, which met in Enugu on the 27th of May, 1967, working on the information available to it at the time, was therefore fully justified in mandating Ojukwu to declare an Independent Biafra at the "earliest practicable date." Was the 30th of May, 1967 that earliest practicable date? We all know now that it was not, even though the Head of State, who had all the facts at the time, still thought it was. Why was it so? Again the answer is simple. As a Military Governor in charge of a Region of Nigeria, Ojukwu must have known that his appointment as a military ruler might be terminated by Lagos and another person appointed in his place. Such an action by Lagos would have greatly embarrassed Ojukwu in addition to introducing doubts in the minds of people about the justness of any attempts he would have made to continue in Office. There were also many top Army officers in the Eastern Region over whom the Military Governor had absolutely no authority as long as that Region remained a part of Nigeria. It was therefore an urgent necessity that Eastern Nigeria became independent of Nigeria as soon as possible to enable him not only to remove all authority of Lagos over him, but to establish himself as an effective leader exercising unlimited powers over the entire population. It was an action that had to be taken before any developments from Lagos made it impossible for him to do so successfully. That is why the 30th of May, 1967 was considered in some quarters as the earliest practicable date for declaring Biafra an independent and sovereign nation.

The Biafran financial disaster, if not a total collapse as a result of the change in currency by Nigeria in January, 1968, was the most important single reason why we lost the war. At the end of the

381

financial chaos which followed in Biafra, we had lost over 50 million pounds which could have made a world of difference in our favour if properly utilised for the execution of the war. This should not have happened if prior arrangements were made to counter the move. After all, as far back as October, 1967, the common man in Biafra was already talking about a possible change of currency by Nigeria. As a result of that fantastic financial loss, Biafra found it difficult to support her Army at war.

Whatever money Biafra ever had during the war was under the control of the Head of State, while the actual spending was the responsibility of Mr. C. C. Mojekwu, a lawyer. It goes without saying that better results may have been achieved with the little we had if the above committee had been expanded to include a few other financial experts, and credible accounts kept. This leads me to the question of purchases made for the Army during the war. Even though there was a government statement before the war that no country in Black Africa could defeat Biafra by air, land, or sea, we still started the war with practically nothing, and could not improve on that situation right to the end. The Biafran Army, despite its gallant efforts, was forced into fighting defensive battles throughout the war and no Army can win a war through defensive battles. The little money available for the purchase of military stores and weapons was wasted by those civilians who were responsible for all military purchases during the war. Rifles arrived either in unserviceable condition or with the wrong calibre of ammunition. Most of the artillery guns and mortars were unserviceable when they arrived in Biafra. For the very few that were serviceable, the shells and bombs for them often arrived without fuzes!

Despite this obvious waste of time and money, these civilians under Mr. Mojekwu continued to buy for the Army until the end of the war. A question uppermost in many minds is why armed forces personnel who are most qualified to do those purchases were not used. For the answer to this question, one guess is as good as the other. If qualified men were used for those purchases perhaps numerous aircrafts which could not fly as soon as they were paid for, would never have been bought. We could have therefore made better use of the limited resources available to us to achieve better results in the battlefield. How could complete honesty be expected when all Biafran funds were raised and spent throughout the war under accounts opened in the name of individuals?

Enough has been said about the importance of an efficient and effective administrative backing for an Army at war to convince anyone that the Biafran Army, which lacked such a backing, suffered serious handicaps as a result. We grossly underrated the important effects which military administration could have on the efficiency and effectiveness of a soldier. If we now know that it is as important as the rifle and ammunition with which the soldier fights, we have learnt a useful lesson. It is wrong to administer an army at war through independent civilian organisations. Such a system is bound to reduce efficiency within that army and hamper its operations through an inevitable loss of flexibility. The best thing is always for an army to administer itself using a system it is familiar with, a system which is normally worked out carefully and modified from time to time to satisfy the needs of the army under a frequently changing war situation. If civilian organisations must assist the army with its administration, for the best results, such organisations should be placed under the control of that army for ease of control.

The civilian population of Biafra suffered even more than the Army as a result of complete lack of any form of administrative arrangements to ensure that their basic needs were met. For this reason, family problems among the troops virtually got out of hand and resulted in loss of morale, if not efficiency. In addition, civil enthusiasm and support for the war decreased as their administrative difficulties increased. If the privileged few had not had a plane and the money for weekly shopping trips abroad, the problem may have been identified, and food rationing introduced like in all countries at war, particularly under a total blockade.

The introduction of a formal revolution into Biafra during the war may have been a good idea but we got into serious trouble immediately after. People conveniently misinterpreted the "Ahiara Declaration" — the Biafran Revolutionary Document — to suit their purpose. The Army became the "people's army" and thereafter, local leaders not only felt entitled to know all that was going on in the Army, including its future plans and intentions, but frequently sat in judgment over Army officers. When the new revolution struck the Army, it swept many experienced and vital officers into jail for offences judged anti-revolutionary by our numerous textbook revolutionaries. This was also true of civilians. We therefore lost the services of those important men in the name of the revolution at the expense of the war. In September, 1969, Count Von Rosen, a Swedish pilot serving with the Biafran Air Force who was commenting on the arrest and detention of some Biafran pilots for "offences" against the "revolution," said that Biafra must choose between a war and a "revolution" before they lose both. In my view, when it was seen that the "revolution" was sweeping our war effort aside, the "Ahiara Declaration" should have been withdrawn and the "revolution" postponed till after the war.

Finally, I think there was by far too much time and energy wasted in frequent struggles for power and position inside Biafra during the war. Those struggles intensified whenever there was a bit of stability in the war fronts. A situation like that should never have been allowed to exist during a war of survival. We posed as experts in everything and that brought about confusion and frustration. It also caused vital omissions in places where people left their jobs to do other people's jobs. If we have learnt to stick to the jobs for which we are trained and give others a chance to do their own jobs, we have learnt a useful lesson.

COUPS D'ETAT IN AFRICA

As we have seen, the Nigerian Revolution which led to the civil war between Biafra and Nigeria was sparked off by a *coup d'état* and the war itself was fought between two opposing military regimes. This brings us to consider briefly the question of *coups d'états* and military regimes in Africa.

A good number of Black African countries today are under military rule as a result of a wave of *coups d'état*. One therefore often wonders why Africans tend to resort to this method to bring about a change of government in preference to more orthodox methods. The simple reason is that very few African governments have ever been removed through "democratic" elections. This fact has therefore made the *coup d'état* an essential and integral part of African governmental systems. A possible military intervention remains, perhaps, the only check on the excesses of politicians who invariably neutralise the power of the ballot paper.

One would ask why it is not always possible to remove an African Government through democratic elections. The difficulty lies not only in the nature of the African politician himself and the peculiar society in which he finds himself, but also in the fact that these governments are constantly under the influence and protection of interested foreign powers. An average African politician regards politics as a business enterprise. Despite the numerous financial obligations he owes to his extended family and clan, he takes a calculated risk of investing all his savings and loans in politics in order to get into parliament. Once there, his primary aim is to make sufficient money so as to meet his financial commitments to his creditors, family and clan, in addition to ensuring his profits.

If in trying to achieve his aim, his country benefits through any actions of his, it is all well and good; if not it is just too bad. It is therefore ridiculous for anyone to expect such a politician to give up his seat in parliament by allowing himself to be defeated in a so-called democratic election. When the ruling party is made up of such individuals, as is the case in many African countries, then you have a situation where the government cannot be removed through elections. Such a government will use its unlimited powers and various agencies available to it to ensure that this does not happen. At this stage a section of the people complains to the army and the army intervenes, sometimes rather too readily.

Only very few African army officers would want to seize political power in their country just for the love of it, as long as all sections of the community are fully satisfied with the government in power. The average African army officer is politically naïve and, unless prompted from within the country or by an interested foreign

385

power, will not seize the reins of government of his country. When a *coup d'état* takes place as a result of secret pressure by a section of the community, the government is invariably an imposed and unpopular one which no longer serves the interest of all sections of the community. If carried out without the knowledge of the foreign power in whose sphere of influence the country lies, the exercise must be very efficiently executed and ruthlessly sustained if it is to succeed. This was the point General Ironsi failed to realise soon enough after the January 1966 revolution in Nigeria. On the other hand, foreign-inspired coups, which are almost always for economic reasons and in complete disregard for the true wishes and aspirations of the people, succeed without difficulty.

Unfortunately, no matter who wants a change of government for whatever reasons, soldiers more often than not, end up being used as tools. The situation today therefore, is that Black African armies are increasingly constituting the greatest threat to the governments they exist to protect.

In conclusion, it is correct to say that African soldiers do not topple their governments just for the love of political power. They are always pushed into it when the politicians themselves have prepared the stage for it. It is only the African politician who can put an end to military coups in Africa. This he can do not by legislating against it, but by placing the interests of his entire people above all others. He must also show at all times in words and deeds that he holds his political office at the pleasure of his people and for the sole purpose of serving their interests. There must be clear indications that he could be removed through democratic means when he no longer satisfies the people's needs. If such a situation truly exists in any African country, there cannot be a military *coup d'état* to overthrow the government.

A military government is a major set-back for any nation and should be avoided at all costs. This is because military men are unqualified for the task of government and either lean too heavily on advice which may not always be in the best interest of their people or, worse still, attempt to rule without it. With the gun in his hand, it is difficult to remove the military leader, particularly when he begins to enjoy full political power. It is however the greatest disservice an army officer can do to his country and people if he plunges them into political darkness and keeps them there simply because he wants political power and wealth. No matter what a politician does, he must always avoid drawing his country's army into politics for, in the final analysis, it cuts both ways, and the results could be contrary to all his expectations.

CONCLUSION AND REFLECTIONS

To say that the Biafran struggle for separate existence was merely a rebellion by one man, General Ojukwu, apart from serving the propaganda interests of Lagos, is an insult to the man in the street, who without doubt is the real hero of this war. I have therefore tried to establish in this book that the Biafrans fought in the belief that it was the only way to protect themselves from possible extermination. We believed that we were fighting to ensure our very survival. It is true we lost the war, but we fought well enough and with sufficient determination to bring our grievances successfully to the notice of the entire world. Despite a negative world reaction, we made a significant impact which is a commendable achievement. What I am trying to say is succinctly summarised in the words of a French deputy, Ambassador Raymond Offroy, who had this to say after visiting the Biafran enclave: "Before I came to Biafra, I was told that Biafrans fought like heroes. But now I know that heroes fight like Biafrans."

Biafrans were not really angry with Gowon for carrying out a coup against the Federal Government of Nigeria because he was as much entitled to do so as anybody who believes he has sufficient justification. We were, however, angry that the Nigeria Army appeared to be used for the complete destruction of a part of the country. We were particularly angry that Britain saw fit, purely for economic reasons, to invite the rest of the world to assist Gowon in completing his coup which, before then was unsuccessful in parts of Nigeria, particularly in the Eastern Region. This action of Britain set a very dangerous precedent in African politics. What it amounts to is that any group of African army officers can initiate a move against their government and ask for foreign assistance to accomplish it successfully.

The aim of the January 15th, 1966 coup in Nigeria was simply to ensure the unity of Nigeria which, at the time, was fast disintegrating. As far as that aim goes, the exercise was a success at the cost of a few lives, but unfortunately left the control of the Nigerian Federal Government for the first time ever, in the hands of the Southerners. This turned out to be a situation some foreign powers could not tolerate for any length of time. Thus, we had the counter coup, which was an attempt by Northern Nigeria to secede from Nigeria, closely followed by a civil war to keep Nigeria one.

In the end, the whole exercise of splitting and re-uniting Nigeria cost us over three million lives. The question is how could anyone ever justify the loss of so many lives in order to gain political control of his country? What alienated Biafrans most during the whole violent period is that even if one were to admit that the May and July killings of 1966 were necessary for the successful carrying out of Gowon's counter revolution and as a revenge for the elimination of some Northern Nigerian leaders in the January Revolution, what happened the subsequent October could be described as sadism, to say the least.

Looking at the entire revolution and the war objectively, one finds it difficult to determine who indeed was rebelling against the Nigerian Government. Could it be Biafrans who were fighting to foil an uncompleted coup by Gowon against the Nigerian Government? Or was it Gowon who was still trying to complete the overthrow of the last legal government of Nigeria under General Ironsi? The most baffling aspect of the whole thing remains the basis upon which the world decided that the Biafrans were the true rebels. From there the revolution moved a step further and we have seen how a massive movement by the people of Northern Nigeria, against the entire people of Southern Nigeria, was quickly transformed into a war against the Ibos. It is clear that this change of attitude was designed to remove the possibility of a co-ordinated and effective resistance by the entire peoples of the South against the North. With the Ibo as the guinea pigs, the other Southern tribes heaved a sigh of relief and were too happy to call the war that followed "an Ibo rebellion."

But the Ibos appear to have learnt a lesson which will make it difficult for them to rebel as readily as they did in the past. It would appear that some people somewhere who always incited the Ibos into rebellion, were never around whenever the confrontation began. If the Ibos can only give others a chance to fight their own wars, there may never be any more wars in Nigeria in which they will be involved directly.

We have seen also how Biafrans made many unnecessary mistakes. If they have learnt through those mistakes they have gained a lot of useful experience which is vital for a mature and progressive society. Biafra inherited a peculiar problem in leadership which operated such that the beleaguered people of Biafra were denied both the professional advice of their military leaders and what is worse, the political sagacity and experience of such astute political leaders as Dr. Michael Okpara, the former Premier of Eastern Nigeria. We often left the straight path leading to our objective in search of such frivolities as personal power, wealth and making of one's name. Those who disappointed the people by so doing did not seem to realise that all they sought were automatic by-products of a successful establishment of a State of Biafra. In the end, Biafra was lost and those who retained big names and wealth must be doing so temporarily.

Yet we all stayed there, boxed in on all sides by a vicious enemy whom we had to fight to a finish as there was no other alternative. As things were, any attempt on the part of anyone to work towards a change of leadership would have been seen by the common man as an act of sabotage designed to aid the enemy. Such an attempt could have failed woefully. Thus, those of us who were aware of the true situation found ourselves immobilized between the devil and the deep blue sea. Moreover because only the Head of State knew all the facts about the actual execution of the war, it would have taken any other officer a long time to find out those facts, thus reducing his chances of success. No one wanted to inherit the mess which had gone beyond repair and take the final blame. It is my belief that if Biafra had gone through the revolution and the war under a civilian leader, we could have emerged much more successfully than we did.

This leads me to further reflections on the earlier stages of the coup when with the hindsight of the "ifs" of history we could have avoided the calamity that befell our people. For unfortunately Biafra's case was not an exception because, throughout the Revolution and the war, Eastern Nigerians were unsuccessful in their leaders. General Ironsi equated his task of ruling Nigeria with doing everything in his power to placate a section of the country and was thus, in a way, following the policy of the former colonial master. The irony of the situation was that every move the General made in this direction further alienated those he tried to please and emboldened them more to plan his ouster. This was as to be expected for the political history of Nigeria has shown that there are those who have always insisted, as a condition for staying part of one Nigeria, on having one of their sons at the head. On this point all those concerned, irrespective of their political and ideological differences are agreed, and are willing to use any means to achieve their aim.

General Ironsi's regime was a real tragedy for the people of Eastern Nigeria in other ways because it created the conditions which led to the killings and the ultimate civil war. In the first place he abolished not only the political parties but also all ethnic organisations such as the Ibo State Union which provided corporate protection for the people, particularly in the somewhat alien environments of some parts of Nigeria. If an organisation like the Ibo State Union had been in existence at the time of the May massacres, it could have organised an effective defence or evacu- ation of the peoples of Eastern Nigeria living in the North just as it did during the 1953 Kano riots. Also, the fact that an Ibo man was at the helm of power gave the Ibos a rather false sense of security, not knowing that the Ibo Ironsi was much more interested in making peace at all costs than in protecting his fellow Ibos in areas where such protection was necessary. By the time the Eastern Nigerians realised the true situation, it had become too late for them to organise their own defence.

Certain people are of the erroneous notion that the "January Boys" as they put it, were only interested in completing the Revolution they started on January 15, 1966 and were not interested in secession as such. It is these same people who argue that the young officers wanted to oust General Ojukwu (then Lt. Colonel) and then fight for a united Nigeria which was their original aim. This is false and smacks of foreign propaganda. What the Boys told me at Nkalagu in 1967 was that they wanted to oust General Ojukwu for personal reasons, and then to continue the struggle under what they regarded as a more honourable leadership.

There is another erroneous notion that Lt. Colonel Unegbe was killed because he refused to surrender the key to the armoury to the "January Boys." Such a statement by anyone only brings out his ignorance of military affairs and procedure. The fact is that Lt. Colonel Unegbe, as the Quartermaster General, holds no keys to any armouries. When Unegbe was told to join the revolution while it was already on, he refused to do so, and having already killed Brigadier Maimalari, a very close friend of Unegbe, the "boys" feared that Unegbe would fight back if he learnt of Maimalari's death. It was simply for that reason that he was also killed.

As pointed out earlier in the book, Major Nzeogwu made a major mistake in the sharing out of tasks to the officers who were to carry out the revolution in the Lagos area. Some of the officers he chose to neutralise certain senior Northern Nigeria officers happened to be those who had personal grudges against these same officers. They saw this then as an opportunity to engage in bloody personal vendettas, oblivious of the harm this would do to the revolution. It was thus that Major Ifeajuna, for example, killed Brigadier Maimalari instead of arresting him as instructed by Nzeogwu, because Ifeajuna had a personal grudge to settle with the Brigadier. This blood-letting eliminated most of the senior Northern officers and thus created a dangerous vacuum at the top of the Army leadership. If these senior men had been alive, particularly the astute and highly articulate Maimalari, they would have been able to hold in check some of the wilder excesses of their fellow Northerners. Perhaps if this had happened, Biafra would not have seceded, the civil war would have been avoided and this book would not have been written.

INDEX

Aba, 252, 260, 281, 283, 284, 288, 289, 309, 330, 356, 358, 367
textile mill, 117
enemy advance to, 240-42
fall of, 267-73 ,
attempts to clear, 273-74, 330-32
spiritualism within Army. *See* spiritualism within Biafran Army
enemy final push, 361, 364, 368
Abagana, 223, 224, 350
Defence Headquarters, 219
battle of, 221-22
destruction of enemy convoy, 224-228
Abagana-Onitsha road. *See* "Onitsha Corridor"
Aba-Ikot-Ekpene road, 241, 363
Abakaliki, 90, 100, 129, 130, 256
battle of, 230-36
Abak-Oko, 262
Aba-Onitsha road, 258
Aba-Opobo road, 261
Aba-Owerri road, 274, 282, 305
Aba Province, 357-58
Aba River, 331
Aba-Umuahia road, 361, 363
Abeokuta, 9,64
barracks, 62
Abi, 206
Abiama, 252
Abor, 173, 174
Abraka, 160
Abriba, 330
Aburi Conference, 93, 97
Aburi Declaration, 87
Aburi, Ghana, 92
Achi, 256
Achuzia, 116, 228, 231, 256, 267, 268, 274, 329, 348, 370
Midwest Operation, 160
invasion of Onitsha, 201
commissioning into Army, 204

attempt to clear Nsukka, 204-05
commander 11 Division, 220-23, 258
invasion of Port Harcourt, 247-55
invasion of Oguta, 276-78
attempt to clear Obilagu airstrip, 285
commander 13 Division, 286-87
attempt to clear Okigwe, 286-89
commander 15 Division, 294-296, 297
attempt to clear Agulu, 294-97
attempt to clear Owerri, 310
defence of Umuahia, 314-18
ROB Brigade commander, 343
attempt to open "Onitsha Corridor," 343-44
Action Group, 5, 7
Adaba, 209, 212
Adani 206, 207, 208
Adazi, 294, 296, 298
Addis Ababa, 268, 269,
Adebayo, Robert (Col.), 31, 56
Adedoyin (Prince), 6
Adegbenro (Chief), 5
Adekunle, Benjamin (Major), 97, 191, 270
Ademoyega, Wole (Major), 8, 28, 159
Ademulegun, Samuel (Brig.), 11, 12, 13, 16, 17, 19
Ad Hoc Constitutional Conference, 81, 82, 87, 92, 93
Adigio (Major), 123, 129 (Lt. Col.) 179, 193, 194
Adoa, 159
Adcru, 129
Advisory Committee of Chiefs. *See* Biafran Government, 93
Afam, 252, 253, 255, 321
Afam Power House, 251
Afikpo, 233, 283
battle of, 237

A. G. *See* Action Group
Agaga, 235
Agala, 138 141, 143, 163, 164
Agaya, 132
Agbani, 250
Agbo, 206
Agbogu (Major), 236 (Col.), 283
Agbogugu, 181, 194, 197, 206, 215
Agbor, 159
  bridge, 159
Aghanya (Col.), 104, 105, 205, 221, 241
Agunta, 284
Aguobu, 216
Agulu, 294, 296, 298, 299
Agwa, 338
Ahaba, 313, 314
"Ahiara Declaration," 383, 384
Ahmadu Bello University, 30, 31, 41
Ahoada, 99, 131, 332, 333, 336, 339
Ahoada-Oguta road, 267
airport. *See* Enugu airport; Ikeja Airport; Kaduna Airport; Kano Airport; Katsina Airstrip; Uga Airport; Uli Airport
Ajalli, 351
Ajasso bridge, 131
Akagbe, 180
Akaghe, Festus (Col.), 256
  Midwest Operation, 158
  invasion of Calabar, 194-97
  commander 12 Division, 239
  invasion of Umuahia, 313
Akahan, Joe (Col.), 57
Akaneze, 313
Akeze, 283
Akilu, Ali 20, 28, 33, 47
Akintola, (Chief) 5, 6, 7, 22
Akonobi (Lt. Col.), 350
Akpan, N. U., 371
Akpanya, 146
Akpoha bridge, 124, 236
Akpuaka (Lt.), 22
(Akri Ogidi) Ndoni 198
Akukwe, Mr., 75, 77, 78
Akwete, 260, 261, 331
Alama River, 236
Ala-Oji, 331, 332
Alele (Major), 145, 147, 166, 167, 168, 169
Aletu, 254
Alexander (General), 311, 349, 350
Aloa, 338, 339
Aloma, 138
Amadi, Pat (Major), 100, 148 (Lt. Col.), 168, 231, 232, 256, 257, 275, 368 (Brig.), 260, 296, 297
  Ogoja battles, 124-25, 139, 151
  commander First Battalion. 137, 138
  commander 51 Brigade, 170
  enemy advance to Enugu, 174-75
  division within 51 Brigade, 231-34
  commander 13 Division, 237
  commander 11 Division, 256, 257

attempt to clear Onitsha, 258-59
  disagreement with Achuzia, 343
  acting Commander of Army, 372
Amadim Olo, 212
  battle of, 209-10
Amafor, 301
Amaia, 282, 338, 370
Amandugba refinery, 115
Amaraku, 372
Ameke, 317, 318
American Government, 167
ammunition, shortage of, 181, 327-28, 339
  Onitsha, 198, 200, 208, 210, 212, 217
  Abakaliki, 232
  Port Harcourt, 246
  Aba, 270, 272, 332
  Oguta, 276, 278
  Owerri, 281-82, 301, 310
  Operation Hiroshima, 293-294
  Owerri, 301, 210
  Umuahia, 313
  Aba, 332
  Okigwe, 342
  Operation Do or Die, 343, 347
  enemy's final push, 354, 355, 356, 361, 362
Amokwe, 213, 216, 312, 313
Amuzu, 236
Anah (Capt.), 126, 127
Anambra River, 207,
Ananaba (Major), 314
Aniebo, Ifeanyi (Col.), 239, 240, 241
Ankpa, 129
Annang Province, 239, 242, 358
Annangs, 242, 258, 362
Anueyiagu (Mr.), 46
Anuforo, Christian (Major), 15, 16, 28
Anuku (Capt.), 255, 267, 268, 275, 276, 372,
Anwunah, Patrick (Lt. Col.), 43, 46, 61, 63
apartheid, 3
Appolo (Major), 98
Araba, 42
Araba riots. *See* riots and rioting
Archibong, 263
Army. *See* Nigeria Army; Biafran Army
Arochukwu, 239, 329, 330, 356, 364
Asa, 280, 281, 308, 331, 332, 337, 350
  junction, 270, 331
Asaba, 160, 198, 200, 202, 203, 259, 328
Asanamafo, 243
Asoya (Major), 279 (Lt. Col.), 279 (Col.), 301, 318, 337
Asse River, 259, 328
Atani, 198, 259
Atim Bo, 191
Atta, 280
Atumaka, (Major), 283, 310
Auchi, 156, 159
Avu, 280, 302, 305, 306, 321

Awarra, 280, 331, 332
Awgu, 205, 232 249, 273, 285, 311
    Army, Tactical Headquarters, 181
    invasion of 256
Awgu-Okigwe road, 283, 339
Awka, 205, 213, 216-19, 221, 259, 294,
    298
Awkunanaw, 179, 180, 186, 214
Awlaw, 350, 351, 354
Awolowo, Obafemi (Chief), 6, 94
Awomama, 372
Aya Adam, 194
Ayalagu, 74, 75
Azikiwe, Nnamdi, 5, 95, 290
Azuago, 249
Azumini, 330, 355, 361
    bridge, 330

Balewa, (Sir) Abubakar Tafewa, 6,
    8, 31, 35
Banjo, Victor (Col.), 91, 145, 146,
    379
    commander 101 Division, 145-51
    attempt to clear Obollo Afor and
        Nsukka, 145
    Midwest Operation, 156-58
    attempt to overthrow Ojukwu,
        168
Banori, 249
BASC. See Biafran Army Service
    Corps
Bassey, Duke (Lt. Col.), 17, 36, 44
BBC, 27, 271, 311, 349, 350
Bello, (Sir) Ahmadu. See Sardauna
    of Sokoto
Bende, 330
Benin, 23, 97, 98, 156, 157, 159, 167
Benin-Asaba road, 160
Benue River. See River Benue,
Biafra, 11, 91, 104, 105, 108, 119,
    137, 148, 163, 197, 204, 251, 278,
    279, 287, 314, 319 328, 329, 331,
    347, 372, 373, 380, 389, 390
    declaration of independence, 88,
        93, 381
    departure of expatriates, 95,
    guerrilla warfare, 105
    sabotage propaganda, 145, 194,
        211, 290, 367
    Midwest Operation, 161
    attempt to overthrow Ojukwu,
        167
    fall of Enugu, 176, 181, 198
    enemy occupation of Onitsha,
        201
    mercenaries, use of, 215, 293
    enemy collaborators within, 240
    fall of Port Harcourt, 255
    ammunition purchase and im-
        portation, 272
    Owerri victory, 321
    collapse of, 332, 349, 350-60, 368,
        369, 370, 377
    Government of. See Biafran
    Government

foreign assistance to, 379
finances of, 382
Ahiara Declaration, 383, 384
See also Biafrans, philosophy of;
    Biafran War; Ojukwu, Chukwu-
    emeka Odumegwu
Biafra-Cameroun border, 131, 189,
    197
Biafran Air Force, 94, 100-01, 175,
    221, 351, 373, 384,
    invasion of Port Harcourt, 243-
        45, 255
    invasion of Oguta, 276, 279
Biafran Armed Forces, 97, 109, 115,
    116, 175, 176. See also Biafran
    Army, administrative support;
    Food Directorate; Directorate
    for Fuel Supply; Transport
    Directorate; Clothing Direc-
    torate, Biafran Air Force; Bia-
    fran Navy
Biafran Army 94, 124, 126, 144, 152,
    166, 168, 170, 171, 173, 175, 195,
    201, 206, 207, 230-33, 250, 259,
    265, 319, 340, 349, 350, 370
    administrative support 107-18,
    149, 175, 181, 190, 229-30, 304, 307,
    310, 327, 338, 349, 354, 355,
    359, 362, 364, 369, 383. See also
    ammunition, shortage of; Bia-
    fra Army Service Corps Direc-
    torate for Fuel Supply; Food
    Directorate; Ojukwu, C. O.,
    control of ammunition pur-
    chase and supply; Petroleum
    Management Hoard; survival
    companies; Transport Direc-
    torate
    ammunition and weapons. See
    ammunition, shortage of; Oju-
    kwu, C. O., control of am-
    munition purchase and supply;
    weapons, Biafran made
    attempt to overthrow Ojukwu,
    effect on, 170
    civilian intervention in. See
    civilian intervention into war
    effort
    Commander of, 161, 169
    crisis of confidence between
    Army and Head of State. See
    crisis of confidence
    guerrilla forces. See guerrilla
    warfare; Biafran Organisation
    of Freedom Fighters
    politics within, 204, 348, 367,
    mercenaries, recruitment of. See
    mercenaries
    Militia, relationship with 102-04.
    See also Biafran Militia, reor-
    ganisation of. See Madiebo,
    A. A., reorganisation of Biafran
    Army
    sabotage within. See sabotage
    propaganda

special units under control of Head of State. *See* Biafran Army, Commando Division, "S" Division

spiritualism within, *See* spiritualism within Biafran Army

troops, recruitment of. *See* recruitment and training, Biafran Army

Commando Division, 362-63; battle of Ugba junction, 360; commander of, 364, destruction of 12 Division, 365, 368, 369, "S" Division, 283, 288, 301, 302, 314, 330; formation of, 181, 273-74; attempt to clear Mbaise, 281-82; attemp to clear Okigwe, 281-82; attempt to clear Okigwe, 309-10, 320, 324; "Jet 77," 324, 337; offensive to disrupt Port Harcourt, 337; placed under Army Headquarters, 337-38; enemy final push through Ibo Heartland, 350; spiritualism within. *See* spiritualism within Biafran Army; recapture of Owerri by Nigerian forces, 371

101 Division, 147; formation of 144, 146; commander of, 146; attempt to clear Obollo Afor, 146; Midwest Operation. *See* Midwest Operation

11 Division, 289, 298, 299, 369; enemy advance to Onitsha, 207, 220-21, 224; formation of, 216; fall of Awka 219-20; commanders of, 21, 219, 220, 247, 257; Abagana disaster, 224; invasion of Port Harcourt, 247-48; attempts to clear Onitsha, 257, 292, 294; invasion of Midwest, 259; attempt to clear Oguta, 276; invasion of Okigwe, 284; battle of Agulu, 297; defence of Umuahia 311, 314; attempt to reopen "Onitsha Corridor," 342-44; defence of "Onitsha Corridor," 350

12 Division, 370; formation of 239; commanders of, 239, 257; attempt to clear Ikot-Ekpene, 260-63; enemy advance to Owerri and Aba, 268-72; attempts to clear Aba, 273-74, 330-32; clearing of Ugba junction, 288; defence of Umuahia, 314; collapse of, 354-69

13 Division, 258; formation of, 236; commanders of, 236, 257; 286; invasion of Okigwe, 283-85; changed to 15 Division, 286; *See also* Biafran Army, 15 Division

14 Division, 116, 350, 369, 370; formation of, 267-68; commanders of, 268; enemy advance to Owerri and Aba, 268-69; battle of Oguta, 275-76, 280; defence of Owerri, 280-82; attempt to clear Owerri, 301, 309, 320; attempt to clear Ohoba, 331-32; defence of Umuahia, 360

15 Division, 51; commanders of, 51, 286, 289; changed from 13 Division, 286; attempts to clear Okigwe 286, 288-89, 339-42; battle of Agulu, 294-97; defence of Umuahia, 312-13; enemy final drive through Ibo heartland, 350, 366, 369

51 Brigade, 123, 151, 152, 176, 180, 193; formation of, 100; commanders of, 100, 170, 283; deployment of, 100, 283; Ogoja battles, 123, 130-32, 139-44; unit of 101 Division, 146; attempt to clear Obollo Afor, 146-51; Midwest Operation, 156; Operation Torch, 162-65; defence of Enugu, 174; attempt to clear Enugu, 185; invasion of Abakaliki, 230-33, 235-36; unit of 13 Division, 236

52 Brigade, 129, 176, 245; formation of, 100; commanders of, 100, 267, 275, 287; deployment of, 100; invasion of Calabar, 189; battle of Onne, 244; attempts to clear Port Harcourt, 254; unit of 14 Division, 267-68; defence of Owerri and Aba 268; battle of Oguta, 275; attempts to clear Owerri, 302, 304-05, 320; attempt to clear Ohoba, 331

53 Brigade, 103, 139, 151, 152, 176, 256, 281; formation of, 130; commander of, 138, 206, 268; deployment of, 130, 206; battle of Obollo Afor, 131-33, 137-38; unit of 101 Division, 146; attempt to clear Obollo Afor, 147; Operation Torch, 162-66; enemy advance to Onitsha, 213, 216; defence of Aba and Owerri, 268; invasion of Okigwe, 283-84; enemy final push through Ibo Heartland, 351, 354

54 Brigade, 289; commanders of, 219, 220, 245, 258; deployment of, 206, 207, 216; unit of 11 Division, 207; enemy advance to Onitsha, 212, 216, 219; attempts to clear Onitsha, 258, 292; defence of Umuahia, 311; attempt to reopen "Onitsha Corridor," 344-45

55 Brigade, 236, 239, 283, 312

56 Brigade, 195, 239, 287
57 Brigade, 216, 299, 300, 342-44, 347-48, 350, 367
58 Brigade, 239, 241-42, 262-63, 331, 360-61
60 Brigade, 283, 318; formation of, 267; commanders of, 267-68, 301; deployment of, 267, 301; unit of 14 Division, 267-68; battle of Oguta, 274-75, 279; attempt to clear Owerri, 301-07, 320; attempt to clear Ohoba, 331
61 Brigade, 261, 331, 361, 363
62 Brigade, 242, 262, 263
63 Brigade: formation of, 259; commanders of, 259, 281, 301; deployment of, 259; attempt to clear Mbaise, 281-82; unit of 14 Division, 301; attempt to clear Owerri 301-05, 306 attempt to disrupt Port Harcourt, 338 recapture of Owerri by enemy, 370
64 Brigade, 313, 340
65 Brigade, 331, 359, 360
66 Brigade, 344, 346
68 Brigade, 309, 338
69 Brigade, 340, 341
71 Brigade, 355
73 Brigade, 369
Republic of Benin Brigade, 328, 343
"S" Brigade: formation of, 180; attempt to clear Enugu, 182, 185; enemy advance to Onitsha, 214-16; commanders of, 250, 273, 283; invasion of Port Harcourt, 250; invasion of Okigwe, 283, 285; attempt to clear Owerri, 310. See also "S" Division
4 Commando Brigade, 368
8 Commando Brigade, 314-17, 368
12 Commando Brigade, 287
First Battalion, 142, 152; formation of, 98; deployment of, 98, 99, 100, 128, 131, 132; commanders of, 100, 137; Ogoja battles, 123, 128; unit of 51 Brigade, 130; battle of Obollo Afor, 131-33, 137; fall of Obollo Eke, 150-51; fall of Eha-Amufu, 154-155; Operation Torch, 165; invasion of Abakaliki, 230-31, 233
4th Battalion, 163, 165, 230
7th Battalion: formation of 98; commanders of, 98, 129, 179, 194; deployment of, 98-100, 179, 192-93; unit of 51 Brigade, 100; Ogoja battles, 123, 129, 131; enemy advance to Enugu, 174; invasion of Calabar, 192-93
8th Battalion, 98, 99, 100, 189
9th Battalion, 100, 189-90, 192-93

11th Battalion, 198
12th Battalion, 163; deployment of, 131, 138, 141, 198; battle of Obollo Afor, 64; fall of Obollo Eke, 147; commander of, 156; Midwest Operation, 156; unit of 54 Brigade, 206; enemy advance to Onitsha, 206-09, 212
14th Battalion, 130, 141, 142; formation of, 100; commanders of, 100, 215; deployment of, 100, 123, battle of Obolla Afor, 132; fall of Obolla Eke, 150; fall of Eha-Amufu, 152, 165; unit of 51 Brigade, 182; attempt to clear Enugu, 182, 185; defence of Enugu, 214-15; enemy advance to Port Harcourt, 250, 252-53
15th Battalion, 193; commanders of, 130, 164, 179; unit of 51 Brigade, 130; deployment of, 130, 176-77; Ogoja battles, 132; Operation Torch, 164; enemy advance to Enugu, 174; invasion of Abakaliki, 230-33
18th Battalion, 198
21st Battalion, 262-63
22nd Battalion, 262-63
23rd Battalion, 263
26th Battalion, 233-34
68th Battalion "S" Division, 320-07. See also Biafran Army 68 Brigade
(Arochukwu), 329-30, 364, 367, Special Task Force (Arochukwn), 329-30, 364-367, 369
Army Eelectrical and Mechanical Engineers Unit, 113
Biafran Army Service Corps, 110, 111
"Biafran Babies." See Minicon aircrafts
Biafran Government, 355 356, 371, 279, 380
Cabinet, 371, 380
Consultive Assembly, 380, 381
See also Joint Planning Committee; Qiukwu, Chukwuemeka O.
"Biafran Mentality," 181. See also sabotage propaganda
Biafran Militia, 102-04
National, 103
Port Harcourt, 103, 180, 245, 248, 254
problem of, 102-03, 107
enemy advance to Nsukka, 132
attempt to clear Obollo Afor and Nsukka, 149-50
Midwest Operation, 156
enemy advance to Enugu, 166
attempt to clear Enugu, 185-86
enemy advance to Onitsha, 206
enemy advance to Port Harcourt, 253-55

399

Biafran Navy, 94 101-02, 254, 255, 279
  invasion of Calabar, 189
  invasion of Port Harcourt, 243-45
  invasion of Oguta, 275-76
  Ebocha Offensive, 333
Biafra-Nigeria border, 124, 132
Biafran Organisation of Freedom
  Fighters, 104-07, 309
Biafran Police, 52, 175
"Biafran Revolution," 256, 380, 383-
  84. See also "Ahiara Declara-
  tion"
Biafrans,philosophyof, 131, 242, 259,
  263, 312, 314, 321, 361-62, 377, 387.
  See also civilian intervention
  into war effort; Civil Defence
  Organizations; Biafran Militia;
  refugees; sabotage propoganda
Biafran Science Group, 202, 204, 255.
  See also weapons, Biafran ma-
  de Biafran War, purpose of,
  255, 377-78 387-88
  why Biafra lost, 379, 389-90
Biafra Sun, 117
Bodo, 243
BOFF. See Biafran Organisation
  of Fredom Fighters
Bomu oil fields, 250
Bonny Island, 99, 152, 189, 243
  invasion of, 152
Bonny River, 190, 243-44
Bori, 248, 250
Boyle (Major), 43
Britain. See Great Britain
British Army, 312
British Broadcasting Corporation.
  See BBC
British Government, 9, 10, 161, 167,
  311-12
Bugaji (Capt.), 140

Calabar, 99, 109, 182, 198, 234, 239
  256
  invasion of, 189-96
Calabar Province, 197
census (1963), 6
Chinwuba (Police Commissioner),
  103
Chokocho, 267, 269, 282
  bridge 338
Chudi-Sokei (Major), 91
Chukwuka (Major), 160
Civil Defense Organisations, 309
  destruction of Annang property,
  242, 358
  Port Harcourt, 251
civilian intervention into war ef-
  fort, 191, 194, 219-20, 361-62, 367,
  383-84. See also sabotage pro-
  poganda
Civil War. See Biafran War
Clothing Directorate, 116-18
"Commands." See Biafran Army,
  Commando Division; Steiner,
  Rudolf

Common Services Organisation, 81
Commonwealth Prime Ministers
  Conference (1966), 8
Congo, 13
constitution:
  Nigerian, 7
  Biafran 84, 93
"Corporal Nwafor," 259, 274, 279,
  286, 332
corruption, 88
counter-coup. See coup d'etat, 29
  July, 1966
Coup d'etat, 13, 43, 44, 50, 56, 86,
  87, 167, 188, 384-87
  15 January, 1966, 8, 9, 12, 15,
  16, 31, 32, 33, 34, 44 52, 56, 87,
  91, 167, 390; planning of 15-16;
  prosecution in the North 17-
  27; prosecution in the South,
  22, 25-26; effect of 27-28; purpose of, 27, 388
  29 July, 1966, 28, 33, 50, 57, 378;
  planning of, 29-34, 45 47, 55-57;
  prosecution in the South 61-
  63, 85-86; prosecution in the
  North 63-65; effect of 81-84, 378;
  purpose of 388
  See also Gowon; Ironsi; Nzeogwu; pogroms; riots; secession
Creation of states, 82, 94
Criminal Investigation Bureau, 31
crisis of confidence, 87, 88, 90, 130,
  379
Cross River, 190, 196-97, 236-37, 283
currency change by Federal Military Government, 237-38, 381-82

Danjuma, T. Y. (Capt.), 86
Daramola (Capt.), 72
declaration of independence (Biafra), 87, 89, 93-94, 108, 381
Decree No. 8, 93
Decree No. 34, 42, 44, 51, 56
detention:
  of Awolowo and supporters, 6
  of originators of January coup,
  in Lagos, 85
  of Ibos, in Benin, 89
  of Banjo in Eastern Nigeria, 91
  of Ibo officers during Midwest
  Operation, in Benin, 158
  of Njoku by Ojukwu, 136
  in Owerri, 308
  of war prisoners, 263, 379, 385
Deyor Chara, 250, 253
Dike, Kenneth, 290
Directorate for Fuel Supply, 114-16
Divide and Rule. See Government,
  types of
"Doctor Wise" 357-58 See also spiritualism within Biafran Army
Douglas, William (Dr.), 91
Dumez, 348
Dunukofia, 223

"earliest practical date." 93, 94, 381. *See also* Biafra, declaration of independence
Eastern Nigeria. *See* Nigeria, Eastern Region of; "Ibo Heartland"
Eastern Nigeria Command, 98. *See also* Regional Military Commands
Eastern Nigeria Regional Government:
    Civilian, 6-7
    Military, 87, 93
    See also Biafran Government
Ebenebe, 343
Eberi, 359, 361
Ebocha, 267, 279,
    bridge, 274, 278, 301, 333, 350
    battle of, 333-37
economic interests (British), 3
economic sanctions on Eastern Nigeria, 93
Edet, Louis, 31
Edicts of Eastern Nigeria, 93
Effim, 236
Efiong, Philip (Col.), 63-66 (Brig.), 102, 108, 129 (Gen.), 246, 299, 325, 362, 369, 371, 380
    acting Brigade Commander, Kaduna, 52, 63
    commander Biafran Militia, 102, 103
    Chief of Staff, Biafran Armed Forces, 246,
    surrender of Biafra, 373
Egbede, 331
Egbema oil fields, 115-16, 278-79, 301, 333, 337, 356
Egbu, 302, 310, 320
Egwang, 189
Eha-Amufu, 131, 132, 146, 150, 163, 165, 230-31
    battles of, 141-43, 152-55
Eha-Amufu-Abakaliki road, 231
Eha Alumona, 133, 137, 162, 164
Ejoor, David (Lt. Col.), 12, 26
Eke, 131, 173,
Eket, 189, 190
Eket Province, 239
Ekpene-Ebam, 262
Ekwegbe, 165, 171
Ekwulobia, 297
electricity, 115, 251, 255
elections:
    federal (1959), 5; (1964), 6
    Western Region (1965) 7, 14, 27
Elele 306, 308, 332, 333
Elelem, 282, 304
Eluelu junction, 315
Emekuku, 301 309
Emelifonwu (Major), 65, 66
Emene, 214, 215
    bridge, 214
Enahoro, Anthony, 6

Enugu:
    capital of Eastern Nigeria, 19, 34, 40, 67, 68, 72, 76, 84, 93, 230, 231, 234
    capital of Biafra, 23, 97, 98, 100, 103, 109, 131, 143, 146, 148, 149, 150, 159, 162, 168, 169
    Prisons, 98
    enemy advance to, 129, 131, 133, 164-67, 171, 173-75
    fall of, 176, 179 181, 190, 198
    attempts to clear, 180-88
    Airport, 18, 185, 214, 215
    enemy occupation, 204, 206, 214, 216
Enugu-Awgu-Okigwe road, 179
Enugu-Ezike, 99, 129, 133, 146, 162
Enugu-Onitsha road, 176, 258, 292, 344. *See also* "Onitsha Corridor"
Esuk Mbai beach, 191
Ete, 129
ethnic balance, 10
ethnic quota system, 10
Etinam, 190
Etiti, 215, 268, 273, 355, 363, 365
exodus of Eastern Nigerians from Northern Nigerian 42, 74-86. *See also* refugees
expatriates, 4, 29, 31, 95, 328,
Ezamgbo, 236
Eze, Anthony (Major), 15 (Col.), 48, 50, 57, 90, 189 191, (Brig.), 265, 324
    Commanding Officer of Lagos Garrison, 48
    escape following counter-coup, 85
    commander 52 Brigade, 100
    commander 53 Brigade, 129, 133, 146, 162
    Operations Officer, 221, 223, 231, 250, 253, 256
    commander 12 Division, 257, 270, 272, 288, 331, 357, 359-60, 362-63
    Chief of Staff, Army Headquarters, 367
Ezeilo W. (Wing Commander), 190
Eziama, 213, 304
Ezillo bridge, 234-35
Ezi-Orsu, 275, 278-79

Fajuyi, Francis 26, 56, 61, 85-86
Federal Government of Nigeria. *See* Nigeria, Federal Government of
Federation of Nigeria. *See* Nigeria, federation of
Food Directorate, 108, 109-112, 113, 175 236, 304. *See also* Biafran Army, administrative support
food-producing areas, 110, 236, 299, 338, 344, 348
"foot cutters," 198. *See also* weapons, Biafran made
Foresythe, Fredrick, 271-72

Fuel Directorate. *See* Directorate for Fuel Supply; refineries and refining of fuel

Gambia, 8
Garkem, 124, 130, 131
battle of, 125-28
Garkem-Adikpo road, 125
Gbulie, Ben (Major), 129, 131
Military Administrator, Aba Province, 358
"Genocide," 153-55. *See also* weapons Biafran made
Ghana, 8, 16, 97. *See also* Aburi Conference
Ginger (Major), 315, 369
Government. Federal. *See* Nigeria, Federal Government of; Nigeria, Federal Military Government; Nigeria, National Military Government
Government, types of:
Divide and Rule, 3
federation. *See* Nigeria, federation of
unitary, 82, 84
See also Nigeria, Federal Military Government; Nigeria, Federal Government of; Nigeria, National Military Government
Gowon, Yakubu, 25, 26, 43
Army Chief of Staff, 31, 49-52, 55, 64, 70
personal relationship with Madiebo, 54
Head of State, Nigeria, 72, 81-82, 84-85, 93, 97, 119, 161, 311, 312, 327, 328, 388
dispute with Ojukwu, 72, 87
rejection of Aburi decisions, 92-93
See also Nigeria, Federal Military Government
Gowon's Government. *See* Nigeria, Federal Military Government
Great Britain, 11, 25, 31, 45, 52, 54, 55
as colonialiser, 3-5, 10
in support of Gowon, 161, 387-88
guerrilla warfare, 101, 104-07, 69, 236. *See also* Biafra Organisation of Freedom Fighters (BOFF)

House of Assembly, Western Nigeria. *See* Western Nigeria Regional Government
Head of State (Biafra). *See* Ojukwu, Chukwuemeka O.

Ibadan, 63, 64
capital of Western, Nigeria, 6, 23, military installations in, 9
kidnap of Ironsi and Fajuyi, 61, 85-86, 88
Biafran Midwest Operation 156-57

Ibagwa Ani, 162
Ibiaku, 262
Ibiam, Francis (Dr.), 168-69, 173
"Ibo Heartland," 201, 229, 240, 311
"Ibo Rebellion". *See coup d'etat,* 15 January, 1966
Ibos, 41, 46, 47, 57, 76, 86, 389, 390
majority of Eastern Nigeria, 5
exodus from the North. *See* exodus of Eastern Nigerians
assurances of safety in the North, 43
from Northern Nigeria
plan to drive away from North, 48
killing of soldiers at Ikeja, 62
massacre in North, 81, 84-85
See also Biafrans, philosophy of
Ibo State Union, 390
Ibrahim, (Sir) Kashim, 20
Ibusa, 259
Idah, 63, 156, 198, 205
Idemili River, 258
Idi, 165, 171
Idika (Capt.), 66
Ifeajuna, Emmanuel (Major), 16, 28, 91, 166-67, 391
Ifite Ukpo junction, 222, 224
Igbo, 267
Igboba, Henry (Col.), 158
Igbos. *See* Ibos
Igobido, 164
Igrita, 254-55, 269, 338-39
Igumale, 141, 163-65
Igweze, Obi, 287 (Major), 320
Ihama, 141
Ihenacho, Lambert (Major), 281 (Col.) 301, 370
Ihube, 285, 286, 297, 340, 341
Ikang, 189, 191
Ikeja, 63
airport, 15, 61
barracks, 62
Ikeji (Major), 301
Ikem, 152-53, 163, 165
Ikem-Nsukka road, 132, 133
Ikolo, 171
Ikom, 130, 131, 236
Ikot Ebak, 262
Ikot Ekpene, 134, 284, 361, 361, 363, 364
fall of, 239-41
combing for saboteurs 242, 358
attempt to clear, 257, 260-65
starvation of inhabitants, 263, 336,
link-up with Umuahia by enemy forces, 367
Ikot-Ekpene-Itu road, 262
Ikot-Ekpene-Uyo road, 262
Ikot-Ntuan-Ukpana, 262
Ikot-Nturen-Ukana, 262
Ikot-Nvoho, 262
Ikot-Okoro, 261
Ikot-Okpara, 287, 330

Ikot-Okpora, 196, 197, 236
Ikpe-Nung-Inyang, 262
Ikwak, 262
Iloanya (Mr.), 72-73
Iloputaife (Capt.), 85
Imo River, 189, 246, 260, 267, 301, 355, 357, 363-65, 369
imprisonment. *See* detention
independence:
  Nigerian 4, 10
  Biafran. *See* Biafra, declaration of independence
Inyi, 281, 343
Inyi-Awlaw road, 351
Inyiogugu, 281, 301
  junction, 281
Irete, 302
Ironsi, U. A. (Brig), 12, 19 (Gen.) 22
  General Officer Commanding, 13, 19
  foiling of 15 January coup in Lagos, 22-26
  Head of State, Nigeria, 26, 27, 29-37, 43-44, 47-51, 55-56, 91, 378, 386, 390
  support of Decree No. 34, 42-43
  decision to tour Regions 56-57
  arrest and execution, 62-63, 85-86
  See also Nigeria, National Military Government; *coup d'etat*, 15 January, 1966
Ironsi's government. *See* Nigeria Federal Military Government
Isele-Uku, 160
Ishangev, 128
Isiokpo bridge, 338, 339
Isiukwuato, 313,
Isi Uzo, 163
Isoba, 338
Isong, Ukpo (Major), 23, 24
Isu, 122, 329, 372
Isuochi, 285
Itak-Ikot, 262
Iva Valley, 174
Ivenso, Mike (Col.) 90, 156, 198, 217-19, 241, 256
Ihahe, 130
  bridge, 138, 236
Izombe, 283, 305

"January Boys." *See coup d'etat*, 15 January, 1966
January 1966 coup. *See* coup d'état, 15 January, 1966
Jebba, 23
  bridge 48, 157
"Jet 77." *See* Biafran Army, "S" Division
Johnson, Mobalaji, 48, 49
Joint Planning Committee, 325, 340, 354, 362, 380
Jos, 16, 36, 41, 76, 84

Kachia, 71
Kaduna. 12, 15, 16, 18, 50, 52, 55,
  location of military installations, 9
  prosecution of 15 January coup within, 20-27
  under Katsina, 32-37, 40, 43, 45, 47
  rioting within, 35-36
  Airport, 37, 61
  exodus of Easterners from, 42-43
  prosecution of 29 July coup within, 63-65
  Madiebo's escape from. *See* Madiebo, Alexander, A., escape from North
Kafanchan, 70-74
Ka Lori, 249
Kalu, Ogbugo (Lt. Col.), 67, 73 (Col.), 246, 255, 259
  involvement in 29 July coup, 65, 66, 67, 73, 78
  commander 8th Battalion, 98, 189
  commander 52 Brigade 243; removal from, 247-49
  attempt to clear Bonny Island, 243
  enemy advance to Port Horcourt, 246
  attempt to clear Mbaise, 281-83
  commander 14 Division, 304
Kampala Peace Talks, 255
Kani Babbe, 247-48
Kano, 45, 47
  location of military installations in, 9
  5th Battalion's participation in 15 January coup, 18, 23, 24
  rioting within, 36-37, 39, 84
  Airport, 37, 84
  prosecution of 29 July coup in, 62
  exodus of Easterners from, 84
Katsina, Hassan (Major), 15, 17, 28, 49, 51
  involvement in 15 January coup, 21-24
  Military Governor of North, 27, 32, 33, 36-41, 43. *See also* Nigeria, Federal Military Government; Kaduna, rioting within; Katsina, rioting within; pogroms; riots and rioting
  involvement in 29 July coup, 47, 62
Katsina, 36, 39, 40-41
Keshi, Alphonsus, 17, 18, 26
Kono, 246, 249
Kreigani, 336
Kurubo, George (Lt. Col.), 18, 91
Kwa Ibo River, 190
Kwale oil fields, 328
Kwashiokor, 112, 263, 336
Kwawa, 247
Kyari (Major), 65

Lagos, 15, 16, 18, 44, 55, 85, 86, 105, 312, 339, 354
  rioting within following Western Regional elections, 7-8
  prosecution of 15 January coup in, 22-28, 391
  seat of National Military Government under Ironsi, 29-33, 35-36, 42, 45, 49-51, 57
  Prosecution of 29 July coup in, 61-63, 80
  Midwestern Operation, 156-57
  See also Nigeria Federal Military Government; Ikeja Airport
Largema (Col.), 22
Leja, 165-66
Lekwesi, 285
LeRois, 207, 210
Leru, 340-41
Lokoja, 47, 49
Lokpauku, 340

Madiebo, Alexander A. (Lt. Col., Nigeria Army; Major General, Biafran Army)
  officer cadet, Nigeria Army, 8
  Regimental Commander, Artillery Regiment (Kaduna), 8, 35
  involvement in 15 January coup, 17-27
  inspection of Kano, Kaduna following May riots, 36-40
  attempt to thwart October, 1966 Northern riots, 47-49
  movement of Artillery Headquarters to Lagos, 50
  return to Kaduna, 29 July 1966, 55-56, 61-69
  escape to East, 69-80
  commander 7th Battalion, 98
  commander 51 Brigade, 100, 123
  Ogoja battles, 123-55, 161-66
  involvement in attempt to overthrow Ojukwu, 166-70
  Commander Biafran Army, 169; reorganisation of Biafran Army, 176-82; Northern Sector battles, 171-88, 198-236, 258-260; Southern Sector battles, 189-97, 239-55, 260-265; enemy drive through Ibo Heartland, 267-319, 349-73; recapture of Owerri by Biafra, 319-25; Biafran Army offensives, May-Sept., 1969, 327-48; collapse of 12 Division, 354-368
  escape to Abidjan, 371-73
Maiduguri, Hammon, 37
Maimalari, Zakari (Brig.), 13, 16, 22, 391
Majekodunmi (Dr.), 6
Makurdi, 23, 72, 73, 77, 123
  bridge, 48, 73, 77
Mamu bridge, 217
Maribu, 247

"Marshall," 344, 345, 347. See also weapons, Biafran made
May Test Riots. See riots and rioting; pogroms
Mbaise, 281 366, 370, 372
Mbala, 284, 285
Mbanefo, (Sir) Louis, 290
Mbawsi, 356, 359, 364
Mbiere, 283
Megwa (Major), 169
mercenaries:
  use of by Nigeria Army at Nsukka 181-82
  demand for by Biafran troops 182
  use of by Biafra, 185, 197, 207, 244, 268-72, 273-74, 291-93,
  desertion by, 196, 210
  formation of "Commandos," 215-16
  See also LeRois; Steiner; Biafran Army, Commando Division
Mgbagu Owo, 212,
Mgbede, 305
Mgbirichi, 302, 306
Midwest Operation, 156-61, 163, 168, 379
Military Government. See Nigeria, National Military Government; Nigeria, Federal Military Government
Military Governor of Eastern Nigeria. See Ojukwu, Chukwu-emeka Odumegwu
military installations, 9-10
Militia. See Biafran Militia
Millikin Hill, 175, 185
Minicon aircrafts, 101, 351
minorities, 5
Mojekwu, Christopher, 91, 169, 174, 176, 382
Morah (Col.), 249
Muhammed, Murtala (Major), 51, 55 (Col.), 158
  formation of Nigeria Army 2 Division, 158
  drive through Midwest, 159-60
  capture of Asaba, 160
  drive to Onitsha, 198, 202, 206-07, 211, 213, 221-23
  See also Nigeria Army, 2 Division

Nadu, 146
napalm, 181, 237, 300, 318, 347
National Convention for Nigerian Citizens, 5, 7
nationalism, 4
Naze, 302
NCNC. See National Convention for Nigerian Citizens
Ndiaboh, 284
Ndiba beach, 237
"Ndidi," 317
Ndiya-Etuk, 262

Nebo (Capt.), 123, 130, 246 (Major), 247 (Col.) 345
Nekede, 320
New Nigerian, 35
Ngbo, 138
Ngene-Ukwa River 219
Ngodo, 285, 340
Ngor complex, 282
Ngusu, 313
Ngwo, 212
Ngwo-Udi road, 213
Nibo, 206
Nigeria Army, 52, 95, 100, 117, 139, 224, 252, 387
northern/sourthern division within, 4, 12, 13
location of military installations prior to January 1966, 9, 10
ethnic quota system of recruitment, 10
military rule by, 22, 24, 31
role in Northern riots, 34-41
discipline within, 51
involvement in 29 July coup, 61-47
in Eastern Nigeria prior to outbreak of war, 87, 89-90, 97-98
strength of, 130, 309
final push through Ibo heartland, 311, 312, 349
formations prior to war: 3rd Battalion, 6, 9, 14, 16, 18, 46, 63, 75; 5th Battalion, 9, 12, 18, 24, 37, 72; 1 Field Battery (Artillery) 9; 1 Field Squadron (Engineers) 9; 88 Transport Regiment 9; 6th Battalion 9; 4th Battalion 9, 22; 2 Field Battery (Artillery) 9; 2 Reconnaissance Squadron 9, 13, 8, 21; 1st Battalion 9, 89, 94; 1 Brigade, 11, 12, 14, 17, 26, 31, 34, 44; 2 Brigade 16, 22, 49
3rd Marine Commando Division, 49, 237, 252, 368
2 Division, 230, 259, 299, 311, 343; formation of, 158; drive through Midwest 158-60; invasion of Onitsha, 202; drive to Onitsha, 205-06, 212-13, 221-24, 228
1 Division, 214, 230, 233, 299, 312, 368
14 Brigade, 324
Nnewi Task Force, 311
Nigeria, Federal Government of, 5, 7, 13, 237, 387
Nigeria federation of, 3, 4, 5, 42, 82, 84, 93
Eastern Region, 5, 10, 23, 42, 51, 72, 76, 86-94, 108, 373, 379, 387, 390; military installations in prior to January, 1966 9; appointment of Military Governor 26; reaction to 15 January

coup 27; refugees from Northern Nigeria. *See* refugees; economic sanctions upon 93; declaration of independence. *See* declaration of independence (Biafra); preparation for war 97-100. *See also* Biafra
Midwestern Region, 10, 23, 57, 89, 97, 103, 105, 205, 259, 314, 344, 370; appointment of Military Governor, 26; reaction to 15 January coup, 27; Midwestern Operation. *See* Midwest Operation; Republic of Benin Brigade
Northern Region, 3-5, 13, 50, 51, 63, 97, 135, 140, 155, 159 161, 162, 180, 198, 217; military installations in prior to January, 1966, 9, 10; Tiv riots 12, 16; prosecution of 15 January coup, 19, 23-27; appointment of Military Governor, 26; political unrest following coup, 29, 32, 34, 43, 36; rioting (May, 1966) 35-41, 43, (October 1966), 81-82, 84-85; exodus of Southerners, 42; desire to secede. *See* secession, Northern Nigeria; invasion of, 164-65
Southern, 3, 11, 22, 29, 34, 48, 64, 65
Western Region, 10, 22, 23, 55, 57, 105, 159; political struggle within 5-6; declaration of State of Emergency, 6, 8; Elections (1965) 8; military installations prior to January, 1966 9; appointment of Military Governor; 26 reaction to 15 January coup, 27; prosecution of 29 29 July coup, 61-62
Nigeria, Federal Military Government 81, 82, 84, 119 388
measures against Eastern Nigeria, 93-94, 378
prosecution of the war, 161, 311-12
Nigeria Military Academy, 9
Nigeria Military School, 9
Nigeria Military Training College (NMTC), 9,14, 17, 25, 66
Nigeria, National Military Government 28, 29, 32, 34, 43, 61, 62, 64, 119
attempts to placate North, 33, 34, 43, 390
Decree No. 34, effect of, 42, 44
Nigeria Navy, 101, 152
"Nigerian Mentality," 181. *See also* sabotage propaganda
Nigerian National Democratic Party 6, 7
Nigerian Revolution, 383-84, 390, 391. *See also coup d'etat*, 15

405

January, 1966
Nise, 296, 298
Njaba bridge, 272
Njoku, Hilary (Lt. Col.), 98, 171
  commander 2 Brigade (Lagos),
    49
  involvement in 29 July coup, 86
  Commander Biafran Army, 88,
    129, 161-63
  compaign against command, 145-
    46, 156-57
  involvement in attempt to over-
    throw Ojukwu, 168, 169
  detention of, 273
Njoku (Major), 296
Nkalagu, 166, 180, 185, 193, 391
  Cement Factory, 141, 150, 230, 231
  junction, 232
Nkpololo, 284
Nkpologu, 204, 206-08
Nkpologu-Agbo road, 162
Nkpor junction, 300, 344-47
Nkwelegwu, 208
Nkwelle, 292, 293, 300
Nkwoagu, 236
Nkwok, 261
Nkwerre, 283, 372
NMTC. See Nigeria Military
  Training College
NNDP. See Nigerian National De-
  mocratic Party
Nnewi, 88, 257, 291, 300, 314, 368,
  371, 372
  storage of weapons, 90
  enemy advance to, 229, 294, 297,
    298
Nnewi Task Force. See Nigeria
  Army, Nnewi Task Force
NNS Nigeria, 101, 243
Nonwa Kebara, 253
Northern independence. See seces-
  sion, Northern Nigeria
Northern Nigeria. See Nigeria,
  Northern Region
Northern People's Congress, 5, 7,
  11
Notem, 249
NPC. See Northern People's Con-
  gress
Nsiak, 262
Nsude, 212
Nsudoh (Major) 198, 201, 217 (Lt.
  Col.) 220, 351
Nsugbe, 198
Nsukka, 95, 98, 99, 103, 109, 123,
  133, 143, 191, 204, 205, 223, 231,
  234, 256
  fall of, 131-32
  enemy occupation of, 133, 137-39,
    151, 156, 161, 182, 204-06
  attempts to clear, 146, 162, 164-
    65, 204-06
Ntak-Afa, 261
Nwafor (Cpl.), 258-59
Nwaigwe bridge, 361, 363

Nwajei, Ben (Col.), 57, 256, 268,
  276, 280, 283
Nwankwo (Capt.), 85-86
Nwawo, Conrad (Col.), 160 (Brig.),
  204, 205, 220, 223, 247, 364
  Military Attaché, Nigerian High
    Commission, London, 26-27
  commander 11 Division, 203
  defence of Onitsha, 203, 205, 206,
    216, 219
  commander 13 Division, 256
  Chief of Staff, Army Headquar-
    ters, 286
  Commander Commando Divi-
    sion, 293
Nweke, Raphael, 68-71
Nweke (Capt.), 209-11
Nwobosi, Emmanuel (Col.), 197
Nzefili (Lt. Col.), 1979
Nweogwu, Chukwuma K. (Major),
  12, 15, 29, 69
  Chief Instructor, NMTC, 14
  leader of 15 January coup, 17-28,
    391
  suspended from military duties
    by Ojukwu, 87-88

Oba, 224
Obeakpu, 250
Obete, 246, 247, 249
Obiakpa, 261
Obido, 336
Obienu (Major), 62
Obigbo, 254, 267
  junction, 252
Obiga, 331
Obigwe, 305
Obilagu Red Cross Airport, 284-85
Obinofia, 216
Obinze, 280, 302, 306
Obioha, Frank (Major), 88 (Lt.
  Col.), 187, 209, 216, 250, 251
Obokwe, 331
Obollo Afor, 99, 139, 140, 152, 202,
  211
  battle of, 130-133, 135-38
  attempts to clear, 146-51, 162
Obollo Afor-Orokam road, 65
Obollo Eke, 99, 132-33, 135, 137,
  152, 154
  battles of, 138-41, 145-51
Obeasi, 258, 347
Obrikon, 334, 336
Obubra, 197, 236
Obudi, 283, 305
Obudu, 124, 131, 211
  battle of, 128
Obunselv, Dr. (Lt. Col.), 180
Ochei (Col.), 159-60, 197, 236
Odigwe (Major), 194, 196, 247
Odo, Wilson (Capt.), 150-51
Odukpani, 194
Ofogwe, 305
Ofoko, 162
Ogbabu, 285

406

Ogbaku, 283, 305
Ogbemudia, Sam (Major), 41, 63, 66
Ogbogwu, 336
Ogbor Hill, 361
Ogbu, Christian (Capt.), 147
"ogbunigwes", 191, 198, 202, 282, 311, 317, 331, 341, 347. *See also* weapons, Biafran made
Ogidi, 201, 223, 344, 345, 347
Ogobido, 139
Ogochia River, 338
Ogoja-Abakaliki road, 130
Ogoja, 100, 109, 123, 124, 129, 130, 133, 140, 144, 236, loss of, 131-32
Ogoja Province, 99, 138, 197
Ogugu, 129, 146
Ogundipe, Babafemi, 31
Ogunewe, David (Col.), 89, 90, 143, 372
Ogunro (Major), 66
Oguta, 280, 283, 284, 301 battle of, 274-79
"Oguta Boy," 278, 316
Oguta Lake, 275-76, 278
Oguta-Mgbirichi road, 274
Oguta-Mgbuisi road, 275
Oguta-Uli road, 275
Ogwashiuku, 160, 259
Ogwe, 331
Ohabian, 331
Ohafia, 330
Ohanehi, Linus (Major), 51 (Col.), 289
   commander 14th Battalion, 100, 130, 142, 155
   Commander 26th Battalion, 233, 234
   commander 54 Brigade, 258
   commander 15 Division, 289, 312-13
   attempt to clear Okigwe, 340-41
Ohanze bridge, 361
Ohoba, 321, 333, 337, 350
   attempt to clear 331-32
Ohum, 171
oil fields. *See* Egbema oil fields; Bomu oil fields; Kwale oil fields; Owazza oil fields; Umuechem oil fields
oil industry, 255. *See also* refineries and refining of fuel; Petroleum Management Board
Ojeh, Mr., 73-75
Oji-Achi road, 216
Oji-Awgu road, 284
Oji, Ogbo (Major) 100 (Lt. Col.), 358, 366
   commander 9th Battalion, 100, 189
   invasion of Calabar, 191
   defence of Umuahia, 241, 364-65
   destruction of property in Annang, Uyo Provinces, 242, 358-59, 362
Principal Staff Offices (Operations) 12 Division, 358
dismissal from Biafran Army, 367
Oji River, 216-17
Ojukwu, Chukwuemeka Odumegwu (Lt. Col.), 18-19 (Col.), 92 (Gen.), 324
   commander 5th Battalion (Kaduna), 18
   involvement in 15th January coup, 22-24, 26, 28
   Military Governor of Eastern Region, 26, 43 82, 87-94
   dispute with Gowon, 87
   Aburi Conference. *See* Aburi Conference
   declaration of Biafran independence. *See* declaration of independence (Biafra)
   Biafran Head of State, 97, 98, 103, 104, 108, 110-11, 113, 115-16, 156-57, 161, 171, 173,187-88, 191-92, 194-95, 197, 211, 216, 219 221, 228, 240-42, 245-46, 255-57, 265, 268, 272-73, 276, 278-79, 281-82, 289, 298-99, 327, 337, 340, 354, 356-58, 369-70, 379-82, 387, 389
   Control of ammunition purchase and supply, 101, 129-30, 187, 192, 196, 204, 207, 209, 253, 272, 276, 304, 309, 319, 382-83. *See also* ammunition, shortage of
   Organisation of Freedom Fighters BOFF, 105, 107
   formation and command of 101 Division, 146
   attempted overthrow, 167-70
   defence of Enugu, 171, 173-75
   formation of "S" Brigade, 180-81
   recruitment and use of mercenaries, 182, 186, 207, 210
   formation and command of commandos, 215-16, 229, 270-71, 291-294
   defence of Onitsha, 219-21
   defence of Port Harcourt, 245-46
   formation and command of "S" Division, 273
   attempt to clear Oguta, 276, 278
   attempt to clear Obilagu airstrip, 285
   attempts to clear Okigwe, 286-87, 288
   dismissal of Col. Ude from Army 286
   attempt to clear Onitsha, 291-93
   attempt to clear Agulu and Adazi, 296-97
   attempt to clear Owerri, 309-10

defence of Umuahia, 313-14, 318
formation of Joint Planning
Committee, 325
destruction of 12 Division, 262-68
dismissal of Brig. Eze and Col.
Oji from Army, 367
escape to Abidjan, 371-73
Ojukwu (Capt.), 124
Okafor, David, 98, 163, 192, 193, 194
Okafor, Donatus, 16, 28
Okafor (Major), 315
Okapatu, 171
Okeke, Emmanuel (Major), 222,
261
Okeke, Joseph (Lt. Col.), 331
(Col.), 363
Okeke, Patrick (Chief), 290
Okigbo, Christopher (Major), 166
Okigwe, 274, 283, 297, 329, 339-40,
342, 369
invasion of, 283-89
Okigwe-Afikpo road, 284
Okigwe-Awgu road, 284
Okigwe Province, 369
Okilo (Major), 281
Okitipupa, 158
Okoanala, 328
Okogbele, 328
Okoloma, 252
Okon (Major), 73
Okoro, Israel (Major), 18-19 (Col),
46-47, 50, 55, 64-66, 75-76
Okotie-Eboh, (Chief) Festus, 22
Okoye (Capt.), 234
Okpantu, 247, 249
Okpara, (Dr.) M. I., 371, 379, 389
Okpoma bridge, 131
Okposo, 189-90
Okpuala, 269, 282, 370-71
bridge, 360
junction, 282, 370
Okpuala-Uvoro road, 281
Okrika, 246, 251, 254
refinery, 251. See also refineries
and refining of fuel
Oku, 259
Okuje, 129, 162
Okuku, 68, 305
Okunweze, Gabriel (Lt. Col.), 62
Okuta, 95
Okutu, 63, 160
Okwechime, Michael (Major), 12,
48, 314, 324-25
Okwuzu, 279
Olakwo, 282
bridge, 371
Olakwo-Obiagwu road, 281
Olehi, Michael (Capt.), 128, 142
(Major) 209-11, 241
Olisakwe (Col.), 250
Olo, 209-10. 212
Olutoye (Major), 97
Omanelu, 269, 306
Omanelu-Umuakpu road, 308
Omeruo (Lt. Col.), 331

Omoku, 333, 336
Onitsha, 90, 99, 117, 141, 147, 156-
57, 160, 230, 241, 247, 256, 257,
261, 265, 289, 350
bridge, 99, 124, 157, 160, 228, 229,
292, 344
textile mill, 117, 230, 292, 344
formation of forces for Midwest Operation, 141, 147, 156
invasion of, 198,-205, 219-21, 223-24
market, 201, 229
attempts to clear, 228-30, 257-59,
291-93. See also Operation
Hiroshima
Fegge Quarters, 228-29, 292, 344
enemy occupation of, 299-300, 311
attempt to clear "Onitsha Corridor." See "Onitsha Corridor"
"Onitsha Corridor":
attempt to reopen, 342-47
enemy attempts to close, 350
Onitsha Province, 257
Onne, 244-45, 255
Onwuatuegwu, Timothy (Capt.), 18,
20, (Lt. Col.), 164, 176-77, 288,
324
involvement in 15 January coup,
18, 20, 25
commander 15th Battalion, 164,
231-32,
commander "S" Brigade, 216,
273
commanding officer, School of
Infantry, 232
commander "S" Division, 273
attempt to clear Okigwe, 288
attempt to clear Owerri, 310
defence of Umuahia, 314, 318
320
removal as commander "S" Di-
vision, 337
commander sector 90, 363
Onwudiwe (Mr.), 253-54
Opara (Major), 215
Oparaji (Lt. Col.), 340
Operation Do or Die. See Onitsha
Corridor"
Operation Hiroshima, 291-93
Operation Torch, 161-66
Opi junction, 132, 136, 138, 164, 204
Opi-Nsukka road, 80
Opobo, 189, 246, 261
Oraifite, 329
Orashi, River, 274, 307, 333
Ordnance Depot (Owerri), 356
Ore, 158
Orji, 302, 305, 320
bridge, 283
Orlu, 283
Orabo, 206
Orodo, 283
Orogbu, 250
Orogwe, 302
Orokam, 135, 139, 140
Oron, 239-40, 263-99

Orukpa, 147, 149
Osuagwu (Major), 344
Otamini bridge, 308
Otamini River, 307
Otuocha, 198, 204, 299-300, 342, 344, 348, 350, 367
Otupocha, 300
Ovim, 313
Owazza, 269, 271, 331
  bridge, 269-70
  oil fields, 332
Owerri, 268, 269, 282, 283, 284, 287, 289, 291, 314, 321, 324, 330, 332, 333, 337, 388, 339, 354, 355
  invasion of, 280
  attempts to clear, 301-10, 319-24
  return of civilians, 331
  recapture by enemy, 350, 370-71
Owerri-Ihiala road, 283, 301, 372
Owerrinta bridge, 282, 305
Owerri-Okigwe road, 282
Owerri-Umuahia road, 281, 301
Owutu, 312
Ozala, 214-15
Ozieh, Christopher, 68-72
Ozuzu-Odufu, 267

Pam, Yakubu (Col.), 16, 22, 54
Parliament, federal, 5, 7
Parrot Island, 190
Petroleum Management Board (PMB), 114-16
pogroms, 33, 40, 81, 378
Port Harcourt, 98, 99, 103, 104, 114, 117, 153, 221, 255, 256, 259, 260, 269, 278, 281, 284, 307, 321, 333
  invasion of, 243-55
  enemy attempt to break out of, 308
  Biafran threat to, 333, 337-39
Port Harcourt-Aba road, 251, 331
Port Harcourt Airport, 181
Port Harcourt-Owerri road, 267, 301
Premier of Eastern Nigeria. See Okpara, M. I.
Premier of Northern Nigeria. See Sardauna of Sokoto
Radio Kaduna, 35
recruitment and training, Biafran Army, 98. See also Enugu, Prisons
Red Cross, 111, 284, 285
refineries and refining of fuel, 114-16, 251, 255, 356. See also Uzuakoli refinery; Amandugbe refinery; Okrika refinery; Port Harcourt refinery
refugees:
  from Northern and Western Nigeria, 84, 89, 98, 108
  in advance of enemy movement 109, 141, 230, 289, 338, 366, 371, 372
Regional Military Commands, 97.

See also Eastern Nigeria Command
Research and Production Board, 114, 198
revolution, Nigerian, 15 19, 20, 22, 25, 26, 31, 391. See also coup d'état, 15 January, 1966
Rhodesia, 8
riots and rioting, 8, 27
  Araba Riots, 35-36, 38 41, 42, 390
  Kano (1953), 390
  See also Nigeria, Northern Region; Kano; Kaduna; Katsina; Sokoto; Zaria; Jos
River Aya, 132
River Benue, 72, 77
River Mamu, 217
River Niger, 200, 202, 203, 216, 217, 259, 292, 329
  bridges. See Jebba bridge; Onitsha bridge
Rivers Province, 333
Royal Military Academy Sandhurst, 52
Royal West Africa Frontier Force, 8
Russian planes, use of by Nigeria, 101, 111, 215
  following fall of Enugu, 181
  invasion of Calabar, 190
  invasion of Onitsha, 202
  invasion of Oguta, 275
  enemy final drive, 336 346, 347

Sabon gari, 4
Sabon Gida, 72, 73
Sabotage propaganda within Biafra, 148, 173, 174, 180, 218-19, 221, 223, 234, 241, 250, 254
  introduction into war effort, 145-46, 179
  effect on war effort, 145, 187, 211, 214, 218, 233, 242, 248, 251 252, 257, 389
  victims of propaganda, 145-46, 179, 187, 191, 194, 214, 223, 233, 237, 256, 290
  perpetrators of, 145, 158, 248
Salem, Kam, 31, 49
Sapele, 156
Sardauna of Sokoto, 5, 7, 12, 13, 17, 22, 35, 46
Scott, Robert, (Major), 13
secession:
  Northern Nigeria 42 47, 378, 388
  Eastern Nigeria, 87, 392
  See also Biafra
Shodeinde, Ralph (Col.), 17
Shuwo, Muhammed (Col.), 37-40
Sokei (Col.), 221, 223
Sokoto, 41, 85
Sotomi, 140
Southern Nigeria. See Nigeria Southern
spiritualism within Biafran Army.

357-58, 359
State of Emergency, declaration of, 6, 8, 93
Steiner, Rudolf (Lt.), 215 (Major), 229 (Col.), 269
commander Commando Brigade, 229
attempts to clear Onitsha, 267, 291-93
defence of Owerri and Aba, 267-70,
removal from Biafra, 293-94
Stranger's quarters. See Sabon gari
students, Northern, 29
Supreme Military Council, 31, 42, 91
"Survival companies," 112

Tiv Division, 12
Transport Directorate, 113
tribes and tribalism, 3, 87

Ubiaja, 159
Ubimini, 331
Uchendu (Major), 225
Udeaja (Col.), 223, 225
Ude, Christian (Capt.), 24 124 (Col.), 162, 210, 211, 216, 218, 256
arrest at Kano, 23
Chief Operations Officer, Army Headquarters, 152
commander 53 Brigade, 171, 206, 284
defence of Udi, 213
commander 51 Brigade, 283
defence of Okigwe, 283-84
dismissal from Army, 286
Udi, 90, 173, 174, 206, 208, 214, 216, 256, 286
Headquarters 51 Brigade, 59
fall of, 212-14
Udi-Oji road, 216
Udo bridge, 366
Ufuma, 351
Uga Airport, 294, 350, 373
Ugba junction, 274, 324, 360, 363-66
attempts to clear, 288, 340-41
recapture by enemy, 361
Ughelli, 156
Ugokwe (Col.), 268 275, 301
Uguozo, 165
Ugwuoba, 216, 217, 218
Ugwuogo, 163
Ukawood, 292
Ukehe, 131-32, 138, 162, 165, 166, 171
Ukpabi-Nibo, 207 208
Ukpata 207, 208
Ukpom-Uwana, 262, 263
Uli airport, 255, 278, 283, 311, 349, 350, 372
Umalo, 163
Umuaba, 249
Umuabayi, 249, 250, 360-62

Umuagwo 268, 302, 306
Umuahia, 186, 191, 241, 242, 256, 274, 279, 285, 287, 296, 310, 313, 314 319, 320, 339, 356, 357, 359, 360, 362, 364-69
capital of Biafra, 186, 187, 197, 210, 229, 246, 272, 276, 278-79, 287
"Umuahia Brigade," 296, 297
Umuahia-Ikot-Ekpene road, 241, 242
Umuakpu, 267, 302, 305, 306, 308, 333
Umu-Aro, 272
Umuchitta, 251
Umuechem oil fields, 338, 339
Umueji, 207
junction, 351
Umueje-Adaba road, 207
Umueze, 212
Umuezike, 313, 314
Umuguma, 320, 321
Umukoroshe, 254
Umulokpa, 207, 208
Umumkpeyi, 363
Umuna, 300
Umunede, 160
Umunekwu, 312, 340, 341
Umunko, 171
Umunwoko, 332
Umunya, 300
Umuoba, 273
Umuogwuwu, 315
Umuoji, 259
Umuokpara, 315, 317
Umutu, 160
Umuwayi, 332
Unegbe, Arthur (Lt. Col.), 10, 12, 22, 391
Unification Decree. See Decree no. 34
United Progressive Grand Alliance, 7
University of Nigeria (Nsukka), 88, 95
University Teaching Hospital, Enugu, 88
UPGA. See United Progressive Grand Alliance
Utonkon, 164
Utuk (Commander 14 Brigade, Nigeria Army), 321, 324
Utukpo, 138
Uturu, 312
airstrip, 341
Uvuru, 101
Uwa bridge, 241
Uwakwe, Simeon (Major), 67 (Col.), 239, 330, 364
Uyo, 129, 240, 262, 131
Uyo-Ikot-Ekpene road, 262
Uyo Province, 239, 241, 242
Uzuakoli, 313-19, 369
refinery, 114
"Uzuakoli Boy," 317

Uzuakoli Leper Colony, 315

Van Rosen, 101, 384
violence, 5, 8

Wakama, 253
warri, 156, 160
weapons, Biafran made
    production of, 198
    use of, 191, 198, 202, 206, 282, 311,
    317, 331, 341, 344-45, 347
    See also "foot cutters," "ogbunig-
    wes," "Marshalls," "Genocide",
    Research and Production Board
Western Nigeria. *See* Nigeria,
    Western Region

Williams, Taffy, 268-71
Wilson, Harold, 312
Wiyakara, 248, 249

Yar 'Adua, 15
Yehe, 250
Yesufu, 21, 28, 31, 49

Zakpong, 248
Zaria, 23, 29
    military installations in, 9
    Ahmadu Bello University. *See*
    Ahmadu Bello University; stu-
    dents, Northern
    rioting within, 36, 41, 85
    planning of, 29 July coup, 45, 47

Printed in the United Kingdom
by Lightning Source UK Ltd.
128572UK00001B/372/A